BRITISH SOCIAL AND ECONOMIC HISTORY
FROM THE 18th CENTURY TO THE PRESENT DAY

MAKING MODERN BRITAIN

CHRISTOPHER CULPIN

with

BRIAN TURNER

D0347634

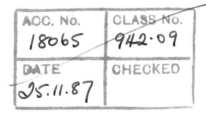
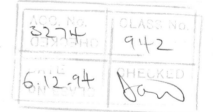

Collins Educational, 8 Grafton Street, London W1X 3LA

© Christopher Culpin

First published 1987

ISBN 0 00 327257 5

Designed by Chris Laver

Artwork by John Booth

Printed and bound in Great Britain by R J Acford

Contents

Preface

Making Modern Britain tells you about the lives of the people of Britain since the 18th century. Things have changed a great deal during this time and the book follows these changes to see how they have affected the way people have worked and lived.

■ Part A explains how Britain became an industrialised country, the first industrialised country in the world. It deals with basic elements in the life of Britain up to 1850: population, agriculture, industry and transport. Part B follows these same basic themes up to the present day. This is not such a success story, but it is important in understanding the position Britain finds herself in today. Part C looks at how these changes have affected every aspect of life in Britain: housing and education, relations between men and women, health, religion, and so on.

■ Historians want to know precisely what happened in the past. This is not easy as accurate statistics were not often kept. Also, such records as were kept have often been destroyed. This book explains some of the difficulties we have in knowing the exact truth.

Any statement an historian makes should be based on evidence. This evidence is gathered by questioning historical sources. This book contains numerous historical sources. Sometimes they just give you information. Sometimes they give you an idea of the problems historians face in deciding what the evidence really means. The questions that go with the sources will help you to understand these problems.

■ Historians also want to know why things happened in the way they did. Different historians may have different theories. For example, why exactly did the cotton industry expand so enormously? The book goes into this and other debates and helps you reach your own conclusions.

■ Many of you reading **Making Modern Britain** will be working for the GCSE examination. At the end of each chapter there are assignments. These can be used as exam practice, or as coursework. An important group of assignments is about 'Empathy'. Empathy means understanding the attitudes, values and beliefs of people in the past. These may be similar to our own, or may be quite different. The empathy assignments try to explain this.

Some assignment sections are headed 'Local Study'. Because the events described in this book affected every part of Britain you may be able to discover what happened in your area. Suggestions are given as to how to do this.

The sections headed 'Understanding Concepts' deal with causes, motives, results and factors which bring about change.

Learning to handle evidence is an important part of studying history. The questions with the sources in the chapters themselves give plenty of practice at this. There are also some more questions on evidence in some of the assignment sections.

All of these tasks are best approached by discussing them with other people first. You do not have to reach agreement but such discussions help to sort out your own ideas. You do not have to agree with what I have written either!

Under 'Themes for Discussion' you are invited to look back over the previous chapter, or several chapters, and reach your own conclusions about what happened, and why. The Britain you will be living in as adults will be shaped by what has gone before.

■ I hope that by reading, thinking and talking about the topics in this book you will see why an understanding of history is so important.

**Christopher Culpin
1987**

1 *People and Industry*

Britain: An Industrial Society

Making Modern Britain will help you understand what kind of country Britain is today, and how it came to be like this. We are going to start by looking at present-day Britain and comparing it with some other countries in the world.

Rich and poor countries

■ *SOURCE 1*

I am sure you know that there are great differences between a rich country like Britain and a poor country like Ethiopia. Source 1 reminds you of some of these differences. When we study social and economic history we need to be precise in what we say. So just how much richer is Britain than Ethiopia? Twice as rich? Ten times as rich? The World Bank collects statistics from 118 countries and lists them, starting at number 1, for the poorest, and ending at number 118 for the richest. (This is called 'the rank order of wealth'.) Source 2 gives some World Bank figures.

You can work out from this table that the average income per person per year in Britain is over 76 times greater than in Ethiopia. This is an enormous difference. Of course, we know that an *average* income of $9200 (£6053) per year does not mean that everyone in Britain earns this much. Some people are very much richer and some much poorer. We also know that money isn't everything. But a higher income does mean that people are generally better off in other ways too. Look at the right hand column of Source 2 which shows life expectancy.

? QUESTIONS

a) What exactly does this column show?
b) Why do the figures increase down the column?
c) What do you think money has got to do with life expectancy?

Not surprisingly, people look at the rich countries to see what they have in common. If you ask yourself one or two questions about your life in Britain today, the answers begin to build up. Think about where your home is, how you and other people travel about, what jobs are done by the adults in your family, what things you have in your home.

Probably most of them are connected with industry. Industry is the

■ *SOURCE 2* **Figures taken from *World Bank Review*, 1985**

Country	Average income per person per year, in dollars	Rank order of wealth	Life expectancy at birth
Ethiopia	120	1	43
India	260	14	55
Brazil	1 880	77	64
Britain	9 200	105	74
Switzerland	16 290	118	79

■ SOURCE 3 Percentage of the working population engaged in agriculture, industry, etc

Country	Agriculture	Industry	Other (Services, etc)
Ethiopia	80	7	13
India	71	13	16
Brazil	30	24	46
Britain	2	42	56
Switzerland	5	46	49

making of goods of all sorts, on a large scale, using machines and powered tools, Britain belongs to a small group of industrial countries including, among others, Switzerland, Germany, Japan, USA, France and Holland. Industrialised countries are generally among the richest in the World Bank table.

How does an industrial country differ from a non-industrial one?
The World Bank statistics tell us something about the kinds of work people do in different countries (see Source 3).

In the poor countries, most people seem to work in agriculture. Their farming methods are simple: even with a large proportion of the population working in farming they only just grow enough food for themselves. Only a few people work in industry. Those who do are often craft workers who are occupied at home, making clothes, tools or other household items to be sold and used in their own village or town. Neither agriculture nor industry produces much for export.

In an industrialised country like Britain, nearly half the population works in industry. The things they make are sold at home and abroad and this creates wealth for the country as a whole. This can then be spent on a whole variety of goods, including food. Very few people actually work in agriculture, and yet, with modern methods, farms produce large amounts of food.

Poorer countries want to know how to create more wealth to spend on a better life for their people. They want to find an answer to the question: how and why does industrialisation happen? There is a particular interest in studying Britain because it was the first country in the world to go through this change. This book tells us the story of how and why industrialisation happened in Britain, how it affected the country, and changed people's lives.

Trying to Find Out the Facts

Britain before the Industrial Revolution

It is not, unfortunately, as easy to get accurate information about the past as it is about the present. There was no World Bank in 1700. There is some information we can use, however. There are many descriptions of places and people which were written or drawn at the time.

■ SOURCE 4B

Exeter is a town very well-built. The streets are well-pitched, spacious, noble streets and a vast trade is carried on ... there is an incredible quantity of serges* made and sold in the town ... the market for meat, fowl, fish, garden things and dairy produce takes up three whole streets ... the whole town and country is employed for at least twenty miles around in spinning, weaving, dressing and scouring, fulling and drying of serges. It turns the most money in a week, of anything in England.

* Serges = a kind of cloth

Celia Fiennes, visiting Exeter, 1698

■ SOURCE 4A Exeter in 1587

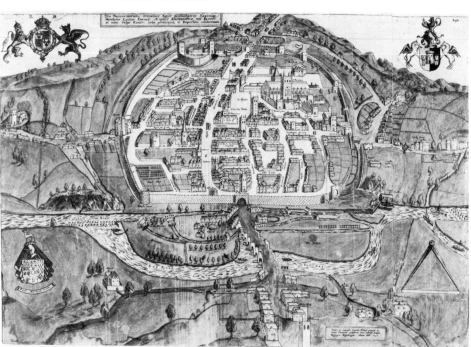

❓ QUESTIONS

a) In Source 4A find: the river, the bridge, the town walls, the cathedral, the castle.
b) How accurate do you think this map is?
c) How could you check its accuracy?
d) How reliable do you think Celia Fiennes' account is?
e) How far do these two sources, 4A and 4B, support each other?
f) Does the fact that there are over 100 years between these two sources mean that they cannot be used to support each other at all? Explain your answer.
g) Source 4A shows a built-up town; Source 4B describes the cloth industry. Do these sources prove that England in the 16th and 17th centuries was an urban, industrial country?
h) How could you use these sources to show that England was *not* an urban, industrial country at that time?

Travellers such as Celia Fiennes, John Leland (1540) and Daniel Defoe (1724), with the occasional map or drawing, such as Source 4A, give us some evidence. They only describe a certain place at a certain time, however, and we cannot be sure how accurate they are. They certainly did not collect accurate statistics: governments only began to do this in the 19th century. Fortunately some people in the 17th century did begin to see the value of statistics. It was very difficult to collect information at that time, but these people, who called themselves 'political arithmeticians', made estimates. One of the most famous was Gregory King, who tried to estimate how many people worked in various jobs.

■ SOURCE 5 Estimates of Gregory King, 1688

Commerce and Industry

Merchants and traders by sea (greater)	2 000
Merchants and traders by sea (lesser)	8 000
Shopkeepers and tradesmen	40 000
Artisans and craftsmen	60 000
	110 000

Agriculture

Freeholders (greater)	40 000
Freeholders (lesser)	140 000
Farmers	150 000
	330 000

Modern historians have tried to check the accuracy of Gregory King's estimates. One form of evidence they can use is parish registers. These record all baptisms, marriages and burials, and often note the job or occupation of those married or buried. Historians take a sample of parish registers and use them to make estimates for the total population. In 1980, P. Lindert used this method to estimate numbers working in different jobs in the late 17th century.

■ SOURCE 6 Estimates of P. Lindert, 1980, for the late 17th century

All commerce	135 333
Manufacturing	179 774
Mining	15 082
Building trades	77 232
	407 421
All agriculture, excluding labourers	241 373

? QUESTIONS

a) Why is it difficult to compare the figures produced by Gregory King (Source 5) and P. Lindert (Source 6)?

b) Are there any groups of workers which appear on one table and not on another? (They might appear under a different name.)

c) Which do you think is likely to be more reliable – the person working at the time (Gregory King, Source 5) or the modern historian (P. Lindert, Source 6)?

d) Why do you think there are such wide differences between the two sources?

e) Compare Sources 5 and 6 with Source 3. Which of the five countries shown in Source 3 seems to be closest to the position of Britain in the late 17th century?

Information from the 19th century

Better, more reliable statistics were collected every 10 years from 1801, using the census. The form shown in Source 7 was used from 1851 onwards and clearly records a great deal of useful information. You will find these forms very interesting and helpful if you prepare a coursework assignment on your own local area. Remember that censuses less than 100 years old are kept secret. (Why do you think this is?)

The Registrar-General (the one person who collected all the census returns for the Government) was able to make some quite accurate calculations about where the people of Britain worked:

■ SOURCE 8 Estimates of percentage distribution of the British working population, based on census returns

	1801
Manufacturing, mining, industry	30%
Trade and transport	11%
Agriculture	36%
Others	23%

Obviously all the figures contained in Sources 5, 6 and 8 are only estimates, and have many inaccuracies. Also, as you have seen, Sources 5 and 6 seem to disagree considerably. Nevertheless, some conclusions are clear: certainly in 1801, and probably even before 1700, Britain had a larger proportion of its population employed in jobs other than agriculture than poor countries have today. Britain's position was more like that of a 'middle-ranking' country such as Brazil today. Probably we would have to go back before 1550 to find a time when Britain had the same employment pattern as Ethiopia has now, and that is well outside the scope of this book. The fact is that Britain in 1700 was already more

■ SOURCE 7 Census enumerator's form, 1851

industrialised than most countries in the world today and Source 4B gives us a clue about what industry was like at that time.

Why Did the Population Grow?

The industrialisation of Britain was accompanied by a rise in population. We know this from looking at the censuses, although these, as we have seen, only began in 1801. The problem is therefore to know how long this rapid population growth had been going on. As there are no census returns for the 17th and 18th centuries, historians have again turned to the parish registers of baptisms, marriages and burials.

There are many problems in using these records. Although parish registers had to be kept from 1537 onwards, very few have survived. Some priests in the past were not very thorough in keeping the register up to date. Some births and deaths may not have been recorded if the baby had not been baptised or if the dead person had not been given a proper burial. From the 1650s many people refused to attend the Church of England, so their baptisms, marriages and burials were not recorded. Historians have, however, managed to find a sample of 404 parishes with good records. Using computers, they have managed to work out a great deal about the population, family size, age at marriage, age at death and many other facts, from the late 16th to the mid 19th centuries.

Source 9 shows what an extraordinary population rise there was. In fact population rose by at least 10 per cent every 10 years from 1781 to 1911. The greatest increase was 17 per cent in the decade 1811–21.

Any variation in population numbers is affected by two factors: the birth rate (the number of babies born, per year, per 1000 people) and the death rate (the number of people dying, per year, per 1000 people).

What was happening to birth rates and death rates in the years 1700–1850?

The birth rate

It seems that about 70 per cent of the reason for the tripling of population in these years was due to an increase in the birth rate and 30 per cent to a decrease in the death rate. The birth rate increased for several reasons: first, the average age of marriage fell from about 26.5 to 23.5. This meant women had three more childbearing years in marriage, and so the size of families increased. Second, many more people married: the number of unmarried people fell from 15 to 7 per cent of the population.

Why did more people marry and marry younger? There were better harvests in the 18th century, partly as a result of agricultural improvements. (These are looked at in

Chapter 2.) Thus food was cheaper, wages went further, and people could afford to get married. The industrial changes of this period (covered in Chapters 3–5) helped the trend. Men and women moved to towns to work (see Chapter 11), earned good wages and were free to make their own decisions without parents or other villagers interfering. The old trades demanded long apprenticeships of seven or nine years, during which marriage was forbidden and apprentices had to live in their employer's house. The new factory-owners paid by the week and took no interest in their employees' personal life. Indeed the average age of marriage in towns was about 20 and the frequency of marriage greater too. In rural areas the average age of marriage remained high, at about 27. Married couples in industrial areas may also have chosen to have bigger families as children could earn money by working in the factories (see Chapter 14).

The death rate

Historians used to think that the tripling of population was caused by a fall in the death rate, and that this was due to medical improvements. In fact, there were hardly any important medical improvements before 1850. The great killer diseases, such as diphtheria, typhoid and tuberculosis were still rampant. Medical knowledge was poor and sanitary conditions were appalling. There were some hospitals, but these were mainly in towns and were careful who they took in, as their benefits were limited. For more information on these aspects of life, read Chapter 13.

There was a small decline in the death rate. Some diseases, such as smallpox, seem not to have been quite such big killers. After 1720 the black rat, which carried the fleas which caused the plague, began to be replaced by the grey rat, so plague gradually disappeared from Britain. The use of bricks and tiles for building, instead of mud and thatch, may have helped decrease the number of germs in houses. There were better harvests in the early 18th century, so people could eat more food and a better variety of food, including vegetables. This may have helped them

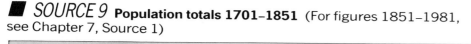

■ *SOURCE 9* Population totals 1701–1851 (For figures 1851–1981, see Chapter 7, Source 1)

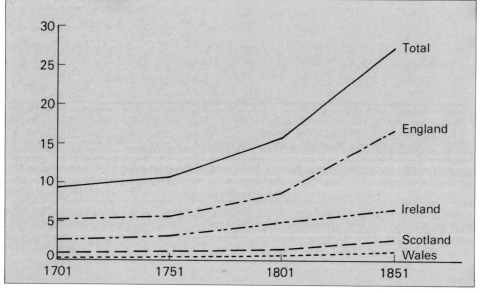

resist disease as well. Nevertheless, it was not until the late 19th and early 20th centuries that any real changes took place in the death rate.

Results of population growth

The huge increase in population was a major factor in the industrialisation of Britain. The changes in agriculture meant that more food could be produced, so that these new mouths could be fed. When workers were needed for the new factories, mines and foundries, the hands were there, ready to start work. The coming together of factories and large numbers of workers led to the growth of cities. The demands of industry led to huge changes in the transport systems of Britain. The new millions were not only producers of goods, but consumers too, buying textiles and pans and all the goods now being manufactured.

Industrialisation and population growth also created huge problems, so that no aspect of life in Britain remained unaffected. The huge new cities posed problems of mass drainage and sanitation, of large-scale law and order, and of local government. A rising population is a young population, and the education system had to change. The Churches had to adapt to meet the changes. People tried to solve their problems by their own actions, so trade unions, co-operatives and new political parties were formed. Parliament attempted to make improvements. Lives, homes, habits – relations between men, women and children – were all utterly changed. You can find out about all these topics in Section C of this book.

Assignments

Local study

1 Census returns are usually available on microfilm for the years 1841, 1851, 1861, 1871 and 1881 at your County Record Office or Public Library. There are many interesting things to be found out from them (see also Chapter 11). Take a rural parish and an urban parish from your area. This chapter has said that people in towns married younger and had more children than people in the countryside. Is this true for your area?

2 Parish registers are much more variable in type and quality, but again your County Record Office can probably help. If you can find good registers you can again build up a picture of age at marriage and age at death of people in a variety of parishes. With parish registers, you might be able to go back beyond 1841.

Understanding concepts

1 Similarity/difference
Look at Sources 4A and 4B.
  a What differences are there between a modern town or city and Exeter as described here?
  b What similarities are there?

2 Similarity/difference
  a How industrialised was Britain in 1700?
  b How do we know?
  c How does this compare with other countries in the world today?

3 Causation
The population of Britain rose from 10.7 million in 1751 to over 27 million in 1851.
  a Why did these changes take place? You should refer to:
   i changes in the birth rate;
   ii changes in the death rate.
  b Did population changes help industrialisation, or did industrialisation help the population changes?

Evidence

1 a What kinds of sources of evidence can we use for studying the population of Britain before 1700?
  b What are the advantages and disadvantages of each?

Themes for discussion

1 a What are the benefits of living in an industrialised country?
  b What are the disadvantages?
  c Do you think there are bound to be both benefits *and* disadvantages?
2 Do you think less-developed countries such as Ethiopia should be encouraged to follow the path of industrialisation that Britain has followed since 1750?
3 a Why do historians have to try and be as accurate as possible about the past?
  b What problems does this create for historians?
  c Why do these problems make History a different kind of subject from Science?

2 Agriculture – New Ways to Feed More People

In the last chapter we saw how the population of this country grew in the years 1700–1850. England, Scotland and Wales contained only 6½ million people in 1700, 11 million in 1801 and an astonishing 21 million by 1851. The big question for us to ask is: how were all these people fed?

There aren't many possible answers to this question. England did not increase in size to grow more food! Perhaps we bought in food from abroad? No, the figures tell us that in fact we sold food abroad; as much as a quarter of our crop in 1750. We imported a little after that, but in the Napoleonic Wars from 1793 to 1815 the French stopped any country in Europe sending us food. So that is not the answer. Perhaps the same land was made to yield more?

■ SOURCE 1A

'Tis more remarkable still how a great part of these downs comes, by a new method of farming to be not only made arable, but bear excellent wheat, and great crops too.

Daniel Defoe, *A Tour through England and Wales*, 1724

■ SOURCE 1B Livestock, 1683

■ SOURCE 1C Sheep, 1859

? QUESTIONS

a) In Source 1A, what does 'arable' mean?
b) In Source 1A, which part of England is Daniel Defoe describing?
c) Because Source 1A is only about a part of England, does this mean it is no help to us?
d) Describe the main differences between the sheep (centre picture in 1B) in 1683 and the sheep in Source 1C.
e) How far do these sources help to answer the question of how the growing population was fed?

Perhaps more land could be used for farming?

■ SOURCE 1D

If the melancholy wastes and commons are enclosed and drained, the land yielding at present 3s 6d [17½p] or 4s 6d [22½p] an acre can be made to yield 10s [50p] an acre.

Arthur Young, 1768

? QUESTIONS

a) In Source 1D, which pieces of land does Arthur Young want to bring into cultivation?
b) How, does he say, can they be improved?

Sources 1A–D give us some clues about how more grain and meat might have been produced from the same land, and how more land might have been brought into use. How did farmers set about doing these things?

Growing Better Crops

The great problem facing all farmers was – and still is – how to keep the soil fertile. You cannot grow the same crop year after year in the same piece of ground. If you do, the land becomes exhausted and will not produce good crops. Nowadays, farmers use chemical fertilisers. These had not been invented in the 18th century, so there was only one answer to the problem of how to keep soil fertile: leave the land fallow, without a crop, and allow animals to graze so that their dung fertilised the land. Most farmers in the early 18th century changed the crops which they grew in each field every year, according to a pattern, as shown in Source 2.

■ SOURCE 2 Crop rotation, 18th century

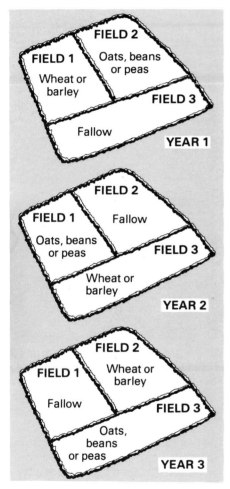

? QUESTIONS

a) The system in Source 2 is called a 3-crop, or 3-course, rotation. Explain why it is called this.
b) Wheat or barley is the most demanding crop for the soil. What happens to a field the year before it is sown with wheat or barley?
c) What fraction of the farm grows no crop at all every year?
d) Animals were most important, as they were the only source of fertiliser. Which crops grown were fodder crops, for animals to eat in winter?

It seemed impossible for farmers to break out of the 3-crop rotation. They could not grow more crops because the land would become exhausted. The only way to improve the soil was to keep more animals, but there were not enough fodder crops to keep them alive in the winter. In fact, humans and animals competed for food in the winter and so many animals were slaughtered each autumn; some were so badly fed in the winter that they had to be carried out to the fields in the spring.

Norfolk rotation

However, there was an answer. After the English Civil War, in the 1650s, many landowners who had fought for the King went into exile in Holland. There they saw different crops being grown, such as turnips and clover, and grasses like lucerne and sainfoin. When they came home, after 1660, they began to grow these new crops in England. The most popular way of using them was in a 4-course, or Norfolk rotation, introduced by Sir Richard Weston.

■ SOURCE 3 Norfolk rotation

Year One After the wheat harvest, harrow up the stubble, then plough the field in November/December.

Year Two Cross-plough and harrow again, removing weeds. June, prepare for turnips with 8 cubic yards of dung per acre. Sow turnips, and hoe twice, removing weeds. November–April, pull biggest turnips and cart them to farmyard. Place in heaps of 12 cartloads, cover with straw. Use as fodder for cattle in yards. Sheep eat smaller turnips in the field, fertilising it with their dung.

Year Three March–April, plough land, sow with barley, clover and grass. Barley yields 50 bushels to 3½ bushels of seed.

Year Four Clover and grass grow through the barley stubble for animals to eat in winter; what is left is mowed as hay in May, about 2 wagon-loads an acre. October, plough and sow 2 bushels of wheat per acre.

Year One Harvest winter wheat: yields about 17 bushels per acre.

From a farmer's evidence, 1813

? QUESTIONS

a) List the ways the animals are fed.
b) Describe how the land is kept fertile.
c) Which of the crops seems to need most work?
d) When are weeds removed?
e) Using this account, make your own diagram of the Norfolk rotation along the lines of Source 2.

There were many advantages to this system, as you can see. The turnips fed animals in winter, so more animals could be kept alive. They produced more manure, so other crops were heavier. Clover provided grazing, hay, and also restored fertility to the soil. The land was always being used, never just lying fallow collecting weeds.

The Norfolk system worked well on light soils, such as north Norfolk. On heavier soils turnips would rot or run to seed. Farmers found that swedes or mangolds grew better in these conditions and did the same job. Sometimes, on heavier land, the clover or grass was left for three years as a 'ley' or temporary meadow. Another idea in low-lying areas was the 'floating meadow', which was also started in the 17th century. This meant diverting a stream to trickle over the land, keeping it very rich, with grass growing nearly all the year. Again, this helped the animal feed problem.

Viscount Townshend

One man whose name has always been linked with the growing of turnips is Viscount Townshend (1674–1738). He was a chief minister in the government of 1714 and brother-in-law of the great Prime Minister, Sir Robert Walpole. In 1730 he quarrelled with Walpole, gave up politics and retired to his farm at Raynham in north Norfolk.

Townshend did not discover turnips or invent the 4-course Norfolk rotation: as we have seen, some farmers had started farming in that way nearly 70 years earlier. Daniel Defoe described turnips as 'common over most of the Eastern and Southern parts of England by the reign of Queen Anne'; she died in 1714. But the biggest problem with bringing changes to farming is telling farmers about a new idea and persuading them to introduce it. Townshend was already a famous politician and soon became a famous farmer. His estate was written up by Arthur Young, Secretary to the Board of Agriculture, some years later.

 **SOURCE 4**

In 1730 it was an extensive heath without tree or shrub, only a sheep walk to another farm. Now in 1780 the whole is laid out in enclosures and cultivated in the Norfolk system in superior style. The whole is let at 15 shillings [75p] an acre, ten times its original value.

Arthur Young, 1780

 QUESTIONS

a) What was the land used for before Townshend took over?
b) What was the reason for the success?

If a farmer had not heard of turnips and the Norfolk system before, their adoption by the famous Viscount Townshend was much more likely to attract attention to them now. Townshend's fame and success persuaded farmers to adopt his farming methods.

Animals

Source 1B shows how poor the animals of the late 17th century were. They were big-boned, with long legs, very little meat and often diseased. There were two main reasons for this: first, the lack of fodder, which meant that herds and flocks were small; second, the system of grazing all the animals in a village together on the common, the fallow or the wasteland. This common grazing meant that good and poor quality animals all bred together, so it was impossible to breed fine animals. Also, disease spread between them very easily.

We have seen that the fodder problem was being solved. The enclosure movement, which is described on page 10, meant that farmers began to keep their own animals separately in their own fenced fields. This meant they could go in for selective breeding, that is, breeding carefully from selected stock to produce certain

qualities such as shorter legs, longer bodies, more meat, better wool, etc.

One of the most famous breeders was Robert Bakewell (1725–95) of Dishley in Leicestershire. By carefully controlling his flock, he produced the New Leicester sheep, double in weight to earlier breeds. It had less bone in proportion to meat. It also put on weight fast, so did not cost so much to keep.

Bakewell's Leicester sheep was actually rather fatty. Fat had more uses at that time than now – in soap and candles for example – but the Leicester is now extinct. However, Bakewell helped in the breeding of the shire horse, and showed others the way. Robert Ellman bred the Southdown sheep, and the Collings brothers the Shorthorn cow. In the early stages of selective breeding, size and weight were admired.

■ *SOURCE 5A* **Leicester rams, 1810**

■ *SOURCE 5B* **Champion Shorthorn, 1856**

❓ QUESTIONS

a) How can you tell who are the shepherds and who are the prosperous farmers in Source 5A?

b) Compare the animals in Source 5A with those in Source 1B. What are the differences?

c) Compare the cow in Source 5B with present-day cattle and describe the differences.

d) Source 5B is a painting: does that mean it is a reliable picture of this animal?

e) Does this mean that historians ought to ignore this source?

There was a general improvement in all types of animal, as the figures in Source 5E show.

■ SOURCE 5C Cattle at Castle Howard, 1840

■ SOURCE 5E Average weight of animals sold at Smithfield Market, 1710 and 1795 (lb)

	1710	1795
Cattle	320	800
Calves	50	143
Sheep	28	80
Lambs	18	50

An average lamb in 1795 weighed as much as a calf in 1710!

New Machines

In many other chapters in this book, you will read of new machines bringing about change. Was this also true in agriculture? Was the great increase in crop yields helped by machines?

An agriculturalist, Jethro Tull (1674–1741), invented several machines, including a seed drill and a horse-drawn hoe. The system of sowing seed in his time was 'broadcasting', that is throwing the seed by hand on to the field. Tull's drill planted the seed in rows, at a steady rate. Hoeing was thus made easier. Tull explained his ideas in *Horse Hoeing Husbandry*, a book published in 1731.

Tull's drill was not taken up very widely until well into the 19th century. This was partly because it did not work very well, partly because industrial methods at the time

■ SOURCE 5D Pig, Surrey, 1798: 4 feet high, 8 feet 9 inches long, 5 inches of fat all over, 2½ years old, weighed nearly half a ton

could not make machines which were strong but light, and partly because farmers were reluctant to change.

Later improvements in industry brought other new products to farming after 1800. Lighter iron ploughs, such as the Rotherham plough, could be made. This could be pulled by two horses, and began to replace the heavy wooden ploughs of earlier years which took six oxen to pull them. Better scythe blades from Sheffield meant that the scythe gradually replaced the sickle as the main harvesting tool. Farm labourers using scythes could cut much more in a day. The threshing machine was invented, and this

■ SOURCE 6 Seed drill, similar to Jethro Tull's, 1730

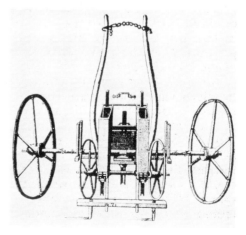

put an end to hours of laborious work with the flail.

However, farmers were slow to take up new inventions. With a high and rising population, there was no shortage of farm labourers to do the work. Why spend money on some new labour-saving gadget? Many changes in farming actually increased the amount of work needed. Turnips demanded hours of hoeing, and enclosure provided lots of work hedging and ditching. The great age of labour-saving farm machines was yet to come.

Enclosures

One of the main obstacles to better farming in the late 18th century was the way much of the land was organised. Many villages in central and southern England still had open fields. (Look at Source 7.)

This system of farming had been in existence for a thousand years. Each villager had a number of strips of land scattered among everybody else's in large, unfenced, open fields. Usually they followed the old 3-crop rotation (see Source 2). There were some good points about this: everyone shared good or bad harvests; good and bad land was evenly shared out. Also, as all ploughing, harvesting and grazing on the fallow had to take place at the same time, it kept the village together. However, there were many disadvantages.

❓ QUESTIONS

a) Why did the open-field system waste a lot of land?
b) In what ways would this system stop you if you wanted:
  i) to change your crop rotation?
  ii) to drain your strips?
  iii) to breed better animals?
  iv) to try out a seed drill?
c) Each strip was divided from the neighbouring one by a narrow piece of land called a balk. Why was this bad farming?
d) What other disadvantages of the open field system can you think of?

In addition to the open field villages, there were other areas of unenclosed land: commons, moors, greens, wide road verges, marshes and fens. These were used, if at all, as shared rough grazing for animals. In 1695 it was estimated that 10 million acres of England were uncultivated. These commons were often the only means of support for poor people, and an essential extra asset for many others. Little cottages had been put up by 'squatters', and these people could just make ends meet by grazing a few animals. Landowners, keen to make more money by cultivating more land, looked eagerly at the open fields and commons (see Source 1D).

Enclosure simply meant taking open land and dividing it up into small parcels according to who had a right to use it. Each person could then put a fence round their piece and use it as they wished. Sometimes, this was arranged by agreement: villagers might swap strips among themselves until they each had several together. These could then be combined, fenced in and treated as one field. Villagers might agree that a common, or a marsh, could be used better if each person had their own piece, instead of sharing it all. We shall never know how many enclosures by agreement were made privately in this way.

However, what if everyone did not agree? If just one person objected, the enclosure could not automatically go ahead. The people who wanted enclosure then had to try to arrange for it to be done by an Act of Parliament. A notice was nailed to the church door saying that enclosure was proposed. If the owners of four-fifths of the land agreed, then a private Act was put through Parliament. When the Act was passed, Commissioners would come to the village and their surveyors would make an accurate map of it.

■ SOURCE 8A Frontispiece of an Act, 1798

AN

A C T

FOR

Dividing and Inclosing the Open and Common Fields, Common Meadows, and other Commonable Lands, within the Parish of *Weston Turville*, in the County of *Buckingham*.

WHEREAS there are within the Parish of *Weston* Pa Turville, in the County of *Buckingham*, certain Open and Common Fields, Common Meadows, and other Commonable Lands, containing One thousand Acres, or thereabouts, and divers Quantities of Meadow and Pasture Land:

❓ QUESTIONS

a) Which village is to be enclosed, according to Source 8A?
b) How many acres are going to be enclosed?
c) What is the difference between 'four-fifths of the landowners' and 'the owners of four-fifths of the land'?
d) Which groups of people would the four-fifths rule benefit?

■ SOURCE 7 Map of open fields at Ingham, 1769

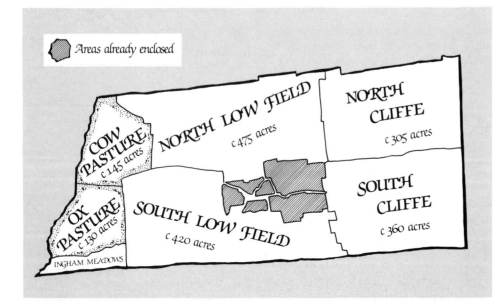

Areas already enclosed

COW PASTURE c 145 acres

NORTH LOW FIELD c 475 acres

NORTH CLIFFE c 305 acres

OX PASTURE c 130 acres

SOUTH LOW FIELD c 420 acres

SOUTH CLIFFE c 360 acres

INGHAM MEADOWS

■ SOURCE 8B Surveyors at work, about 1798

lion acres were enclosed, of which two-thirds were open field and commons combined, and one-third was commons only.

What were the results of enclosure?

Of course, enclosure on its own did not bring about better farming. There are some examples of improved farming in open fields and old-fashioned farming in enclosed fields. However, there is no doubt that better farming methods could really only start to work properly after enclosure. Also, enclosure brought into cultivation over 2 million acres of land which had not been farmed before. This was mainly common land and wasteland, but also included some of the Fens. In Norfolk alone, common land declined from 149 000 acres in 1784 to 27 000 acres in 1844.

Who benefited?
It was the better-off farmers and landowners who gained most. Enclosure was expensive: it cost money in lawyers' fees to draw up documents; the Commissioners charged expenses of up to £3 per day. Then there was the cost of hedging and ditching the new enclosed fields. Enclosure could cost

? QUESTIONS

a) What is the state of the fields in Source 8B?
b) What sort of instruments are they using?

The Commissioners would also investigate people's rights to the land. How much land was theirs? What rights did they have? Did they have written proof? And so on. They were busy men, because of the hundreds of Enclosure Acts passed at this time.

■ SOURCE 8C Diary of an Enclosure Commissioner, Arthur Elliott

December 31, 1795 At the Grange settling Kimberworth Enclosure with Lord Effingham.
January 1, 1796 Took a ride with his Lordship and Rev. Redhead.
February 19, 1796 Settling Draft (arrangement of land) for Upper Hallam.
February 25, 1796 Attended to Heeley Draft. Dined at the Angel with Gentlemen of the Hunt.

? QUESTIONS

a) Which villages are involved in the enclosure?
b) Who are Arthur Elliott's friends?
c) How do you think this might affect his decision when it came to dividing up the enclosed land?

When the Commissioner had made his decision a new map was made.

? QUESTIONS

a) Look at Source 8D. Find the old strips: have the Commissioners used the old fields in laying out their new boundaries?
b) What do you notice about the new hedges?

As the 18th century wore on, there was a great increase in the number of Enclosure Acts passed. Before 1750, there were about 30–40 per year; from 1770 to 1780 there were 642, and from 1801 to 1810 there were 906. In all, 7 mil-

■ SOURCE 8D Modern aerial photograph of land enclosed in 1795

anything from £1.50 to £3 per acre. Clearly, only those who had some money to start with could afford it. If you could afford it, then you probably went on and prospered. Prices for farm produce rose and rose, especially during the Napoleonic Wars.

Who lost out?

Smallholders often could not afford enclosure. The cost per acre was highest to them anyway, as small fields needed more hedging and ditching per acre than larger ones. Many smallholders and cottagers lived on common land to which they had no written title, even though they had lived there for years. They therefore received nothing. The common rights which helped people to make ends meet before enclosure were not provided for in the same way afterwards. The right to graze a cow, some hens and some geese on the common could not be replaced by the granting of a plot of half an acre by a Commissioner. Enclosures made many cottagers give up their little independent holdings and work for wages. When wages were low, their poverty and unhappiness were great.

■ SOURCE 9A

LORD TORRINGTON: **Has Meriden Common long been enclosed?**
WOMAN: **A lackaday Sir, that was a bad job, and ruined all us poor folk ...**
LORD TORRINGTON: **Why so?**
WOMAN: **Because we had our garden, our bees, our share of a flock of sheep, and the feeding of our geese. And could cut turf for our fuel. Now that is gone! ... My cottage with many others is pulled down and the poor are sadly put to it to get a house to put their heads in.**

The Torrington Diaries, 1782

? QUESTIONS

a) What rights did the woman lose?
b) Why do you think her cottage was pulled down?

Even Arthur Young, who encouraged all forms of improvement, was horrified at the results. He reported that one farm labourer told him, 'All I know is I had a cow and an Act of Parliament has taken it from me.' There were riots in some villages, and there was a famous rhyme:

■ SOURCE 9B

The law arrests the man or woman
Who steals the goose from off the common
But leaves the greater rascal loose
Who steals the common from the goose.

? QUESTIONS

a) Explain this in your own words.
b) Who was 'the greater rascal'?

Many people blamed the Commissioners for the bad effects of enclosures, but this was unfair. Most of them probably did their job properly, trying not to be influenced by their connections with the big landowners. It was not their fault that the law gave no support to common rights.

Reasons For Change

We have seen what changes were introduced into farming, but why did people agree to them? What made them change the habits of generations?

To answer this we need to know who owned and who farmed the land in Britain in the 18th century. At the top of the scale were the big landowners of the country, people who owned 5000 acres or more, with an income over £10 000 per year. They held all the important posts in the government, and in fact, ran the country. Below them were the gentry, or squires, with incomes from £5000 to £10 000 per year. Neither of these groups farmed the land themselves; the actual farming was carried out by tenants, who paid them rents. Some tenant farms could be quite large, up to 1000 acres. There were also many thousands of smaller farmers who owned their own land. This meant anything from quite good-sized farms (for that time) of 300 acres or more, down to smallholdings of 20 acres or less. At the bottom of the heap were the labourers. Their wages might only amount to £20 a year, but with a pig, or a patch of ground, or by doing some other work, they just kept themselves and their families alive.

Large landowners

The main thrust for improvement came from the top. The big landowners of the 18th century found that their lifestyle was expensive. Many built new houses. Prime Minister Sir Robert Walpole, for example, built Houghton Hall.

This is perhaps an exceptional house, larger than most. However, many landowners great and small were building or rebuilding their houses at this time. They were fitting them out, too, with Chippendale furniture, silver and paintings from Italy. To raise the money for this lavish lifestyle, they had to raise the rents for their farms. This could only be done if they improved the land to increase its value.

■ SOURCE 10 Houghton Hall, Norfolk, built 1722–35

An interest in improved farming methods therefore became vital for the great men of the time. Sir Robert Walpole, for example, is said to have always opened letters from his estate before he began on State papers. Lord Althorp and the Marquis of Rockingham were famous improvers, so was Viscount Townshend (see earlier, page 7). Even the King, George III, loved to be called Farmer George, and wrote articles on farming under the name of his shepherd, Ralph Robinson. It was as important for a fashionable aristocrat to own a good bull as a good racehorse. This explains the picture of Castle Howard in Source 5C, and also perhaps the clothes of some of the men in Source 11.

Improvements cost money, as we have seen, but in the 18th century it was easy for landowners to borrow money on a mortgage. Merchants, too, often bought estates with their profits from trade. Being a landowner carried a higher status than being a merchant. They brought business methods into farming and wanted to be up-to-date.

The spread of ideas

Books were written to pass on new ideas. Arthur Young (1741–1820), who has already been quoted in this chapter, was made Secretary to the Board of Agriculture in 1793. He ordered descriptions of the farming in every county to be written. Many he wrote himself.

Farming, however, is a practical business, and farmers began to want to meet, talk about and sample new ideas. Agricultural societies and shows were started.

The Duke of Bedford raised the rents on his estate to a total of £31 000 a year. He held a five-day sheep-shearing at Woburn Abbey, where people from all over England met to discuss farming.

? QUESTIONS

a) Notice the different classes of people in Source 11, ranging from aristocrats, to farmers, to shepherds. How can you tell them apart?
b) Describe the buildings.
c) What other animals can be seen?
d) What topics do you think were discussed?
e) Imagine you were one of the people there. Describe your day to a friend or relative on arriving home.

The most famous improver of all was Sir Thomas Coke (pronounced Cook) of Holkham, in Norfolk (1754–1832). He had taken over a poor estate, quite near Viscount Townshend's, in 1776. It was then worth £2000 a year. He used all the new ideas, including the Norfolk 4-course rotation and enclosure. He added some of his own, such as using bone-meal as fertiliser. By 1816, his estates were worth £20 000 per year. He used to hold huge sheep-shearings, at which as many as 7000 people would come and see his latest ideas. Farmers and dukes would rub shoulders and compare seed samples.

Coke's system for improving his estate was to write into the leases of his tenants that they must farm in

■ *SOURCE 11* **Sheep-shearing at Woburn, 1811**

an improved way. His tenants had to take notice of what his steward said, or their leases were not renewed. If they did, their yields increased and they continued to make money, even though their rents were high. In this way, the new methods were gradually spread across the country from the centres shown in Map 1.

The Speed of Change

■ SOURCE 12

When I passed from the conversation of the farmers I was recommended to call upon to that of men whom chance threw in my way, I seemed to have lost a century in time, or to have moved 1000 miles in a day. There was a dark ignorance under the cover of a wise suspicion.

Arthur Young, *Oxfordshire*, 1809

❓ QUESTIONS

a) Who were the two groups of farmers?

b) Why should this make us careful when we read descriptions of new methods of farming at this time?

Some people have talked of an Agricultural Revolution. A revolution means a *rapid* change, though, and Source 12 reminds us how slowly things change in farming. Arthur Young could write his books, but he could not make farmers read them or act on his suggestions. Coke could do great things in Norfolk and show them to many people, but only those people who were interested travelled to Holkham. The change was slow and patchy. Arthur Young was probably right to say in Source 12 that the difference between farmers in the same county could be 100 years of change.

We have seen that some methods dated back to the mid-17th century, and were really only used widely by the mid-19th century. This is hardly a revolution! What we do see is a gradual, steady spread of new methods, until a few, rare, bright ideas became the normal practice of most farmers.

■ *MAP 1* **Centres of innovation in farming**

Results of the Changes in Farming

1 The massive rising population could be fed. Indeed it could be fed quite well (see Chapter 17).

2 The number of people employed in agriculture actually rose, as there was lots of work to be done. (In 1801 there were 1.7 million employed in agriculture; by 1851 there were 2.1 million.) However, this is nothing like the rise in population. Workers were thus available for the new industries.

3 Many trades and businesses prospered as farming prospered. Corn provided raw material for millers, bakers, starch-makers, book-binders, linen printers and paper hangers. Barley was needed by maltsters, brewers, distillers and innkeepers, and animals by butchers, harness-makers, soap-makers, candle-makers, shoe-makers, cutlers and glue-makers. An improved supply of cheap agricultural produce helped all their businesses.

4 Plentiful, cheap food meant that wages in industry did not have to be all that high. Businessmen therefore had good profits to invest in their enterprises.

5 Although there were times of low wages, this was not always the case. When wages were good and food cheap, the rural people were very ready to buy industrial products, such as cloth, furniture, household supplies and ornaments. They were a good market.

6 As the landowners became richer through improved farming, so they began to invest their money. Country banks spread in the early 19th century as a way of making funds available to business. Many schemes for canals, turnpikes, railways and industrial businesses had money put into them by successful farmers.

Assignments

Empathy

1 Get into groups of four. Each member of the group should take one of the following characters:
   i the squire, running into debt because he has just re-built and re-furnished his house;
   ii a young tenant-farmer, interested in agricultural improvement;
   iii an older landowner, happy with the old ways;
   iv a shepherd and smallholder with a house on the edge of the common.
   Each person should give his or her view on a proposal to enclose the village's open fields.

2 Read Source 12. Imagine a conversation between 2 farmers, one from each of the types mentioned by Arthur Young, and write it down.

Understanding concepts

1 **Cause/effect**
   a Why was it difficult to break out of the 3-course rotation cycle?
   b How did the growing of turnips allow farming to break out of the 3-course rotation?
   c In what ways did the 4-course rotation make farming more productive?

2 **Change/continuity**
   In what ways did farming methods improve in the years 1700–1850? You should mention:

i crops grown;
ii types of animals;
iii use of machinery.

3 **Cause/effect**

> Farmers want to breed better animals
> More food grown
> Farmers became richer
> Need to make land yield more
> More employment on the land
> Farmers want to change their crop rotation
> Squatters lost their homes
> Smallholders sold up their land

a Choose 2 important *causes* of the enclosure movement from the box above, and explain why they are important.
b Choose 2 important *effects* of the enclosure movement from the box above, and explain why they are important.

Themes for discussion

1 a Who benefited from enclosures, and why?
   b Who lost from the enclosures, and why?
   c What other changes can you think of which have been good for some groups of people and bad for others?

2 The phrase 'Agrarian Revolution' is often used to describe the changes outlined in this chapter. Do you think the changes described amount to a 'Revolution', or not?

3 Textiles: The Marvel of Machines

If we wanted a picture to sum up the Industrial Revolution, then we might well choose Source 1. There is the huge city sprawling right across the picture. There are the smutty clouds of smoke blotting out the light. Most of all there is the forest of great chimneys towering above the old church spires and towers. These chimneys belonged to cotton factories – Manchester was the centre of the cotton textile industry.

The cotton industry is a good place to start exploring the Industrial Revolution. It was the industry foreign visitors commented on. It made use of other industrial products such as coal, iron and steam engines. Its factories, as we can see, changed the face of Britain. By 1850, cotton goods were the leading British export. The story of the cotton industry may not be typical of all industries, but it is at the centre of the story of the Industrial Revolution.

The Early Textile Industry

Textiles are woven cloth. They can be made of cotton, linen, silk or wool. In fact, Britain had had a successful woollen textile industry for centuries before the 'Industrial Revolution'. The processes of making textiles were still much the same whatever the material.

1 Cleaning
The natural raw materials – fleece for woollens, flax for linen, silkworm cocoons or cotton bolls – had to be sorted out. Dirt and rubbish were removed and the materials were cleaned with soap or alkali.

2 Carding (see Source 2A)
This was done with a pair of boards. Each was covered with leather with wire points sticking through it. The boards were pulled gently across each other and so the fibres were untangled. When this had been done they were all pulled off together in a roll or 'sliver'.

3 Spinning (see Source 2B)
This was done with a spinning wheel. The fibres were pulled, stretched and twisted together. This made a continuous thread, or yarn. The yarn was then wound on to a bobbin – see the container of bobbins between the two women in the picture.

4 Weaving (see Source 2C)
This was done on a loom. One set of threads, called the warp, ran from one end of the loom to the other, away from the weaver. Alternate threads were raised or lowered by foot pedals to give a triangular gap. Through this the weaver passed a shuttle containing the weft thread from side to side.

5 Finishing
Many things could now be done to the cloth, such as bleaching or dyeing. Cotton often had patterns printed on it. (Note: some woollens were dyed as yarn, not cloth.)

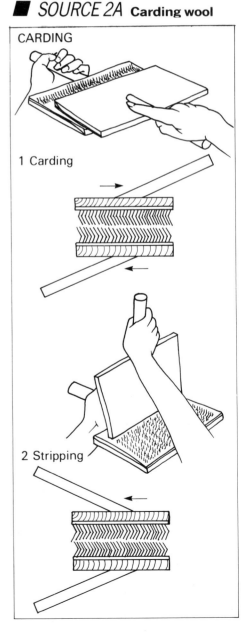

CARDING

1 Carding

2 Stripping

■ SOURCE 2B **Spinning yarn**

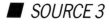

■ SOURCE 2C **Weaving cloth**

? QUESTIONS

a) What are the machines or tools in Sources 2A–C made of?

b) Where are the workers in Sources 2B and 2C working?

c) Note the sex of the workers. How do you think working in the textile industry fitted in with family life?

d) Which member of the family might do the carding?

e) What can you tell from these pictures about how well off textile workers were in the 18th century?

f) What else would you want to know before making a reliable statement about question e)?

It is clear from Sources 2B and 2C that people used to work in their own homes. The tools of their trade were small; even the loom only took up a small spare room. The power used was only their own muscles. Either a family would share the different jobs, or the merchants would arrange for the fleece, yarn or cloth to be carried from worker to worker

in their own homes. This was called the Domestic System.

■ SOURCE 3

We came to Halifax, we found the houses thicker and the villages greater in every bottom; and not only so, but the sides of the hills which were very steep every way were spread with houses and that very thick. There was not a beggar nor an idle person to be seen because of their always being in business. This business is the clothing trade ... at almost every house there was a tenter* and on every tenter a piece of cloth ... Among the manufacturers' houses are scattered a number of cottages in which dwell the workmen, the women and children of whom are always busy carding, spinning etc. so that no hands being unemployed all can gain their bread, even from the youngest to the most ancient.

* tenter – a wooden frame for drying and stretching cloth

Daniel Defoe, *A Tour through the Whole Island of Britain*, 1724

? QUESTIONS

a) Why, according to Defoe, are there no beggars?

b) What jobs does he describe?

c) What evidence is there that weaving was done as well?

Reasons for Change

This, then, was the textile industry before the Industrial Revolution. Source 1 shows a very different picture from that described in Source 3. Why did the change happen? Historians have suggested different theories to explain this.

Theory 1

This says that, as the population was rising (see Chapter 1), there were millions more people needing textiles. From 1750 to 1850 there were 17 million more British people, each needing clothes and household items such as curtains and tablecloths. This means there was a demand for more textiles, so people who made them decided they could get richer by making and selling more.

SOURCE 4 Imports of cotton, wool (including home production), linen and silk (lb million)

	Cotton	Wool	Linen	Silk
1740–9	2	57	3	½
1772–4	4	85	9	1
1795–1800	42	98	8	1
1819–21	141	140	–	–

To test this theory we would need to know exactly how much textile production increased: was it the same, or more, or less than the population rise? Unfortunately, exact figures for how much was made were not kept at that time. Historians have to use such evidence as we can find. For example, people wrote about changes in their times, and travellers wrote about their journeys. The government kept note of raw materials coming into or going out of the country, for tax reasons. This gives us some interesting statistics as shown in Source 4.

? QUESTIONS

a) Which was the most important raw product in 1740–9?
b) Which was the smallest? Why do you think this was?
c) Which put on the greatest growth up to 1821?
d) Compare the rise in figures for cotton imports with the population figures in Chapter 1, Source 9. Which goes up the fastest?

SOURCE 5A Fashionable dress of the 18th century

It is clear that the cotton industry grew far faster than the population. Theory 1 will not serve as a complete explanation, therefore.

Theory 2

This suggests that people were more extravagant in the 18th century. They wanted more and richer clothes, so again there was more demand. This is difficult to prove, but we do have some evidence.

SOURCE 5B Belongings of a Colchester weaver in 1744 before she went to the workhouse

2 bedsteads, 2 beds, 1 pair curtains, 7 sheets, 3 blankets, 2 coverlets, 4 pillows, 4 pairs pillowcases, 2 bolsters, 2 pairs drawers.

SOURCE 5C

Females of all ages and conditions hardly use any woollens at present, except those of the finest texture, and made of the finest woollens. Silks, cottons and linens, combined in a thousand forms, these are now almost the universal wear, from Her Grace in the drawing-room down to the lowest scullion in the kitchen.

Dean Tucker's *Observations*, 1749

? QUESTIONS

a) How do Sources 5A–C suggest that it was not just the rich who bought more fabrics?
b) Use these sources to write a paragraph in support of Theory 2.
c) In what ways are these sources a different type of evidence from Source 4?
d) Which is the more reliable – Source 4 or these sources?
e) Which source is the more useful to a historian trying to decide on a big national issue like the textile revolution?
f) Write a paragraph criticising Theory 2, using Sources 4 and 5.

Both Theory 1 and Theory 2 explain the growth of the industry by saying that *demand* in Britain grew, so it was worth making more textiles. If this were true, the price of cotton would have gone up as more people wanted cotton goods. In fact, the price of cotton fell: fine yarn prices went down from £1.90 per lb in 1786 to 26p per lb in 1812, coarse yarn from 80p per lb in 1779 to 12½p per lb in 1812.

If cotton was becoming cheaper, more people could afford to buy it. But is this sufficient to explain that huge rise in cotton imports in Source 4? Was it all sold in Britain? What about exports? Exports of cotton goods were worth only £11 000 per year in the 1740s; this had risen to £¼ million by the 1760s, £10 million by 1805, £17 million by 1820 – the first year that cotton exports were worth more than woollens.

Theory 3

We can now begin to put together Theory 3: something (we are not yet sure what) brought the price of cotton goods tumbling down. This meant more cotton goods could be sold, both inside and outside Britain. This 'something' could only be one of two things: the raw material or the cost of making it, since anything that is made has these two parts to its price. Let us look at each in turn.

Perhaps there was a sudden huge drop in the cost of raw cotton. Before 1760 most cotton came from India or Egypt. It was grown in the West Indies, too. When America was a British colony the growing of cotton was banned in order to protect the British trade with India and the West Indies. After America's independence in 1783, the Americans looked for new products to grow and sell. A Stockport cotton merchant, John Milne, had a son who became a friend of George Washington, first President of the USA. He suggested growing cotton in the southern states. The idea was taken up and American cotton plantations became very successful. They increased output from 100 lb an acre to 340 lb or more. In 1793 Eli Whitney invented a simple machine, called a cotton gin, which stripped the seeds from the raw cotton quickly and easily. Imports of raw cotton from the USA into Britain grew from under ½ million lb in 1790 to 55 million lb by 1810.

However, although all the raw cotton Britain needed could be supplied, it was not at lower prices. The American plantations grew to meet the demand for raw cotton. They didn't cause the industry to change by supplying the raw cotton cheaply. Therefore the fall in the price of cotton yarn must be due to a fall in the cost of making it.

Theory 3 can now be more clearly stated: the cost of making cotton goods fell so much that lots more could be sold, at home and abroad, so more was made. The reason the costs of making cotton goods fell is due to a few remarkable inventors. Their inventions greatly increased the amount of textiles each worker could make and so the price of cotton goods fell rapidly.

Inventors and Their Machines

Because there are so many processes in the textile industry, any speeding-up of one process will cause a problem in another. For example, if the weavers are able to work faster because of some new invention, they will soon run out of yarn. Unless spinning changes too, there will be a bottleneck, or hold-up. These bottlenecks sometimes held up the industry for some time. They were also a powerful reason for someone to invent another machine to reduce the bottleneck.

Kay's flying shuttle, 1733

John Kay was a Lancashire weaver and clock-maker. He fitted wheels to the shuttle, and a spring at each side to drive the shuttle to and fro across the loom. This simple improvement meant that one weaver could weave as much cloth as two weavers did before.

New machines are not always welcomed and handloom weavers in the woollen industry were very afraid that if too much cloth was made their wages would fall. Kay was driven from his home in Colchester; his house in Bury, Lancashire, was attacked, and he fled to France for a while.

Later, in the 1760s, there was some increase in the demand for cotton goods. This was probably as a result of the rise in population and the desire for better clothes (see Theories 1 and 2). Weavers began to use the flying shuttle, and were soon running out of yarn. They often spent days going round visiting spinners, trying to get more yarn. There was a bottleneck in the spinning process.

Hargreaves' spinning jenny, 1764

James Hargreaves was a weaver and carpenter from Blackburn, Lancashire. A 'jenny' is just an engine or any sort of machine. He is said to have got the idea in 1764 from seeing a spinning wheel, like those in Source 2B, knocked over and carrying on spinning. You can see the big wheel in Source 6A.

❓ QUESTIONS

a) How many spindles can the machine in Source 6A spin at once?
b) What is it made of?
c) What power is used to make it work?
d) Could it be used in the spinner's own home?

Hargreaves' first jenny had eight spindles. The version he patented in 1770 had 16. (If you patent an invention you register your idea with the government and no-one else is allowed to use it unless they pay you money, called a royalty.) However, once again the inventor was not popular.

■ *SOURCE 6B*

It was generally known that he had made a spinning machine and his wife having boasted of having spun a pound of cotton during a short absence from the sick-bed of a neighbouring friend, the minds of the ignorant and misguided multitude became alarmed and they shortly after broke into his house, destroyed his machine and part of his furniture.

From a description of Hargreaves's invention, published in 1808

❓ QUESTIONS

a) How did the neighbours find out about the invention?
b) Why were they angry and hostile?
c) What is the attitude of the writer of this source to the neighbours? How can you tell? Do you agree with the writer?

Hargreaves and his family fled to Nottingham, where he set up a factory. He earned some money from his inventions, but lots of jennies were made and used without the makers paying him royalties. By the 1780s jennies capable of spinning 80 spindles were in use in many spinners' homes. They spun a fine but weak thread, suitable for the weft.

Arkwright's frame, 1769

Richard Arkwright was working as a barber and wig-maker in Bolton, Lancashire in the 1760s. He must have heard people talk of the need

■ *SOURCE 6A* Hargreaves' spinning jenny

■ *SOURCE 7A* Arkwright's waterframe

for a better, faster spinning machine. He was interested in inventions, and became friendly with the clock-maker, John Kay. Kay had heard of an idea of spinning where the thread was drawn through four pairs of rollers, each moving faster than the pair before. It was not Arkwright's and Kay's idea, but they worked on it together. When Hargreaves fled to Nottingham in 1767, Arkwright, worried for his own invention, went there too. He needed money, and went into partnership with Jedediah Strutt of Derby. In 1769 he patented his waterframe.

■ QUESTIONS

a) How many spindles does the machine in Source 7A spin?
b) Can you tell, from the size, or name, of this machine what form of power was used?

■ *SOURCE 7B* A modern photograph of Arkwright's factory at Cromford

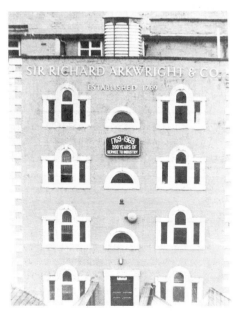

The frame was too large and too expensive for the cottage-spinner. At first it was built to be driven by a horse, but was soon adapted to water-power, and therefore could only be used in factories. In 1717 the first factory had been set up in Derby by the Lombe Brothers. It used water-power to drive silk-spinning machines, but did not last long. Arkwright and Strutt learnt from this example and built a factory at Cromford, near Derby, in 1771.

■ *SOURCE 7C*

The fame of Arkwright resounded through the land; and capitalists flocked to him, to buy his patent machines, or permission to use them ... Mr Arkwright spent, in large buildings in Derbyshire and elsewhere, upwards of £30000. Thus a business was formed which already [i.e. in 1782] employed upwards of 5000 persons and a capital of not less than £200000 ... The factory system in England takes rise from this period.

Edward Baines, *History of the Cotton Manufacture in Great Britain*, 1835

■ QUESTIONS

a) What title did Arkwright receive? (See Source 7B.)
b) What effect would his invention have had on where the cotton-spinning industry was set up?

It would have been quite easy to have built smaller versions of the frame for use in spinners' homes. However, Arkwright would only issue licences for large machines. The factory system began to drive out the home-based hand-spinner. (For more on factories, see later and Chapter 14.)

Crompton's mule, 1779

Samuel Crompton lived near Bolton, Lancashire, and was a weaver. He knew that the yarn produced by the jenny was fine, but weak, while that produced by the frame was strong, but coarse. He came up with a machine which produced a fine, strong yarn. It was a combination of the jenny and the frame, and was called a mule. It was another machine which required water or steam power, so it had to be used in a factory. Soon mules capable of

■ *SOURCE 8* **Crompton's mule**

spinning 300–400 spindles were built. In 1825 Richard Roberts devised a mule which could spin 2000 spindles. They worked in pairs, face to face, with one operator for both.

? QUESTIONS

a) Describe the factory room in Source 8.
b) How does the power reach the machines?
c) Describe the workers you can see.
d) Does the work seem dangerous?

Crompton estimated that in 1811 in Britain there were 4.2 million mule spindles, 0.3 million frame spindles, and 0.15 million jenny spindles. In spite of this he did not become rich. Arkwright left £½ million when he died. Crompton never patented the mule and only received a grant of £5000 from Parliament for his work.

Cartwright's power loom, 1785

All these changes in spinning affected the hand-weavers. Large quantities of yarn were being made, and the weavers could demand high wages to turn it into cloth. Their numbers rose from 75 000 in 1795 to 250 000 in 1833, carrying on

their hand craft in the new age of spinning factories. Their weekly wage was over £2 a week when most other wages were less than £1 a week.

■ *SOURCE 9A*

They brought home their work in top boots and ruffled shirts, carried a cane, and in some instances took a coach. Many weavers at that time used to walk about the streets with a £5 note spread out under their hat-bands. They would smoke none but long 'Church-warden' pipes and objected to the intrusion of any other handicrafts-men into the particular rooms in the public houses which they frequented.

G. French, *The Life and Times of Samuel Crompton*, pub. 1856

There was clearly a bottleneck in the weaving section of the industry. Weaving was such a complicated job that it seemed unlikely that it could ever be done by a powered machine. Edmund Cartwright, a poet and clergyman, decided to try to invent a power-loom. He had never even seen a loom when he started, but in 1785 produced one that did, just, weave cloth. It was very clumsy, and factories attempting to use power-looms were attacked by the hand-loom weavers.

Others refined Cartwright's ideas, but it was not until the 1820s that a good, workable power-loom was available.

■ *SOURCE 9B* **Weavers' cottages, from the late 18th century**

? QUESTIONS

a) How did the hand-loom weavers show off their wealth?
b) What invention would put an end to their prosperity?
c) How can you tell that Source 9B shows weavers' cottages?
d) Why were they built like this?

■ SOURCE 9C Power-looms in the 1840s

? QUESTIONS

a) What are the looms in Source 9C made of?
b) Who are the workers?
c) How are the looms powered?

The number of power-looms soon grew rapidly. In England there were 60 000 by 1830, 250 000 by 1850; in Scotland there were 2000 in 1820, 17 000 by 1845. The effect on the hand-loom weavers was catastrophic. Their wages fell and fell as they tried to compete with the machines. In 1797 they could receive £1.45 for weaving 24 yards of cambric muslin (a kind of cotton cloth); by 1827 the price was 32½p.

■ SOURCE 9D

A very good number of the weavers are unable to provide for themselves and their families a sufficiency of food of the plainest and cheapest kind; they are clothed in rags ... they have scarcely anything like furniture in their houses; their beds and bedding are of the most wretched description ... despite their poverty they have full employment; in fact their labour is excessive, not infrequently 16 hours a day.

Parliamentary Committee Report, 1835

? QUESTIONS

a) What are the main problems the weavers are facing?
b) Why is Parliament becoming interested?
c) Is there any solution to their problems?
d) What workers today face similar problems from new technology?

The Growth of Factories

By the 1830s cotton was almost entirely produced in factories. Here, with the aid of water or steam power, one person could produce much more than by hand.

■ SOURCE 10A Jedediah Strutt's cotton mill at Belper, Derbyshire, 1819

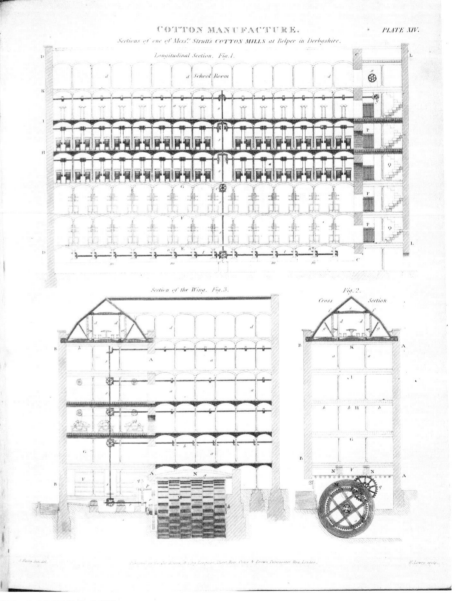

■ SOURCE 10B

Number of hours needed to spin 100 lb of cotton		
18th century	Hand spinning	50 000
1780s	Crompton's mule	2000
1790	100-spindle mule	1000
1825	Roberts' automatic mule	135
1980s	Most modern machines	35

QUESTIONS

a) In Source 10A, how many working floors are there?
b) What is the top floor used for?
c) What form of power is used in this factory?
d) How is power transmitted to all the floors?
e) Why was the factory built high and narrow rather than low and wide?
f) What would be the effect of the figures in Source 10B on the *price* and the *amount* of cotton goods made?

In 1782 James Watt invented a way of using steam power to turn a flywheel. Factories could now use steam power instead of water, and the first steam-powered spinning factory was started at Papplewick, Nottinghamshire in 1785. Factories could now be built wherever there was plenty of coal for the furnace. People at the time were amazed and enthusiastic.

SOURCE 10C

A cotton-spinning establishment offers a remarkable example of how, by the use of very great power, an enormous quantity of the easiest work can be accomplished. Often we may see in a single building a 100 horse-power steam-engine, which has the strength of 880 men, set in motion 50 000 spindles. The whole requires the service of but 750 workers. But these machines, with the assistance of that mighty power can produce as much yarn as formerly could hardly have been spun by 200 000 men, so that each man can now produce as much as formerly required 166! In 12 hours the factory produces a thread 62 000 miles in length, that is to say which would encircle the whole earth 2½ times!

Edward Baines, *History of the Cotton Manufacture in Great Britain*, 1835

QUESTIONS

a) How many workers are there in the factory?
b) How can you tell that the writer finds the whole thing almost incredible?

MAP 1 (right) Centres of the textile industry in 1850

SOURCE 10D Water- and steam-powered mills, 1835

	No. of mills	Steam horsepower	Water horsepower
Northern England	934	27 000	6000
Scotland	125	3000	2500
Midlands	54	400	1000

The location of cotton factories

The first factories, like Arkwright's and Strutt's, were built near rivers in Derbyshire or Lancashire. The use of steam-power led to the growth of cotton factories on, or near coal-fields, particularly in south Lancashire and central Scotland (see Source 10D and Map 1).

QUESTION

Why was steam-power used so much more than water-power?

Manchester was the most important city in the cotton industry. There were 23 factories there in 1801, 34 by 1811 and 66 by 1821. The growth by 1851 can be seen in Source 1 (page 16).

There are several reasons why the cotton industry flourished in Lancashire. The port of Liverpool was convenient for the import of raw cotton. Transport was good. There was abundant soft water for cleaning, dyeing, bleaching and other finishing processes. There were

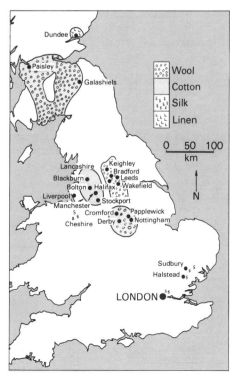

plenty of skilled workers in the dyeing, printing and machine-building trades. Manchester was a good banking and trading centre; also the damp climate helped, as cotton tends to snap easily if it gets too dry. Finally there was plenty of coal for the steam-engines.

Central Scotland had several of these advantages too. High-quality textiles of many types were produced there, including the famous Paisley products.

The Textile Industry in 1850

Cotton

Source 4 showed that although there was growth in the other textiles it was the cotton industry which expanded far faster than the others. There are several reasons for this. First, as we have seen, the rise of the cotton plantations of the southern USA meant that the huge demand of the British cotton factories could be met. It was not nearly so easy to increase the supply of wool, flax or silk suddenly: they have what is called an 'inelastic' supply.

Second, the machines which were invented were particularly suitable for use with cotton. However, a most important factor is simply that cotton cloth was very popular. It was light, easily washable and took colourful printed patterns well. The British exported cotton textiles wherever they had trading links in the world. At that time this was in hotter semi-tropical countries of Asia, Africa, the Far East and South America. Traditional British woollens did not sell nearly so well in these areas.

Wool

Nevertheless, there was some growth in the woollen industry. It came a little later. Although the first woollen factory was set up in Leeds in the 1790s, the great expansion was in the 1830s, by which time machines had been adapted for use with wool. The industry flourished in West Yorkshire, around Leeds, Bradford, Halifax, Wakefield, Keighley and Huddersfield. These towns soon had the tall factories and chimneys typical of Manchester. The woollen industry was an important one, worth £10 million in exports in 1850.

Linen

The linen industry expanded particularly successfully in Northern Ireland. The skills had been learnt there in the 18th century, and the first factory was started in County Down in 1805. Again there was a delay before machines were adapted to the fibre, but there was growth from the 1830s, with many factories set up in Belfast. There were also linen factories in Scotland, centred on Dundee.

Silk

Silk is rather different – a luxury product. Nevertheless there were new inventions and a growth in the number of silk factories. The Jacquard loom, for example, invented in 1805, allowed the weaving of complicated patterns. Silkworks grew in several areas of Britain, including Cheshire, London and East Anglia.

The overall picture

With over 5000 factories and nearly 600 000 employees, the British textile industry was a very important part of the British economy. Both Lancashire and the West Riding of Yorkshire had been transformed by the rapid growth of the industry. Most of all, it contributed a great deal to the prosperity of Britain. In the 1850s, total textile exports were worth £60 million, or 60% of all British exports. Cotton goods accounted for over 50% of this figure. The story of how the industry developed over the years after 1850 is told in Chapter 9. You can find out more what conditions were like in the textile factories in Chapter 14.

■ SOURCE 11 **The importance of the different industries in 1850**

	Number of factories 1850	Number of workers 1850
Cotton	1932	331000
Wool	1998	154000
Linen	1141	68000
Silk	277	43000

QUESTIONS

a) Which industry had the greatest number of factories?
b) Which industry had the greatest number of workers?
c) Which industry had the biggest factories?
d) How many people were employed in the British textile industry as a whole?

Assignments

Empathy

1 In pairs, look at Sources 2B, 2C and 9B, then Sources 8, 9C and 10A. Discuss what it would have been like to work at home, as in the first three sources. What would it have been like to work in a factory, as in the second three? What would have been the good and bad aspects of each environment?
2 Write a short speech made by one of the people who attacked Kay and Hargreaves for their new inventions, explaining why you are worried. Then, as Kay or Hargreaves, write a short speech in reply.

Understanding concepts

1 **Causation**
Take each of the ideas below, in turn, and explain how far it explains the tremendous growth of the cotton textile industry in the years 1740–1830.
a Rising population caused rising demand for textiles.
b Changing fashions caused rising demand for textiles.
c More cotton textiles were made more cheaply because raw cotton was cheaper.
d More cotton textiles were made more cheaply because of new technology.

2 **Cause/effect**
1733 Kay's Flying Shuttle
1764 Hargreaves' Spinning Jenny
1769 Arkwright's Frame
1779 Crompton's Mule
1785 Cartwright's Power Loom
a Explain the effect of each of these inventions on:
i the cotton industry and
ii the people who worked in it.
b There was often a time-lag between the invention and the impact it had on the industry. Sometimes other inventors were as important as the person who had the original idea. Choose two of the inventions above and show how far these statements are true in each case.

3 **Cause/effect**
a Why did new inventions in the textile industry lead to the growth of factories?
b Where were factories built?
c Why did the cotton industry flourish in Lancashire?

Themes for discussion

1 Changing technology brought, first, prosperity then poverty to the hand-loom weavers. Why was this so? How have changes in technology in our own times brought both prosperity for some and poverty for others?
2 What do you think are the advantages and disadvantages of working at home, or in a factory, nowadays?

4 The New Age of Iron

■ SOURCE 1 A song called Humphrey Hardfeature's Descriptions of Cast-iron Inventions

Since cast iron is now all the rage
And scarce anything's made
   without it
As I live in a cast-iron age
I mean to say something about it.

Here's cast-iron wagons and
   carts
Cast-iron bridges and boats
Corn-sellers with cast-iron hearts
That I'd hang up in cast-iron
   coats.

We have cast-iron gates and
   posts
Cast-iron mortars and mills too;
And our enemies know to their
   cost
We have plenty of cast-iron wills
   too . . .

Iron bedsteads have long been in
   use
With cast-iron they now pave our
   streets
Each tailor has a cast-iron goose*
And we soon shall have cast-iron
   sheets . . .

* goose – a kind of smoothing iron

? QUESTIONS

a) List the items which the song-writer names which really were made of iron.
b) List the items which the song-writer names which could not possibly be made out of iron.
c) Using the evidence, what date do you think this song was written?
d) What is the value of this source to a historian of the iron industry?

The early Industrial Revolution was, as the songwriter says, a cast-iron age. Cast iron replaced wood in the manufacture of many items, from ploughs to textile machines; it was used to make all sorts of new things from steamships to toys. All these new uses meant that the demand for iron rose and so much more iron had to be produced. New methods were invented and the iron industry was set up in new areas. These sources show how great the changes were.

■ SOURCE 2A Blast furnace, early 18th century

■ SOURCE 2B Lilleshall furnaces, mid-19th century

? QUESTIONS

a) In Source 2A, how is the furnace kept hot?
b) In Source 2A, how is the furnace fed with material?
c) In Source 2A, how much iron is pouring out of the bottom?
d) Estimate the heights of the furnaces in Sources 2A and 2B.
e) Why is it difficult to answer questions a), b), and c) for Source 2B?

The Iron Industry Before the Changes

Iron is mined as iron ore, a reddish-brown earthy material. If it is heated to very high temperatures, pure, or nearly pure, iron melts and separates from the impurities. This process is called smelting. Iron has been smelted ever since ancient Egyptian times. The method used

■ *DIAGRAM 1* Smelting iron ore to produce cast iron and wrought iron

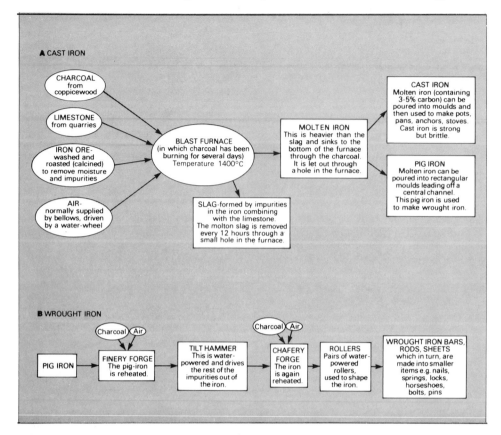

▲ CAST IRON

- CHARCOAL from coppicewood
- LIMESTONE from quarries
- IRON ORE – washed and roasted (calcined) to remove moisture and impurities
- AIR – normally supplied by bellows, driven by a water-wheel

→ BLAST FURNACE (in which charcoal has been burning for several days) Temperature 1400°C

→ MOLTEN IRON
This is heavier than the slag and sinks to the bottom of the furnace through the charcoal. It is let out through a hole in the furnace.

→ CAST IRON
Molten iron (containing 3-5% carbon) can be poured into moulds and then used to make pots, pans, anchors, stoves. Cast iron is strong but brittle.

→ PIG IRON
Molten iron can be poured into rectangular moulds leading off a central channel. This pig iron is used to make wrought iron.

→ SLAG – formed by impurities in the iron combining with the limestone. The molton slag is removed every 12 hours through a small hole in the furnace.

B WROUGHT IRON

PIG IRON → FINERY FORGE The pig-iron is reheated. → (Charcoal / Air) TILT HAMMER This is water-powered and drives the rest of the impurities out of the iron. → (Charcoal / Air) CHAFERY FORGE The iron is again reheated. → ROLLERS Pairs of water-powered rollers, used to shape the iron. → WROUGHT IRON BARS, RODS, SHEETS which in turn, are made into smaller items e.g. nails, springs, locks, horseshoes, bolts, pins

■ *SOURCE 3* Tilt-hammer, a painting from 1772

by the early 18th century, in blast furnaces like that shown in Source 2A, is shown in Diagram 1. The iron from the furnace could be treated in different ways for different uses. This is also shown in Diagram 1.

■ *QUESTION*

What clues are there in Source 3 that this is a small workshop near the worker's home?

Growth of the Iron Industry

As shown in Diagram 1, the iron industry before the Industrial Revolution needed large quantities of charcoal and water-power. If the industry was to expand, it needed either more of these, or else cheap and plentiful alternatives.

Meeting the iron industry's need for fuel

Early blast furnaces used huge quantities of charcoal – about an acre of woodland was needed to smelt a ton of iron. The system of coppicing provided enough charcoal for a small industry, but production could not be rapidly stepped up. Coal could not be used as fuel because the sulphur in it ruined the iron.

■ *SOURCE 4A*

About the year 1709, my husband's father came to Shropshire, to Coalbrookdale ... He here cast iron goods in sand out of the blast furnace that blow'd with wood charcoal ... Some time after he thought that it might be practicable to smelt the iron from the ore in the blast furnace with pit coal. Upon this, he tried with raw coal as it came out of the mines, but it did not answer. He, not discouraged, had the coal coked, as is done for drying malt, and it then succeeded to his satisfaction. But he found only one sort of pit-coal would best suit.

Mrs Abiah Darby, wife of Abraham Darby II, writing about her father-in-law, also called Abraham Darby, 1755

■ SOURCE 4B Charcoal and coke production, 1750–90

Year	Number of charcoal furnaces	Output (in tons)	Number of coke furnaces	Output (in tons)	Total output (in tons)	Coke production as % of total
1750	71	26 625	3	1500	28 125	5
1760	64	25 600	14	9800	34 400	28
1775	44	19 800	30	24 000	43 800	55
1790	25	12 500	81	74 925	87 425	86

? QUESTIONS

a) According to Source 4A, what fuel did Abraham Darby try first and with what result?

b) What fuel did he then use successfully?

c) Comment on the usefulness and the reliability of this source to a historian of the iron industry.

d) From Source 4B:
   i) From which year did coke furnaces produce more than charcoal furnaces?
   ii) By which year were there more coke furnaces than charcoal furnaces?
   iii) By how much did total production rise, 1750–90?
   iv) Which furnaces were bigger: coke or charcoal? How can you tell?

At first sight these two pieces of evidence seem to suggest that the problem of supplying fuel was easily solved: they used coke and the first person to try it successfully was Abraham Darby. But this explanation presents a problem for us. Look at the dates – Abraham Darby successfully used coke soon after 1709; there were only three coke furnaces in 1750, and it was not until the 1770s that coke furnaces overtook charcoal in production.

Why the delay? Perhaps Darby did not tell anyone about his new method. Maybe it wasn't worth using coke until later in the century. Perhaps coke-produced pig-iron was no good for making wrought iron. Perhaps there wasn't a great demand for iron. Let us look at each of these explanations in turn.

Darby did not take out a patent on his method of coke smelting. He joined up with other owners – ironmasters – to build other furnaces. His workers travelled to work at other ironworks. In 1712, Darby himself explained his method to William Rawlinson, an ironmaster who was, like Darby, a Quaker. There was therefore no secret about coke-smelting at all.

On the other hand the price of charcoal remained quite low and steady up to 1750, so there was no advantage in using coke. Further, coke-smelted pig-iron took longer to turn into wrought iron, so used more fuel. Why then did Darby continue with coke?

Most ironmasters used their furnaces to make pig-iron which was then turned into wrought iron for many uses, but especially for guns. Quakers are pacifists, and Darby used his iron in a different way. In 1707 he invented a way of casting iron cooking pots in sand. The coke-smelted iron produced good pots, thin-walled, light but strong, using half the metal of other manufacturers. Darby's iron therefore suited his own trade, but not the trade of other iron masters.

■ SOURCE 5A Modern photograph of one of Darby's furnaces at Coalbrookdale

The change came in the 1750s. There was an increase in the demand for iron, to make cannons to fight the Seven Years' War. This led to more demand for charcoal, which could not be met. Charcoal prices rose, and by 1760 coke was £3 a ton cheaper than charcoal. Abraham Darby II made coke in ovens. This produced coke-smelted pig-iron which was suitable for making into wrought iron.

Meeting the need for power

The other problem which faced the operators of blast-furnaces was the need for power to drive the bellows. Most furnaces could only operate about 30 weeks a year because of shortages of water to drive the water-wheels. From 1742 Abraham Darby II used a Newcomen engine (Chapter 5, page 39) to pump water up to the furnace pool so that it could drive the water wheel. By 1775 half the furnaces in Britain had a Newcomen engine doing this job.

Another great ironmaster was John Wilkinson – nicknamed 'iron-mad Wilkinson'. He built three furnaces, in Cheshire, Shropshire and Staffordshire, all using Abraham Darby's coke-smelting process. His business prospered with the demand for cannon in the Seven Years' War (1756–63). He built a boring machine to make the barrels of cannons accurately. James Watt, working on improvements to the steam-engine, realised that this method could be used to make accurately-bored cylinders. In 1776 Wilkinson provided the cylinder for Watt's first successful engine (Chapter 5, page 40). In turn Wilkinson used the engine to pump the bellows for the blast furnace. This method was soon widely used. It freed ironmasters from the limitations of water-power.

Wilkinson was always on the look out for new ideas and uses for iron. He built an iron chapel for his workers, and his own house had iron window frames. He launched an iron boat in 1787, and provided 65 km of iron pipes for the sewers of Paris. His most visible relic is the cast-iron bridge, at Ironbridge in Coalbrookdale, built in partnership with Abraham Darby III (Source 5B).

Meeting the need for transport

All the raw materials for iron-smelting: coal, iron ore, limestone, and even the finished castings, were heavy and bulky. Good transport would be needed for the British iron industry to grow. The Sheffield iron and steel industry, for example, used imported Swedish pig-iron because it could be brought in cheaply

■ *SOURCE 5B* Ironbridge, 1779

by water. Poor transport made British iron too expensive. Once again the Darby family showed the way forward.

■ *SOURCE 5C*

Many other improvements he was the author of. He got roads made and laid with sleepers and rails and brings them to the furnaces in waggons. And one waggon with three horses will bring as much as twenty horses used to bring on their backs. Of late years the laying of the rails of cast iron was substituted; which, altho' expensive, answers well for wear and duration ... Had not these discoveries [using coke for smelting] been made, the iron trade of our own produce would have dwindled away, for woods for charcoal became very scarce and landed Gentlemen raised the prices of wood exceeding high.

Mrs Abiah Darby, writing about her husband, Abraham Darby II, 1783

■ *SOURCE 5D* View of Coalbrookdale, 1758

❓ QUESTIONS

a) In Source 5C, who does Mrs Darby blame for rising charcoal prices?

b) How did Abraham Darby II improve transport to his ironworks?

c) In Source 5D find:
  i) the blast furnaces,
  ii) coal being burnt to coke in heaps,
  iii) the furnace pool which provided water for the water-powered bellows,
  iv) a heavy iron casting pulled away by at least six horses,
  v) a waggon on a railway coming down an incline.

Darby built six furnaces in Coalbrookdale, and a railway down to a wharf on the River Severn. Other ironmasters were closely involved in canal-building: it is estimated that a quarter of all canals had the iron trade as a major part of their business.

The Location of Ironworks

In the early 18th century ironworks were built near to woodland, where there were streams. (Why?) From the middle of the century they were built on coalfields and on good transport routes (see Map 1 right). Coalbrookdale was well situated, near to coal mines, limestone quarries and the River Severn. Other ironworks were set up in South Yorkshire. At Walker's of Rotherham, the Rotherham plough was made. In 1759 Dr Roebuck set up a huge ironworks at Carron, beside the Clyde in Scotland. But what was to be the largest ironworks in Britain was set up in the same year at Dowlais, in South Wales by John Guest. Together with Richard Crawshay's Cyfarthfa Works at Merthyr Tydfil, started in the 1760s, and Penydarren in the 1780s, these works made South Wales the iron-making centre of the world. Merthyr had six blast furnaces, two mills and four steam-engines, turning out 200 tons of iron a week by the 1790s, and employing 2000 workers.

■ MAP 1 Location of ironworks and coalfields

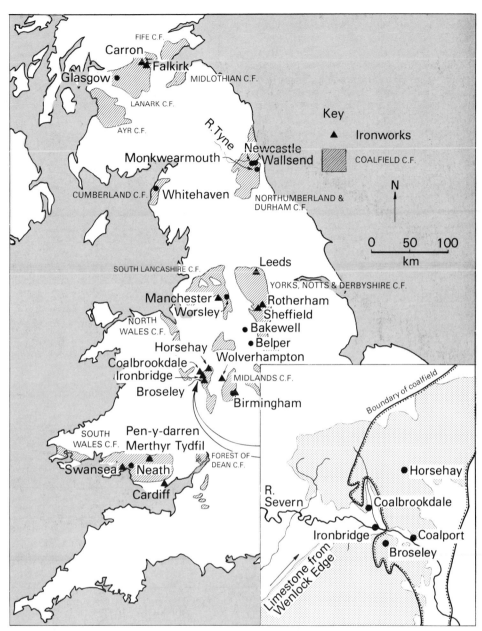

■ SOURCE 6A Dowlais in about 1840

■ SOURCE 6B

Four blast furnaces, forty-five feet high, devour day and night immense quantities of coal and ore. We can therefore realise the amount of air needed to keep alive these fiery furnaces, which, every six hours, pour forth streams of liquid iron. Each furnace is kept going by four air-pumps, from which the air, driven through a single tube, produces such a piercing whistle that anyone who did not know what was coming would certainly feel terrified. These wind machines, a kind of huge bellows, are set in motion by the action of water ... The current of air is so rapid and strong that it produces a live and bright flame ten feet above the top of the furnace.

French visitor to the Carron Works, 1761

■ SOURCE 6C

All the way along from Leeds to Sheffield it is coal and iron, and iron and coal. It was dark before we reached Sheffield so that we saw the iron furnaces in all the horrible splendour of their everlasting blaze. Nature has placed the beds of iron and the beds of coal alongside of each other, and art has taught man to make one to operate upon the other ... The furnace stands fifty feet up in the air, the ever-blazing mouth of which is kept supplied with coal and coke and ironstone from little iron waggons forced up by steam, and brought down again to be refilled. It is impossible to behold without being convinced that other nations will never equal England with regard to things made of iron and steel.

William Cobbett, 1830

？ QUESTIONS

a) In Source 6A, what is the landscape like around the ironworks?

b) What problems would making iron in such a remote, hilly area pose for the ironmasters?

c) Compare Sources 6B and 6C. What kind of power is being used in each case?

d) What impression did the furnaces make on the writers of Sources 6B and 6C?

The Napoleonic Wars produced a great demand for iron for cannon and other guns. Lord Nelson went to Merthyr Tydfil to see where his guns

■ SOURCE 7A Cort's puddling furnace

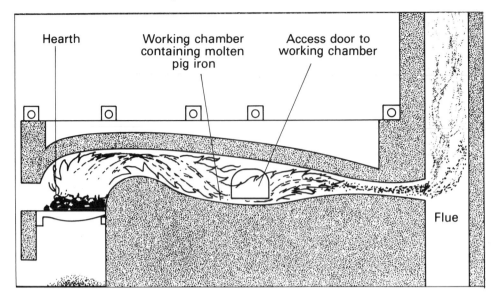

came from. Production of iron continued to increase through the 19th century: 68 000 tons in 1788, 250 000 tons by 1804, 680 000 tons by 1830, 2 250 000 tons by 1850. Furnaces were built in groups of three, four or more, so that the steam-engines could supply them all with air-blast (see Source 2B, page 25: the steam-engine house is on the right). They were built larger – average sizes for furnaces increased from 600 cubic feet to 2600 cubic feet by 1830. Round furnaces were found to be much more efficient than square ones (compare Sources 5A and 2B). In 1828 Neilson heated the air going into the furnace, which reduced the amount of fuel needed by 30%. Neilson's hot-blast was soon widespread, and later furnaces economised further by using the heat of the furnace itself to heat the blast.

Changes in the Way Wrought Iron was Produced

Changes were slower in the wrought iron side of the industry. Coke could not be used in forging, as it spoilt the iron, so charcoal continued to be used. In the 1760s the Wood brothers invented a process of putting the iron to heat up in pots in a coal furnace. This process – the Staffordshire process, as it was called – kept the iron separate from the coal and was widely used. However, it

■ SOURCE 7B Cort's puddling furnace – puddlers at work. An illustration from 1848

only made limited quantities of wrought iron.

Several people got close to solving this problem. The Cranage brothers, working in Coalbrookdale, used a furnace which separated the fuel and the iron; Payne invented an improved system of rollers, and Onions the 'puddling' process, in which the molten iron was stirred to remove all the impurities. Eventually, in 1784 Henry Cort brought these discoveries together in his puddling furnace. As Source 7A shows, the heat from the fire is led over the iron, which is kept separate by a bridge. The heat reverberates on the iron, which is stirred. The spongy balls of molten iron are pulled together and lifted out (see Source 7B), and then rolled while still hot.

■ *SOURCE 7C* **Mills and forge at Horsehay, Coalbrookdale. An illustration from 1848**

■ *SOURCE 7D* **Nasmyth's steam-hammer, photographed in 1855**

? *QUESTIONS*

a) Use Source 7A to explain what the people in Source 7B are doing.
b) How do the workers hold the iron in Source 7C? Why?
c) In what ways would these processes be dangerous?

The method was not an immediate success – only six of these furnaces were in use by 1790, and two of those soon closed. Cort himself was very unlucky and joined up with a partner who was dishonest. When his partner was convicted of fraud, Cort lost all his own money too. It was the Cyfarthfa works in Wales which developed his ideas. They increased production from 2300 tons in 1793 to 6000 tons in 1798, with a price fall from £12.30 a ton to £11 a ton. Cort's original furnace only produced one ton of wrought iron from two tons of pig iron. Later methods, lining the furnace with slag, produced one ton of wrought iron from 21 cwt of pig iron. In 1839 Nasmyth invented a powerful and accurate steam-hammer which made forging much easier and faster (Source 7D).

Links With Other Industries

You can read how iron was used in all the new industries in other chapters of this book. Textile machines

(see Chapter 3), which at first were built of wood, were much stronger made from cast iron. They could be used 24 hours a day without shaking to pieces. Cast iron had many uses in the coal industry (see Chapter 5) from waggons to pithead winding gear. The manufacture of steam engines used large amounts of cast iron.

In fact the coal, steam and iron industries were all very closely linked, each industry helping the growth of the other (see Diagram 2).

The great transport engineers, such as Telford and Brunel, were quick to see the advantages of iron. Telford used an iron trough to hold

the water on the Pont Cysyllte canal aqueduct. His Menai Suspension Bridge (Chapter 6, Source 5B, page 45) used 16 iron chains. Brunel used cast iron for his Royal Albert Bridge outside Plymouth, and built two huge iron ships, the *Great Britain* and the *Great Eastern* (Chapter 10, Source 15A, page 117).

Foundries produced a large range of iron items for industry. The one shown in Source 8A (over) started in 1814 in Manchester.

■ *DIAGRAM 2* **Links between the coal, steam and iron industries**

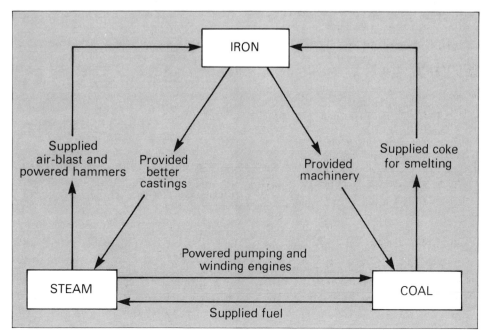

Skilled engineers were needed who could work in iron, and accurate machines were essential. Henry Bramah invented an unpickable lock which required small, accurate parts. He developed the modern lathe to make them. One of his workers, Maudsley, developed a screw-cutting lathe, and Whitworth's of Manchester developed a wide range of precision machine tools. The Whitworth standard of screw sizes is still used today.

Cheap, good iron was the raw material for many small workshops all over Birmingham and the Black Country. Here, in backyard forges, locks, bolts, pins, buttons, nails, gates, fences and hundreds of small items were made. The bar iron was bought from the ironworks by 'foggers', who supplied it to the little shops. They then bought the finished products and sold them to customers.

■ *SOURCE 8B*

The Black Country is not pretty. The earth seems to have been born inside out, nearly all the surface of the ground is covered with cinder heaps. By day and night the country is glowing with fire and the smoke of the ironworks hovers over it. There is a rumbling and clanking of iron forges and rolling mills. Workmen covered with smuts and with wild fierce white eyes are seen among the glowing iron and dull thud of the hammers.

Nasmyth, writing in the 1850s

? *QUESTIONS*

a) Identify as many iron items as you can in the yard of the foundry in Source 8A.

b) How are heavy products taken to and from the foundry in Source 8A?

c) What impression of the Black Country does Nasmyth give in Source 8B?

■ *SOURCE 8A* Peel and Williams foundry, an engraving of 1814

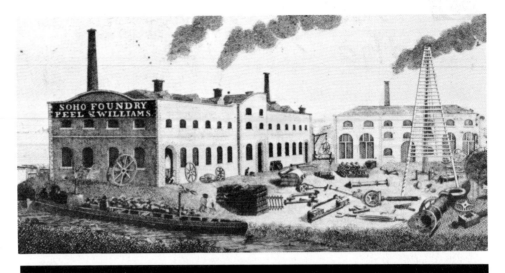

Assignments

Empathy

1 Look at Sources 6A, 6B, 6C, 7B, 7C, 8B. Use these sources to describe what it was like to work in the iron industry in the early 19th century. Concentrate on the actual jobs people did, the sounds, sights, smells, feelings, dangers and skills involved.

2 **a** Look at Sources 2B, 5D, 6A, 7B and 8A. What impression do you get of the iron industry in the early 19th century?

b Read Sources 6C and 8B. What impression did it make on visitors at the time?

c Explain why the 19th century visitors might have reacted in the ways they did.

d Explain any differences between your own impressions and those of 19th century writers.

Understanding concepts

1 **Continuity/change**
Look at Sources 2A and 2B.
a In what ways are the two furnaces the same?
b In what ways are they different?
c Explain why the later furnaces are different.

2 **Causation**
In order to expand rapidly, the iron industry had to overcome

the problems of:
 i fuel supply;
 ii cheap, reliable power, and
iii cheap transport.
Show how each of these problems was overcome in this period.

3 **Factors causing change**
a Use this chapter to illustrate how:
 i war, and
 ii famous individuals, bring about change in History.
b Use this chapter to show that:
 i peace, and
 ii lesser-known people also bring about changes.

Themes for discussion

Get into groups to discuss these questions which should help you to understand more about the nature of change in History. Coke smelting was discovered by Abraham Darby soon after 1709.
a What other factors had to be present before this discovery could make a great difference to the iron industry?
b Was it inevitable that the iron industry would grow, once Darby had made his discovery?
c Of the discoveries described in this chapter, which *caused* change, and which *helped* change?

5 *Coal and Steam: Powering the Wheels of Industry*

Energy and Industrialisation

■ *SOURCE 1*

? *QUESTIONS*

a) Look at these pictures. Which kinds of energy are being used in each of them?

b) Which kinds of energy in these pictures are natural, and which are converted or generated?

c) Which countries do you think use the most converted or generated energy: industrialised countries like Britain, or non-industrialised ones?

Source 2 shows clearly that it is industrialised countries which use and produce much more energy than non-industrialised ones.

SOURCE 2 National energy consumption, 1981

Country	Coal per head (kg) equivalent
Britain	5365
USA	11626
Kenya	208
Ethiopia	25

In an industrialised country, lots of generated energy is used at almost every stage in making something for sale. Take the example of a loaf of bread. Energy is used to make the fertiliser which is put on the field; diesel-powered tractors and combines sow and harvest the grain; and energy is used to run the machines that turn it into flour. Electric or gas-heated ovens bake the bread, and lorries use fuel to carry it to shops. Shops need energy for lighting, heating and the electronic cash register which is used when we buy the loaf. It is not surprising that one of the definitions of industrialisation is 'a high-energy economy'.

Britain today uses large quantities of oil, petrol, coal, gas and electricity. This chapter shows how the increasing energy needs of the early Industrial Revolution were met, by changes in the coal industry and by the invention of steam power.

The Increasing Demand for Coal

One kind of energy that we need, for homes and for many types of industry, is heat. Before the Industrial Revolution this need was met, as it still is in many parts of the world, by burning wood. Coal was used less. There were several places in Britain where coal was found at or near the surface, but transport was too slow and expensive to send it very far. Local people would simply burn it on their own fires.

In the 16th and 17th centuries, London began to need more and

more fuel. Not only were there half a million people wanting to warm their homes, but industries were starting to make things on a larger scale. The manufacture of soap, bricks, beer, salt, sugar and dyes all needed lots of heat.

In north-east England, near the River Tyne, coal was found near the surface. It could be sent by water cheaply to London. This trade in sea-coal (so-called because it came to London by sea), grew from under a quarter of a million tons in 1550 to over two and a half million tons by 1700. (It was also the basis of Britain's coastal shipping trade – see Chapter 6, page 47.) Even in 1661 John Evelyn complained about 'the hellish and dismall cloude of sea-coale'.

This increase in the demand for coal, which had been going on for some time, continued through the 18th century. Historians' estimates of coal production show a rise to 11 million tons per year in 1800 and 25 million by 1830. It was being used in many industries, but particularly for making iron and as fuel for the increasing number of steam engines.

Meeting the demand

This increase in demand was met by sinking new pits in Northumberland and Durham as well as in new areas such as Lancashire, Yorkshire, South Wales, Scotland and the Midlands (see Map 1, page 29). People did not really understand where coal seams were until the Geological Survey was set up in 1835. However, long before then miners had become skilled at deciding where coal might be found and in which direction known seams continued. They learnt to take test bores, using a sequence of poles attached to each other like a chimney-sweep's brushes. In the 1820s James Ryan invented a drill which removed a solid core of rock, so miners could actually see if coal was present, at what depth, and how thick the seam was.

Once coal had been discovered, a shaft was dug down to the seam. If the seam was not very deep, it would be mined by being worked outwards from the base of the shaft. Source 3A shows this type of pit, and how it got its name of bell-pit. Deeper pits were worked at first by

SOURCE 3A Bell-pit; bell-pits which have fallen in can be found all over the coalfields of Britain

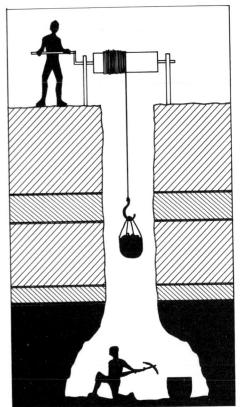

SOURCE 3B Modern open-cast mining (where huge draglines simply remove the upper layers of rock down to the coal) has exposed this 18th century bord-and-pillar mine. You can see that some roadways have been deepened to make height for ponies to haul the tubs of coal

■ *SOURCE 3C* **Undercutting a long wall in Wales, about 1900**

■ *SOURCE 3D* **Working in a thin seam in a Durham pit**

The thin seams of Durham are a nightmare, and many's the nightmare I've had about them since .... Crawling down the seam, only inches would separate the roof from your prostrate body, your head would be turned to the side, flat against the floor, with maybe a two-inch space above you before you made contact with the roof.... You would 'swim' forwards, arms straight out in front, legs spread-eagled behind, pushing, striving, wriggling forward and always the roof, bumping and creaking above your head.

David Douglass, *Pit Life in County Durham*, pub. 1983

the pillar-and-stall or bord-and-pillar method. Roadways were cut at right angles from the bottom of the shaft, and square blocks of coal were left to keep the roof up. Later the long-wall system, which started in Lancashire and Shropshire, was used. Here the miner cut under the coal-face with a pick, to a depth of about 4 feet. As he worked, small props held the rest of the face up. These were then knocked away, so that the face collapsed and could be taken away (Sources 3C and 3D).

The huge rise in demand for coal led to an increase in the depth and size of pits. Most 18th-century pits were less than 200 feet deep. In the 1760s John Roebuck sank a shaft to 420 feet at Kinneil, in Scotland. By 1793 the deepest pit was the King

pit, at Whitehaven in Cumbria, at 993 feet. By the 1830s the deepest pits were in north-east England, where Monkwearmouth colliery reached 1578 feet in 1834, and 1000 feet was common.

? QUESTIONS

a) Which of the methods shown in Sources 3A–D would leave the most coal behind?

b) What were the dangers of working a bell-pit (Source 3A)?

c) What were the dangers of undercutting the long wall (Sources 3C and 3D)?

d) Apart from the dangers, what else would be physically unpleasant about working in any of these pits?

Dangers and Problems

Bigger and deeper pits brought new dangers and problems for the miners and mining engineers. The most important were flooding, dangerous gases and bringing the coal to the surface. Early pits were drained by digging drainage tunnels called soughs to come out on to the hillside at a lower level. Deeper pits made this impossible. Ordinary water pumps could only lift water 30 feet or less. Chains of buckets, driven by horses, were used, but failed to cope with bigger, deeper and wetter pits.

The Newcomen steam-engine, as we shall see later in this chapter, was large, inefficient and needed huge quantities of coal. However, coal was cheap at pitheads, and the Newcomen engine began to solve the problem of flooding. It was widely-used in coalfields by the 1760s. At that time there were at least 100 such engines in use on Tyneside and 60 in the Midlands. From the 1780s, the much more efficient steam-engine invented by James Watt gradually replaced the Newcomen engines. The steam-engines made many deep mines workable by pumping out the water, day and night.

■ *SOURCE 4* **Pumping engine at an old pithead in Wales, built in 1845**

Dangerous gases also built up in coal mines. Choke-damp (carbonic acid gas) made breathing difficult, and could cause death if the miner was not rushed to the surface for some fresh air. Firedamp (methane) was even more dangerous, as it could cause huge explosions. In 1708, at Wear colliery: '69 were killed, the blast blew the bodies of two men and a woman 350 feet up the shaft and out of the pit. The explosion was like a thunderclap'. Mining disasters were so common that it was not considered necessary to hold an inquest on a miner who had died in an accident.

■ SOURCE 5A

One of the greatest colliery disasters took place in Cannock in the 1860s, the explosion taking place as the day and night shifts were changing over. 660 lost their lives.

In another pit explosion, at Nine Locks, Quarry Bank, miners were entombed for a long period; it was rumoured they had eaten the pit ponies and harness and had reached the decision of cannibalism. Lots were drawn for the first victim and it fell on a young boy. The hardened old colliers could not carry their plan through. Later, they were rescued, and the boy was often pointed out to people as 'the boy that should have been eaten'.

J. W. Jones *A History of the Black Country*, 19th century

■ SOURCE 5B Wives and other relations waiting at the pithead, Morfa, South Wales, after an explosion underground, 1863 (coffins are waiting in the building on the left)

■ DIAGRAM 1 Mine ventilation system

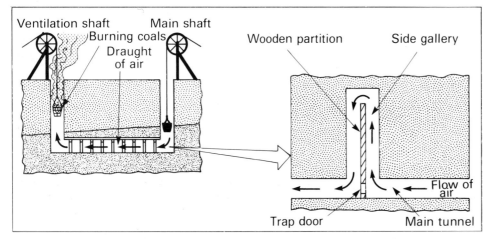

? QUESTIONS

a) In Source 5B, how is coal taken away from the pithead? What kind of power is used to lift coal up the shaft?
Making Modern Britain Galley 4

b) How far do Sources 3C, 3D, 5A and 5B support these statements:
  i) miners were strong;
  ii) miners were brave;
  iii) miners were uncaring;
  iv) miners had close working friendships;
  v) miners lived in close-knit villages?

One solution to the problem was to dig two shafts, and keep a fire burning at the bottom of one of them. This would suck fresh air down the other shaft. A system of trap-doors ensured that the air had to travel through all the roadways and faces before reaching the fire (see Diagram 1). Opening and shutting the trap-doors was a job given to small children. (Working conditions in the coal mines are dealt with in greater detail in Chapter 14.)

In 1796 John Buddle, of Wallsend, set up huge fans in a mine to suck foul air and gas out. However, this idea was slow in being taken up.

The problem of lighting was a serious hazard in pits where gas built up. Candles were generally used (see Source 3C), and the naked flame could set off an explosion. In 1815 the Society for the Prevention of Accidents in Coal

■ SOURCE 6A Boy leading a pit-pony in a Nottinghamshire pit, about 1910. (He is also carrying a safety lamp similar to the one Davy invented)

Mines called for a safety lamp. The famous scientist, Sir Humphrey Davy, and George Stephenson, the railway engineer, came up with the same solution: a lamp in which the flame was surrounded by a metal gauze. This cooled the flame so that it could not ignite the gas. It also burned blue when methane gas was present, giving warning of the danger (see Source 6A). Safety lamps unfortunately meant that deeper and more dangerous pits could be used. They gave a rather poorer light, so many miners still used candles and there were still horrific accidents.

Getting the Coal Out

As pits got deeper, with longer underground roadways, the problem of getting all the coal out quickly and efficiently increased. In early years wooden boxes, tubs, or wicker baskets (corves) were used. Pulling these along galleries, or carrying them up ladders, was one of the jobs which women did in some mining areas. By the late 18th century some of the best pits had small tubs or trucks running on rails. This made the job of moving the coal about much easier. The miners were pleased:

God bless the man with peace
   and plenty,
That first invented metal plates,
Draw out his years to five times
   twenty,
Then slide him through the
   heavenly gates.
**(Verse of a song from a mining
   area)**

The Lowther Mine in Cumbria had 20 miles of underground rail in 1813. Many pit owners had also switched to pit-ponies by 1800. These ponies spent all their lives underground, hauling the tubs of coal (see Source 6A).

The ordinary windlass, shown in Source 3A, was a slow and dangerous method of winding coal, and people, up the shaft. In the 18th century many pits used 'whims' or horse-powered winding systems. Source 6B shows one in operation in Wales in 1798. The horse walks round and round the drum, turning it. The rope passes from the drum

into the thatched house, where it runs over a pulley and down the pitshaft. From the 1780s they were replaced by steam-engines (see Sources 6C and 6D).

One of the most important changes came in the 1830s, when cages, with iron guide-rails, were introduced into shafts. Before this, tubs, corves and miners had been lowered freely down the shaft. Now tubs could be wheeled into the cage, hauled up the shaft and wheeled away, as in Source 6E.

■ *SOURCE 6B* **Horse-gin at coal mine near Neath, 1798**

■ *SOURCE 6C* **Steam-engine at coal mine in Staffordshire, mid-19th century**

■ *SOURCE 6D*

Several steam engines, erected for the purpose of raising coal from the pits are now in almost general use instead of horses, performing the business much quicker, and at considerably less expense. The apparatus is so simple, yet so strong, that the person who controls it has it so far at his command as to stop the machine in a moment.
Coalbrookdale, 1801

■ SOURCE 6E Tubs and cage underground, about 1860

the shaft, dangling on a rope. There was now the Davy lamp as well. However, despite these improvements, coal mining throughout the 19th century remained a dangerous occupation. The threat of floods, explosions and roof-falls was ever-present. There was no medical knowledge of the deadly lung diseases which miners developed as a result of spending their working lives breathing in coal-dust, so nothing was done about that problem. Mining also remained an entirely manual occupation: machines did not replace picks and shovels until well into the 20th century (see Chapter 9).

Power for Industry

We have seen that steam-engines helped the expansion of the coal-mining industry. The rapid growth in the use of steam-engines in turn brought an increase in demand for coal. However, it was not until after 1850 that steam power became

? QUESTIONS

a) Write a comparison of Sources 6B and 6C. You should comment on the strength of the two methods, the surrounding landscape, the way that coal is carried away once it has come up from the pit, and the amount of money involved in setting up the coal mine.

b) Source 6D says steam-engines were cheaper than horses. How do you think this could be?

c) In what ways would the system of cages shown in Source 6E be more efficient (more coal carried and faster) than Source 3A?

The introduction of cages, with steam-powered winding engines, increased fourfold the rate at which coal could be extracted. The problem of transporting coal to customers was mainly solved by canals, and then by railways. In Chapter 6, you can read how the need to get coal cheaply to market was the main reason for the first really successful canal – the Bridgewater Canal. In fact the Duke of Bridgewater had the canal extended into his mines at Worsley, with several miles of underground waterways.

As the coal industry expanded with deeper, bigger and more pro-

ductive pits, so the number of miners grew. There were 40 000 in 1800, but over 150 000 in 1850. To some extent mining was safer. As Source 6D explains, steam-engines were powerful, but could stop and start easily. The use of cages was better than sending miners down

? QUESTIONS

a) What is the wheel made of?

b) At what times of year could the wheel not be used?

■ SOURCE 7 Water-wheel used to drive tilt hammers at Clay Wheel Forge, Sheffield

really important. Before that, horses, wind and especially water had provided adequate power.

Water-wheels

Water-wheels had been in use on almost every river in Britain since the Middle Ages. They were used mainly for grinding corn, but also for other industrial tasks such as fulling cloth, or driving bellows or tilt-hammers. It took a great deal of money, and skilled work, to set up a water-wheel. A weir might have to be built, and a mill-race or leat – a small stream – led off the main river. This had to fall over the wheel back into the river. You can still see many of these mill-races even if the mill has gone. Once installed, however, the water-wheels were extremely cheap to run. The power they provided was regular and strong, unlike early steam-engines, which had a jerky motion.

As Chapter 3 explained, water-wheels powered the early textile factories in Derbyshire, Lancashire and Yorkshire. Abraham Darby II introduced a steam-engine at Coalbrookdale, but only to lift water up to a pond. A water-wheel was used for the strong steady blast of the bellows for his furnace. Better iron-making produced bigger and stronger water-wheels. Jedediah Strutt built one 23 feet wide for his mill at Belper, and the Cyfarthfa ironworks had a wheel 50 feet in diameter. Skilled engineers were able to build wheels to generate 200 horsepower by the early 19th century. This was far more than any steam-engine of the time.

The biggest problem with water-wheels was that they needed a steady flow of water. On average, two weeks a year were lost through streams freezing over or running dry. In the end, of course, there would have to be a limit on how much power a water-wheel could generate. Why?

Steam power

The Newcomen engine

The power of steam had been known about for centuries before it was harnessed to do a job of work. In 1698 Thomas Savery invented a sort of steam-engine to pump water out of mines which he called 'The Miner's Friend'. However, Savery's

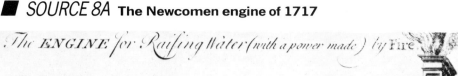

■ SOURCE 8A The Newcomen engine of 1717

The ENGINE for Raising Water (with a power made) by Fire

machine did not work very well – among other faults it had no safety valve! Thomas Newcomen, a Devon locksmith and blacksmith, tried to improve Savery's design. In 1706 he was successful, and five years later he formed a company to make his engines. He attached the engine to a beam to operate pumps in mines.

In Source 8A the furnace, at the bottom of the steps, heats the boiler. Steam then enters the big cylinder above the boiler. When this is full, cold water is injected into it. The steam cools, a near-vacuum is created, and the piston in the cylinder is forced down by atmospheric pressure. This pulls down the right-hand end of the beam, so the left-hand end rises, lifting water from the mine. Steam is then let into the cylinder again, so the vacuum is filled, and the beam returns to the position in the picture.

Newcomen's engine was slow, inefficient and expensive. It was difficult to get good quality iron at that time, so it was difficult to make

the piston fit tightly into the cylinder. The cylinder was continually being heated and cooled, so huge quantities of coal were used. However, many were sold in coal mining areas of the Midlands and the North-East as well as in Cornwall, where they were used for pumping water out of tin mines.

Watt's engine

The improvements that were later made to this engine by James Watt made it a virtually new invention. James Watt was well educated, the son of an architect and shipbuilder in Scotland. He was working as an instrument-maker to Glasgow University when, in 1763, he was asked to repair a model of a Newcomen engine. He realised that he could make the engine much more efficient if:

a) The steam was led out of the main cylinder into a separate cylinder, and condensed there. This condenser could be kept cool; the cylinder could then be kept hot, by giving it a 'jacket' containing steam (see Source 8C).

■ *SOURCE 8B* **Watt's engine made for the Birmingham Canal in 1777, being dismantled in 1898. The cylinder, with lid and steam-jacket, can be seen lower right**

■ *SOURCE 8C* **Diagram of Watt's engine. (Note that the sun-and-planet gear was not invented until 1781. The engine in Source 8B merely pumps up and down)**

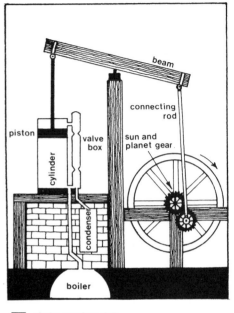

b) The cylinder was closed at the top (Newcomen's was open). Steam could then be used both to push the piston up and to push it down. This required a valve box to let steam into the right part of the cylinder at the right time of the stroke. This made much better use of the steam.

? QUESTIONS

a) Look at Sources 8A and 8B. How long was the beam in each case?

b) Why were beams made so large?

c) The Watt engine in Source 8B was used at a canal. What use would a canal have for such a machine?

d) These engines were very slow: why would this not matter for the jobs they were used for?

Although Watt completed his invention in 1765, numerous problems meant that it could not go into production. Even more than Newcomen, he needed accurately-made cylinders. He also needed accurate small parts for the valve-box. At first he teamed up with John Roebuck, at the Carron Works, but Roebuck went bankrupt. The creditors included Matthew Boulton, who ran a factory in Birmingham producing small, precision-made items. Boulton realised that there was a great deal of work to be done on Watt's engine, and suggested that they went into partnership.

The Boulton/Watt partnership

Boulton's factory could make accurate valves, and he knew the iron-master, John Wilkinson. Wilkinson had devised a technique for boring the barrels of cannon accurately, and used the same method to make accurate cylinders. In 1775 the first Boulton and Watt engine was built. It was used to pump water out of a coal mine (see Source 8E). Wilkinson himself took the second, to power the bellows for his blast-furnaces. Forty more were built in the next five years, mostly for Cornwall, where the improvement in coal consumption over the Newcomen engine was appreciated, as coal was expensive there.

Boulton and Watt set up a new factory to meet this demand. If you ordered an engine, you were expected to supply most of the building and some parts. Boulton would try to persuade you to go to Wilkinson for the cylinder. Boulton and Watt's would supply the small precision parts. The price was one-third of the difference in running costs compared with a Newcomen engine.

■ SOURCE 8D

Dear Watt,

I had two motives in offering my assistance, which were love of you and love of a money-getting idea.

I realised that your engine would require money, very accurate workmanship and good selling to make the most of it, and that the best way of doing the invention justice was to keep it out of the hands of ordinary engineers who from ignorance and lack of experience would be liable to produce bad and inaccurate workmanship. To remedy this, my idea was to set up a factory near to my own, by the side of our canal, where I would erect all necessary for the completion of the engines, and from which factory we would serve the world with engines of all sizes. It would not be worth my while to make for three countries, but I find it very well worth my while to make for all the world.

Letter from M. Boulton, 7 February, 1769 (adapted)

? QUESTIONS

a) What skills does Boulton think he can offer Watt?

b) What does Boulton hope to get out of the co-operation with Watt?

c) What impression of Boulton's personality do you get from this letter?

■ SOURCE 8E

On Friday last a steam-engine constructed upon Mr Watt's new principles was set to work at Bloomfield Colliery near Dudley ... The workmanship ... did not pass unnoticed, or unadmired. All the Iron Foundry parts were executed by Mr Wilkinson. The condenser, with the valves, pistons and all the small work at Soho.

From the first moment of its setting to work it made about 14 to 15 strokes per minute and emptied the engine-pit, which stood 57 feet deep in water, in less than an hour. The Gentlemen then adjourned to dinner ... and the workmen followed their example. After which a name was given to the machine: 'The Parliament Engine'. This engine is applied to the working of a pump which is capable of going to the depth of 300 feet with one-fourth of the fuel that a common engine would require. The cylinder is 50 inches in diameter and the length of the stroke is 7 feet.

Birmingham Gazette, **11 March, 1776**

❓ QUESTIONS

a) What aspects of this first James Watt engine impressed the reporter?
b) What special events marked the first day's work done by the engine?

All the engines so far had provided only up-and-down motion. Watt worked on a way of providing rotary motion, only to find that the most obvious, the crank, was patented. His foreman at Soho, William Murdock, then invented the sun-and-planet gear, which can be seen in Source 8C. The engines could now be used in factories of all kinds.

Results of Improvements in Steam Power

The effects on the textile industry are described in Chapter 3. Steam power was also used in the iron and steel industries (see Chapter 4) for bellows, rollers and hammers, and in the pottery industry for flint and pug mills. Most of all, steam power freed many factory-owners from having to site their factories by rivers. Provided there was good transport and coal supply, the factory could be built anywhere, and it could be built larger.

It would be wrong to overestimate the speed of the growth of steam power. In 1800 there were probably 500 Boulton and Watt engines, 450 other steam-engines like Watt's, and about 300 Newcomen engines. Together they accounted for only about 10% of Britain's industrial power requirements. Only by 1850 was steam really replacing water-power on a large scale.

It is common to overestimate the importance of James Watt, too. Other people had their part to play. We have already seen the contribution of Boulton and Murdock. Watt himself was uninterested in new developments in steam for use on the roads, in boats, or in high-pressure engines. It was other inventors who took these ideas on – including Murdock, who built an early locomotive. It was other inventors, too, who improved on Watt's engine in the early 19th century, greatly increasing its economy and efficiency. Britain's steam-engineering industry built engines for the world, as Boulton had foreseen, throughout the next century.

Assignments

Empathy

Look at Sources 3C, 3D, 5A and 5B. Imagine you are *either* the miner in Source 3C, *or* one of the relations waiting at the pithead in Source 5B. Describe the job of a miner, as you see it, and the hardships and dangers. Explain why you, or your family continue to do the job despite the dangers.

Understanding concepts

1 Change/continuity
The demand for more coal meant that several problems in coal-mining had to be overcome.
  a Explain how attempts were made to deal with each of these problems:
    i flooding;
    ii gas and bad air;
    iii getting the coal out of the pit;
    iv getting the coal away from the pithead.
  b Why was very little done to deal with problems of dust?

2 Change/continuity
  a In what ways did a miner's job change between 1750 and 1850?
  b In what ways was it the same in 1850 as it had been in 1750?

3 Role of individuals
  i Savery ii Newcomen iii Boulton iv Wilkinson v Murdock
  a Discuss the importance of each of these to the growth of steam power.
  b Savery's invention did not work. Boulton was not an inventor. Why are both these people still important?

Themes for discussion

1 Use this chapter and Chapter 4 on the iron industry to explain the links between coal, iron and steam.
2 Using Chapters 3, 4 and 5, make a list of the motives of the inventors during this period of industrial development. Do they all have the same motive? What motives lead people to work on new discoveries nowadays?

6 *Road, Water, Rail – People and Goods on the Move*

Road Transport

Roads Before the Industrial Revolution

Because it is difficult to imagine just how bad the roads of Britain were before the Industrial Revolution, we need to look at the evidence from that time. Daniel Defoe, in 1724, saw a woman in Sussex arrive at church in a cart pulled by six oxen because the road was so bad that horses couldn't get through. Before 1750 it was impossible to get from Leeds to Manchester in winter.

■ *SOURCE 1A*

I know not, in the whole range of language, words sufficiently accurate to describe this damned road. Let me warn all travellers who decide to travel through this terrible northern country to avoid it as they would the devil ... They will meet here with ruts which actually measured four feet deep and floating with mud after a wet summer. What can it be like after a winter? The only mending the road gets is the tumbling in of some loose stones which serve no other purpose than to jolt the carriage around in the most intolerable manner. I actually passed three carts broken down in these 18 miles of ghastly memory.

Arthur Young, *A Tour Through the North of England*, 1771

The evidence is clear that roads were channels of mud in winter, with hard-baked ruts in summer. But why were they like this? Nowadays, local and central governments repair the roads. At that time the government took little notice of the problem. Some people actually feared that good roads would allow an army to move about quickly and take over the country. Many centur-

ies earlier, the Romans had built fine roads. Almost nothing had been done since then apart from building some better bridges. By an Act of 1555, still in force, everybody in a parish had to work four days (later six days) a year on the roads of the parish. Richer people had to supply carts, tools and materials. This was the only roadwork that was done.

■ *SOURCE 1B*

They know not how to lay a foundation, nor to make the proper slopes and drains. They pour a heap of loose, huge stones into a swampy hole which make the best of their way to the centre of the earth. They might as well expect that a musket ball would stick on the surface of custard.

***Gentlemen's Magazine*, 1752**

? QUESTIONS

a) In what ways do Sources 1A, 1B and 1C agree with each other?
b) In what ways do they disagree with each other?
c) Arthur Young's writings are full of complaints about the roads. Does this mean that all the roads of England were bad?
d) Why would the villagers not work very hard at road-mending?
e) The 1555 Act also made each parish appoint a surveyor (unpaid), to organise the work. How does Source 1B suggest that this was not done well? Why do you think it wasn't?
f) If you lived in a parish crossed by a busy main route, what would you find unfair about the system?

In Scotland, between 1726 and 1737, General Wade built some 200 miles of good road and 40 bridges. This was under govern-

■ *SOURCE 1C* **Road-menders in Yorkshire, early 19th century**

■ **SOURCE 2** **Wide-wheeled wagon, 18th century**

change enormously to meet these needs. On the roads, on water and then on rails, a transport revolution took place. By 1850 transport itself was an essential new industry, with 5% of the working population employed in it.

The Growth of Turnpikes

If the government would do nothing about improving roads, another way had to be found.

One method of improving roads was for local businessmen and landowners to get together to build turnpikes. A turnpike was a section of road with gates. All road users had to pay a toll to pass through the gates, and the money was spent on improving the road. The first was set up in 1663 along the Great North Road in Hertfordshire. Local people would form a turnpike trust and arrange a private Act of Parliament. This allowed them to raise money, put up gates, build toll-houses, and pay a surveyor, a clerk, a treasurer and labourers. A trust was not a business: it was not supposed to make a profit for the trustees, but they obviously thought they would benefit from better roads in other ways.

There was a large growth in the number of turnpikes in the 18th century, especially after 1750. About 1600 trusts had been set up by 1800, 2450 by 1830, controlling some 22 000 miles of road (see Map 1, over).

ment orders, to deal with any rebellions from the Highland clans. However, nothing was done in other areas. In fact, the government gave up trying to improve the roads and began to try to limit the damage. They put weight restrictions on wagons – but there were no accurate weighing machines. In 1753 all wagons had to have wheels which were at least nine inches wide as they thought narrow wheels dug up the roads.

QUESTIONS

a) How many horses are needed to pull the wagon in Source 2?
b) How fast do you think it would go?
c) Do you think it would stop the road from being damaged?

In these conditions freight charges were as high as 10*d* (4p) per ton per mile. At that price it was not worth trying to send goods very far: they would be so expensive at the other end that no one would buy them.

Think of all the lorries pounding up and down the motorways nowadays. In 1778 one wagon a day took all the necessary freight from Leicester to London.

■ **SOURCE 3**

About half a century ago, the heavy goods passing through Leicester for London and the South, and on the great northern routes to Leeds and Manchester, did not require more than about one wagon a day each way ... One weekly wagon to and fro served Coventry, Warwick, Birmingham and so on to Bristol and the West of England. At present there are about two wagons, two vans, and two fly-boats daily to London; the same number extend the connection not only to Leeds and Manchester, but by means of canal to the ports of Liverpool and Hull. There are at least six weekly wagons to Birmingham ...

Mr Philip of Leicester, 1828 (adapted)

QUESTIONS

a) From Map 1, page 23, what goods would be carried from Leicester in such quantities by 1828?
b) What other methods of transport does Mr Philip mention, apart from wagons?

Why did transport develop?

Mr Philip gives us a clue that by 1828 changes in transport were taking place. Other chapters in this section have told us about industry. Industrial output in Britain was increasing at 9% per decade after 1780. Without improvements in transport this just would not have been possible. Industry needed cheap, regular, reliable supplies of raw materials, including coal, iron, timber, bricks and stone. Industry needed to sell its products across the country and abroad. Businessmen needed to travel rapidly and safely around the country. The transport system of Britain had to

■ **SOURCE 4A** **Tolls at Llanfair Gate, 19th century**

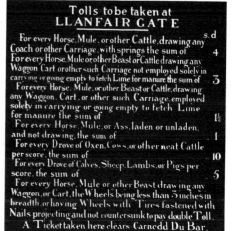

■ *MAP 1* **Roads built by General Wade, Metcalf and Telford**

Roads built by Metcalf ┈┈┈┈
Gen. Wade's roads ┅┅┅┅
Telford's roads ┈┈┈┈

0   50   100
km

N ↑

■ *SOURCE 4B* **Tollhouse in Shropshire, built in the 1830s**

■ *SOURCE 4C*

On the 26th July, 1749, between 10 and 11 at night, a large body of Somersetshire people came with drums beating and loud shouts, armed with cutting instruments fixed in long staves, and some disguised in women's apparel, and demolished the turnpike erections newly fixed.

***Gentlemen's Magazine*, 1749**

? QUESTIONS

a) In Source 4A, how did the trust try to help farmers?
b) In Source 4A, how did they penalise narrow wheels?
c) Why do you think there was such opposition to turnpikes from local people (Source 4C)?
d) How did the rioters in Source 4C disguise themselves?
e) Try to find toll-houses, like the one in Source 4B, in your area.

Road Builders

Now that surveyors were paid, it became a worthwhile job to have. They began to work out better ways of designing and surfacing roads. One of the most remarkable was John Metcalf (1717–1810). He was blind, but nevertheless built over 180 miles of road in Lancashire and Yorkshire. Perhaps his blindness gave him an extra sense of how steep a road was, and how solid its foundation. His roads were made of small stones packed together to make a smooth surface.

Thomas Telford (1757–1834) started life as a stonemason, and went on to build many other things, including canals. He built nearly 1000 miles of road, of which the most famous was the London–Holyhead route. He carefully engineered his roads to avoid steep hills and sharp bends, and the A5 through North Wales largely follows his route to this day. He also built careful foundations of large stones, covered with loosely-packed stones of not more than 2¼ inches in diameter. He supplied his road-builders with a ring to check the size of stones. Traffic was then allowed to run on the road to make the surface smoother, and this was then covered with 1½ inches of gravel to help drainage.

But John Loudon Macadam (1756–1836) felt that this was too complicated and expensive. He insisted that the main need was a well-drained, solid foundation. After that, a layer of small stones was placed on top, just thick enough to make sure they didn't let water through. He helped this by building the road with a camber, which means it is slightly higher in the middle than at the sides.

■ *SOURCE 5A*

I have generally made roads three inches higher in the centre than they are at the sides; if the road be smooth and well-made the water will run off easily on such a slope.

Any piece of stone put into a road which is more than one inch in diameter is mischievous. I always make my surveyors carry a pair of scales and a six ounce weight in their pockets. When they come to a heap of stones, they weigh the largest.

J. Macadam, *Remarks upon the Present System of Roadmaking, 1820*

Macadam and his three sons were hired by many turnpike trusts. Between them they were responsible for over 2000 miles of road by 1820. Years later road surfaces were made with bitumen – tarmacadam (or tarmac), named after him.

Stage-coaches

Better road surfaces meant much faster journey times: London to Manchester took four days in 1754, three days in 1760, two days by 1784. London to Edinburgh took ten days in summer and 12 in winter (if you were lucky) in the 1750s; by the 1830s it could be done in 45½ hours. London to Oxford took two days in 1751 and six hours in 1828. By changing the four horses every 10–15 miles the stage-coach could keep up an average speed of 10 mph on the fastest routes. Only four or five minutes was allowed for changing horses.

From 1720 to 1762 the mail service was run by Ralph Allen, for his own profit. Post-boys used horses or light carriages and the service was slow and irregular. A Bath theatre owner called John Palmer used

■ *SOURCE 5B* **Thomas Telford's Menai Bridge, 1826, with a stage-coach crossing from North Wales to Anglesey**

stage-coaches to deliver notices of his plays and found them much more reliable. In 1784 he suggested that the mail be sent by stage-coach, and offered to run a mail-coach on the Bristol–Bath–London route. It was a great success: the growth in business and industry had brought a fast-growing need for quick, reliable ways of getting business letters around the country. The new mail-coach was the fastest vehicle on the road. It carried an armed guard, with a horn to let toll-gate keepers know they were coming and open the gate so they could get through without stopping. There was also strict control of times and the first reliable timetables.

■ *SOURCE 6A* **Sudbury, Hedingham and Braintree Coach, 1800**

■ SOURCE 6B

I must observe that they have a curious way of riding, not in, but upon, a stage-coach. Persons to whom it is not convenient to pay a full price, instead of the inside sit on top of the coach, without any seats or even a rail .... When I was up I was obliged to sit just at the corner of the coach, with nothing to hold by but a sort of little handle fastened on the side. I sat nearest the wheel, and the moment we set off, I fancied I saw certain death await me. The machine now rolled along over the stones through the town, and every moment we seemed to fly into the air .... My neighbour every now and then fell asleep, and perpetually rolled against me with the whole weight of his body. We at last reached Northampton, where I immediately went to bed and slept until noon.

C. P. Moritz, *Travels through Several Parts of England*, 1782

De Quincey describes carrying the news of British victories in the Napoleonic Wars in 1810–15 by mail-coach out from London to other towns (Source 6D).

■ SOURCE 6C The Devonport Mail

■ SOURCE 6D

Five years of life it was worth paying for an outside place on a mail coach when carrying down the first tidings of such an event. On any night the spectacle was beautiful: the absolute perfection of all the appointments about the carriage and the harness, their strength, their cleanliness, but more than all, the royal magnificence of the horses, were what first fixed the attention. Every carriage on every morning of the year was taken down to an inspector for examination – wheels, axles, linch-pins, pole, glasses, lamps were all probed and tested. Every horse had been groomed with as much rigour as if they had belonged to a private gentleman.

De Quincey, 1849

■ SOURCE 6E

Every minute should be used on the road. I have to direct you at the peril of your job that you do not quit your coach, to go into any public house, or stop at any place on the road, but where you have letters to leave, or real coach business to perform. See to this, and if coachmen will stop, write me of their misconduct.

Harker's Directive to the Mail Guards, 1800

? QUESTIONS

a) Compare the two coaches in Sources 6A and 6C. What differences in design are there? How many inside passengers are there in each case? How many outside?

b) How far do Sources 6A and 6C support, or contradict, the impression of travelling as an outside passenger given in Source 6B?

c) How reliable is Source 6D in the impression it gives of the coaching age?

d) Suggest reasons for the different impressions of coach travel given in Sources 6B and 6D.

e) In Source 6C, find the coach-horn, the lamps, the turnpike gate, the paddle-steamer.

f) In what ways does Source 6E show how control was kept over the operations of the mail-coach? Why do you think this was necessary?

The coaches had to be very well built to withstand the terrible state of the roads. The mail coaches were hired from the coachmaker, John Vidler, at 1¼d (½p) per mile, so it was worth his while building them to last. Even so, travel was not comfortable, as Source 6B suggests. Early coaches were heavy and high, and swayed about, making passengers feel sick. There was no protection from the weather for 'outsides' (passengers sitting outside the coach). One winter's day in 1812 the coachman found two of his outsides dead, and one dying, from exposure, on arrival at Bath. In 1804 a new method of springing, Elliott's elliptical spring, was invented. This gave coaches a lower centre of gravity, allowing faster speeds, and up to 12 outside passengers. The difference can be seen by comparing Sources 6A and 6C.

Nevertheless, there was a huge increase in the number of passengers – about eight times as many from 1790 to 1830. By 1835 there were 700 mail-coach and 3300 stage-coach routes in Britain. Routes were mainly centred on London, where three big firms – Chaplin, Horne and Sherman – supplied most of the routes. Most coaches operated from inns, which provided food and accommodation for the horses and for passengers. At the peak of stage-coach activity, Chaplin employed 2000 people and 200 horses at just one inn, the Swan with Two Necks, with another 1600 horses at other inns.

Coach travel was not cheap: average prices were about 4*d* (1.75p) a mile inside, 5*d* (2p) in a mail-coach, and 3*d* (1.25p) a mile outside. In addition there were other costs to the traveller: a tip to the coachman – usually 2*s* (10p), breakfast – about 1*s* (5p), dinner – 3*s* (15p), overnight stay at inns, with more tips, and so on. All this meant that stage-coaches were quite beyond the means of most people. If they did have to travel, and most still did not, they walked, or took a wagon. A stage-wagon, rather like the one in Source 2, cost about ½*d* (0.2p) a mile and averaged about 3 mph. Passengers were expected to walk beside the wagon, except when it rained, but could sleep in it overnight. The very rich, on the other hand, owned their own coaches and would hire horses as they travelled.

Results of Road Improvements

● The improvements in road-building brought about by the turnpike trusts meant faster travel for people, letters and small items. This was a great help in building up businesses all over the country. Josiah Wedgwood, for example, set up a network of travelling salesmen so that his china and pottery could be sold across Britain. He was able to keep in contact with them, and run the factory to meet their orders, because there was a fast, reliable mail service. Such a system would not have been possible in 1750.

● The changes on the roads had much less impact on goods haulage, which increased by 130% between 1790 and 1830, barely keeping pace with the rise in population. The bulky raw materials of industry: coal, cotton, clay, iron as well as timber or grain, were still far too expensive to move by road. A wagon might need fewer horses to pull it on a better road surface, but it was still slow. A journey of several days meant several days' wages for

the carrier and fodder for his horses, so prices remained too high.

● It would be wrong, however, to think that there was no change at all in road freight. There was a large increase in the amount of food, especially fruit and vegetables, coming into London, and in the

distance it came from. This was made possible by turnpikes and the road improvement carried out by the trusts. In rural areas lime, marl and manure were carried cheaply over shorter distances. In many areas there was a growth of road traffic on short hauls from river or canal wharves to local firms.

Water Transport

Coastal Shipping

Ships are especially good carriers of bulky items. Adam Smith, in 1776, pointed out that a ship, with a crew of six or eight, could carry as much as 50 wagons, pulled by 400 horses, and led by 100 men. We have seen that road transport in the 18th century was slow and expensive. However, nowhere in Britain is far from the sea, and for centuries ships had carried goods around the coasts.

In the 16th and 17th centuries there was an increase in the demand for coal. Apart from heating homes, it was used in making glass, paper, salt, bricks and beer. The

coalfield which could supply this demand most easily was on Tyneside, where ships could sail upriver, close to the pits, and then bring the coal down the coast to London. For this reason Londoners called it sea-coal.

This coal trade was by far the biggest coastal shipping trade, making up 84% of all coastal shipping tonnage in 1824. However, other products were also carried, such as corn from ports around the Wash, stone from quarries in south-west England and huge amounts of hay for all London's horses. The trouble was that it was all dependent on the wind. This meant that journey times were uncertain. Sometimes there was a terrible shortage, when no ships could sail,

■ *SOURCE 7* **Coal drop at Wallsend, 1839. The coal can be dropped down the chute into small boats, but here the wagon itself is lowered into the collier and the coal unloaded direct**

■ *SOURCE 8* **Two paddle-steamers off Gravesend, 1840s**

or a glut, when lots of them arrived together. Sailing ships could also be wrecked in storms.

Steamers

Inventors were quick to apply steam-engines to ships. William Symington experimented with a James Watt engine in 1788, and in 1802 the *Charlotte Dundas* successfully sailed on the Forth and Clyde Canal. Henry Bell's *Comet* began operating a steamship service on the Clyde from 1812. By 1821 there were 188 steamers in service, and by 1853 there were 639. At first they were used as tugs and estuary boats on the Thames, Clyde, Tyne, Humber, Solent, Mersey and the Bristol Channel. These early boats were paddle steamers, and could travel around the waterways regardless of wind or tide. The invention of the screw propeller, in 1836, brought greater speeds and more reliable progress in rough weather.

In the 1820s and 1830s steamers were the fastest and cheapest way of travelling. On the Edinburgh to London route the *Monarch* ran a service at £2 10s (£2.50) on deck, £4 4s (£4.20) with cabin, both including meals. The coach fare was £3 10s (£3.50) outside, £6 15s (£6.75) inside, but this did not include the continual outlay of tips

and meals which nearly doubled the fare. Except in bad weather, the *Monarch* was also extremely comfortable, with a dining salon for 100 people. By the 1840s steamers were running some 1400 route miles, visiting 90 ports. Even as late as 1849, nearly 12000 people travelled from Edinburgh to London by steamer, compared with 6000 by train.

? QUESTIONS

a) How do you think travelling on a paddle-steamer, such as those shown in Source 8, would compare with travelling on a passenger liner today? What would be the main differences?

b) What other forms of water transport are shown in Source 8?

The punctuality, comfort and cheapness of the steamer made it popular very quickly, but these qualities are not important for carrying coal. Sailing brigs still plied up and down the east coast until early in the 20th century. The coastal trade remained important to many little ports and harbours for the same period, and money was spent on dredging, building harbour walls and piers. Not until 1906 did the tonnage from foreign trade exceed the tonnage of Britain's own coastal shipping trade.

Waterways Before 1750

The rivers of Britain had been used to carry goods for centuries. Even quite small rivers, miles inland, were used for big, bulky items, such as stone, coal or corn which were difficult to carry by road. In 1768 a list was made of 580 water-ports in the country. There were, however, problems in using rivers for transport. Many were very winding, making journeys long. They might flood in winter, or dry up in summer. Millers might wish to build weirs to provide power for their waterwheels. Landowners might not want a tow-path along the bank. Local merchants might not want goods brought in from afar, as this could upset their control of local prices. Most important, there might not be a good-sized river going to the place you wanted to reach.

Over many years, people had learnt to improve rivers for transport. Cuts were made to avoid bends, and locks built to by-pass weirs. In the 18th century, the River Weaver, linking the Cheshire saltfields with Liverpool, was improved. In 1757, the Sankey Brook was made navigable from the St Helens coalfield down to the River Mersey and then to Liverpool.

■ SOURCE 9A Barton Bridge over the River Irwell, engraving of 1760s

Canal Builders

Canals had been built in Britain before the 1750s. In 1564 the Exeter Canal by-passed weirs on the River Exe, and in 1724 the Newry Canal took coal down to the port of Newry, in Ireland. However, the first canal of the canal age is usually held to be the Duke of Bridgewater's Canal, which ran from his coal mines at Worsley into Manchester and was completed in 1761 (Map 2, page 50).

Although Worsley was only ten miles from Manchester, the cost of taking coal from the Duke's mines, by packhorse, meant that it was too expensive to sell well in the city. He, and his agent, James Gilbert, hired James Brindley to design the canal. It was built so that it led straight into the mine at the Worsley end. Brindley had to take the canal over a bog, Trafford Moss, and over the River Irwell. This he did with an aqueduct, at Barton, which was marvelled at by everybody.

■ SOURCE 9B

At Barton Bridge he has erected a navigable canal in the air, for it is as high as the top of the trees. Whilst I was surveying it with a mixture of wonder and delight four barges passed me in the space of about three minutes, two of them being chained together and dragged by two horses who went on the terrace of the canal, whereon, I must own, I durst hardly walk, as I trembled to behold the large River Irwell beneath me.

Annual Register **1763**

The canal did exactly what the Duke of Bridgewater hoped: the price of his coal in Manchester fell from 7*d* (3p) to 3½*d* (1½p) per hundredweight. The next stage was to extend the canal to Liverpool, and this was completed by 1767. The two great cities now had a really cheap means of freight transport between them, as canal charges were a sixth of the cost of carrying goods by road.

Once Brindley had shown how to overcome the major problems of canal building, many others were built. Some were small enterprises – short canals, with few if any locks. However, Brindley was soon engaged on a much bigger plan. The great rivers of England, Mersey, Trent, Thames and Severn, had always presented two problems – how to get from one to the other, and how to reach towns which lay between them. The most obvious example of this latter problem was Birmingham, which had no good river link with the rest of England.

The first step to improving links was the Trent and Mersey, or Grand Trunk Canal, started in 1766 but not

■ SOURCE 9C

The smith's forges, the carpenter's and mason's workshops were covered workshops, which floated in the canal and followed the work from place to place. The Duke made the rubbish of one help to build another. Thus the stones which were dug up to form the basin for the boats at Worsley were cut into different shapes to build the bridges over the rivers, brooks or highways, or the arches of the aqueduct. The clay, gravel and earth taken up to preserve the level at one place were carried down the canal to raise the land in another.

J. Philips, *A General History of Inland Navigation*, 1793

? QUESTIONS

a) What can you see in Source 9A which clearly prevents the River Irwell being used for boats any further upstream than Barton?
b) How does the barge in Source 9A move, other than being pulled by horses?
c) What is the aqueduct made of?
d) What are the attitudes of the writers of Sources 9B and 9C to the canal?
e) What different things does each writer admire about the canal?

completed until 1777 (see Map 2). A major promoter of this canal was Josiah Wedgwood, who set up a new factory and his own home, by the canal, at Etruria. He could bring in Cornish clay by sea to Liverpool, and then by canal, and send out his fragile pottery on the gently-running canal barges. When the canal was complete his freight charges from Etruria to Manchester dropped from £2 15*s* (£2.75) per ton to 15*s* (75p) per ton.

The next link was the Staffordshire and Worcester Canal which linked the Grand Trunk with the Severn, via Wolverhampton, with a branch to Birmingham. This was completed by 1772. The last arm of the 'Grand Cross', as it was called, was the Oxford Canal. This linked the system with the Thames and was finished in 1790. Many other short links were built, especially in the Birmingham area.

Canal mania

These early canals made good profits, but building ceased for a while in

■ *MAP 2* **The main canal and river systems**

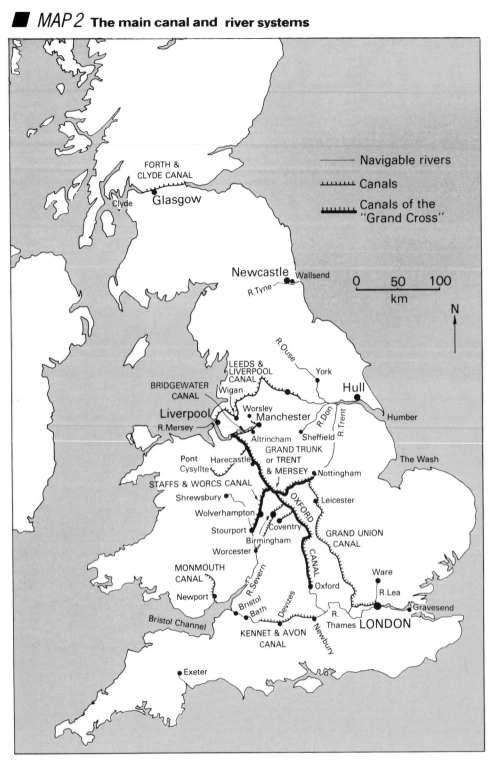

FORTH & CLYDE CANAL

Clyde — Glasgow

— Navigable rivers

⊥⊥⊥⊥⊥ Canals

▬▬▬ Canals of the "Grand Cross"

Newcastle — Wallsend
R.Tyne

0   50   100
km

N

R.Ouse

LEEDS & LIVERPOOL CANAL
York

BRIDGEWATER CANAL — Wigan

Hull

Liverpool
R.Mersey

Worsley — Manchester
R.Don   R.Trent   Humber

Altrincham — Sheffield

Pont Cysyllte — Harecastle
GRAND TRUNK or TRENT & MERSEY

The Wash

STAFFS & WORCS CANAL
Nottingham

Shrewsbury
OXFORD
Leicester

Wolverhampton

Stourport — Coventry
CANAL
GRAND UNION CANAL

Birmingham
Worcester

MONMOUTH CANAL
R.Severn
Ware

Newport
Oxford
R.Lea

Bristol — Bath
Devizes
Gravesend

Bristol Channel
R. Thames   LONDON
Newbury

KENNET & AVON CANAL

Exeter

---

and dashed through the night to Devizes, hoping to get rich. In this situation some canals were built, especially in the South of England, away from industrial areas, which could never possibly make a profit.

In the early 19th century some improvements were made to the initial 'Grand Cross'. The Grand Junction Canal, 1805, was a better link between London and the Midlands. The Leeds and Liverpool Canal, 1816, provided a more direct route between Yorkshire and Lancashire across the Pennines. The Government then built the Royal Military Canal in Scotland in 1822.

Brindley's early canals were usually contour canals: that is, they followed the same level, avoiding locks or very large engineering works. This meant that they were often rather winding. Later canal engineers, such as Smeaton, Rennie, Green and Thomas Telford built more direct routes, using cuttings, tunnels, embankments, aqueducts and inclined planes. Telford's most spectacular construction was the Pont Cysyllte (pronounced Pont-Kersulty), 127 feet above the River Dee on the Ellesmere Canal. Canal engineering improved over the years in the speed of building, too. Brindley's first Harecastle Tunnel took eleven years to build; Telford's larger tunnel, completed in 1827, took only three years. By the 1820s Telford was helping to build canals in Sweden as well.

■❓ *QUESTIONS*

a) Look at Source 10A. Explain the ways in which Telford's tunnel is an improvement on Brindley's.

b) Source 10B is an artist's impression. The tunnel is over 1½ miles long, and the hill is not as high as this source makes it. Does this mean that Source 10B has no value to someone studying canal history? Explain your answer.

c) Compare the sizes of the locks in Sources 10C and 10D. What does this tell us about the amount of traffic in each case?

d) Note the width of the canal in Source 10C. Why do you think it was built so narrow? What effect do you think this would have on the amount of goods it could carry?

---

the 1780s when war with the American colonies led to a business slump. When peace came, business revived. Industrialists in coal, iron and textile industries wanted to expand, and needed cheap transport. Investors remembered the good profits of the early canals. This brought about a 'canal mania' during 1791–4, when 42 canals were started at a total cost of over £6 million.

Canals were very expensive to build: the Duke of Bridgewater calculated the cost at £10 000 a mile. Nevertheless, many schemes were put forward, and investors were anxious to put money into them. One plan, for a canal from Bristol to Southampton and London, was announced in Devizes, in 1792, with one day's notice to buy shares. Thousands of people wanting to buy shares rushed to hire horses

e) In Source 10E (over), what jobs are being done? What tools and machines are being used? How many workmen are there?

f) What would be the differences between the way the work in Source 10E was done in 1845 and how it would be done now?

The Canal Age

Canal families

There were 25000 canal barges in the middle of the 19th century, employing some 50000 people. In early years boatmen kept a home in one town and worked the barge with a horse and a boy for help. When railways produced such fierce competition, wages were cut and the boatman and his family had to abandon their home and move into the barge. Here whole families lived in the tiny cabins – the worst living conditions in the country. The children received no education, as they were continually on the move. Even as late as 1938 there were still 600 children living on the canal barges.

■ **SOURCE 10D** **Top lock of a flight of five at Allt-yr-yn, Newport, on the Monmouthshire Canal, 1796**

■ **SOURCE 10A** **The northern end of the two Harecastle Tunnels on the Trent and Mersey; you can see Brindley's from the 1770s on the right, and Telford's on the left, completed in 1827**

■ **SOURCE 10B** **Artist's impression of the Harecastle Tunnel, 1785**

■ **SOURCE 10C** **Double lock on the Regent's Canal, 1801; Islington Canal in the distance**

■ SOURCE 10E The building of Worcester locks, about 1845

■ SOURCE 11A 'An Evening Halt' from the *Illustrated London News*, 1874

❓ QUESTION

Imagine you are one of the people in Source 11A; use both Sources 11A and 11B to describe your life on the barge and how you feel about it.

Goods carried

The main item the barges carried was freight, especially coal. In fact the Duke of Bridgewater said that any successful canal 'had coal at the heel of it'. In addition to coal, canals also carried iron ore, stone,

■ SOURCE 11B

Mr Smith said that he had had brought to his notice the case of a woman who, during the last 20 years had not slept in a dwelling-house. She had brought up a family of eight children in a cabin measuring 7 feet by 6 feet by 5 feet which must have borne a strong resemblance to a rabbit hutch. One of the children slept at her and her husband's head, another at their feet, two in a cupboard and the rest where she could put them ...

An average of the persons who occupied the cabins of the boats would be a man, his wife and two or three children. When a boy reached the age of eight or nine he generally left his parents and went to work for another boatman, while the younger members of the family were employed in driving the horses or steering their parents' boat.

Warrington Guardian, 1875

brick, slate, timber and clay. In rural areas they usually brought in coal, seed and fertiliser, and took out grain. Some barges were built to carry cattle and sheep, which previously walked to market on their own legs.

Despite their slowness some canals carried passengers as well as freight. On the Johnstone Canal, in Scotland, an 11-mile, lock-free canal, passengers were carried at speeds of up to 10 mph by horses that were changed regularly. From 1774 a regular passenger service ran from Altrincham to Manchester. It was very comfortable, and there was 'a coffee-room at the head, from whence wines etc. are sold by the Captain's wife. Next to this is the first cabin, at 2s 6d (12½p), the second, at 1s 6d (7½p) and the third, at 1s (5p).' The Scottish canals, such as the Caledonian, with stone banks, carried passengers for many years, but fears for the erosion of the earth banks prevented the adoption of steamers on English canals. Locks, which slowed up the journey, and the grimy industrial landscape which canals went through, also rather put people off.

Industry

The cheap transport of bulk goods by canal came at an important time

■ SOURCE 12A Stourport, 1776

However, some did not. Canals in south-western and southern England never paid back their costs. The average canal boat was 72 feet long, 7 feet wide, carrying a load of 30 tons. Some canals were wider than this, but barges – narrow-boats – making cross-country journeys had to fit into the narrowest canal they could use. Indeed, some locks were only 64 feet long, which cut the size of barge still further. The large profits some canals made were not usually ploughed back into widening or deepening canals, which would have made bigger loads possible. Another problem was that several canal companies were involved in all but the shortest journey. Travelling from Liverpool to London might involve dealing with nine or ten companies; the waste of time and paperwork was unnecessarily expensive. There was never a goods clearing house, such as the railways opened up (see later). As we shall see, competition from railways hit the canal business hard.

in the Industrial Revolution. From the 1770s to the 1840s it was the canals which met the transport needs of industry. Further expansion in coal, textiles, iron and pottery could now take place: raw materials could be provided and finished products transported around the country at a time when road haulage was slow and expensive.

It was the Midlands which benefited most: an area previously cut off from good, cheap transport. The network of canals fed coal and iron to the wharves and factories of the Black Country. The population of the Potteries, an area largely opened up by canals, rose from 7000 in 1760, to 20 000 in 1785.

Where the Staffordshire and Worcester Canal joined the River Severn a whole new town sprang up, called Stourport (see Source 12A).

■ SOURCE 12B

The cottage, instead of being half-covered with miserable thatch, is now covered with a substantial covering of tiles or slates, brought from the distant hills of Wales or Cumberland. The fields, which before were barren, are now drained, and by the assistance of manure, clothed with a beautiful green-ness. Places which rarely

knew the use of coal are plentifully supplied with it, at reasonable prices. And what is the still greater public benefit, corn merchants are prevented from charging high prices. Communication being opened between Liverpool, Bristol and Hull, and the line of canal being through counties abundant in grain, it brings in corn in a way unknown in the past.

Thomas Pennant, 1782 (adapted)

? *QUESTIONS*

a) In Source 12A, find: the river, the canal, locks, sailing boats, warehouses.

b) List the benefits of canals, as Thomas Pennant sees them in Source 12B.

c) How did the canals prevent corn prices from being too high?

d) Read the following paragraph, and compare it with Source 12B. How far do they differ? Why do you think Pennant and this author make different points? Which is the most useful piece of text to someone studying canals?

Problems

Some canals did extremely well, paying their shareholders dividends of 25% well into the 1840s.

Longer-term effects of canal-building

The task of building canals brought several new practices into British life:

a) *The civil engineers*, men like Brindley and Telford, invented all sorts of new methods of building. Tunnels, bridges, cuttings, embankments, locks and aqueducts all posed new engineering problems. The solutions which these men worked out provided the basis of civil engineering for the future, first in the days of railways, then of modern roads.

b) *The men who actually did the work* were the 'navigators' or 'navvies'. Without any modern machinery, with only picks and shovels, they built 2200 miles of canal by 1815. Shovelling earth was not a new job, but the sheer scale of operations was. When the huge railway building boom took place, the navvies were ready to take on the work.

c) Canal building required *considerable organisation*. A great deal of capital had to be laid out before there was any return. The canal companies had to find ways of raising this money and did so without relying too much on the Stock Exchange. The preference share, on which a dividend was always paid after essential running expenses had been met, was devised to meet this need. Each canal required a private Act of Parliament, and considerable experience was gained in getting these passed. (It was also, incidentally, the beginning of the rights of the public to question big projects, now done through public inquiries.) Each canal had to deal with many property owners, and simple ways had to be found to compensate them. In all these matters, experience gained in canal companies proved invaluable when the railway boom took place.

Railways

■ **SOURCE 13A** **Horses pulling coal-wagons, Derbyshire, 19th century**

? QUESTION

Look at Source 13A. Would you call this a railway? In what ways is it like a railway as we know it? In what ways is it different from a railway?

We would expect a railway to have a steam-engine (later diesel or electric) pulling the trucks. The rails would be different, and it would be open to any member of the public to travel, or send goods on it. Clearly several different inventions had to come together to make the steam railway system of 19th-century Britain.

Early Railways

Some of these inventions go back quite a long way. As with so many other changes, the roots lie in the coal industry. We have seen that there was an increased demand for coal as far back as the 16th century for such industries as brewing, making salt, paper, glass and bricks. The coal boats described in the earlier section on coastal shipping (page 47) carried large quantities of coal, but did not sail much in the winter months. The coal mines produced coal all the year round, and could not store it at the pit-heads. They had to find an easy way of getting lots of coal down to the staithes (see Source 7 on page 47) where it could await the summer sailings. It was calculated that while a horse could pull a ton of coal in a wagon on a road, it could pull 8 tons on a track. Wooden tracks were laid down as early as 1604 in Nottinghamshire, and 1605 at Bedlington, County Durham. These wooden tracks lasted only two or three years before wearing out. In 1767 the first cast-iron rails were used in Coalbrookdale (see Chapter 4, Source 5C, page 28) and from 1776 cast-iron L-shaped rails were widely used. These were like the rails shown in Source 13A, and could take wagons with ordinary wheels. In 1801 the Surrey Iron Railway opened, the first railway open to the public. There were 300 miles of track in Britain by 1810, mainly in coal fields. These were called plateways.

■ **SOURCE 13B** **The opening of the wagonway from Bewick Main Colliery to the Tyne**

At eleven o'clock four wagons of small coal were brought up the first plane by the steam engine. In the evening, in order to prove the excellency of the level railway, six men, without horses, took with the greatest ease, four laden wagons, each with ten men on top from Ayton Cottage to the Tyne.

The level part of the railway is so calculated that one horse could take with ease four laden wagons.

Newcastle Courant, **May 20, 1809**

■ SOURCE 13C Tyneside scene, 1787

Plan of the COLLIERIES on the RIVERS Tyne and Wear also Blyth, Bedlington and Hartley; with the Country 11 Miles round Newcastle Taken from actual Surveys by JOHN GIBSON 1787

? QUESTIONS

a) Which kinds of power are described in Source 13B?

b) How do we know the wagonway was skilfully laid out?

c) Compare Source 13C with Source 7: what differences are there in the way the boats are loaded?

d) In what way does the wagonway in Source 13C seem inferior to the one described in Source 13B?

New Engines

The steam-engine described in Source 13B was a stationary engine: it hauled the wagons up a slope, then they were unhitched and pulled by horses. At that time steam-engines were very large, low-pressure engines. What was needed was a way of making one small but strong enough to go on rails.

The first successful steam locomotive was invented by Richard Trevithick (1771–1833). Trevithick was a big, burly Cornishman, an expert wrestler, the son of a mining engineer and a mine-manager himself. There were many steam engines in use in Cornish mines at that time. Trevithick began to experiment with what he called 'strong steam' – steam under pressure – which gave more power. He built a steam carriage to travel on the roads, and in 1804 was asked to build a locomotive to pull wagons on the Pen-y-darren plateway in Wales (see also Source 16C).

■ SOURCE 14 Trevithick's own account of the event

Sir,

Yesterday we proceeded on our journey with the engine we carryd ten tons of iron five waggons and 70 men riding on them the whole of the journey, its above 9 miles which we performed in 4 Hours and 5 Mints, but we had to cutt down som trees and remove some large rocks out of road the engine while working went near 5 miles pr Hour ...

We shall take forty tons the next journey, the publick untill now called mee a scheming fellow but now their tone is altered.

Penydarren, 22 February, 1804

? QUESTIONS

a) Trevithick seemed to be better at locomotive design than at spelling: how many mistakes can you find?

b) What kind of man does Trevithick seem to be, based on Source 14 and what you have read so far?

The Pen-y-darren experiment was only a partial success, as the locomotive was so heavy it broke many of the rails.

All the basic ideas needed for a successful steam locomotive were invented by Trevithick: the piston was linked directly to the wheels; the steam exhaust was used to create a draught to make the fire hotter; the locomotive gripped the rails by sheer weight, not by cogs or any other means. The problem was now to make stronger rails and more powerful engines. The next steps were taken in the coalfield railways of Northumberland and Durham. William Hedley, at Wylam Colliery, built the 'Puffing Billy', in 1813 (see Source 16D). George Stephenson, at Killingworth Colliery, built his first locomotive in 1814, and by 1823 there were over 20 others in use, all on colliery lines.

George Stephenson

George Stephenson came from a poor family, and had started work at the age of eight. He became interested in locomotives and in other inventions in the coal-mining industry. He was a blunt, practical person who had already built a number of railway lines as well as designing and driving the locomotives to go on them.

In 1821 a Quaker businessman, Edward Pease, asked Stephenson to design a much longer line. It would go from coal mines near Darlington, 25 miles down to the port of Stockton-on-Tees. When he asked George Stephenson to design the line, he proposed to use horses and stationary engines to pull wagons. Stephenson persuaded him to use some locomotives and built Locomotion No. 1 for the job.

■ *SOURCE 15* **Opening of the Stockton–Darlington Railway, 1825**

Train of Waggons crossing the Turnpike Road near Darlington.

? QUESTIONS

a) What does the picture in Source 15 tell you about the strength of the engine?

b) What does this picture tell you about the speed of the train?

c) What are the people riding in?

d) What obstacles has Stephenson had to overcome in building the line?

The Stockton–Darlington Railway gave plenty of ideas to Stephenson, and to businessmen in northern England. The railway made a good profit. It used horses, stationary engines and steam-engines, and this meant that comparisons could be made between them. Stephenson found that steam-engines were 30% cheaper than any alternative for coal haulage. Locomotion No. 1 could pull 75 tons of coal at a steady 5 mph – downhill it reached 12 mph, which terrified many people. Lastly, Stephenson fixed the gauge of the railway, the distance between the rails, at 4 feet 8½ inches. He did this by measuring over a hundred colliery wagons and taking the average distance between the wheels. This gauge is still the gauge of British railways, and many railways all over the world.

At this time most industrial traffic was taken by canal barge. It was only because it would have been very expensive to build a canal over the hills between Stockton and Darlington that Pease decided on a railway. But there were other disadvantages of canals. The Bridgewater Canal between Liverpool and Manchester had been hailed as a great success when it opened in 1767. By the 1820s the prospering port of Liverpool and the booming city of Manchester found the link inadequate. The canal company took advantage of their monopoly by charging heavy tolls – 15s (75p) a ton. Canal journeys were slow as well. Cotton was said to take as long getting from Liverpool to Manchester as it took to get from the USA across to Liverpool. A group of businessmen, observing the success of the Stockton–Darlington, therefore decided to build a railway from Liverpool to Manchester.

George Stephenson was appointed Chief Engineer, and his son Robert was Chief Surveyor. Robert had been to Edinburgh University, but was too ill to work as a mining engineer down a pit, and so joined his father. People at the time were amused to see the tall father and the slightly-built son discussing their problems in a broad Northumbrian accent no one could understand.

There were several problems. The line was opposed by the canal company and by local landowners. The surveys had to be done secretly after local farmers had attacked the surveyors. An Act of Parliament was needed, and George Stephenson was questioned by a Parliamentary Committee, an experience he hated. Then there were obstacles for the line to cross: Olive Mount, near Liverpool; the wide valley of the River Sankey; the huge bog at Chat Moss.

When the line was nearly ready, the directors decided to hold a competition for the best locomotive to operate it. The prize was £500, and the contract to supply locomotives. Four were entered, but George Stephenson's Rocket won easily (see Source 16E). It had to pull three times its own weight, forward and reverse, 20 times, over the 1½ miles of level track at Rainhill (the distance from Liverpool to Manchester is 35 miles). The Rocket did this at an average speed of 10 mph, often going over 20 mph. After this triumph at Rainhill in 1829, George Stephenson drove the Rocket himself at the opening of the railway in the next year.

■ *SOURCE 16A* **Olive Mount Cutting, 1830**

■ *SOURCE 16B* **Sankey Viaduct, 1830**

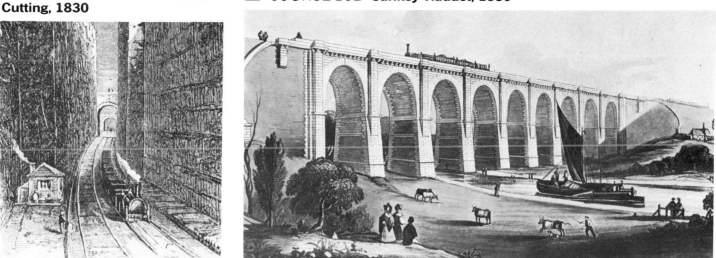

■ *SOURCE 16C* **Trevithick's Pen-y-darren locomotive, 1804**

■ *SOURCE 16D* **Puffing Billy, 1813**

❓ QUESTIONS

a) The Duke of Wellington described the various engineering achievements of the Liverpool–Manchester line as 'magnificent' and 'stupendous'. Look at Sources 16A and 16B. Do you agree with his opinion?

b) In what ways do we look at things differently today from an observer in 1830?

c) Compare Sources 16C, 16D, 16E, and 16F. In what ways are these engines the same and in what ways are they different?

d) Obviously the engine in Source 16F (next page), is the fastest and strongest: how do you think this was achieved?

e) What protection from the weather is given to the driver in all four of these locomotives?

■ *SOURCE 16E* **Rocket, 1829**

SOURCE 16F Broad-gauge express locomotive, 1848

MAP 3 Railway network in 1845

The Railway Age

The Rocket and the Liverpool–Manchester Railway opened up the Railway Age. The problems faced by Trevithick were overcome: the multi-tube boiler of the Rocket gave more steam under pressure from the same boiler size. Wrought-iron rails were strong enough for the weight. From the first the Liverpool–Manchester Railway was run entirely by steam engines and was open to the public for goods and passengers. It provided transport that was faster than the stagecoach, but as cheap as the canal. It was an immediate success.

SOURCE 17 Traffic on the Liverpool–Manchester Railway

	1831	1835
Goods	88 000 tons	156 000 tons
Coal	11 000 tons	116 000 tons
Passengers	445 000	474 000

The fact that the Liverpool–Manchester Railway paid a dividend of 9½% attracted the attention of investors. In the first wave of enthusiasm, up to 1838, 500 miles of railway were built, and 1500 were planned. London was linked to Birmingham by 1838, to Southampton by 1840, and Dover by 1843. The Taff Vale Railway linked Merthyr Tydfil to Cardiff by 1841, and Glasgow and Edinburgh were joined in 1842 (see Map 3).

In the West of England the great engineer Isambard Kingdom Brunel built lines to a 7-foot gauge. This meant that his trains were more stable. He also built his lines as level as possible. To this day, trains to the West can travel very fast. His first line was the London–Bristol, opened in 1841.

Railway mania

There was a brief halt to new lines in the early 1840s, but then, during 1844–47 came 'railway mania': 626 railway companies were set up, with plans to build some 9536 miles of railway. Money poured into railway schemes – £252 million by 1847, or nearly 7% of the national income of Britain. Everyone wanted to make money out of promoting or owning shares in a railway. Some of the lines planned were, of course, quite sensible. But in the rush, lines were proposed which were parallel to others, or which underestimated the cost of building, or which went to places which would never provide enough traffic to pay for a railway.

The government made no effort to plan the railways at all. They did not believe that it was their job to interfere in economic affairs. There were lots of small companies, which made journeys across country difficult. One man, George Hudson, tried to join together, or amalgamate, several companies. By the late 1840s he controlled over 1000 miles of railway, and had become an MP. However, he was found guilty of dishonest use of funds in 1849, and forced to resign. At the same time several railway schemes ran into trouble and many people who had put money into them lost all their savings. Over 2000 miles of the proposed railways were never built.

By 1852 all the major routes of Britain had been built (see Map 4). Some historians have argued that railways in Britain were built too expensively. The average costs per mile in Britain were £42 500, in Belgium £36 500 and in France £27 700. In a big country like the USA they were much less. They point out the high extra costs: there had to be an Act of Parliament for every line. This cost a great deal in lawyers' fees: the parliamentary expenses on the London–Brighton line cost £180 000 and on the Great Northern £433 000. Then there were landowners to compensate. They very often protested loudly to increase the sum they would receive to drop their objections. The extra costs, while not huge, did mean that Britain had a railway network which was not only unplanned, but rather expensive. You can read about the effects of this in Section B, Chapter 10.

The navvies

All these new miles of railway, with their cuttings and embankments, tunnels and bridges, had to be built by hand. Mechanical steam shovels were not introduced until later in the 19th century. The men who did

■ *MAP 4* **Railway network in 1852**

this were the navvies, the successors of the canal-builders of the 18th century (see above). By 1847 there were 256 000 navvies working in Britain. Men joined because of the high wages – 5s (25p) a day for skilled workers, 3s (15p) or 2s (10p) a day for unskilled. The system was that a contractor would agree to build a length of line for a certain price. He would arrange

with a 'ganger' to do part of the job. The ganger paid the navvies by the 'set': a set was a train of 14 wagons, each holding 2 cubic yards of earth, and a pair of navvies would be expected to fill the set in a day. This meant shifting 10 tons of earth each. It is small wonder that they had the reputation of being fierce, strong, big eaters, drinkers and fighters.

■ SOURCE 18A Navvies at work on the Tring Cutting, London-to-Birmingham line, 1837: 1½ million tons of earth were removed to make this cutting

■ SOURCE 18B

Rude, rugged and uncultivated, possessed of great animal strength, collected in large numbers, living and working entirely together, they are a class by themselves. Collected from the wild hills of Yorkshire and Lancashire, coming in troops from the fens of Lincolnshire, and afterwards pouring in masses from every country in the empire, displaying an unbending vigour and an independent bearing; unable to read and unwilling to be taught, impetuous, impulsive and brute-like, they increased from thousands to hundreds of thousands. They lived but for the present; they cared not for the past, they were indifferent to the future ... Insolent and insulting, they were dreaded by the good and welcomed by the bad.

J. R. Francis, *History of the English Railway*, 1851

The navvies moved on as the railway moved on, so they often had no permanent homes.

■ SOURCE 18C

They made their houses where they got their work. Some slept in huts made of damp turf, too low to stand upright in, while small sticks, covered in straw, served as rafters. Barns were better places than the navvies' dwellings. Others formed a room of stones without mortar, placed thatch or flags across the roof, and took possession of it with their families.

J. R. Francis, *ibid*.

? QUESTIONS

a) Look at Source 18A. In what ways would the barrow-ways be regarded as dangerous nowadays?

b) What is the attitude of the author of Source 18B to the navvies?

c) Do you think Source 18B is a primary or a secondary source?

d) How far does the information in Sources 18A and 18C explain the opinions of the navvies given in Source 18B?

e) Many navvies were Irish, but Source 18B does not mention this fact. Does this mean that Source 18B is unreliable?

The navvies were paid once a month, so if they needed anything before pay day they had to buy it from the 'tommy-shop'. Here they got credit against their next pay. Despite the good wages there was often very little cash left to receive on pay day. As soon as they were paid navvies would go 'on the randy', drinking and refusing to work. Sometimes they would go into a local town in huge numbers and terrorise the place. All work on the railway stopped for two or three days until the money ran out.

The bigger contractors, such as Samual Morton Peto or Thomas Brassey, employed thousands of men, and even took gangs of British navvies to work abroad. They usually treated their men better, and provided better living accommodation. Other contractors tried to make more profit by speeding up the work. It was always a dangerous

job, with no regard to safety measures. In building the Woodhead Tunnel through the Pennines, in 1839–45, 3% of all the navvies were killed, and 14% injured. This was a worse casualty record than soldiers under the Duke of Wellington in the Peninsular War! It is no wonder that there were hardly any old navvies.

Public reaction

The reaction of the public to railways was very varied.

■ SOURCE 19A Travelling on the Liverpool–Manchester line

I had the satisfaction, for I can't call it pleasure, of taking a trip of five miles in it, which we did in just under a quarter of an hour – that is twenty miles an hour .... It is impossible to get rid of the idea of instant death to all upon the least accident happening. It gave me a headache which has not left me yet.

Thomas Creevey, 1830

■ SOURCE 19B

Neither the railwaymen nor the public had yet learned to treat railway trains with the necessary caution. Engine-drivers fancied that a collision between two engines was much the same thing as the interlocking wheels of two stage-coaches. Passengers tried to jump on and off trains moving at speed with the utmost recklessness. Again and again it is recorded: 'injured, jumped out after his hat', 'fell off, riding on the side of a wagon'.

W. Acworth, *The Railways of England*, 1900

(Two hundred people were killed on the railways in 1848.)

■ SOURCE 19C A journey on the Liverpool–Birmingham, 1837

The first sensation is a slight degree of nervousness, and a feeling of being run away with, but one soon feels safe, and the speed is delightful. Town after town, one park and mansion after another are left behind with the rapid variety of a moving panorama, and the continual hustle of the stops and changes make the journey very entertaining. It certainly makes all other travelling boring by comparison.

The Greville Memoirs (adapted)

■ SOURCE 19D Railway disaster at Kentish Town, 1861

■ SOURCE 19E Opposition to the Great Western Railway, 1834

The people would be smothered in tunnels, and those that escaped suffocation would be burned in the carriages. Eton College opposed it because it would harm the discipline of the school. A farmer objected because his cows might be killed in passing under an archway. The water in the Thames would be decreased, and the supply to Windsor Castle destroyed.

J. Francis, *A History of the English Railway*, 1851

❓ QUESTIONS

a) Why did the writer of Source 19A dislike railway travel?

b) How far do Sources 19B and 19D prove that his fears were justified?

c) What other reasons can you suggest for the high casualty figures on early railways, apart from those in Source 19B?

d) What does the writer of Source 19C like about railway travel?

e) By 1850 railways were very popular as a form of travel. Does Source 19C explain this popularity?

f) What other reasons might there be for this popularity?

g) What reasons might the people mentioned in Source 19E have had for objecting to railways?

h) What do you think is the attitude of the author of Source 19E to the objectors?

Look again at Source 17. You can see that in 1831, which was its first full year of operation, the Liverpool–Manchester carried over 400000 people. It was the same on other lines, especially near cities: the London–Greenwich, opened in 1838, carried 650000 passengers in its first 15 months of operation. This kind of huge, and sudden, passenger traffic astonished the railway companies. They had expected to carry only a few passengers in addition to goods.

One reason why people preferred to travel by train was the combination of speed and cheapness. On the Leeds to York run, for example, the stage-coach took four hours, at a cost of 3s (15p) outside, while the railway took 1 hour 20 minutes, at a cost of 2/6 (12½p). The outside seats on stage-coaches were, anyway, as we have seen, very uncomfortable. A better comparison would be to compare inside coach fares which were about 4d (2p) a mile, against second-class rail fares which were about 2d (1p) a mile. There were no irritating tips and other extras to pay on the train either. Indeed, the train offered half-fares for children, so family outings could be planned. It was exciting, speedy and new.

■ SOURCE 20A Paddington Station, a painting by Frith, 1862

■ SOURCE 20B First-class train, 1831

■ SOURCE 20C Third-class travel, 1840s

? QUESTION

a) Imagine you are one of the people in the crowd at Paddington in Source 20A (previous page). Write an account of what you saw and how you felt as you made your first train journey. Use these sources, and the others in this section, to help you.

You will see from Source 20C that third-class rail travel was pretty uncomfortable. The railway companies did not expect poorer people to travel by train, and did not encourage it. When asked about travel for the poor, a director of the Great Western Railway said, in 1839, 'I think the directors will probably send carriages once a day, perhaps with goods; carriages of an inferior design, at very slow speed, and at a very low price; perhaps too it may only be done at night.' In fact, the railways opened up a huge market for poorer people wanting to travel. Britain's working people in the 1840s were on the move: leaving home, finding jobs, visiting relatives. The railways increased this many times over.

In 1844 Gladstone's Railway Act ensured that one train a day ran in each direction, stopping at every station, at a rate of not more than 1d (½p) a mile. This increased third-

class travel until it was soon well over 50% of revenues.

Goods traffic

Goods traffic did not develop as early as passenger traffic.

■ SOURCE 21 Receipts from railway traffic (£ million)

	1843	1852
Passengers	3.1	7.7
Goods	1.4	7.9

There were several reasons for this slow start. In most areas canals were quite good enough. Speed did not matter much and canals were still very cheap. Early railway lines were very short (average length 41 miles) as all the small companies built their separate lines. This made long-distance freight journeys hard and was also made worse because in the early days the railway companies did not provide many of their own trucks. Carriers provided trucks, and had to arrange their own transfer at each changeover point. The Railway Clearing House, set up in 1842, began to deal with this problem after 1847 under the management of Braithwaite Poole. Railway companies became the sole

carriers of goods, and so they did all of the management. This kept rates low, and the tonnage travelling by rail overtook canal tonnage in the 1850s, just as it overtook passenger revenues (see Source 21).

? QUESTION

Look at Source 22. What kind of goods are being carried?

Although Source 22 shows many different kinds of freight, coal in fact accounted for over half of all goods traffic. This may have been good for the coal industry, but slow-moving coal trains clogged up the railway system in many areas.

Results of the Growth of Railways

This new, fast, cheap means of carrying people and goods was bound to affect many aspects of people's lives. Hardly any side of British economic or social life remained unaffected.

1 Effects on iron and other industries

There was a huge demand for iron, which alone boosted the growth of the iron and steel industry. The con-

■ SOURCE 22 Goods trains on the Liverpool–Manchester line, 1830s

tract for the London to Southampton Railway, in 1834 specified: '6000 tons of wrought-iron rails, and a suitable quantity of cast-iron chairs. 1000 tons of above to be delivered every 2 months from beginning of contract.' (Chairs are the things which grip the rail and hold it to the sleeper.)

Such large quantities were repeated up and down the country during the boom of the 1830s and 1840s. It has been estimated that rails alone took 15% of all iron output in the 1840s. To this must be added engines, signals, trucks, carriages and buildings – perhaps a 25% increase in demand for iron.

In addition, the building of railways took millions of bricks – perhaps one-third of all brick production in the 1840s. Thousands of tons of timber were used in sleepers, trucks, carriages and buildings. There was also an increased demand for coal. Thus the railways were not only a service to other industries, helping carry goods around faster and cheaper; they were an industry in their own right, with a big demand for raw materials of several kinds. New branches of industry grew up to meet this demand, such as new ironworks in Wales, Middlesbrough and Barrow-in-Furness, as well as several new brickworks in Essex.

2 Jobs

The railways created many new jobs. There were jobs in the industries described above. There were

the gangs of navvies described earlier. There were also all the people employed on the railways as drivers, firemen, guards, signalmen, porters, booking clerks, loaders, builders, carpenters, engineers as well as more middle-class jobs such as stationmasters and managers. A job on the railway was highly-regarded and there were probably 50 000 of these 'railway servants', as they were called, by 1850.

3 Food

The railways finished what the turnpikes and canals had started: the break-up of local control of food prices. No longer could there be a shortage, with high food prices in

one area and a good supply in another. It was for this reason that farmers often objected to railways, fearing that cheap food would put them out of business. Later, they found that railways could help them a great deal: fertiliser, seed and machines could be brought to them cheaply. Their own produce could be taken to distant markets cheaply.

The old system of driving cattle (and also geese, turkeys and other livestock) hundreds of miles to market came to an end. Under that system the animals lost lots of weight on the drive. Being taken by train (see Source 22) was faster, and there was no loss of weight. Cattle yards grew up at collection

■ SOURCE 23 Milk churns being taken by train from the West Country to London

points instead, such as Ludlow and Craven Arms on the Welsh Border.

Milk was another product which the trains could carry. Fresh milk from the West Country was carried overnight into London, putting an end to the need to keep cattle in London itself. Other dairy products and fresh vegetables, fruit and flowers could also be sold in the cities in good condition. The speed of trains also helped the fishing industry. Fresh fish could now be brought from Hull, Grimsby, Lowestoft and Wick in Scotland to customers in the cities.

4 Shops

Before the coming of railways shops had only been able to stock locally-made items. The shop-keepers were often local craftsmen, who made and sold their own work. Now goods could be brought to every High Street from anywhere in Britain. For the shopper, this meant much more choice in every shop and a great increase in the range of goods. The shop-keeper's job changed too: he or she became more of a trader, ordering and selling goods which were made somewhere else.

5 Management skills

By 1850, because of amalgamation of smaller companies, 75% of the rail mileage was operated by the 15 largest companies. These larger railway companies were, by 19th century standards, quite large and complex organisations. There were many different sides to a railway company's operation and this presented quite different problems from managing say, a factory, however big. New methods of accountancy, costing and management had to be worked out, which became useful in the 20th century when companies became larger.

6 Effects on road transport

The effect of the opening of railway routes on stage-coach operators was, as you can imagine from what has been said above, catastrophic.

■ *SOURCE 24A* **Evidence of E. Sherman, stage-coach proprietor**

Q: **You are now working two coaches?**

A: **Yes, between London and Birmingham**

■ *SOURCE 24B* **Painting called *Past and Present Through Victorian Eyes*, 1850**

Q: **How many did you work before the railway opened?**

A: **Nine.**

Q: **You said you were thinking of getting rid of most of the coaches?**

A: **Yes, we now carry mostly timid people who do not like to go by the railroads except when they offer very low fares indeed. That attracts the lower order of people. These people are so poor that coachmen say they get nothing besides the passage money.**

Select Committee on Turnpike Trusts, 1839

❓ QUESTIONS

a) What sort of people travelled by coach, according to Sherman in Source 24A?

b) What does he mean by 'the coachmen get nothing besides the passage money'?

c) Explain why people preferred to go by rail.

d) Explain what the artist of Source 24B is trying to say.

e) How does the fact that Source 24B is a painting affect its reliability as evidence?

f) How does the fact that Source 24B was painted in 1850 affect its reliability as evidence?

The first reaction of the stage-coach companies was to cut costs to meet the railway competition: the fare from London to Brighton was cut from 15s (75p) to 5s (25p) plus a free glass of wine. However, the coaches could not cut costs too much, and anyway could not match the speed of the railway. The number of horses in towns dropped as a result: Doncaster had 258 horses in 1839 and only 60 in 1845.

The coach companies did find a way of surviving by fitting in with the railways. In the early days, when there were only a few lines, coaches ran to meet the trains from all over a wide area. Thus when the London–Leeds line opened, coaches met the train from as far away as Scarborough and the Lake District. The early railways even agreed to carry coaches on specially designed trucks – a bit like the Motor-rail service today. Later, when more lines were built, coaches and drivers continued to find work driving cabs around the town, meeting trains and carrying people into the surrounding countryside. Many people had their own private horse-drawn vehicles; it was not until 1926 that the number of private cars exceeded the number of private horse-drawn vehicles.

The turnpike trusts suffered

badly from railway competition. There had been few amalgamations, so only short lengths were looked after by each trust, often with big debts. Any attempt to put up tolls met with great opposition. In 1843–4 the 'Rebecca Riots' broke out in Wales against raising of tolls. Such tolls had never been popular (see Source 4C on page 44), and local people were afraid of the effect high tolls would have on food prices. Turnpikes on station approach roads, or those which were not parallel to a railway, did quite well. However in general the roads, for another 60–70 years, became quite empty, serving only local people.

7 Effects on canal transport

Canals were actually cheaper for goods traffic than railways, and the decline of canals was much longer and slower. In 1850 two-thirds of the freight between Liverpool and Manchester still went by canal, and only by 1890 was the canal link seriously short of business.

Some railway companies were aware of the advantages of canals. They bought up the canal companies and put up the charges so they were no longer competitive. On long routes they only needed to buy part of the way and charge high prices on that, for canal rates to exceed railway charges. Thus a railway company bought control of the Rochdale Canal and put up charges. This affected the whole of the Leeds–Manchester–Liverpool route.

Thus to some extent the decline of canals was due to these unfair actions. Some people have pointed out that in other countries, such as France, the canals were improved and are still used for many kinds of freight. British canal companies did not take advantage of their 60-year lead over railways to improve, amalgamate and so become competitive. When railways were starting, many canal companies spent lots of money opposing them, then sold out in a panic when railways were opened.

8 Landscape

The landscape and appearance of the cities, towns and countryside of Britain was changed in major ways by the railways. The bridges, embankments, tunnels and cuttings altered the appearance of rural areas. At the time many lovers of

SOURCE 25 Viaduct near Consett, County Durham

landscape, such as the poet Wordsworth and the critic Ruskin, objected strongly. At Witham, in Essex, the railway cuts through the ramparts of a castle; at York a line was allowed to breach the medieval walls; in Devon a long stretch of track was built right on the edge of the beach; in cities thousands of houses were destroyed to build new stations and tracks. Such actions nowadays would not be allowed. Yet some features, such as viaducts, are now, a hundred years on, regarded with great affection and are even said to add to the landscape.

? QUESTION

Do you regard the viaduct in Source 25 as an eyesore or an attractive addition to the landscape?

SOURCE 26 Swindon in 1849

9 Railway towns

The building and repairing of engines, coaches and trucks was a new industry. Each company set up a works where this was done, either in a new town, or part of an existing town. Wolverton, on the London–Birmingham, Doncaster, Crewe and Swindon are examples of railway towns. There was no town at all at Crewe in 1841, but 42000 people by 1901. About 14000 employees worked at the Great Western works in Swindon in 1905.

? QUESTION

In Source 26 find: the railway line, the engineering works, the new streets of houses for the workers.

The Stratford area of London and the Gorton area of Manchester were railway suburbs. Carriage building led to the growth of Ashford in Kent and, at Chippenham in Wiltshire, signalling equipment was made.

10 Growth of cities

This is dealt with in Chapter 11, but it is worth pointing out the huge growth of cities which railways made possible. Horse-drawn vehicles, buses and trams began the growth as people found they could live and work in different places. It was the railway which brought the greatest growth of suburbs. It was not only the better-off who could afford to commute. Several suburban lines ran 'workmen's trains', with cheap return tickets valid before 7 a.m. and after 6 p.m. In this way different classes of suburb grew up and the cities sprawled further.

11 Excursions and holidays

People did not only travel to work by train. From early days special excursions, at reduced prices, were offered. Probably the first was in 1831 when 120 Sunday-school teachers went on an outing on the Manchester–Liverpool line. Thomas Cook offered his first excursion ticket in 1841. The Great Exhibition of 1851, in Hyde Park, London, encouraged family outings, and all the main lines offered cheap tickets. The London and North Western Railway took 775 000 tourists to the Great Exhibition at a fare of 5s (25p) return from Lancashire.

This led to the growth of seaside towns. Some places resisted the arrival of the railway – no tracks were laid on the Isle of Wight until 1862. But it was soon realised that a railway provided a huge opportun-

■ *SOURCE 27* **The new Victoria Station, London, in 1861**

ity for the holiday trade, and many lines were built for that alone. Sometimes, as at Cromer in Norfolk, the company also built and owned hotels as well as the railway to take holidaymakers there.

12 Politics

Railways allowed other kinds of activity to take place. As we shall see in Chapters 19 and 20, trade unions and political parties grew in the second half of the 19th century. It would not have been possible to run national political campaigns, or organise national unions, without the railways. Speakers, organisers and pamphlets could be sent rapidly all over the country.

13 Breakdown of local isolation

Local differences were broken down in many ways. One of the most significant was time. Before the railways, clocks in Reading were 4 minutes later than London, Cirencester

was 7½ minutes later and Bridgewater 14 minutes later. Obviously trains could not run to these times, so Greenwich mean time was enforced over the whole country.

Local differences disappeared with the railways in other respects, too. National newspapers could now be printed in Fleet Street, London, and sent all over the country. Each morning everyone could read the same news stories. Local building materials were used less as railways brought standard bricks, glass and slate to any builder who wanted them. With people able to travel so easily around Britain, for work or pleasure, local dialects and accents became less extreme. All these processes have increased in the 20th century, aided by 20th-century inventions such as cars, telephones, radio and TV, but it was the Railway Age in which they began.

Assignments

Local studies

Local study uses evidence from historical records as well as the landscape itself. Transport history has left plenty of evidence of both types.

1 Turnpike Trusts often have good records. Try to get hold of a map and trace the line of turnpikes on it to see how far modern roads still use them. Tollhouses often remain.
2 Many canals still exist. You could use a camera to record features such as bridges, locks, cottages and inns which date from the time the canal was built. Several canals have closed and been drained, but their routes can still be followed on maps and on foot.
3 The same can be done with railways. Learn to tell the difference between early features and modern improvements. As with canals, tracing old, disused tracks on foot can be an interesting activity. There are also many working steam railways to visit.

Empathy

1 **Travelling by stage-coach**
   a How would *you* feel about riding on the outside of a stage-coach?
   b How did passengers feel at the time?
   c Some passengers found it unpleasant; it was also expensive. Yet there was an eight-fold increase in passengers between 1790 and 1830. How do you explain this?
2 **Roads and canals**
   The coming of stage-coaches and canals meant lots of new jobs for all sorts of people.

   a Make a list of these new jobs.
   b What do you think people felt about doing each of these jobs? What were the good and bad points of each?
   c How do you think these people were regarded by those still doing traditional jobs on the land or in towns?
3 **Railway navvies**
   a What was the attitude of many people towards the railway navvies?
   b Why did they feel this way?
   c Was such an attitude justified?

Understanding concepts

1 **Causation**
   a How did a Turnpike Trust work?
   b Why were many of them successful?
   c Why did most of them collapse in the end?
2 **Cause/effect**
   What were the effects of the improvements in road transport brought about by the Turnpike Trusts on: the rich, the poor, business, letters, bulky freight?
3 **Change/continuity**
   Coastal shipping continued to be an important part of Britain's freight transport throughout the whole of this period.
   a What kinds of goods were carried by sea?
   b What were the advantages of using ships at sea, compared to i roads ii canals iii railways?
4 **Factors causing change**
   a In what ways did canals help the growth of industry in the years 1790–1850?
   b Why did it not matter that travel on them was so slow?
   c Why did they decline?

5 **Factors causing change**
   Building roads, canals and railways cost a great deal of money.
   a Why were they so expensive?
   b How was the money raised, in each case?
   c Why were so many people eager to put money into them?
   d What were the results of the financial arrangement in each case?
6 **Role of individuals**
   George Stephenson was obviously very important in the early history of railways.
   a Which other individuals made contributions, and what were they?
   b How far do you think the growth of railways was due to the work of Stephenson and the other people you have listed in a?
   c What other factors were important in the successful growth of railways in Britain?
7 **Cause/effect**
   a Who benefited from the growth of railways, and why?
   b Who suffered, and why?

Themes for discussion

1 a Stage-coaches have a romantic image nowadays – they are shown on Christmas cards and pictures. Yet they were expensive, slow and often uncomfortable methods of transport. Why do they have this image?
   b Does the same apply to steam railways?
2 Which had the greatest impact on the life of the average person in Britain today – the coming of railways in the 1840s, or the coming of TV in the 1950s?

7 Population – New Patterns of Living

What Happened to Population Growth?

In Chapter 1 we saw that population increased dramatically in the 150 years up to 1850. Did this rise continue?

The figures in Source 1 show that the population growth continued (except in Ireland) into the 20th century. They also show a slowing down of growth as the 20th century went on. Why did this happen?

As we saw in Chapter 1, changes in the population depend on what is happening to the birth rate and the death rate. The extraordinary growth in population during the years 1750–1850 was caused partly by a fall in the death rate, but mainly by a rise in the birth rate. More people got married and got married younger. Contraception was almost unknown, so lots more babies were born. Have things changed back again in recent years, to fewer, later marriages? This is not, in fact, the case. More people are marrying than before – and at even younger ages. In 1911, 55% of women aged 20–39 were married. In 1951 it was 73%. The average age of marriage is now 22 for men and 20 for women. Why, then, is the population only rising slowly? What is happening to the birth and death rates?

One of the problems we met with in Chapter 1 was the lack of reliable information for the 18th century. Fortunately we have better statistics for the later 19th century. The census was started in 1801, and has been carried out every ten years since. The Factory Act 1833 (Chapter 14, page 157) laid down the ages at which children could work. However, with no other records, the only people who could state the age of the children were their parents. In 1837 therefore, registration of births, marriages and deaths began. At first this was voluntary, but we have good information from about 1850.

■ *SOURCE 1* **Population of Britain 1851–1981, millions**

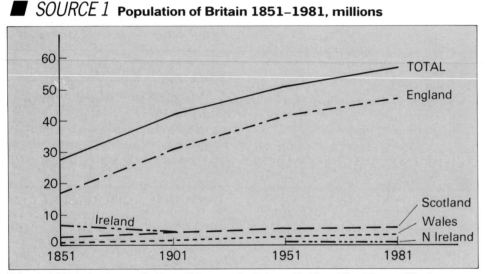

(Note: In 1921 Ireland was split. Most of it became the independent Republic of Eire, and Northern Ireland remained part of the United Kingdom.)

■ *SOURCE 2* **Birth rates and death rates, 1850–1980**

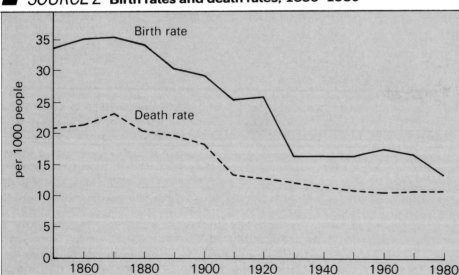

? QUESTIONS

The general trend of the graphs in Source 2 is downwards, but:
a) What happened to the birth rate between 1850 and 1870?
b) What happened to the birth rate in the 1920s?
c) What happened to the birth rate around 1960?
d) What happened to the death rate between 1850 and 1870?
e) What has happened to the death rate since 1930?

Try and think of the reasons why these small changes took place as we look at the general changes in the birth and death rates.

Why Did the Birth Rate Decline?

Smaller families

Contraception

In the early days of the Industrial Revolution, greater prosperity seemed to bring an increase in the birth rate. As this prosperity has continued into the 20th century, however, it has brought a dramatic decline in the birth rate. It is very difficult to give firm reasons for this fall. That is because it is almost entirely due to contraception, and so to private decisions taken by couples to limit their families. Upper-class families began to use contraception from the 1850s. Most forms of contraception at that time were expensive and not easily available. Poorer families either didn't know about contraception or didn't want to use it or couldn't afford it. In fact there was a lot of opposition, from doctors, the government and the Church, to giving advice on contraception.

One of the pioneers in making information about contraception available was Marie Stopes. She trained as a doctor and opened a clinic in 1921 in London to give free advice and cheap contraceptives. Most of the people who came to her were women. Marie Stopes knew that regular pregnancies and too many children ruined the health and happiness of working-class women.

■ SOURCE 3A A patient's letter to Marie Stopes' clinic, 1920s

I belong to the working classes and I know only too well how bitterly we need the help Dr Stopes is giving .... What do our lives become? We get broken in health, have sickly babies and go out to work to make ends meet. And our poor husbands have to suffer for it: you nag at them and then they pay toll at the nearest public house. I wish Dr Stopes was a multi-millionaire so she could open clinics at every town in England.

■ SOURCE 3B Case histories from the clinic

B8: 17 pregnancies, 10 living. Husband and wife can neither read nor write.

B7: Has had four confinements in two years; three dead.

B14: Has had six criminal abortions.

E8: Has had 17 pregnancies and seven living children. Quarrels with husband regarding too frequent unions.

G20: 12 pregnancies. One child died and one induced abortion. Husband refuses to take any precautions.

[Note to Case B14: abortion was illegal at that time.]

From *The First Five Thousand*, 1925

? QUESTIONS

a) From these two sources, what effect was the lack of contraception having on the lives of women?

b) Why do you think the authorities were opposed to giving advice on contraception?

c) What does Source 3A tell us about who funded Dr Stopes' clinic?

Many people in authority were still opposed to giving the public any information on contraception. Health visitors employed by the government were not allowed to give advice on contraceptives. Change only came slowly. In 1930 the voluntary groups joined together in what was later called the Family Planning Association. By 1935 there were 47 clinics, and local health authorities had also started 66 clinics of their own. However, it was not until 1967 that every local authority was obliged to offer advice on contraception.

In spite of these difficulties, many couples seem to have limited the size of their families, as Source 2 shows. This seems to have begun at least as early as the 1870s and had a dramatic effect from the 1920s.

A smaller family – a better standard of living

We can only suggest some of the reasons for smaller families. Improvements in child care meant that from the late 19th century fewer babies died (see later). This allowed a couple to plan how many children they wanted. Before, as

Source 3B shows, women may have had many more pregnancies than children who survived. Factory Acts and Education Acts meant that children were no longer able to earn money by working. Couples began to choose to limit the size of their family in order to have a better standard of living for themselves and their children. Life for working people became less of a hand-to-mouth struggle. They wanted to be able to enjoy life, to have holidays, decent clothes and furniture. In the 1920s radios, motorbikes and even cheap cars were available to families who had a little money to spare. By the 1960s there were more and more glittering consumer items: cars, fridges, television sets, washing machines, foreign holidays, even a home of your own. Couples wanted to have money left over after feeding and clothing their family to buy some of these things. In the 1860s the average family contained six children who survived to become adults. By 1900 it was four children; now it is fewer than two.

The economic health of Britain

Various other clues suggest that family income, and the economic health of the country as a whole, affect the birth rate. In the hard times of the 1930s the birth rate dropped a great deal. With good wages in the 1950s and 1960s, the birth rate went up again, producing what was called a 'baby boom'. By then, child allowances also helped to reduce the cost of having children. Then the birth rate dropped again during the recent unemployment crisis. Also the class with the smallest families, on average, are white-collar workers. Their pay is often not very good, but they want to 'keep up appearances'. Having fewer children helps them to do this.

Changes in women's lives

Further, women have seen contraception as a key factor in allowing them to lead healthier, more independent lives. When a couple could choose the number and timing of their children, women's health improved.

They could also go out to work – and more jobs were steadily opened up to them, as Chapter 21 shows. The pattern for most of the century has been for women to have their children while quite young, and then return to work when the children start school. A recent trend has been for women to build up their careers until their early thirties, and then have children. The Employment Protection Act 1975 has assisted this by guaranteeing a woman's job and pay for 29 weeks during pregnancy and after childbirth.

Why Did the Death Rate Fall?

Source 2 shows us that the death rate fell overall during the period after 1850. The usual reason given for this is the improvement in medicine, particularly the discovery of cures for the great killer infectious diseases such as cholera, typhoid, tuberculosis, etc. We will see how far these discoveries explain the fall in the death rate.

Medical improvements

The French scientist, Louis Pasteur, proved conclusively in 1864 that germs caused decay and disease. Even then it was some years before doctors fully accepted this. The next problem was to identify which germ caused which disease. Robert Koch, a German doctor, discovered in 1878 the germ which caused blood poisoning, and in 1882 the germ causing tuberculosis. The cholera germ was discovered in 1883, diphtheria in 1885 and polio not until 1949. Then the vaccine had to be developed. Pasteur made the first successful experiment on a human being with his rabies vaccine in 1885. Diphtheria vaccine was discovered in 1890, and many others followed, but the first polio vaccine was not discovered until 1954. Also, by no means everyone chose to be vaccinated. It often cost money, and it was not until the National Health Service was started in 1948 that treatment could cover the whole population of Britain.

? QUESTIONS

a) In Source 4A, why do deaths continue to rise after the cause has been discovered?
b) Why do you think there was little reduction in the death rate from diphtheria from 1920–40?

■ *SOURCE 4A* **Effect of the diphtheria vaccine on the survival of children under 15 in England and Wales**

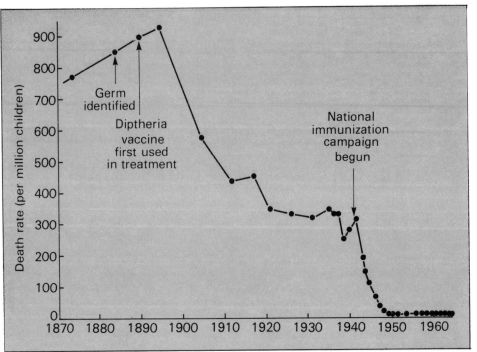

■ *SOURCE 4B* **Poster, 1940s**

PLEASE have me immunised

against

DIPHTHERIA

Ask your family doctor or at the Welfare Centre

? QUESTIONS

a) What was the purpose of the poster, Source 4B?
b) Why do you think it was necessary?
c) From Source 4A, how successful does the poster seem to have been in persuading mothers to have their babies vaccinated?

The full story of the attack on the terrible infectious diseases is also shown in Source 5.

? QUESTIONS

a) Look at Source 5. What happened to deaths from infectious diseases between 1848 and 1901?
b) What has happened to deaths from infectious diseases this century?
c) How far does the discovery of vaccines explain your answers to questions a) and b)?
d) What has happened to deaths from non-infectious causes since 1848–54?
e) Explain why they have not shown the same trend as deaths from infectious diseases.
f) Look again at Source 2. The death rate in Britain seems to have been almost the same for the last 50 years. How far do the figures in Source 5 explain this?

■ SOURCE 5 **Deaths from various diseases, per million population**

		1848–54	1901	1971
Tuberculosis		2901	1268	13
Bronchitis/pneumonia/flu		2239	2747	603
Cholera/diarrhoea/dysentery	Infectious	1819	1232	33
Scarlet fever/diphtheria	diseases	1016	407	0
Typhoid/typhus		990	155	0
Measles		342	278	0
Smallpox		263	10	0
Stroke	Non-	890	803	603
Heart disease	infectious	698	1673	1776
Cancer	diseases	307	844	1169
Violence		761	840	345

Source 5 seems to suggest that the death rate from disease was falling even before cures were available. The same trend can be seen in another example: deaths from scarlet fever. Here the death rate was falling even before scientists had worked out which germ was causing the disease (see Source 6).

We have statistics for the period since 1850 which allow us to see how different age-groups were affected by disease and death (see Source 7).

There seem to be different patterns for different age-groups. The death rate for the elderly has remained largely unchanged: if you reached old age in the late 19th century, you probably lived as long as people do nowadays. Most of the rest of the population, with the exception of babies under one year old, shows more or less the same pattern: a falling death rate in the late nineteenth century (in the case of 5–14-year-olds, falling rapidly even from 1840). The terrible flu epidemic of 1919–20 interrupts this trend, but a dramatic fall takes place from the 1940s. The National Health Service began in 1948, and many treatments and vaccines became widely available for the first time.

Better living conditions

Certainly Sources 4A, 5 and 6 show that new drugs and vaccines have helped to bring the death rate down to its present figure. But these cures were not widely used until about 1900. How can we explain the decline in the death rate before 1900 shown in Sources 2 and 7? Perhaps people were better off: more and better food does help keep people healthy. Historians argue about when this happened; however, there is no argument that the quality of the environment began to improve from about 1850. Piped, clean water, decent sewage systems and street cleaning (see Chapter 13) cut down the spread of disease. More and better housing cut down overcrowding. Although

■ SOURCE 6 **Deaths from scarlet fever, children under 15**

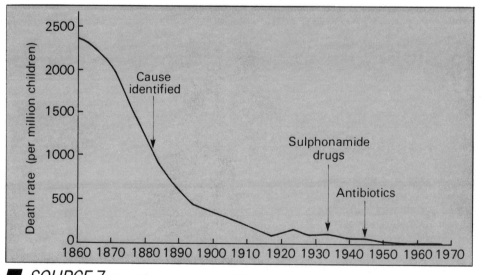

■ SOURCE 7 **Death rates per 1000, England and Wales, in different age-groups**

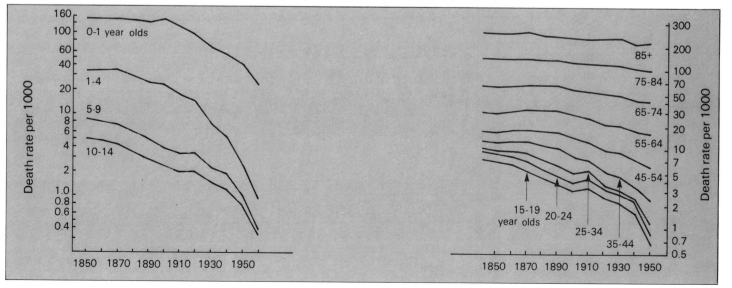

people did not always know *why* such measures worked, proposals for town improvements do seem to have had a positive effect on people's health.

Better health care for babies

These improvements do not seem, however, to have lowered the death rate among babies (see Source 7, age 0–1), where the figures show no improvement at all until after 1900. Here change came with better education, better diet and better maternity care. The Midwives Act 1902 began the training of midwives. The Notification of Births Act 1907 meant that the Medical Officer of Health had to be informed of every baby born. A Health Visitor would then call to help the mother keep the baby healthy.

Changes in population have not been as dramatic in the years since 1850 as they were in the previous 100 years. Nevertheless, population change can have major effects on the country. The 'baby boom' of the 1960s led to a huge demand for more schools; the recent decline in the birth rate has in turn brought school closures. The growing numbers of elderly people have put great pressure on the Health Service and there is an urgent need for more housing suited to the elderly. The government is also finding itself paying out a lot more in old age pensions.

You will find out more about working and living conditions in this period in Chapters 13 and 14. Chapter 21 deals with how these changes affected women in particular.

■ *SOURCE 8* **Pensioners demanding bigger pension increases, 1970s**

Assignments

Empathy

1 **a** Why do you think it was a woman, Marie Stopes, who began the campaign for birth control?

   b Why do you think it was mainly men, in government, the churches and so on who opposed her?

2 Read Sources 3A and 3B.

   a What attitudes among men and women to birth control are revealed here?

   b How have these attitudes changed in the last 60 years?

3 How have attitudes to death changed in the last 100 years?

Understanding concepts

1 **Factors causing change**

   a Why is the population not rising as fast in the 20th century as in the years 1750–1850? You should examine the part played in this change by the birth rate and the death rate.

   b Which two factors do you think are the most important in the current population situation?

2 **Factors causing change**

   a What has happened to the death rate in Britain since 1850?

   b How has this change been affected by changes in medicine?

   c How has this change been affected by non-medical factors?

Themes for discussion

1 **a** How many children do you want to have?

   b What are your reasons for this decision?

   c Would this decision be different if you were:

   i unemployed for a long time;

   ii earning a lot of money?

2 **a** How many brothers or sisters do you have?

   b Do you like being in a family group of this size?

   c Do you think the factors explained on pages 69–70 have been important in deciding the size of your family?

8 Changing Fortunes in Agriculture

British agriculture today is a very efficient industry, using some of the most mechanised farming methods in the world. At the end of Chapter 2 we saw how British farmers in the early 19th century were gradually taking up new farming methods. Have there simply been continuous improvements, or have other factors influenced agriculture from 1850 to the present?

High Farming 1850–75

When the Corn Laws were repealed in 1846 (see Chapter 25, page 258), British farmers feared the worst. They were afraid that cheap foreign corn would flood into Britain and that prices would collapse. The Corn Laws had been passed in 1815 in order to protect British farmers from this threat. However, the period 1850–75 was one of prosperity and rich harvests. These were the golden years of 'high farming'.

Farmers did not find Britain was swamped by cheap imported grain. In Europe the population was rising, and foreign farmers found ready markets at home. Wars in many parts of Europe also disrupted trade. Corn-growing was only just beginning in Canada, the USA and Australia. For the time being, transport and shipping costs were too high for them to undercut British farmers. In Britain, the huge home market in industrial towns and cities continued to grow. Some improvements in wages in these years brought an increased demand for bread, meat, vegetables, milk and dairy products. Farmers who could supply the new towns and cities easily did very well.

? QUESTIONS

a) Source 1A shows prices varied a great deal from year to year. Why do you think this was?
b) What were prices like in the years 1840–95, generally?
c) What effect does the repeal of the Corn Laws seem to have had?
d) How far does this graph support the view that the years 1850–75 were the 'golden years' of British farming?

Many farmers invested money in agricultural improvements in order to make their farms more productive. Some of these were ideas which had been first suggested in the 18th century, but could only now be taken up. Bakewell's ideas on selective breeding, for example, and seed drills based on Jethro Tull's now became widespread. There were also many new ideas.

Fertilisers

The German scientist, Justus van Liebig, and Sir Humphrey Davy had shown that nitrates and phosphates made the soil fertile. At first this was done by adding crushed bones. Van Liebig accused British merchants of raiding the battlefields of Europe in the search for bones! Certainly cattle bones were imported from Russia and South America, crushed, and put on the soil as powder. 120 000 tons of bone-powder per year were being used by the 1860s. There was also a growing trade in guano, a natural fertiliser of bird-droppings from South America. Coprolite – the dung and bones of prehistoric animals – was also mined in parts of East Anglia at this time. In 1843 Bennet and Lawes invented a method of making super-phosphate fertiliser, by treating bones with sulphuric acid. This was easier to use than bone powder. In their efforts to make their land more productive, farmers were spending nearly £8 million per year on fertilisers in the 1870s, compared to only £100 000 earlier in the century.

Feedstuffs

Animal feedstuffs, made from linseed, rapeseed and cotton seed, were also being produced. Firms such as Thorley's of Hull and Paul's of Ipswich specialised in this. Over £5 million worth of artificial feed was being sold per year by the 1870s.

Up to the 1850s most farmers carried on mixed farming. They needed animal dung as manure, and needed to grow grain to feed the animals. With artificial fertilisers and feedstuffs farmers could now specialise in livestock or cereals. They could use their land in whichever way was best. As a result of these developments wheat yield rose from about 22 bushels per acre in the 1820s to about 35 bushels per acre in the 1850s.

■ SOURCE 1A Wheat prices 1840–95

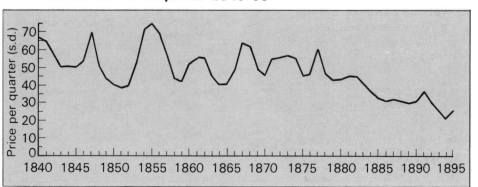

Drainage

Many farmers put money into better drainage. Hand-made drainage pipes were expensive – about 50s(£2.50) per 100. By the 1850s machine-made pipes could be bought for £1.00 per 1000. The price of draining land fell to under £5 an acre, and the Agricultural Drainage Act 1846 made loans available to farmers for this work. Heavy land could now be made more workable.

■ *SOURCE 1B* **Laying drainage pipes in Suffolk. (The trench for pipes was either dug by hand, or made by a steam-hauled plough)**

■ *SOURCE 2A* **Chaff-cutter, from a catalogue, 1846**

New machinery

The mid-19th century was a time when machines came to be used on farms on quite a wide scale. First there were small-scale hand machines which saved time and labour, such as chaff-cutters and beet-slicers (see Source 2A). Iron ploughs, harrows, hoes and rollers were also produced easily and cheaply by the new iron industry (see Chapter 4). Specialist firms grew up to make a huge range of tools and machines for agriculture. Many were based in rural areas, such as Ransome's of Ipswich and Howard's of Bedford.

■ *SOURCE 2B* **Advertisement for Ransome's, about 1890**

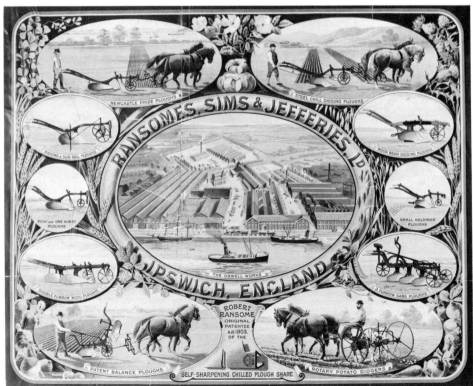

■ *SOURCE 2C* **A seed-drill on display in Dorset, 1850**

It was the new agricultural machine called the horse-drill, then unknown in this part of the country, where the seed-basket was still used for sowing. Its arrival created about as much sensation in the market-place as a flying-machine would create at Charing Cross. The farmers crowded round it, women drew near it, children crept under and into it. The machine was painted in bright shades of green, yellow and red and the whole thing looked like a mixture of hornet, grasshopper and shrimp combined.

? QUESTIONS

a) What kind of power is used to operate the chaff-cutter (Source 2A)?

b) Where on the farm would you find such a machine?

c) Which kind of farm implement do Ransome's (Source 2B) seem to specialise in?

d) How does this advertisement (Source 2B) give the impression that if you use their products you will get good crops?

e) Jethro Tull produced plans for a seed-drill in the 1730s. What does Source 2C tell us about how widely Tull's invention was used by 1850?

f) What do you think the author of Source 2C thought about the machine?

Steam-powered machines

Steam power (see Chapter 5) had brought such great changes to the other industries of Britain that it is not surprising it was also applied to agriculture. Some of the results were successful, such as the steam-powered threshing machine (see Source 2D). These were usually owned by contractors and hired by farmers on a daily basis. A steam engine, called a traction engine, provided the power; unthreshed corn was fed in at the top of the threshing machine, grain poured into sacks at the back, and straw was stacked at the far left. It is estimated that about two-thirds of the corn-harvest was threshed by machine by 1880.

Steam-ploughing was more complicated (see Source 2E). The traction engine stood at one side of the field and a long rope passed right across the field and round a wheel on the other side. A special balance-plough was then hauled from side to side of the field. At the end of each furrow the driver would change round, and tip the plough so that the other side dug into the ground. Unfortunately, steam-ploughing was not successful except on really large fields, as so much was left unploughed.

■ *SOURCE 2D* **Steam-threshing, about 1900**

■ *SOURCE 2E* **Advertisement for Fowler's steam plough, 1859**

■ *SOURCE 2F* **Steam-powered reaper, 1851**

? QUESTIONS

a) In Source 2D look for: the big fly-wheel on the traction engine, the long belt across to the threshing-machine, the sacks of corn, the straw-stack.

b) How many people seem to be needed to do the threshing in Source 2D?

c) Give three reasons why steam-ploughing (Source 2E) was not taken up by many farmers.

d) Suggest reasons why the steam-powered reaper (Source 2F) was not very successful.

e) The introduction of threshing machines in the 1830s led to the Captain Swing Riots (Chapter 18, page 191). Why do you think there was no opposition to the threshing-machines by the 1850s and 1860s?

You can see for yourself that the steam-powered reaper, Source 2F, was a heavy and elaborate machine. Much more successful was the mechanical horse-drawn reaper made by an American firm, McCormick's.

This was only a half-way stage in the mechanisation of British agriculture. Many farmers preferred to carry on with their old methods, perhaps buying a small machine or hiring a gang to do the threshing. Steam-power proved too cumbersome for most farmers, and horse and hand power were still widely used.

■ SOURCE 3A Description of the limits of machines on farms in the 1890s

For a few days ... the fields stood 'ripe unto harvest'. It was the one perfect period of the hamlet year ...

In the fields where the harvest had begun all was bustle and activity. At that time the mechanical reaper, with long, red revolving arms like windmill sails had already appeared in the locality; but it was looked upon by the men as ... a farmer's toy. The scythe still did most of the work, and they did not dream it would ever be superseded. So while the red sails revolved in one field ... in the next field a band of men would be whetting their scythes and mowing by hand as their fathers had done before them ...

After the mowing and reaping and binding came the carrying, the busiest time of all. Every man and boy put his best foot forward then, for when the corn was cut and dried it was imperative to get it stacked and thatched before the weather broke. All day and far into the twilight the yellow-and-blue painted wagons passed and re-passed along the roads between the field and the stackyard. Big carthorses returning with an empty wagon were made to gallop like two-year-olds ...

At last, in the cool dusk of an August evening the last load was brought in, with a nest of merry boys' faces among the sheaves at the top and the men walking alongside with pitchforks on their shoulders.

F. Thompson, *Lark Rise to Candleford*, 1945

■ SOURCE 3B Labourers in Suffolk mowing hay, 1880

? QUESTIONS

a) What was the attitude of the men in Source 3A to the mechanical reaper?

b) What reasons would a farmer have for buying and using a mechanical reaper?

c) Why did other farmers continue to employ teams of men to get in the harvest?

d) Source 3A was written in the 1940s. How does that affect its reliability as evidence of farming methods in the 1890s?

e) Source 3B appears to confirm the picture of farming given in Source 3A, and it is a contemporary photograph. Does that mean that Source 3A must be correct?

f) What are the dangers of using pictures from catalogues, such as Sources 2E and 2F as evidence of farming practice?

g) Write a paragraph on how far machines had changed farming in Britain by 1880, based on Sources 2A–2F, 3A and 3B.

Links with industry and science

Farming and industry were drawing closer together now: industry made machines, tools, fertilisers and feed for farmers. Railways delivered these things cheaply to rural stations. The same railways then carried wheat, milk, meat and dairy products into the cities to feed the millions of people who lived there. No longer were cattle driven hundreds of miles from Scotland or Wales into the industrial areas. Railways – or, from Ireland and parts of Scotland, steamships – did the work. London no longer had resident herds of milk-cattle. Now the railway brought fresh milk daily from the West Country into the capital.

In order to encourage a scientific attitude to farming the Royal Agricultural Society was set up in 1838. Shows and exhibitions were held, and an experimental farm set up at Rothamstead in 1842. With an increased income many farmers invested in better buildings. Advice was available on how to build them economically and efficiently. Queen Victoria's husband, Prince Albert, had two of these 'model' farms built at Windsor.

Gang-workers

These years of high farming were the last period of dominance and prosperity for the landowners of Britain. Labourers' wages also improved although they were still lower than those of factory workers. However, for one group of workers at this time, toiling on the land was cruel and hard. Many of the jobs on the farm under new methods demanded lots of extra labour for just a few days or weeks per year. For these jobs, such as hoeing, or beet-lifting, for example, farmers would hire gangs of labourers. The gang system started in East Anglia in the 1820s. Men, women and children were organised by one person who offered to do a job for a farmer at a fixed price. His profit depended on getting as much work out of the gang as possible. Children were often included in the gangs.

■ *SOURCE 5A* **Father, talking of his 11-year-old daughter, 1843**

They drive them along ... and make them work very hard. Gathering stones has hurt my girl's back at times. Pulling turnips is the hardest work .... My girl went 5 miles yesterday to her work turniping; she set off between 7 and 8; she walked, had a piece of bread before she went; she did not stop work in the middle of the day; ate nothing till she left off. She came home between 3 and 4 o'clock; she is sometimes so tired she can't eat no victuals when she comes home.

? QUESTIONS

a) What work are the children in Source 5B doing?
b) Why did farmers and gang-leaders prefer to hire children?
c) Do you think the hardship in Source 5A is worse than factory children endured? (See Chapter 14, page 153.)

After a parliamentary investigation, the Gangs Act was passed in 1867. No child under 8 was to work; gang-masters had to be licensed and gangs had to be single-sex.

■ *SOURCE 4* **The Norfolk Homestead, built by Prince Albert at Windsor**

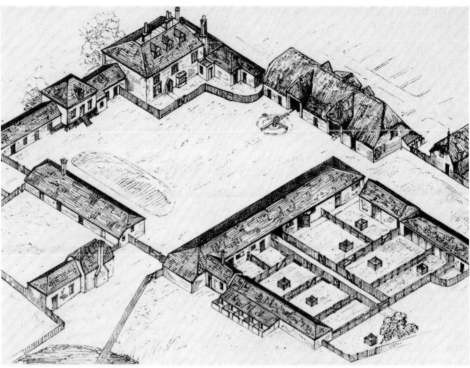

■ *SOURCE 5B* **Children's field gang, 1860s**

Gang-work does, in fact, continue up to the present day. Gangs are often made up of women workers doing seasonal jobs, such as fruit-picking.

The Great Depression, 1875–95

High farming came to an end in the 1870s. A series of wet seasons brought bad harvests and diseases of crops and animals such as mildew and liver rot. By the 1870s foreign corn began to be imported. Farmers in Canada, Australia and the USA were producing large surpluses. Fast iron steamships could bring grain from Canada, the USA and Australia to Britain cheaply. For example, freight charges on the Chicago-to-Liverpool route fell from £3 5s 0d(£3.25) per ton to £1 4s 0d(£1.20) per ton from 1868 to 1882. In 1870, 40% of British wheat was imported; by 1895, 80% was imported.

By the 1880s refrigerated ships were bringing beef and mutton from South America, the USA and New Zealand, too. By 1900 cattle and sheep prices had fallen by 30%.

? QUESTIONS

a) What methods of powering ships can be seen in Source 6?
b) What were the advantages of steam-power for ships?

By the 1870s landowners were no longer in control of the country. Agriculture was less important than industry, and industrialists liked the fall in food prices. The average price of a loaf of bread, for example, fell from 8d(3p) to 5d(2p). This helped the industrial workers, and wages were kept down. Farmers, particularly grain farmers, complained bitterly, but the government was not prepared to protect them. Government policy was one of free trade. They believed that foreign countries should be able to sell food to Britain because this gave them the money to buy British industrial products (see Chapter 25, page 258).

? QUESTIONS

Look again at Source 1A, page 73.

a) What happened to wheat prices generally in the years 1875–95?
b) What effect would these prices have had on British cereal farmers?

c) How far does this part of the graph justify the fears farmers had in 1846?
d) Which types of people in Britain would benefit from the fall in prices?
e) Is the graph evidence that the years 1875–95 were years of a Great Depression in British farming?

Was it really a Great Depression?

In fact, the complaints of the grain farmers did not reflect the situation all over Britain. Farmers who produced milk, beef or mutton did quite well. A fall in the price of grain was, after all, a fall in the price of cattle feed. An improvement in industrial wages led to a swing in the demand from basic items, such as bread, to other things such as meat. British farmers reacted to these changes quite quickly. Those farmers who saw the way prices were going changed from grain to dairying, or beef, obeying the old slogan, 'Down corn, up horn'. Cereal farmers complained that there was a fall in the acreage of cereals planted, but this was less than the rise in the acreage of pasture land.

Certainly the bad harvests and imported corn did hit some farmers badly: incomes fell and some farmers went bankrupt. However other farmers, and especially farmers willing to change their ways, did quite well. Although this period is always called the Great Depression, it is hardly the correct name if the whole of British farming is taken into account.

Recovery, 1895–1914

Those farmers who were willing to adapt to change showed the way forward over the next few years. Many began to specialise according to local needs: market gardening near towns and cities, fruit in the Vale of Evesham, milk and cheese in the West Country. Jam and pickles factories were set up to meet the demand for canned and bottled goods in shops. This encouraged the growing of fruit and vegetables nearby.

■ SOURCE 6 Unloading wheat at London Docks, 1870s

■ *SOURCE 7* **Pickle factory in Lincoln**

? QUESTIONS

a) What sex are most of the workers?
b) What do you think was the purpose of:
   i) the barrels; ii) the jars;
   iii) the straw-filled crate?

Leaving the land

These were the years when the 'drift from the countryside' began to accelerate. Often the first to go were young girls, looking for jobs as servants in the towns. By 1900 there were only 864 females for every 1000 males in rural areas. Under the pressure of the depression, farmers began to lay off workers. When a slight recovery came, they thought hard about how many men to take on. The Agricultural Labourers' Union (Chapter 19, page 201) collapsed in 1896, but it did bring a rise in wages. This led farmers to look with increased interest at new machines to save hiring labourers.

The years 1850–1911 saw a 23% fall in the agricultural workforce; by 1911 only 8% of all workers were in agriculture. This had its effect on village life, too as the number of local craftsmen declined (see Source 8).

Some country people looked for jobs in towns and cities, but some looked further afield – to Canada, the USA, Australia and New Zealand. Emigration offered them a chance for a new, better life – even a farm of their own – which Britain could never offer (see Chapter 26).

However, as usual in agriculture, the true picture is complicated. For all the changes which were taking place, many farms remained exactly the same. There were still one and a half million agricultural labourers in 1914. The main source of power was still the horse.

■ *SOURCE 8* **Craftsmen in Rutland, 1851–1911**

	1851	1911
Millers	63	22
Brickmakers	38	15
Cabinetmakers	31	10
Blacksmiths	116	83
Saddlers	31	24
Tailors	173	63
Shoemakers	236	138

? QUESTIONS

a) Which jobs have shown the most decline, and which the least?
b) Suggest reasons for these differences.

■ *SOURCE 9* **Ploughing with horses. This refers to the 1920s, but things were just the same before the First World War**

The head horseman was called the 'lord' – that's what he was, lord of all the horses .... The place ran like clockwork .... The ploughing teams left and returned to the stableyards according to the rank of the ploughman ...

The horses were friends and loved like men. Some men would do more for a horse than they would for a wife. The ploughmen talked softly to their teams all day long, and you could hear the horses listening ...

A farmer could walk on a field ploughed by ten different teams and tell which bit was ploughed by which.

R. Blythe, *Akenfield*, 1969

? QUESTION

Which machine was eventually to replace the horse on British farms, later in the 20th century?

The World Wars and Agriculture

The First World War brought a big change in farming policy. German U-boats sank millions of tons of shipping which was bringing food to Britain. Production fell as workers were conscripted into the army. At one point, in 1916, there was only two weeks' supply of food left in the country. Suddenly it became vital to grow more food in Britain. Land was ploughed up again, including parks, playing fields and roadside verges. Children were allowed to be let off school to help on the farms; two and a half million more acres were eventually brought into cultivation. In 1917 farmers were given price guarantees for many crops: the freedom to let prices find their own levels was broken for the first time since 1846. Tractors, rare before 1914, were imported from the USA in large numbers.

When the First World War ended, foreign competition began again. Wheat prices tumbled from 86s 4d (£4.31½p) a quarter in 1920 to 40s 9d (£2.03½p) a quarter in 1922. The government refused to continue its price guarantees, and many farmers were ruined. Over the next few years farms became derelict as farmers gave up the struggle to make a living. There was no money to invest in improvements. Hedges became overgrown and buildings were allowed to fall down. Wages were low, and life for farm labourers was hard.

With wages falling, the move out of villages continued. Thirty thousand people moved from rural to urban areas in the years 1911–31. Another reason for moving was bad housing. By the early 20th century housing in towns and cities was improving. In the country there was no such change. Half the houses in rural areas had no mains water supply in 1920.

■ *SOURCE 10*

The slump set in during the great hot summer of 1921. I remember it well. We had no rain from March right through to October. The corn didn't grow no more than a foot high and most of that didn't even come to the ear. We harvested what we could and the last loads were leaving the field when we heard: 'The wages are coming down this week.' It was true. The farmers told the men that they would be given 42s 6d (£2.12½p). Then it was 38s 6d (£1.92½p). A fortnight later on the farm where I worked it was 'The boss can only afford to give you 27s 6d (£1.37½p).'

It was the Government's fault. They ended the Corn Act less than a year after it had been made law. The price of wheat was quartered

in a year. Cattle were sold for next to nothing because the farmers couldn't afford to keep them. The farmers became broke and frightened, so they took it out on us men.

R. Blythe, *Akenfield*, 1969

? QUESTIONS

a) This speaker blames the hot summer and the government for the fall in prices. Do you agree?

b) Do you think the farmers were right to cut wages so drastically?

Government help

By the 1930s the government realised that British farming was in a very bad state and must be helped. The De-Rating Act 1929 freed agricultural land and buildings from paying rates. Then in the 1930s a system of subsidies to farmers was set up: £40 million was being paid out by 1936. There were duties on foreign food imports and strict quotas on how much could come in. Production at home was controlled in order to prevent too much of something being grown. All these things kept up prices paid to British farmers, and marked the end of the free trade policy.

Marketing Boards were set up for certain products: milk, hops, potatoes, bacon and pigs. The Marketing Boards controlled output and fixed prices. Farmers knew they would get a return for their work and gained confidence to invest again. The lack of competition may have cut profits for the really efficient producer, but it kept many other farmers in business.

Once again it was corn-farmers who were in the greatest difficulties. The acreage of land producing grain fell by 3.7 million acres between 1918 and 1939. However other types of farming succeeded in making a profit, such as dairying and horticulture. The sugar-beet industry was started, almost from scratch, to prevent Britain becoming dependent on imported sugar. Some farmers were able to buy tractors, and the first combine-harvesters appeared. There were 200 000 tractors and 3500 combines on British farms by 1945.

The Agricultural Wages Board was set up in 1924 and began to try to stabilise farm-workers' wages. Government protection of the

farmers in the 1930s also helped keep wages up. There was a programme of building council houses in rural areas, and bringing water and electricity to more houses. The big increase in rural bus services also helped to break down the isolation felt by many villagers. Thus, to some extent, the Depression of the inter-war years was lessened.

The Second World War

Nevertheless, the outbreak of the Second World War in 1939 found agriculture in a poor state. Once again, as in 1914, submarines threatened Britain's food supply. Once again there was the frantic effort to grow more food in this country. Farmers were paid £2 an acre to plough up grassland. Thus 50% more land was brought into cultivation and output increased by 70%. Conscription of men into the army brought a shortage of farm-workers, so the Women's Land Army was formed. This organised teams of women to go and work on the farms. People were also persuaded to 'Dig For Victory' by growing their own food.

Helped by a policy of rationing food, these measures managed to keep the British people fed. The war forced the government, however, to consider seriously the importance of British agriculture. Growing our

■ *SOURCE 11A* Second World War 'Dig For Victory' poster

■ *SOURCE 11B* **Women's Land Army: ploughing with a tractor, 1939**

own food, and preventing a repetition of the situation that had occurred during the 1920s, became a priority for all governments after 1945.

Farming Since 1945

The impact of science and technology

In many ways the real Agricultural Revolution has taken place since 1945. After nearly two centuries of gradual change, farming methods altered abruptly. The change can be seen in the appearance of the landscape of Britain, particularly in the cereal-growing areas where many hedges have been removed. It can also be seen in the figures for labourers and for horse-power.

? *QUESTIONS*

a) Look at Source 12. Agricultural production has risen a great deal in these years, yet the number of workers and horses has declined. How do you explain this?

b) What does this source tell us about the productivity of British farming in the 1980s?

c) Why do you think farmers have chosen to replace workers and horses by machines?

■ *SOURCE 12* **Number of agricultural workers and working horses on British farms, 1946–86**

Key
▨ Agricultural workers
▧ Working horses

Millions	1946	1968	1986
Agricultural workers	1.2	0.45	0.2
Working horses	0.5	0.05	0

The diesel-powered tractor and combine-harvester have now become widespread. The result is that although, as the figures in Source 12 show, the number of workers has declined enormously, output has doubled. Productivity per worker has shown the greatest increase of any industry in Britain. One combine, like that in Source 13A, can now do all the work previously done by all the people in Sources 2D and 3B put together. Horse-drawn, single-furrow ploughs like those described in Source 9 could plough 1 acre in a day. The modern ploughman does 2–3 acres in a day.

■ *SOURCE 13B*

I have been ploughing continuously since last June. Now it's February and I haven't stopped. I have ploughed every day, Sundays too, for eight months .... There will be a break until after the harvest, then, as soon as a field is cleared, I'll be in it. There are about 400 acres of corn-land, and I plough it all. All the fields are different. They have their names .... and I wouldn't like the village to become a Tannington where the hedges have gone and the ploughman doesn't know where he is .... The hedges belong to the village.

R. Blythe, *Akenfield*, **1969**

Machines have also replaced human labour in dairying, where automatic milking machines were successfully introduced in the 1950s and 1960s.

Science has also been applied to all branches of agriculture in recent

■ *SOURCE 13A* **A combine-harvester, 1980s**

years. Chemical pesticides ensure that crops are not lost to diseases or pests. New strains of wheat have been bred, which can yield up to one and a half tons of grain per acre. Cattle can be scientifically bred using artificial insemination. Milking cattle now produce 30% more milk than they did before the Second World War. New breeds, and cross-breeds, from other countries have been introduced to improve yields, such as the Charollais from France. However, some modern farming methods have generated widespread controversy.

Factory farming

Business methods are now brought into farming. In fact many farms are now owned by businesses rather than by working farmers. Farming is organised to gain maximum profit. One form of specialisation is factory-farming. This was first applied to chickens (see Source 14A), in the 1950s, then to pigs, calves and turkeys. Large numbers of chickens are kept in a small area by using stacks of cages. Heat, light and food are controlled. Their eggs are taken away by conveyor belt, and they live for about 7 weeks. Calves, pigs, turkeys, ducks and other animals are also kept in factory-farming conditions.

? QUESTIONS

a) Farmers say that these methods (i) produce meat more cheaply and (ii) produce the kind of meat customers want. In your opinion, does either of these arguments justify the kind of farming shown in Sources 14A–C? Explain your answer.

b) Why have these new methods of keeping animals been invented in recent years?

Larger farms

The pressure for profits has brought a move to larger farms. The average arable farm is now 300 acres. Many of these are combined into larger farm-estates, so the average economic unit is now nearly 1000 acres. Bigger farms are cheaper to run, as they can use machines more efficiently. Such use of machines demands bigger fields: so many hedges have been uprooted.

■ *SOURCE 14A* **Battery farm hens, 1980s**

■ *SOURCE 14B* **These calves live all their lives indoors in these crates, with only liquid food. This produces the kind of light-coloured veal that buyers nowadays want**

■ *SOURCE 14C* **Pigs in narrow stalls, lying on concrete, 1980s**

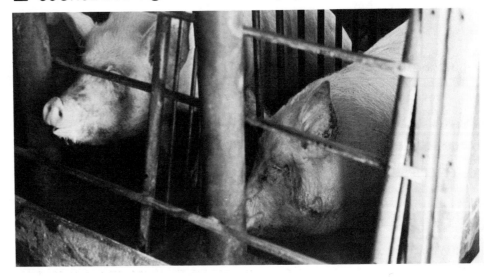

Common Market policies

The economics of farming has also changed utterly from the inter-war years. The Agriculture Act 1947 began a system of guaranteeing prices to farmers and offering grants to improve their farming methods. This policy has been continued by governments of both parties. It has led to a huge investment in modern farming methods.

In 1973 Britain joined the European Economic Community (EEC), and the subsidy passed to the EEC's Common Agricultural Policy (CAP). To protect all farmers in the Common Market, the CAP has an agreed price each year for each product. If the price falls below this, the EEC buys the produce until the price rises. If it continues to fall, the EEC buys it and stores it. Thus, even if farmers over-produce, they cannot lose. The EEC is left with large 'mountains' or 'lakes' of farm produce. Much of this has to be destroyed, or stored indefinitely. The cost of storing 7 million tons of grain from the 1985 harvest is estimated at £150 million a year.

Controversy

Recent changes in farming have brought criticism from conservationists. People are worried about the disappearance of hedges. These may be less than 150 or more than 1500 years old and provide a habitat for many kinds of wildlife. Others object to factory-farming, which they say is cruel to animals. The amount of nitrate fertilisers used on the land has caused river pollution in many parts of the country, notably the Norfolk Broads. The huge profits to be made in cereal farming have led some dairy farmers to want to plough up their meadows. This has brought protests in some areas where ancient pastures, such as the Somerset Levels, are threatened. People are now beginning to question whether farmers have a right to do exactly what they like with the land. The Wildlife and Countryside Act 1981 recognises the need for more control. The Act arranges for farmers to be paid for leaving land unchanged. However, this may not be workable owing to the heavy costs involved.

Not all these changes are, of course, the farmers' fault. Governments have wanted cheap food in order not to have to buy imports. Farmers have responded by using all the high technology methods that money can buy. In 1983, for the first time for over 200 years, Britain exported grain. Nor do the criticisms apply to all farmers. Chemicals and machines cannot be applied to dairy, beef or sheep-farming to anything like the same extent, though the use of hormones and antibiotics to increase yields is very common. Nevertheless, farming in the highland areas of Britain is probably still very much the same as it always was.

The question remains whether, when almost every other British industry is in recession, cereal farming should be so heavily protected. Many people also question whether it is right to pay subsidies to farmers to produce surplus crops in Britain when two-thirds of the world's people are starving.

Assignments

Empathy

1 Read Source 5A. What do you think would be the feelings of the father as he saw his daughter go off to work?
2 Read Source 10, and page 80. The speaker in Source 10 has just received a letter from his brother in Oxford, saying there are jobs going in a car factory. Write his reply.

Understanding concepts

1 **Causation**
   a Once the Corn Laws were repealed in 1846, was it inevitable that British farming would face a crisis?
   b Why was this crisis delayed for 25 years?

2 **Similarity/difference**
   a How far is it true to talk of a 'Great Depression' in British farming in the years after 1875?
   b Which farmers suffered?
   c Which farmers survived?

   d What were the similarities and differences between the two groups?

3 **Similarity/difference**
   a Why did British farmers do well:
      i in the years 1850–75 and
      ii in the years after 1945?
   b In what ways did they use these good conditions to make improvements on their farms, in both periods?
   c What are the similarities and what are the differences between the two periods?

1 **Change/continuity**
   a Summarise the ups and downs of British farming since 1850.
   b What part has the government played in each of these changes?

Evidence

This chapter uses several kinds of sources of evidence: photographs, advertisements, drawings,

reminiscences, a painting, statistics, a poster as well as the text itself – a secondary source in its own right. For a history of farming:
   a Classify each of the sources in this chapter according to its type.
   b Comment on the reliability of the evidence in each type of source.
   c Comment on the usefulness to a historian of the evidence given by each type of source.

Themes for discussion

1 Compare the changes in farming described in Chapter 2 with those described in the last part of this chapter – 'Farming since 1945'. Which can best be described as a 'Revolution' in agriculture?
2 Do you feel that the need for cheap food justifies the kinds of factory farming methods described on page 82?

9 The Rise and Fall of Industrial Britain

The Great Exhibition

In 1851 the Great Exhibition was held in Hyde Park, in London. Even the building itself was a marvel: 600 yards long, big enough to contain some of the trees growing in the park, and made entirely of cast-iron and glass. It was called the Crystal Palace.

The Exhibition was the idea of Prince Albert, Queen Victoria's husband. It was an 'Exhibition of the Works of Industry of all Nations'. British and foreign industrialists set out to show their newest and cleverest ideas. There were 7381 British exhibitors and 6556 from all other

countries. Queen Victoria wrote in her diary: 'I came back quite beaten, and my head bewildered, from the myriads of wonderful and beautiful things which now quite dazzle one's eyes.' Most of the 6 million visitors, who came to the Exhibition from all over Britain and abroad, felt much the same. It made a large profit, which was used to buy the land where the Albert Hall, Science Museum and Victoria and Albert Museum now stand. After the Exhibition, the Crystal Palace was moved to a site in South London, where it burned down in 1936. Only the name of the area remains.

What the Great Exhibition showed to Queen Victoria and the other visitors was the clear lead British industry had over all other

countries. British textiles, railway engines, boats, machines, pottery and manufactured items of all kinds were the best on show. The industrial changes which produced this lead have been looked at in Section A of this book. Britain was described at that time as 'the workshop of the world' – making the goods the world needed, and exporting them.

When another Great Exhibition was held in Paris in 1867 British visitors returned with a different story. British goods were still impressive, but so were items from the USA, Germany, France and other countries. Source 2 in Chapter 1 shows the situation in our own time: Britain is still a rich industrial country, but no longer the richest. How has this happened? Is it a story of steady decline, or have there been ups and downs? Have all industries declined together?

The changes which have taken place have not been easy to adjust to. There are over 3 million unemployed in 1987, and many people look back over the years to 1851 to try and see what went wrong. Perhaps, by understanding the past, we can learn how to go on to new successes. In this chapter we will look first at the most important industries in the country to see how each has changed. Then we will examine how the economy as a whole has changed up to the present-day.

■ SOURCE 1 Crystal Palace, 1851

? QUESTIONS

a) The designer of the Crystal Palace, Joseph Paxton, was a head gardener. What kind of building was the Crystal Palace based on?

b) The Crystal Palace was *prefabricated*, that is, it was made of lots of pieces, all the same, which could be put together on the site in Hyde Park. How did this make it
i) quick to make?
ii) quick to build?

Changes in the Old Industries

Textiles

1850–1914: boom years

The phenomenal rise of the cotton textile industry has been described in Chapter 3. New inventions and steam-driven machines helped businessmen to set up a factory system, especially in Lancashire, to make and sell cotton goods to the world. In 1830, British textiles made up two-thirds of the country's exports. This growth continued up to the First World War. In 1850 Britain imported 589 million lb of raw cotton, and in 1913 2179 million lb. This raw cotton was then made into many different kinds of cloth, nearly all of which was exported – 86% of cotton cloth was exported in 1913. Low-quality, un-dyed cloth went to poorer countries such as India, the Middle East, Africa and South America. British colonies in particular provided a ready market. Good-quality, finished cloth (that is, dyed, printed and ready to use) went to Australia, Canada and China.

There was no change in the way British cloth was made in this period. Machines were bigger but still worked in the same way as before (see Source 2A). New methods of spinning and weaving were taken up by some other countries: ring-spinning, for example, was adopted in the USA, where by 1914 87% of their spinning machines were of this type. At that date only 19% of British machines operated on the ring-spinning method. Then the Northrop automatic loom was invented in 1893 in the USA. By 1914, 40% of US cloth was woven on these machines; at the same period, in Britain, only one firm was using the new looms.

There seemed to be good reasons for the British refusal to take up new ideas. The cotton industry was made up of lots of little firms. Each carried out one stage in the making of the cloth. No one controlled the whole process from buying the raw cotton to selling the finished cloth. This made it very difficult to bring in changes, as they would affect several different firms. Also, buying new machines was expensive and especially so for small companies. The ring-spinning machines and the Northrop loom produced a cheaper, coarser cloth; Lancashire firms had built up their reputation on the finer cloth produced by the old methods, and were reluctant to change. The new machines did not require as much skill to operate as the earlier ones. This made them attractive in the USA, which had a shortage of skilled workers. Lancashire workers had the skill, and were proud of it: why throw it away? Mill-owners realised that introducing new machines would lead to conflicts with the skilled workers' unions which would fight to keep their members' jobs and their good wages. This was an argument that most employers were not prepared to get involved in.

These may have been short-sighted decisions, but the Lancashire cotton industry was doing very well up to 1914. In fact the years 1895–1914 saw a boom in trade, and many new mills were built. It was a boom based on methods, skills and products which were old-fashioned by 1914. But who could know that a crisis was approaching?

1914–45: years of crisis

During the First World War the British economy turned to war production. The war at sea made exporting very difficult. Britain's customers around the world looked for new suppliers of textile goods. It was not hard to find these. One of the successes of British industry in the years 1850–1914 was in exporting machines of all sorts. British-made spinning and weaving machines in India, the Far East and the USA geared up to supply the markets Britain could not reach.

After the war there was a brief boom while factories caught up with orders, and then a slump. In 1922 production was only 61% of the 1913 level; in 1929 only 53%. Throughout the world there was less trade in the years between the wars; Britain was now having to compete with other producers for such trade as there was.

❓ QUESTIONS

a) Compare the size of spinning-machines in Source 2A with Chapter 3, Source 8 on page 21. How have they changed?

b) All the workers you can see are women. What jobs are they doing? Who was doing their job in Chapter 3, Source 9C (page 22)?

■ *SOURCE 2A* Cotton mill, 1926

■ SOURCE 2B Cotton mills, 1920s

c) What form of power was used in the mills in Source 2B, and how did the power in Source 2A get to the machines?

d) How can you tell that the mills in Source 2B are not working?

e) Does this picture, Source 2B, prove that the cotton industry was in Depression in the 1920s?

f) If you had not been given the dates, how could you tell when these two photographs were taken?

Many mill-owners who before the war had borrowed money to build new factories just went bankrupt. Others had mills working 'short-time' – only a few days a week. Wages fell and times were hard for workingpeople. There was no money for new machines, and the banks would not lend any to a sick industry. The government tried to persuade the small companies to join together (amalgamate) in order to be stronger. Ninety-six companies did combine eventually into the Lancashire Cotton Corporation. In 1936 the Spindles Act was passed. This Act ordered the scrapping of machines of firms who went out of business, to force firms to buy new equipment. In fact firms tried desperately to reduce their costs by making poorer yarn and cloth.

The textile industry since 1945

There was a small boom in textiles after the Second World War, just as after the First, but by then the cotton industry was in poor shape. In 1951, 92% of spinning machines and 94% of weaving machines were pre-1939 or even pre-1914. There were even worse signs: cotton textiles began to be imported into Britain from India, Singapore and Hong

Kong. In 1937, 3% of cotton goods sold in Britain were imported; by 1951, it was 16%. By the 1960s imported jeans and other cotton and denim goods had knocked the British cotton industry still further.

The problem of there being lots of small firms, which blocked the introduction of any new processes, was overcome in the 1960s. The huge chemical firms, ICI and Courtaulds, had discovered how to make artificial fibres such as nylon, rayon, terylene, etc. (see page 97). They wanted to control the whole process of manufacture, from making the fibres to selling the finished goods. They also had the size and money to ensure they could do this. In 1962 Courtaulds bought up the Lancashire Cotton Corporation and Fine Spinners and Doublers. Several other companies were brought

together and their factories either scrapped or totally re-equipped. By 1968 just five companies controlled half the spinning and one-third of the weaving. With these changes productivity increased by 86%, and the number of workers halved.

These amalgamations and innovations have helped the textile industry to survive, to some extent. It is no longer the huge exporting giant of the pre-1914 years, but a much smaller industry employing far fewer people. International competition is very stiff, and even since 1979 this has led to drop of about one-third in the amount of cloth produced in this country.

Iron and Steel

Rise of the steel industry

In Chapter 4 we saw that iron was the great material of the early stages of the Industrial Revolution. The most important material of the next stage of industrialisation was steel. Steel is a form of iron which has had impurities removed and small quantities of other metals added to give it strength. It is more pliable than cast-iron, which is too brittle for many modern uses.

In the 1740s Benjamin Hunts-

■ SOURCE 3A Abbeydale Works, Sheffield, which began making steel in 1833

■ *SOURCE 3B* **Crucibles and furnace holes, Abbeydale**

man invented the crucible method of making steel – see Sources 3A and 3B. This melted steel in small clay crucibles, or pots, at intense heat. Small amounts of steel were produced for clocks, springs and scythe blades, mainly in Sheffield. The steel made was good quality, but it took about three hours to make the small amount being poured in Source 3B.

❓ *QUESTIONS*

a) In Source 3A find: the mill-pond, the furnace chimney (a two-storey building) and the forge chimney (a single-storey building).

b) How can you tell, from both these pictures, that production of steel was in small quantities? (Compare also Source 2B on page 25 and Sources 4D and 4H of this chapter.)

In 1856 Sir Henry Bessemer, a professional inventor, produced an answer to this problem. His converter turned molten iron into steel in just 20 minutes. In Source 4A the molten iron was poured into the converter (a). The converter was then turned upright and cold air forced in through the bottom. With a huge roar and sheets of flame the impurities were burnt off (b). The steel could then be poured into whatever mould was needed (c).

Bessemer's invention reduced the price of steel from £70 to £10

■ *SOURCE 4A* **Bessemer converter, 1850s**

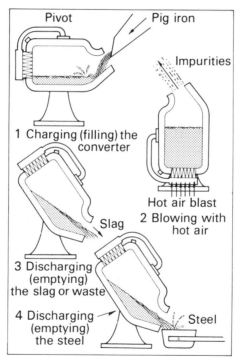

1 Charging (filling) the converter
2 Blowing with hot air
3 Discharging (emptying) the slag or waste
4 Discharging (emptying) the steel

■ *SOURCE 4B*

The oxygen, uniting with the carbon, sent up an ever-increasing stream of sparks and white flames. Then followed a series of mild explosions, throwing molten slag and splashes of metal high in the air, the machine becoming a real volcano in a state of eruption. No one could approach the converter to turn off the blast and some low flat roofs close at hand were in danger of being set on fire by the

shower of red-hot matter falling on them .... I had in no way expected such violent results. However, in ten minutes more the eruption ceased, the flame died down, and the process was complete.

Henry Bessemer's own account, published in 1905

❓ *QUESTIONS*

a) In what ways is the Bessemer method an improvement on the crucible method as regards
  i) quantity made?
  ii) time taken to make it?
b) How would these improvements have affected the cost of the steel?
c) From Source 4B, how much control does Henry Bessemer appear to have over the process?

per ton. He went on to make a fortune in the next ten years. However, the converter only worked with iron ores which did not contain phosphorus. These could be found in Britain only in Cumbria, where steelworks grew up at Workington, Whitehaven and Maryport.

In 1866 William Siemens, a German living in Britain, invented the open-hearth furnace (Sources 4C and 4D). Molten iron or pig-iron and scrap is put in the hearth (A). Cold air enters at (B) and is passed through two heated chambers (C) and over the metal in the hearth. The hot air heats the metal and removes the impurities as hot waste gases. These gases then heat the chambers (D). The process is then reversed. Air enters at (E) and passes through the chambers (D). The whole process is reversed again and again, while carbon and other materials are added to make steel.

■ *SOURCE 4C* **Diagram of an open-hearth furnace**

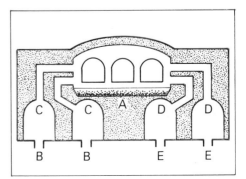

■ *SOURCE 4D* Open-hearth furnace, 20th century

■ *SOURCE 4E* Growth in steel production, 1870–1914

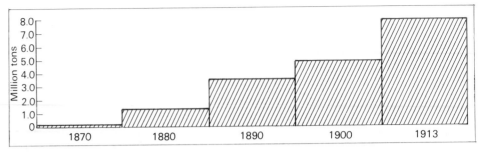

■ *SOURCE 4F* Advertisement for Sheffield steel ropes, 1890s

USED ALL OVER THE WORLD.

Chili, 1875.
Brussels, 1876.
Cape Town, 1877.
Paris, 1878.
Torino, 1879.
London, 1851.
International
Fisheries,
Sweden, 1883.

Glasgow, 1884.
Port Elizabeth, 1885.
Liverpool, 1886.
Adelaide, 1887.
Barcelona, 1888.
Sydney, 1832.
Melbourne, 1889.
Dunedin, 1890.

JOHN SHAW, SHEFFIELD, ENGLAND.

SPECIAL IMPROVED

Steel Wire Ropes

OF THE FINEST QUALITY, FOR

MINING, PLOUGH ROPES. INCLINES,

SHIPS' HAWSERS, CABLES,
TRAWL WARPS, HOISTING GEAR, &c.

Wire all carefully tested and quality guaranteed.

SPECIAL STEEL WOVE WORK for Gold Dressing.

Copper Rone Lightning Conductors, Sash. Cords, Gilt & Silver Picture Cord, &c.

PATENT LOCKWEDGE AND ALL KINDS OF FENCING.

? QUESTION

a) In what way was the open-hearth furnace better than the Bessemer converter?

In fact, although the Bessemer converter was a great breakthrough, it was soon overtaken in importance by the open-earth method. In 1871, 90% of British steel was made by Bessemer's method, by 1890 it was 52% and by 1914 less than 20%. The open-hearth was easier to control, more reliable, and more economical in its use of fuel. It could also be used for smaller quantities of steel, whereas the Bessemer converter was only cheap if large quantities were made. This suited the rather small steel companies of British industry (see Source 4G).

The problem of how to use phosphoric ores was overcome by two amateur scientists, cousins, working together: Sidney Gilchrist-Thomas and Percy Gilchrist. They lined the furnace with limestone, and this absorbed the phosphorus. The steel town of Middlesbrough grew up, as the phosphoric ores of the Cleveland hills could now be used, and steelworks were also started elsewhere.

British steel production rose steadily between 1870 and 1914.

Steel was used for ships, railway engines, mining equipment, trams, bridges and machines of all sorts (see Source 4F). However, other countries took up the discoveries of Bessemer, Siemens and Gilchrist-

■ *SOURCE 4G*

Some American furnaces, with complete equipment, cost over £200 000 each whereas the average cost of British furnaces is probably not over £25 000.

English engineers, on visiting American workshops, have been surprised to see so few men about. Automatic machinery is much more largely used there than in this country ... Our American rivals produce plates at a cost of only about 3/6 [17½p] per ton for labour, averaging 225 tons per shift. These results are not equalled in our own mills.

Report of the (unofficial) Tariff Commission, 1904

Thomas in an even bigger way: in 1913 German steel production was 13.5 million tons, and US 31 million tons. Furnaces in these countries were larger, and productivity (amount produced per worker) far greater.

? QUESTIONS

a) What uses do steel wire ropes have, from Source 4F?

b) How can you tell that the manufacturers exported much of their product?

c) In what ways was British steel-making different from steel-making in the USA?

d) What reasons can you suggest for these differences?

e) In what ways does the account in Source 4G suggest problems for the future of the British steel industry?

f) Why do you think the British steel industry was still able to grow even though it seems to be less efficient than US steel-works?

Iron and steel since 1918

In the 1920s the iron and steel industry suffered from the slump in trade and manufacturing. Tariffs

■ *SOURCE 4H* **Irlam Steelworks, Manchester, closed 1980**

(Chapter 25 page 260) were introduced in the 1930s to prevent foreign steel coming into Britain more cheaply than it could be made here. New steelworks were set up at Scunthorpe and Corby, and production increased, from 5 million tons in 1931 to 13 million tons by 1939. This was mainly because of re-armament: by 1938 the British government was spending nearly one-third of its budget on tanks, planes, ships and guns which were huge consumers of steel. The growing car industry also took steel in large quantities. However, at the price British firms could make it, very little steel was exported.

After the Second World War the industry suffered from changes of government policy. Labour felt that such an important industry as steel needed to be planned and run by government, so it was nationalised in 1949. The Conservatives felt that private enterprise was better for the steel industry, and it was de-nationalised in 1952. In 1967 Labour re-nationalised it as the British Steel Corporation. Try as they might, it was difficult to make British steel competitive in world trade.

Japanese and US steelworks used the latest automated equipment; British steelworks were too small and outdated. In 1980 Mrs Thatcher brought an American steel manager, Ian McGregor, over to Britain to run British Steel. He halved the size of the industry, closing down all but the most efficient works. In some areas, 200 years of iron and steel-making came to an end.

■ *QUESTIONS*

a) Was the steelworks in operation when the photograph was taken?

b) Compare this Source with Source 3A. How can you tell that the steel industry has grown?

c) How can you tell that lots of people worked at Irlam? How many workers do you think there were?

d) What would have been the effect on all these people when the works closed?

Shipbuilding

The growth of the industry

Chapter 10 explores the changes in ship design which took place in the later 19th century. Wood gave way to iron, then steel, and sail to steam. This gave British shipbuilders some advantages. Cheap iron and steel was available; British engineering firms made the new compound engines, and later the turbines. British firms needed to import and export their goods so there were plenty of orders. In the years 1910–14, 60% of ships built in the world were built in Britain, taking one-third of British steel production.

Making the new steel steamships was a large-scale task – see Sources 5A and 5B. Large numbers of skilled workers were needed, as well as many other different trades and huge amounts of capital. These craft and managerial skills were built up in Scotland, along the Clyde, in Belfast, Liverpool, Barrow-in-Furness and along the Tyne.

■ *SOURCE 5A* **Some tasks in shipbuilding, 1866**

■ *QUESTIONS*

a) What kinds of machines are being used to shape the metal in Source 5A?

b) Does shipbuilding seem to employ lots of workers?

c) In what ways does the work seem hard and physically demanding?

d) Using Source 5B, and your own knowledge, make a list of the other skills and trades which would have been needed to complete a liner like the Queen Mary, apart from workers such as those in Source 5A.

Shipbuilding since 1918

The decline in trade in the years between the wars hit British shipbuilding badly. There were not enough goods to fill those ships already afloat, so new orders were hard to get. At that time, other countries carried out a 'scrap-and-build' policy to update their fleets and keep their shipbuilders busy. Britain did not do this, nor did shipbuilders try to build new kinds of ships, such as oil tankers. Changes in the yards meant that fewer workers were needed to build each

ship. This, and the shortage of orders meant that unemployment in shipbuilding towns was very bad. The North Atlantic Shipping Act 1934 gave government subsidies for building passenger liners, such as the *Queen Mary* (Source 5B). Then the re-armament programme in the late 1930s gave rise to orders for battleships.

After the war there was a demand for new ships to replace those sunk, but by this time many British shipyards were out of date and expensive to operate. New, faster, cheaper methods of working were introduced in Japan, Poland and other countries. In Britain there was union opposition to changes which could affect the special skills, and pay, of different workers. In Source 5C, the figures for British shipbuilding, looked at against world figures, show how far Britain has fallen behind.

■ *SOURCE 5C* **Millions of tons of shipping built, Britain and the world**

	World	Britain
1938	2.7	0.8
1950	4.8	2.0
1975	34.6	1.5
1979	12.7	0.5

■ *QUESTIONS*

a) What proportion of world tonnage did Britain build at each date?

b) What has happened to world shipbuilding in the last 10 years?

Clearly Britain's share of shipbuilding orders has fallen. Even British shipping firms found it cheaper to have their vessels built overseas. Many of the yards at

■ *SOURCE 5B* **The liner *Queen Mary* being built on the Clyde in the 1930s**

Belfast, Liverpool, Clydeside and Tyneside have closed. In 1977 the industry was nationalised as British Shipbuilders. However, the 1979 figure shows that by then little new shipbuilding was taking place. There were and are too many ships for the amount of trade in a world depression. In the 1980s shipbuilding is, if anything, in greater difficulties than it was in the 1930s.

Coal-mining

1850–1914: years of growth

The huge demand for coal, growing throughout the years up to 1850 (see Chapter 5), continued up to 1914.

Nor was there much attempt to mechanise the industry: of the 287 million tons extracted in 1913, 92% was dug simply by pick and shovel. In fact productivity – the average amount dug per man – actually fell in the 19th century from 324 tons per miner in 1800, to 287 tons in 1864, to 255 tons in 1913.

Coal was used on the railways, in steam-engines in all types of industry and in ships, for making gas and for home heating. In the years 1890–1914 large amounts were exported as well (98 million tons in 1900). These huge production figures, shown in Source 6A, were achieved by sinking more and deeper mines. There were no new inventions, although some measures were introduced to improve safety.

1918 to the present: years of decline

During the First World War Britain's coal customers found other suppliers – Germany, Belgium, Poland, USA. Productivity in many of these countries was greater, so their coal was cheaper. British coalmine-owners found it difficult to compete, and cut the miners' wages. Bad relations between miners and owners led to the bitter coal-strike and General Strike of 1926 (see Chapter 19 pages 205–7).

Things did not improve in the 1930s, as people changed from coal or gas to electricity for many

■ *SOURCE 6A* **British coal production, 1850–1985**

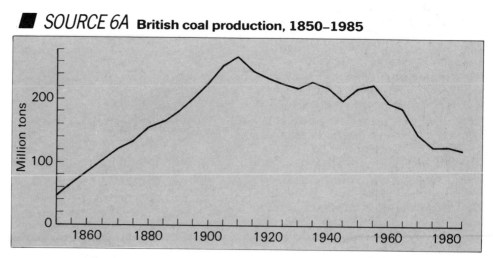

■ *SOURCE 6B* **Coal-mining, 1920s**

■ *SOURCE 6C* **Coal-cutting by machine, 1930s**

❓ QUESTIONS

a) Look at Source 6A. Which was the peak year for coal production?

b) How much was mined in that year?

c) What were the main uses of coal before the First World War?

d) Suggest reasons why coal production has declined over the last 70 years.

e) Look at Sources 6B and 6C. In what ways was the work of a miner in the 1920s the same, and in what ways was it different from his work 100 years earlier?

f) Why do you think there was no great increase in mechanised coal-mining until the 1930s?

g) In what ways would a machine, such as the one in Source 6C, reduce the price of coal?

h) In what ways would a machine, such as the one in Source 6C, change the job of the miner?

home and industrial uses. The electric furnace, for example, replaced the gas-fired open-hearth furnace for making steel.

Although most electricity came from coal-fired power-stations, only certain types of coal could be used in them. Petrol and oil also began to replace coal-fired steam engines. Diesel engines began to be used in ships. Cars and buses took passengers from steam trains. By 1936 coal exports were half the 1913 figure. Some efforts were made to mechanise coal-mining, but in 1936 only 60% of coal was cut by machine.

It was, therefore, a declining coal industry which was nationalised in 1947. The miners had long wanted to see their industry nationalised. They saw the need to invest more money in the good pits than their private owners could afford. They also wanted to plan the run-down of exhausted pits so that hundreds of miners were not thrown out of work in the same village at the same time.

The National Coal Board invested money so that productivity rose

■ *SOURCE 6D* Notice of nationalisation, 1947

? QUESTIONS

a) From Source 6D, what do the miners feel about nationalisation?

b) Why would the village of Cwmparc in Source 6E be badly hit if the local colliery closed?

■ *SOURCE 6E* Cwmparc, South Wales, mid-20th century

from 300 tons per miner per year in 1948, to 439 tons per miner per year by 1970, to 490 tons per miner per year in 1981. Many pits were closed and miners left the industry. There were 1000 pits and over a million miners before the Second World War. By 1981 there were under 200 pits and 230 000 miners. After arranging the drastic cut-down of the steel industry, Ian McGregor was moved by Mrs Thatcher to run the Coal Board from 1984 to 1986. His policy of more pit closures led him into conflict with the miners' union, resulting in the

bitter miners' strike of 1984–5 (see page 211).

The run-down of the coal-industry has been halted to some extent by changes in the electricity industry (see below). The huge rise in the price of oil in 1973 led the government to realise that they should not be too dependent on it as a fuel. Coal-mines in the Vale of Belvoir and at Selby have been opened up and new coal-fired power stations built. With two-thirds of all British coal going to generate electricity, the two industries are now closely linked.

Changes in Power Production

Gas

Coal gas, as a form of lighting, had been known about since the 17th century. In 1765 Lord Lonsdale's mine office was lit by methane gas; in 1798 William Murdock, Chief Engineer to Boulton and Watt, lit their Soho factory with gas lights. George Lee set up a gasworks to light his Salford factory in 1805. F. A. Winsor's Gas, Light and Coke Company provided street lighting in London in 1812.

■ *SOURCE 7A*

What can occasion such a ferment in every house, in every street, in every shop, in every garret about

London? It is the Light and Heat Company. It is Mr Winsor and his lecture, and his gas, and his patent, and his shares .... That strong light that has lit up Pall Mall for this year past has all at once blazed up like a comet.

Lady Bessborough, 1812

? QUESTIONS

a) Why do you think London was so amazed at F. A. Winsor's street lights in 1840? (Think what it would have been like with no streetlights.)

b) In Source 7A, what are people so excited about, apart from the lights themselves?

c) Working in a gasworks was very hard. Use Source 7B to explain why the job was so demanding.

■ SOURCE 7B Charging the retorts at Westminster Gasworks, 1840

By the second half of the 19th century, gas had been installed in most towns and cities. It lit streets, shops, pubs and factories. Some richer people had it installed into their homes, and towards the end of the century gas cookers were invented. Gas was also used in some industrial processes requiring heat, such as Siemens' open-hearth furnace.

In the 20th century, the use of gas slowly gave way to electricity until, in 1959, huge natural gas reserves were found under the North Sea. These were tapped and piped ashore. Gradually, through the 1960s, every gas appliance in the country was adapted for natural gas. It now supplies about 15% of our fuel needs, nearly all of it for home heating and cooking.

Electricity

Scientists knew about electricity, too, long before its use became widespread. Michael Faraday invented a battery in 1809 and a dynamo in 1831. However, the only widespread use of electricity before about 1875 was in the electric telegraph (see Chapter 24, page 245).

In 1878 Joseph Swan invented a light bulb in Britain. Then in 1881 Thomas Edison in the USA, and St George Lane-Fox, also invented a light bulb, all independently of each other.

■ SOURCE 8A Edison's light bulb, 1881

■ SOURCE 8B Notice about electric lighting, late 19th century

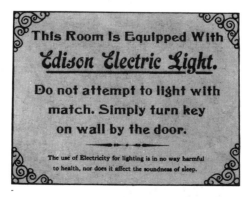

Electricity was used for street lighting and indoor lighting. It was first produced by steam-powered generators, but they could not get up the speed to be really successful. Then in 1884 Charles Parsons invented the steam turbine. This used steam to spin rotor-blades at very high speeds. Successful electricity generating stations could now be set up, and there were 500 of these in Britain in 1914. Control and switchgear for them was invented and produced by Sebastian de Ferranti. Steam turbines were later used for ships, and are still used in generating electricity.

Electrical engineering began only slowly in Britain. The first electric tram ran in Berlin, and when the first London tube was electrified in 1900 it was the American firm of Westinghouse which supplied the system. British industrialists were slow to change from steam to electric power in their factories. Far more electricity was being generated in Germany and the USA in 1914 than in Britain. This meant that other countries wishing to start electric power generation turned to these countries for their orders.

? QUESTIONS

a) Why do you think three people invented the light bulb at more or less the same time?

b) What does Source 8B tell us about people's attitudes to electric light in the early years?

c) Why did people react in this way?

Growth in electric power

Gradually the advantages of electricity became clear. It is clean, it starts at once with no fire to be lit and no boiler to heat, and it can be used in any part of the country. Industry could now be set up where transport and markets were good: it did not have to be on a coalfield. Electric power could be used in awkward places – for example, shipbuilding workers could take electric-powered drills and riveters wherever they were working on a ship. Gradually, too, in the 1920s and 1930s, more and more electrically powered domestic appliances were made – cleaners, radios, clocks, kettles, heaters, washing machines, cookers. The number of households using electricity rose from three-quarters of a million (6% of households) to 9 million (70% of households) between 1919 and 1939.

The Central Electricity Board was set up in 1926. This set about constructing a National Grid to take electricity anywhere in the country. It was completed by 1934, with power-stations at convenient sites, and power lines, on pylons, crossing the country. A hundred thousand people were employed on this job, in addition to all those employed to make domestic electrical appliances and electrical equipment for the new industry. In fact the numbers employed in electrical engineering and construction rose by 142% between 1923–1939.

The electricity supply industry was nationalised after the war, in 1947. The Central Electricity Generating Board (CEGB) was responsible for generation, and local boards for distributing the electricity. Most power-stations were coal-fired, with some hydro-electric power. As oil became cheap, oil-fired stations were built. From the 1960s the CEGB began to turn to more nuclear power stations.

Nuclear power

The work of a huge team of American scientists on splitting the atom had led to the building of the atom bombs dropped on Hiroshima and Nagasaki in 1945. Britain wanted to develop her own nuclear weapons, so set up a reactor at Windscale to produce plutonium (the essential material in a nuclear bomb). Large amounts of heat are generated in the reactors. This can be used to heat water, the steam from which will drive a turbine to make electricity. Thus the next two plutonium reactors, opened in 1956, at Calder Hall in Cumberland and Chapelcross in Scotland, also produced electricity. From then on, reactors were built for the main purpose of generating electricity, until by the present day, over 15% of Britain's electricity is being produced by 18 nuclear reactors.

Nuclear power has become very controversial. The CEGB wants to have a variety of types of power station so as not to be too dependent on one fuel, such as coal or oil. It also claims that nuclear electricity is cheaper. The Conservative government under Mrs Thatcher wanted to develop nuclear power so that electricity supplies should not be too dependent on coal. They felt

■ *SOURCE 8C* **Nuclear power station at Bradwell, Essex**

this gave too much power to the miners' union.

Opponents of nuclear power point out the dangers to health through radiation from accidents or leaks. They cite the fire at Windscale in 1957, the disaster at Three Mile Island in the USA in 1979, and at Chernobyl in the USSR in 1986. Lots of radioactive waste is produced by nuclear reactors, and this has to be stored or disposed of by some means, causing a further possible risk to the environment. The opponents of nuclear power argue that the cost of all this, added to the fall in the price of coal and oil, makes nuclear electricity more expensive.

▨ *QUESTIONS*

a) Why do you think the nuclear power station in Source 8C is built on a remote part of the Essex coast?

b) What arguments are there against putting these power stations in remote rural areas?

Oil

The demand for oil rose enormously in the years before and after the Second World War. It was being used as fuel for cars, buses, lorries and aeroplanes, for heating and as raw material in the plastics industry. By 1970 it was by far Britain's largest import: 113 million tons were imported. Refineries had been set up near several ports, at Milford Haven, Fawley and Canvey Island. Because oil played so big a part in the industrial life of Britain, the huge price rise of the early 1970s caused a rise in the price of nearly every item in the country.

During the 1970s Britain was, however, able to develop its own oil industry. Oil had been discovered in the North Sea in 1969, and the first barrels were brought ashore in 1975. Two huge fields, the Brent and the Forties, have now been developed, reaching a peak of production in 1986. Workers have to drill for oil on huge oil rigs far out at sea off the coast of Scotland. The

■ *SOURCE 8D* **Oil rig in the North Sea**

building and maintenance of the rigs has provided many jobs both on and off shore.

In order that Britain should benefit from the finds, the government set up the British National Oil Company in 1976. BNOC invested in exploration and shared the trading profits. By the 1980s Britain was actually exporting oil. In 1982 the Conservative government sold off BNOC to private investors.

As an industrialised country Britain needs large amounts of energy. Meeting this need is one of the major problems facing the country in the future. The table below shows the changes which have taken place.

■ *SOURCE 8E* **Energy consumption (in millions of tons of coal equivalent)**

	1959	1979
Coal	190	130
Petrol	58	139
Natural gas	0.1	71
Nuclear	0.5	14
Total	248.6	354

? *QUESTIONS*

a) What special problems are there in getting oil from beneath the sea?

b) How do these problems affect the price of oil?

c) What has happened to the total amount of energy needed? What reasons are there for this?

d) What has happened to the amount of each type of energy used?

e) Explain the reasons for these changes.

Growth of New Industries

The Motor Industry

Up to 1945

The early development of the motor-car is described in Chapter 10. Before 1914 Britain lagged behind other countries in the development of the motor industry. Cars were seen as an expensive toy for the rich, and no attempt was made to reach a mass market.

■ *SOURCE 9A*

An American engineer tried to sell the Delco self-starter to the head of a famous British motor-car firm, who said: 'It will cost £20 or £30 more. Why should we put it on the car?'

'Well, if you have this starter on the car, when the car stops the owner won't have to get out and crank the engine; he can put his foot on the pedal and start it.'

'You know, people who use our cars have their own chauffeurs: they wouldn't dream of driving a car themselves.'

The American was baffled but not beaten, so he said: 'I'll tell you, you will sell a lot more cars with this starter on because then women can drive.'

The Englishman replied: 'Women drive, God forbid!'

Quoted in G. E. Folk, *Patents and Industrial Progress*, 1956

? *QUESTION*

What does this story tell us about the British motor industry before 1914?

Quite a different attitude was adopted by the American, Henry Ford, who was making half a million cars per year in the USA before 1914. After the war, two British businessmen applied his ideas to their firms. William Morris set up his factory in Oxford in 1912, but did not introduce assembly-line methods until the 1920s. He also reduced his Morris Oxford in price from £325 to £225, selling enough cars at the lower price to justify the reduction. He also produced the Morris Minor, a very small car, to sell at about £100. His main rival was Herbert Austin, who also produced a small car, the Austin 7.

■ *SOURCE 9B* Austin 7, 1922

■ *SOURCE 9C*

The way to make automobiles is to make one automobile like another automobile, to make them come through the factory just alike, just as one pin is like another pin when it comes from pin factory .... You need not fear about the market. The people will buy them alright. When you get to making cars in quantity you can make them cheaper, and when you make them cheaper you find people with enough money to buy them.

Henry Ford, 1903

? QUESTIONS

a) Which of Sources 9D or 9E shows Henry Ford's methods of car-building?

b) Explain how the cars were made in each of Sources 9D and 9E.

c) Why could the cars made in Source 9E be cheaper?

d) What effect does cheapness have on the number of cars sold, according to Henry Ford in Source 9C?

Between the wars, the British car industry grew, using new production-line methods, until it was second in the world. Britain put a tax on cars, based on their

■ *SOURCE 9D* Early car factory, 1913

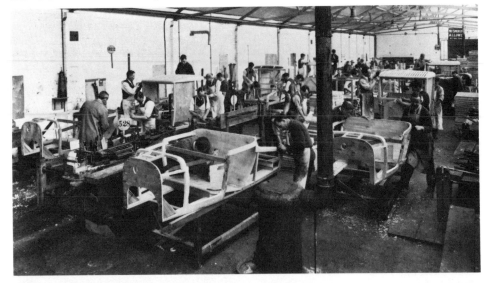

■ *SOURCE 9E* Morris assembly line, 1946

horsepower. This encouraged the making of small cars. These sold well in Britain, but not many were exported. There were also lorry and bus manufacturers, like Leyland and Seddon Atkinson. By 1939 there were three million vehicles of all kinds on British roads.

Building a motor car involves bringing together lots of different parts. These were often made by other, specialist firms, such as Dunlop (tyres) and Lucas (batteries). Car factories used electric power, so they could choose where to set themselves up, near to suppliers and their markets. These were mainly in the Midlands and south-east England, in Coventry, Birmingham, Oxford, Bedford, Luton and Dagenham.

Since 1945

After the war, the British motor industry expanded still further, exporting to much of the world. By 1973 two million vehicles a year were being built. Then things began to go wrong: Britain's share of world vehicle orders fell from 11% in 1964 to 4% in 1980. Foreign-made cars began to be imported into Britain – first the Volkswagen, but then Fiat,

■ SOURCE 9F **Cars produced by Britain, France and Japan, 1940–80 (in thousands)**

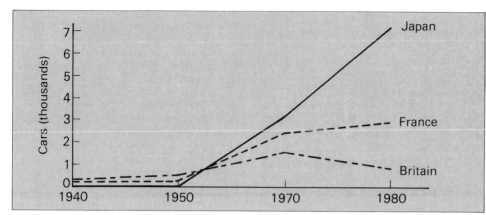

The car industry's response to the crisis was to form bigger and bigger companies in order to compete with the huge foreign companies. By the mid-1980s there remained only four car-builders in Britain: Ford, Vauxhall, Talbot and British Leyland. BL was formed in 1968, by merging Austin, Morris, Leyland as well as Rover, Triumph and Jaguar. Large amounts of government money have been put into BL to modernise factories and help it through this difficult period.

The Chemical Industry

In the later 19th century many industries began to make more use of chemical products: bleaching and dyeing textiles, making soap, fertilisers and glass, for example. In 1856 William Perkin discovered how to make a purple dye from coal tar. Soon a whole range of strong colours were being made from coal products. However, in all these fields Germany established a lead and the British chemical industry lagged behind. When war broke out in 1914, the War Office was horrified to find out that all khaki dyes were made in Germany.

Between the wars the chemical industry expanded in Britain. Four firms joined together in 1926 to make Imperial Chemical Industries (ICI), one of the biggest chemical firms in Europe. Production of fertiliser, plastics, disinfectants, drugs and artificial fibres expanded at several factories. Courtaulds produced an artificial fibre, rayon, in 1937.

The chemical industry has continued to grow since 1945. A huge range of plastics such as polythene, terylene and polyester is now made, as well as many other products for industrial and personal use.

Volvo, Renault and vehicles from all over Europe as well as Japan. In 1965 nearly all the cars sold in Britain were made here; by 1979 over half the cars sold were imported and by 1980 63%.

Source 9F shows that Britain's share of car production was much smaller than either France's or Japan's by 1970 and had slumped further by 1980. Why did this happen? One reason was that British production methods were not very good. There were too many small, old-fashioned, ill-equipped factories. Industrial relations in them were poor, and strikes held up production. The result was that British cars were too expensive, were not well-made and were delivered late. British designs were often good: the Mini, for example, de-

signed in 1959, was a world best-seller. However, it was not priced properly and so did not produce the profits which could have been used to modernise British factories.

By the late 1970s, many foreign companies had invested in modern computerised robot car factories. British firms did not make these changes quickly enough, and so lost their competitive edge.

? QUESTIONS

a) Compare Source 9G with Source 9E. In what ways is this factory faster and cheaper to operate?

b) Why would the cars coming out of the factory in Source 9G be cheaper and possibly more reliable?

? QUESTIONS

a) Look at Source 10 (over). In what ways do Courtaulds in this advertisement try to give rayon an image that is fashionable and luxurious?

b) In what ways does this advertisement differ from the kind we see today?

■ SOURCE 9G **Automated car plant at Austin Rover, 1980s**

SOURCE 10 Advertisement for rayon

Computers and High-Tech Industries

It has taken a long series of inventions to develop the calculating machines of early 19th century mathematicians into the modern computer. Electricity helped to speed up the calculators. Mathematical discoveries were made by Boole and Turing. Electronic valve computers were built in the Second World War as code-breakers; in use they could scan thousands of symbols very fast. After the war the first modern computer was built at Manchester University. It took up several rooms, but later the invention of the transistor and the integrated circuit allowed computers to be built smaller. The microchip brought the size and price of computers within the reach of most firms and many households in the 1980s.

Britain was well placed to take the lead in computer design, but the huge American firms, such as IBM, gained a large share of the world business market. The small British company, Sinclair, had initial successes with small, cheap microcomputers for use in the home. Computers are increasingly being used now in all sorts of businesses, from banking and insurance to controlling production in factories (see Source 9G). The Stock Exchange was computerised in 1986. Computers are also used in weather forecasting, quality control and printing.

Computers, and a whole range of electronic industries such as telecommunications and navigational equipment, have become an important industry. The main centres are in 'Silicon Valley' (the Thames Valley) and 'Silicon Glen' in Scotland, as well as in and around Cambridge. Against the new jobs created in high-tech industries must be set job losses in other industries where workers have been replaced by computers. One of the most spectacular examples of this has been the shift to computerised methods in newspaper production. This has put thousands of printers out of work, and a large-scale dispute blew up in 1986, between the print unions and News International, publisher of the *Sun*, *The Times* and *The Sunday Times*.

SOURCE 11

In 1959 electronics in Scotland employed 7400; in 1966 18000. This is the result of the arrival of American and British technology in Scotland's main industrial area, where one worker in 20 has a job in electronics ...

One firm was so delighted with conditions that it opened a second plant, increasing the number of employees to over a thousand. Another, in Cowdenbeath, a mining town, employed men whose working lives had been spent in the pits.

Lord Clydesmuir, Chairman of Scotland's Development and Industry Council, 1967

QUESTIONS

a) Does the writer suggest that the new industries provided more jobs, or reduced jobs?

b) Which old industry was running down in the area he describes?

The British Economy Since 1850

We have looked at what has happened to the major industries of Britain since 1850. But what has happened to the British economy *as a whole* over the years? And what did people at the time think was happening?

1850–1918

The prosperity of Britain in 1850 was based on narrow foundations: cotton, iron and coal, together with engineering. The early growth of these industries had given Britain a lead of several years over other countries. But there was nothing to stop them catching up. In fact, Britain helped this process in more than one way: machines were exported to many countries, which could then make the goods that Britain made. Also the money made by Britain in earlier years had made London the financial capital of the world. If a country needed money for railways, blast furnaces or other big projects they could raise it in 'the City'. Britain thus supplied the money for the development of other countries.

The Great Depression?

The years 1873–96 were called by many people at the time the Great Depression. Certainly some people were in difficulties: corn farmers, for example, hit by cheap corn imports from USA and Canada. Some manufacturers were hit by cheaper goods coming from other countries for the first time. Many of these people, especially landowners, complained long and hard. They seemed to be the only voices to be heard. There was severe unemployment in some areas. When Parliament looked at the problem, they indeed saw other countries doing well: the USA overtook Britain in total manufacturing production in 1890, Germany overtook Britain in 1904. This rivalry was all the more

■ SOURCE 12 **One of the first Boot's stores**

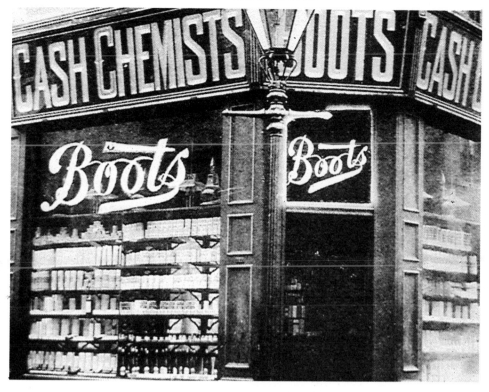

Between the Wars

When Britain tried to restart her trade after the First World War from where it had been in 1914, she found a changed world. Britain's former customers now either had new suppliers, or were manufacturers themselves. Trade was now much more competitive, and many British industries were not in a state to compete. Production was often old-fashioned, inefficient and expensive. This was especially true in just those industries on which the prosperity of the mid-19th century was based: cotton, coal, iron and shipbuilding. The Wall Street Crash of 1929 and the resultant Depression only made things worse. World trade dropped from $2998 million in 1930 to $992 million in 1933.

The decline of old industries

The Jarrow march
The old heavy industries employed lots of workers in areas where there were few other jobs. Jarrow, for example, a town on the River Tyne, was utterly dependent on shipbuilding. With no ships being built, unemployment in Jarrow reached 68%.

■ *SOURCE 13A*

Jarrow is dead. Even at its best, when everyone was working in it, it can only have been a mean little collection of narrow, monotonous streets of stunted and ugly houses. But in those days at least they were working. Now Jarrow is a derelict town. One out of every two shops appeared to be permanently closed. Wherever we went there were men hanging about, not scores of them but hundreds and thousands of them.

J. B. Priestley, 1933

In 1936 the people of Jarrow, led by their MP, Ellen Wilkinson, arranged a march from Jarrow to London. They carried a petition, asking the government to give work to the shipyards. The march was called the Jarrow Crusade (see Source 13B over the page).

Unemployment was bad in other areas too. Source 13C (over) describes the situation in Manchester.

upsetting for Britain because it was completely new. Source 4G (see page 88) is part of one of several investigations into the problem.

The British economy was still growing at this time, even if more slowly than before. Some farmers, and some businesses such as shipbuilding, were doing quite well. They were not perhaps making profits as large as in earlier years, but certainly they were not going under. Prices fell faster than wages, so those people who had jobs saw a rise in their standard of living. Better houses and better food were available. This was the time when chain stores, such as Sainsbury's, Boot's and Lipton's were established (Source 12). It was not a Great Depression for all.

There were some more serious problems taking root at this time, but their effects were not seen until later. As we saw earlier, there was little investment in new equipment in the cotton and coal industries. British manufacturers were proud of their machinery, which was built to last. British workers were proud of their skill in working these machines. Both sides of industry therefore went in for repairs and replacements rather than investing in new and better machinery.

Prosperity from earlier years brought its own problems too.

Factory-owners had grown to expect high profits and complained when they did not get them (a good deal of the feeling of a Great Depression was because of this). They were used to taking their profits rather than going without for a few years in order to invest in new plant. Banks, too, found it much easier to lend money to new, profitable schemes abroad, than to lend it at home.

The earlier part of this chapter revealed another British problem: failure to come to terms with the new science-based industries, such as chemical and electrical engineering. In 1872, Cambridge University produced only 12 graduates in science subjects, and most of these were going on to be doctors. At that time Germany had 11 Technical Universities; the USA had science courses of most of its 70 universities, including the Massachusetts Institute of Technology, set up in 1861. This British lack of interest in science was not as evident in Scotland, but south of the border it was to have serious results. Education in the grammar and public schools was based on the Classics. Britain was never short of inventors, but the bankers, civil servants and business people with the knowledge to support them were sadly lacking.

SOURCE 13B The Jarrow Crusade, 1936

SOURCE 13D Hunger marchers, 1930s

SOURCE 13C

Two thousand people assembled in pouring rain outside the Broadway Theatre, Eccles Cross, today, to apply for 35 jobs. Two men had walked from Oldham, a distance of 12 miles, and after being interviewed were faced with the prospect of another long walk home in the rain. The morning was the time appointed for interviews for the jobs. Applicants came early. Half a dozen men waited all night. Some women came at a quarter to six. Then the crowd began to gather in earnest. The rain drenched the overcoatless, and ran in streams from umbrellas, but no one would give up his or her position.
Manchester Evening News, 1932

? QUESTIONS

a) What does J. B. Priestley (Source 13A) think of the town of Jarrow?

b) Why had the shipbuilding industry collapsed, and why did shipbuilding towns have such high unemployment?

c) What music are the marchers in Source 13B marching to?

d) Why was unemployment in the Manchester area so high?

e) What is the attitude of the reporter on the *Manchester Evening News* to the situation (Source 13C)?

f) Where is the hunger march from (Source 13D)?

g) When the Jarrow Crusaders returned home they found their unemployment pay had been stopped while they were on the march. The government took little notice of their petition, or the march. How do you explain these facts?

The growth of new industries

The economy grew by an average of about 2% per year between the wars, a slightly better growth rate than before the war. Manufacturing output rose 3.1% per year and productivity rose 2.4% per worker. The familiar pictures and descriptions of Sources 13A–D are obviously not the whole picture. This was a time of growth for many industries, often new industries producing new goods: motor cars, motor parts, electrical goods, plastics, aircraft, radios and household articles.

SOURCE 14A Hoover factory, 1930s

SOURCE 14B

Years of living in the West Riding have fixed forever what my idea of a factory should look like: a grim, blackened rectangle, with a tall chimney at one corner. These decorative little buildings, all glass and concrete and chromium plate seem to my mind to be merely playing at factories. Actually I know that they are evidence to prove that the new industries have moved south. You notice them decorating all the western borders of London. But while these new industries look so much prettier than the old, they also look far less substantial. Potato crisps, scent, toothpaste, bathing costumes ...: they seem to belong to an England of luxury trades.

J. B. Priestley, 1933

❓ QUESTIONS

a) What kinds of goods does the firm in Source 14A make?
b) Why did they want a site next to the Great West Road?
c) Does the factory seem to be the kind of building J. B. Priestley describes in Source 14B?
d) J. B. Priestley was brought up in the West Riding of Yorkshire. What kinds of factories was he used to? What form of power did they use?
e) What is his attitude to the 'new' industries he describes in Source 14B?

The new industries sited their factories in the Midlands and the South-East of England. Electricity from the National Grid drove their machines, so they did not need to be near coalfields; lorries carried their products to their buyers, so they preferred to be on good roads, not by a canal. Their products sold mainly to the better-off people in Britain, and the factories were built where they lived, in the South-East.

For people who had jobs, the 1920s and 1930s were good times to live. The price of food and housing fell in relation to wages – real wages rose 20% between 1920 and 1938. There were also new and interesting items to spend money on, as cars and electric gadgets became cheaper and easier to buy. Nearly all the production of the new industries was sold in Britain, or exported to the British colonies (see Chapter 25). For the time being, that was enough to account for the growth figures quoted above.

Regional differences

While unemployment in Jarrow was 68%, Merthyr Tydfil (an iron-making town in Wales) had 62%, Maryport (a coal and iron town) had 57% and Greenock (Clydeside shipbuilding) 36%. On the other hand, unemployment was under 9% in London, 6% in Birmingham and about 5% in Oxford. It is little wonder that many people moved from the great industrial areas of the 19th century – the North, South Wales and Scotland – to south-east England. But this migration still left millions behind in the poorer regions.

The government did not do a great deal to help this imbalance. In fact their policy of returning to the Gold Standard (Chapter 25, page 259) made things worse by making exports expensive. Nevertheless, in the 1930s the government began to help agriculture with subsidies. The North Atlantic Shipping Act 1934 gave firms grants to build ships. The Ottawa Conference of 1932 gave preference to British goods in British colonies. An attempt was made to provide work in the hard-hit older industrial areas by the Special Areas Act 1934. This gave grants to make parks and recreation centres in towns. Only in 1937 were trading estates started. These were areas near industrial towns where factories were set up with substantial financial help in order to provide long-term employment rather than temporary jobs.

The Post-War Boom

As well as death and destruction, the Second World War brought problems and benefits to the British economy. Britain ended the war with £3000 million of debts and £1000 million of her foreign investments sold off. Life was desperately hard for British people at least until 1950, and only US loans prevented a total economic disaster. On the other hand, war brought forward several ideas that would never have gone ahead so fast in peacetime. Frank Whittle invented the jet engine; other important developments were made in aircraft design, plastics, computers, radar and radio. Factories had to turn out goods on a large scale, and new methods and management were brought in. Attitudes towards women working began to change (see Chapter 21).

The Labour governments of 1945–51 believed that the government should take over key industries for the benefit of the country as a whole – and for the workers in them. Accordingly coal, steel and electricity as well as the railways were nationalised. By then, these were declining industries, and all the government could do was manage their run-down as reasonably as they could.

In spite of the growth of new industries in the years between the wars the British economy in 1952 was not so very different from what it was in 1914. Britain was still a manufacturing country, importing raw materials and exporting manufactured goods. Greater changes lay ahead.

Up to the late 1970s there was a boom throughout all industrialised countries. It was particularly a boom in consumer goods: clothes, cars, television sets, radios, furniture and household goods. British industry prospered and expanded, and the standard of living of the British people improved a great deal.

Old industrial areas, which had suffered so badly in the 1930s, were helped by being made Development Areas. New factories, with reduced (or zero) rents and rates were built in these areas. All kinds of industries took advantage of this policy, including car-building at Liverpool and on Clydeside, and steel at Ebbw Vale, in South Wales.

■ *SOURCE 15A*

A question of finding a suitable site arose. A site in the Midlands would have been preferred, but the government policy of encouraging firms to set up plants in Development Areas meant that one of these areas had to be selected .... Nylon yarn needs clean air, away from the dust of industrial areas, but a plant on the scale planned, with a million square feet of floor space must be served by efficient fuel and water supplies and have easy access to road and rail. A site of 112 acres was finally chosen. It was near Pontypool in Monmouth.

D. C. Hague, *The Economics of Man-Made Fibres*, 1957

? QUESTIONS

a) Why would ICI have preferred to put their factory in the Midlands?
b) What seems to have driven them to the South Wales Development Area?
c) Describe the surroundings of this factory (Source 15B).
d) How can you tell from Source 15B that the workers are quite well off?

Inability to compete

However, although the British economy grew, many other industrial countries grew faster. Some

■ *SOURCE 15B* ICI Nylon plant at Pontypool, opened 1948

countries, such as Germany and Japan, had to start industry almost from nothing, because of the war. Others, such as the USA, had continued to prosper and keep their industry up to date. As we saw, the years between the wars had been difficult for British industry. There had not been much money to spare for new investment in machines and equipment in the older industries. The result was that, compared to other industrial countries, key sectors of British industry were still old-fashioned, and deeply rooted in 19th century methods. Even many of the new industries which had grown up in the 1930s were not able to meet the stiff competition from abroad. They had prospered by selling to the home market in Britain or British colonies.

Since the Late 1970s

Towards the end of the 1970s the world trade and industry boom began to slacken off. Britain was particularly badly hit. Some products, such as textiles and cars, which had once been Britain's strengths, were pushed out as foreign imports began to flood in. The uncompetitive basis of industry in

Britain became only too clear. It was in the Common Market by that time, so EEC imports could come into the country easily and home industry had no protection.

The Conservative governments of Mrs Thatcher, which began in 1979, offered no protection either. They believed that competition was inevitable and good for industry in the long term: it would drive inefficient firms out of business and encourage new, efficient, competitive firms to grow and prosper.

By 1987 British manufacturing output had fallen significantly and unemployment was over 3 million. Only one thing kept Britain from total bankruptcy – North Sea oil. In fact, Britain in the 1980s is an exporter of raw material (oil) and an importer of manufactured goods. This is the exact reverse of the situation during the 150 years up to the 1970s, when Britain imported raw materials and exported finished goods.

Assignments

Empathy

1 Look at Sources 2A, 5A, 6B, 9E and 14A. Imagine what it was like to work in each of these places and write a short description of each.

2 Look at Sources 13A, 13B, 13C and 13D. Imagine you were one of the people in Source 13C. Describe in a short paragraph, your feelings as you wait to be interviewed.

3 Get into groups of four. You are the Board of Directors of a cotton mill in Lancashire in 1900. One is a banker, one has just returned from a visit to the USA, one is responsible for sales and one is responsible for relations with the unions. You have to decide whether to invest all your profits for the next eight years in new ring-spinning machines. Each put forward your own views and then try to reach a Board decision, explaining your reasoning to the rest of the class.

Understanding concepts

1 **Causation**
 a There were several weaknesses in the British cotton industry before 1914, yet it was doing well. How do you explain this?
 b Why did it go into decline after 1920?
 c Why did this decline continue in the 1950s and 1960s?

2 **Causation**
 a Foreign competition caused serious difficulties to several British industries in the 1920s

and 1930s. How did competition affect i cotton ii coal iii shipbuilding iv steel in these years?
 b Was it inevitable that competition would cause difficulties to British industry sooner or later after 1851?

3 **Causation**

> lack of investment in new machines
> falling demand
> union hostility to change
> old factories and methods
> lack of government help
> too much British investment abroad

 a Choose three of the above factors that you think were the most important causes of the decline of British industry in the 1920s *and* the 1980s. Explain your choice.
 b Choose one of the above factors which you think was *not* an important cause of British industrial decline in the 1980s. Explain your choice.

4 **Causation**
 a Explain why the British motor industry expanded in the 1930s, at a time when most British industry was in difficulties.
 b Explain why the British motor industry has declined in the last 20 years.

5 **Similarity/difference**
 a In what ways is electric power an improved form of power for industry over steam power?

 b What have been the results of the change to electric power in industry for:
  i the location of industry;
  ii working conditions?

6 **Change/continuity**
 a How far is British industry's decline in the 1980s caused by the same factors as its decline in the 1920s and 1930s?
 b In what ways is the recent decline different from the situation between the wars?
 c In what ways are the results of the decline for the people of Britain the same, and in what ways are they different?

7 **Similarity/difference**
 a How far can the 1930s be fairly described as years of 'Depression' in Britain?
 b Why were some areas of Britain hit so severely by unemployment at this time?

Themes for discussion

1 New inventions played a big part in the success of British industry up to 1850. Several new inventions have been made since 1850, yet industry does not seem to have benefitted. How do you explain this?

2 a Do you think the decline of British industry in the years between the wars could have been prevented? If so, how, and when?
 b Do you think the decline of British industry in the 1980s could have been prevented? If so, how, and when?

10 Transport for All

Railways

1850–1914

The years 1850–1914 were the heyday of the railways. Most main lines had been laid by the 1850s (see Map 4, page 59). The next years saw the filling-out of the network, with local and branch lines, sidings and better stations. At its peak there were 23000 miles of rail in Britain (Map 1). The big river estuaries which cut into the British landscape were bridged over or tunnelled under. The Severn Tunnel was built, at great expense. In 1859 Brunel designed the Saltash Bridge, over the Tamar, bringing railways into Cornwall (see Source 1A.) The Tay was bridged in 1887 (an earlier bridge of 1879 collapsed). The Forth Bridge was completed in 1890.

Greater speed and comfort

There was also a great increase in the speed and comfort of passenger travel. Main-line expresses managed average speeds over 60 m.p.h. In 1895 there was serious competition between two railway companies on the London to Aberdeen route. The fastest did the 524-mile journey in just over eight and a half hours. Improved locomotives made these new speeds possible (Source 1B). Heating and lighting were gradually introduced into passenger trains. Restaurant cars were started in the 1890s – before this people could only buy food at stations (Source 1C). Lavatories and corridors made longer non-stop journeys possible, and sleeping cars made overnight travel more comfortable.

Class differences were preserved. For the rich, travelling first class, the standard of service and luxury was high, with elegant saloon coaches (Sources 1D and 1E). Even the poor third-class traveller gained

■ SOURCE 1A **Building the Saltash Bridge, 1858 (opened 1859)**

■ SOURCE 1B **Express engine, 1901**

some improvements. Roofs and windows were added to third-class coaches, and then in 1875 the Midland Railway offered upholstered seats in all of their third-class carriages (Source 1F). Other railway companies did the same.

❓ QUESTIONS

a) What materials are being used to build the Saltash Bridge (Source 1A)? Which would not have been available 100 years earlier?

b) Compare the engine in Source 1B with Chapter 6, Source 16F, page 58. What changes have been made?

c) Compare Sources 1E and 1F. Read Source 1D. What do these sources tell us about class differences in Victorian Britain?

d) Compare these three sources with facilities on a train today. What differences are there? What does this tell us about 'class' in Britain today compared to Victorian times?

■ SOURCE 1C Food available at Derby for taking on the train, 1875

MIDLAND HOTEL
AND
REFRESHMENT ROOMS.
DERBY.
NOTICE.
On and after MARCH 1st, 1875,

LUNCHEON BASKETS

Will be provided at the DERBY STATION, at the following charges:--

No 1. containing Half-a-Chicken, with Ham or Tongue, Salad, Bread, Cheese, Butter, &c., and a Half-Bottle of Claret or Burgundy - - - - | **3s.**

No 2. containing Veal and Ham Pie, with Salad, Bread, Cheese, Butter, &c., and a Bottle of Stout. - - - - | **2s.**

The Baskets will be fitted with the necessary appointments, which it is earnestly requested may be replaced in their proper position, and the Baskets handed to one of the Company's Servants that they may be returned to DERBY.

WILLIAM TOWLE,
Midland Hotel, Derby

■ SOURCE 1D First-class rail travel

The first-class passenger keeps himself to himself .... He knows the gentlemen's seats along the line and the character of the county foxhounds .... At stations he asks to see the guard, who touches his cap, and says they have thirty-five miles to go.

The Comic Bradshaw, 1848

■ MAP 1 Railway network, 1921

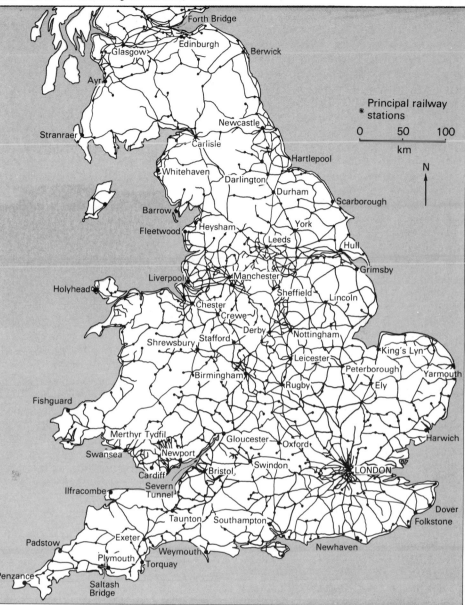

Principal railway stations

0   50   100
km

N

■ SOURCE 1E First-class drawing room car, 1897

■ SOURCE 1F Midland Railway, third-class carriage, 1870s

More attention was paid to safety than before. Block signalling and continuous brakes were made compulsory after a dreadful accident at Armagh in 1889 which killed 78 people. Little attention had been paid to safety of employees in the early days of railways. Three thousand were killed in the period 1870–5, and their employers normally only gave a £10 death grant to their families. One of the main tasks of the railway unions was to press the government to act. Safety measures were tightened up and Workmen's Compensation Acts passed.

Suburban lines expanded, allowing people to live far away from where they worked. Cheap workmen's trains allowed working-class people to do this too. As London's streets grew more crowded, a faster means of getting about was required. The first London Underground line was opened in 1863, to link Paddington, Euston, King's Cross and the City. This route is now part of the Metropolitan Line and was operated by steam for many years (Source 1G). The smoke and soot in the tunnels must have been terrible for railway staff and the public. However the service was popular at 3*d* (1.25p) a ticket and trains every 10 minutes. Electric trains were introduced in 1890, and more lines were built, starting with the Circle Line in 1884. Glasgow was the only other city to introduce Underground trains, although much more recently Tyneside has built a system, completed in 1980.

Independent railway companies

The railway system in 1900 was operated by 15 major independent companies and about 100 small ones. Competition between them wasted their resources, with different lines running between the same towns. Cross-country journeys for goods or passengers were complicated. There was also waste in shunting trucks from one system to another, and waste in having many different managements.

The networks had been built in a great rush in the 1840s and 1850s, with no idea of planning for national needs. There was, for example, no main line through London, and lots of branch lines went through quiet, rural areas with not enough trade to

■ *SOURCE 1G* **Steam Underground train, late 19th century**

keep them profitable. In France and Belgium railways had, from the beginning, been planned and run by the government. Gladstone had considered this in 1844, but the idea was rejected. In the 19th century the rail system's inefficiencies did not matter, as the railways suffered no real competition. The 20th century brought new crises which revealed these problems only too clearly.

1914–45

Central control during the First World War

The first of these crises was the First World War. The whole country was organised for war. Government control of the transport system was regarded as essential in wartime. A Railway Executive Committee took over all the railways, but at first it was left alone to run the railways as in peacetime. As the war went on, huge numbers of men and amounts of equipment had to be moved around: 7 million troops passed through Southampton in four years, for example, and the Great Eastern Railway had to run 13000 special trains to carry troops. All the wastefulness of different companies, of different lines doing the same job, was revealed under this strain. From 1917, the

government began to run the railways as a single system in order to make full use of freight wagons and to run through-trains.

After the war there was a strong move to keep the railways under one controlling body. The advantages of this had been made clear by the war. The Prime Minister, Lloyd George, agreed. Some wanted to reorganise the companies. Others wanted the government to nationalise all transport – that is, to take it over and plan it for the national interest.

■ *SOURCE 2A*

There was a gigantic waste caused by competition with too many trains serving one district merely because there were 3 or 4 companies competing for custom while others had a shortage of facilities.

Lloyd George, 1919

■ *SOURCE 2B*

In a highly-organised modern state, living in an age of fierce international competition, the movement of men and materials is a matter far too vital to be left to private enterprise .... The railways are only part of the national transport system, and in order to be efficient, every possible means of transport must be co-ordinated so as to give the best service possible.

Memorandum to the Cabinet, 1919

a) Put in your own words the criticisms made of the railway system by Lloyd George and the solution suggested in Source 2B.

b) What would be the benefit of the transport policy put forward in Source 2B? What would be the drawbacks?

However, after the war Lloyd George, the Liberal Prime Minister, was dependent on Conservative support. They opposed nationalisation. The Railway Act 1921 cut the number of companies from 123 to four: the London and North-Eastern Railway (LNER), the London Midland and Scottish (LMS), the Southern Railway (SR) and the Great Western Railway (GWR) (see Map 2). The aim was to cut out the wasteful results of competition, but still keep the railways in private hands.

■ *MAP 2* **The four railway companies, 1921**

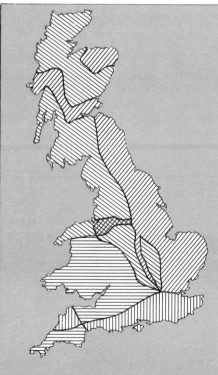

Key

- London and North Eastern Railway (LNER)
- London, Midland and Scottish (LMS)
- Great Western Railway (GWR)
- Southern Railway (SR)

Competition from road transport

The problem was that now the competition to the railways came not from other railways, but from another form of transport. As we shall see later, the road haulage industry grew up and expanded in the years between the wars. For the first time since railways began there was now a serious rival for carrying freight. Unfortunately for the railways, the law still acted as if the railways had no rivals. They were obliged, by law, to carry any freight which a customer required. Lorry owners, on the other hand, could pick and choose, taking the profitable jobs and leaving the rest. Railways also had to publish their rates for freight carriage. Road hauliers did not have to publish theirs, and could easily undercut the railways.

Railways were also closely linked to the 'old' industries of the 19th century such as coal, iron and textiles. As Chapter 9 makes clear, these industries were in serious decline in the inter-war years, and railway freight declined with them (see Source 3A). New industries in the South and East were built on main roads, not on railway lines. For all these reasons the railways lost business in these years.

Rail passenger transport was also being challenged by coach, bus, car

■ *SOURCE 3B* **Silver Jubilee Express, 1935**

■ *SOURCE 3A* **The decline in rail freight (million tonnes)**

	Coal carried by rail	Other rail freight
1913	226	139
1937	188	109

and even air travel. In fact the number of passengers carried remained about the same. However the number of journeys of any kind made by the people of Britain increased. Railways therefore suffered a *relative*, not an *absolute* decline in passenger business. They held on to their business by making trains faster, and by offering more special, cheap tickets. The fastest steam trains in the world were built at this time, with 107 services scheduled to run at over 60 m.p.h.

■ *SOURCE 3C*

Something went wrong with the speedometer and I didn't know what speed we were doing. They had a speed-recording machine in one of the coaches behind. I judged it to be about 90 m.p.h. when Mr Gresley, who had designed the engine, came through the corridor and shouted in my ear: 'Ease your arm, young man! Do you know we've touched 112 twice? Go a bit easier, we've got an old gentleman of a director in the back and he's getting a bit touchy.'

Driver on the test-run of the Silver Link express, 1935

? QUESTIONS

a) Compare Source 3B with Source 1B: what changes had been made in 34 years?

b) Why did aeroplanes find it difficult to compete with train services of this kind?

c) What kinds of passengers find fast express trains most useful?

The loss of income from freight, and cutting fares to hold on to passengers, meant that railways did not make much profit in the interwar years. Only the Southern Railway carried out a major improvement programme by electrifying many of its lines. They found that electric trains had better acceleration, so could offer a better service to commuters. They were quicker to start in the mornings, cleaner and easier to maintain. Their running costs were cut by nearly half. There were plans to electrify other lines, but the Depression of 1931 cut out any new expenditure on railway improvement.

The Second World War proved an even greater crisis for the railways than the First. Once again, the government took over the whole system, and once again it was put under great strain. By the end of the war, bomb damage, a lack of repairs and hard wear left many locomotives, trucks and carriages useless. With the railways in great difficulties, road haulage came to the rescue of freight transport. Many firms never went back to using railways.

Railways Since 1945

Nationalisation

Transport since the Second World War has suffered from changes in government bringing changes in policy. Labour governments have been in favour of nationalisation and a planned transport policy for the country. Conservative governments have been in favour of private enterprise and competition.

The Labour government passed the Transport Act 1947, putting railways, canals, docks, steamers and many road haulage companies under government control. They were all to be planned and run as a whole by the British Transport Commission. There was little money for new investment, but the BTC tried to pull the whole railway network together. They had some success: in 1952 the railways carried 12 million tons more freight than they did in 1948. They did this with 40 000 fewer employees, 1500 fewer locomotives and 100 000 fewer wagons than in 1948.

Then in 1954 the Conservative government returned the road transport side to private companies. This stopped any cross-subsidy, that is profits from road haulage being used to modernise the railways. British Railways began to run at a loss in 1956, as the drift of passengers and freight from rail to road continued. Modernisation was begun afresh in 1954, however: diesel engines were introduced, and no more steam-engines were built after 1960.

The Beeching Report, 1963

British Railways continued to run at a loss, and in 1962 the Conservative government set up the British Railways Board, with Dr Beeching as Chairman. He was a businessman and was told to make British Railways more profitable. His Report, in 1963, pointed out that Britain in the late 20th century still had a Victorian railway system. The rural branch lines made huge losses: the quietest third of the mileage carried only 1% of the passengers and 1·5% of the freight. On the other hand, the busiest 118 stations (out of over 7000) handled 52% of the traffic.

■ SOURCE 4A

Stopping train services developed as the main form of rural public transport in the last century, when the only alternative was the horse-drawn vehicle. Today buses carry the greater part of passengers in rural areas, and these are fighting a losing battle against the private car ... It is questionable if British Railways meet as much as 10% of the total and declining demand for public rural transport ... most of the trains carry less than a busload and lose nearly twice as much as they collect in fares.

Beeching Report, 1963

■ SOURCE 4B Branch line train, 1956

■ SOURCE 4C Branch line goods train and diesel train, 1956

? QUESTIONS

a) Why was a train, like that in Source 4B, more expensive to run than a bus?
b) Why might the diesel in Source 4C be cheaper to run than the train in Source 4B?
c) How many lorries could handle the goods on the train on the right in Source 4C?
d) In what ways were goods trains like that in Source 4C
   i) expensive to run?
   ii) slow to move goods around?
   iii) similar to goods trains 100 years earlier?

Beeching recommended that British Railways should close nearly 9000 miles of its 23 000-mile network. It should concentrate on the things which railways could do well: carry large numbers of people on suburban services and run fast inter-city trains hauled by clean, cheap diesel and electric locomotives. Railways should only handle bulky freight such as coal, or run fast, containerised freight trains. Small freight loads (see Source 4C) should be left to the roads.

■ SOURCE 4D Percentage of freight and passengers carried by road and rail

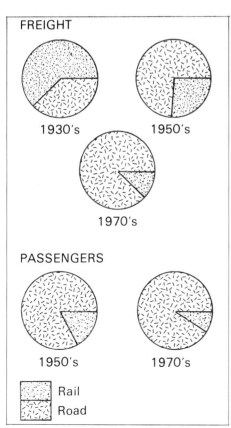

FREIGHT

1930's 1950's

1970's

PASSENGERS

1950's 1970's

□ Rail
□ Road

Beeching was never asked to consider the social cost to a rural area of losing its train service. Supporters of the railways felt that the government did not consider the cost to safety and the environment of an increase in the number of cars and lorries. They argued that the real costs of road transport are hidden because every taxpayer pays for the roads. Railways have only their customers to pay for their system. In 1971, for example, £687 million was spent on road repairs and improvements, and only £26 million on railways.

In the end the government did save some rural lines, for the sake of the people in those areas. Nevertheless, 6000 miles of track and over 2000 stations were closed. Other changes took much longer to put into effect, and meanwhile the loss of traffic continued, as Source 4D shows.

Improvements of the 1970s

By the 1970s some of Beeching's changes were beginning to take effect. Inter-City 125 trains were introduced, at first on the London–Bristol line, and later on many other main lines (Source 5A). They are the fastest diesel trains in the world, capable of 125 m.p.h., with air-conditioning and double-glazing. They have cut journey times to many cities dramatically. Freightliner trains have been intro-

■ SOURCE 5A Inter-city 125 train, 1980s

duced, although since 1970 income from passenger services has exceeded that from freight – a return to the pre-1852 situation (see Source 5B). Many suburban services still need improvement, but governments are unwilling to put the large sums needed into a transport system which now carries less than 10% of the travelling population.

? QUESTIONS

a) Compare Source 5A with Source 3B. What are the similarities and differences in 50 years?
b) Compare Source 5B with Source 4C. What are the improvements in:
   i) speed?
   ii) ease of handling?

■ SOURCE 5B Freightliner, 1980s

Private Road Transport

Bicycles

The coming of the railways brought a rapid end to the stage-coach trade before the middle of the 19th century (see Chapter 6). For a few years hardly anyone used the roads of Britain for long journeys. Traffic was only local: many people rode horses, richer people had horse-drawn carriages, and the wagoner's cart still trundled along for the poor. Then came the bicycle.

Bicycles of the 18th century were heavy and uncomfortable, and called, for good reasons, 'bone-shakers'. Improved engineering in the 19th century made steel bicycles possible. The first were the 'penny farthings' (Source 6A), invented in 1869. These were hard to steer and mount, and the 'safety bicycle' of 1885 was much more popular. The invention of pneumatic tyres by Dunlop in 1888 gave cyclists a more comfortable ride and increased the sales of bicycles.

❓ QUESTIONS

a) What do you think is the date of Source 6B? How can you tell?

b) In what ways do the bicycles in Source 6B offer an easier ride than those in Source 6A?

c) In what ways would cycling offer women more freedom? Do you think the clothes worn by the women in Source 6B were easy to cycle in?

Several firms which had been making other machines turned to making bicycles. This is why the industry centred on the engineering towns of the Midlands. By 1907, 600 000 bicycles were being made per year, by such firms as Rudge, Triumph, Humber and Sunbeam. At that time bicycles did for the general public what the car did later: they gave people freedom to travel wherever they wanted. People in industrial towns could get out to the countryside or the seaside, cycling alone, or with friends, or in clubs.

■ *SOURCE 6A* **Penny-farthing race, 1875**

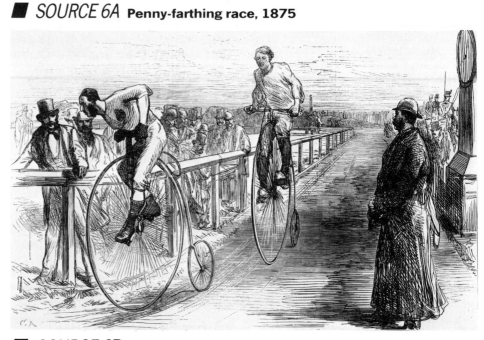

■ *SOURCE 6B* **Cycle outing**

The Motor Car

Early models

The problem with the steam-engine was that, with its furnace and boiler and water-tank, it was very big and heavy. Inventors tried to find a lighter, simpler alternative which would deliver the same power. In 1860, a Frenchman, Lenoir, invented an engine in which gas was let into the cylinders and ignited. Because the power came from inside the engine, it came to be called an internal combustion engine. In 1876, a German, Karl Otto, developed this further by using petrol and a four-stroke cycle (see Source 7).

In 1884 Daimler fixed a petrol

■ *SOURCE 7* **How an internal combustion engine works**

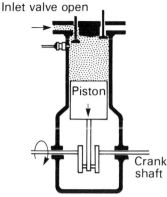
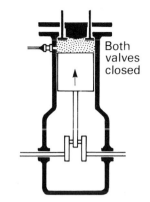
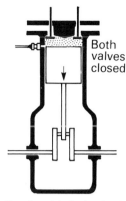

Inlet valve open

Piston

Crank shaft

On the first stroke, air and petrol is sucked into the cylinder as the piston moves down

Both valves closed

On the second, the piston moves back compressing the fuel

Both valves closed

On the third, the fuel is ignited, forcing the piston down.

Exhaust valve open

On the fourth, the piston pushes the burnt exhaust gases out of the cylinder.

engine to a motorcycle and in 1885 Benz drove a motor-powered carriage at 8 m.p.h. Progress in Britain was blocked by the Red Flag Act (see later) which restricted the running of 'horseless carriages' on the open road. When this Act was repealed in 1896, 40 cars took part in a drive from London to Brighton to celebrate. Nearly all were foreign-made, mainly French.

■ *SOURCE 8A* **Motoring, 1904**

■ *SOURCE 8B*

9 December 1895: Motor sparked at once and went well. After lunch came home in motor. Spotted by police round by Fareham. Awful crowd followed us... had to beat them off with an umbrella.

10 December 1895: Policeman called at 1.30 p.m., took our names about driving in Fareham without red flag ahead.

14 December 1895: Went for drive on common. Tyre came off.

16 December 1895: Took train for Fareham and went to court. Silly old magistrate fined us one shilling [5p] and costs 15/7*d* [78p].

27 December 1895: Frightened an unattended horse attached to a milk cart which bolted and set milk cans flying in all directions.

Diary of a motorist, 1895

? *QUESTIONS*

a) What were the main problems of motoring in the early days, as described in these sources?

b) What clues are there in these sources that motoring was confined to better-off people at that time?

Problems with motoring

As these sources make clear, in the early days motoring was difficult. Road surfaces were dusty and threw up clouds of grit. Hats, and often goggles, had to be worn. There was very little protection from wind and rain. Cars were unreliable – tyres came off, radiators boiled, brakes were bad, steering uncertain. They sometimes did not have a reverse gear. The speed limit was 12 m.p.h. until 1903, when it was raised to 20 m.p.h. Cars were capable of going faster than this, and the police set speed traps. The AA (Automobile Association) started in 1905. It placed cyclists on the road with instructions to salute AA members. If the cyclist did not salute, the car-driver knew there was a speed-trap ahead. The Royal Automobile Club (RAC) was set up in 1897.

Cars were also expensive. They were hand-built in small numbers by lots of small firms. In 1913 there were 59 different firms making cars, and 198 different models. Not surprisingly, motor-cars were bought by better-off people.

There was a good deal of opposition to cars. The Motor Car Act 1903 required cars to have lights, horns and numberplates, and to pay a 5*s* (25p) licence. There were 130 000 motor vehicles on British roads in 1914.

The First World War transformed motoring. The Army used lorries and buses a good deal. People learnt how to drive and repair motor vehicles. The petrol tax was removed in 1921, and better tyres were available.

More cars – more cheaply

The main change, however, came in the way cars were made (refer back to page 96). William Morris produced the Morris Minor, a very small car, to sell at about £100. His main rival was Herbert Austin, who had been in the car business since 1905. The Austin 7 (see Chapter 9, Source 9B, page 96) was also just over £100. At these prices motoring became a real prospect for millions of ordinary people. Cars improved – they were built with better brakes, windscreen wipers, stop lights and indicators. By the 1930s Britain had the second largest motor industry in the world.

Motorbikes with sidecars were popular in the 1920s as a cheap way of motoring for a small family. There were 600 000 motorbikes on the roads in 1932. With good cheap cars available later in the 1930s, this had dropped to 470 000 by 1938.

■ *SOURCE 9A* **Car ownership per head of population**

Year	Ratio of cars to people
1914	1:232
1922	1:78
1938	1:15
1963	1:7

■ *MAP 3* **Motorways in Britain, 1987**

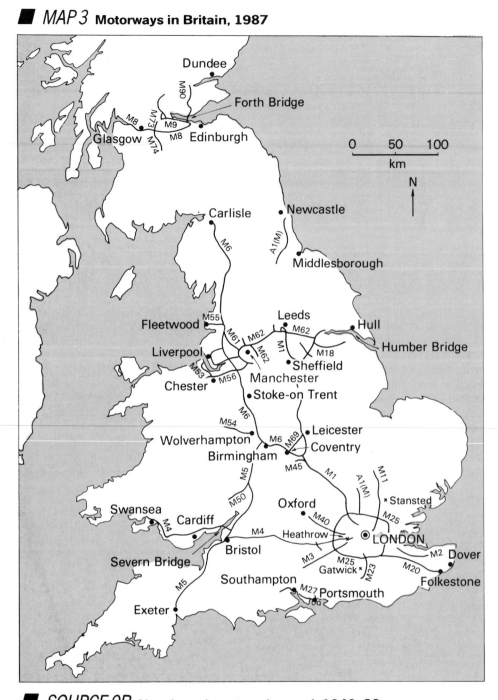

■ *SOURCE 9B* **Number of cars on the road, 1940–80**

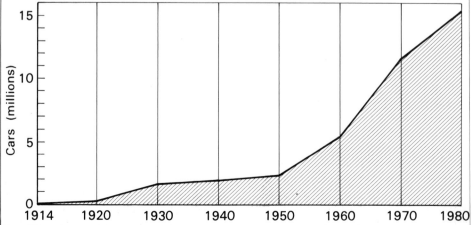

Problems of road safety

The number of accidents on the roads began to go up alarmingly. In 1930, with only just over a million cars, there were 7300 people killed and over 200 000 injured. (This was more than in 1980, with 15 times more cars.) Driving tests were introduced in 1934, and various road safety measures: traffic lights, roundabouts, pedestrian crossings and speed limits. The Highway Code was drawn up and road signs standardised.

The Second World War set back motoring, as petrol was strictly rationed. After the war, however, the motor industry started up again. As Sources 9A and 9B show, car ownership became more and more widespread. Improvements introduced in the 1950s included heaters, de-icers and radios. Cars became much more comfortable, faster, and more economical on petrol. As road accidents began to rise again to 8000 deaths in 1966, new measures were brought in: the MOT for old cars, seat-belts, and the 'breathalyser' to discourage drinking and driving.

Improvements to the roads

The huge increase in car ownership, as well as the growing bus and lorry traffic, brought a demand for better roads. The turnpike trusts (see page 43) had nearly all come to an end in the late 19th century because of competition from the railways. The job of maintaining the roads passed to local councils. They did very little apart from laying tarmac over the dusty surfaces. In 1939 Britain still had much the same road network as in 1850, with the exception of a few by-passes around some towns. Only 4% of roads were dual carriageways. Germany built the first motorways in the 1930s. In Britain the Ministry of Transport had responsibility for trunk roads, but no improvements were made until well after the Second World War.

The result was that by the 1950s British roads were quite inadequate for that traffic they had to take. A pressure-group spoke of 'bottle-necks, sharp turns, blind bends, narrow and hump-back bridges and congested built-up areas'. A

■ SOURCE 10 Traffic in towns

photograph showed a bicycle leaning against the kerb in Retford reducing the A1 to a single line of traffic. In 1958 the M1 was opened, and by the mid-1980s there were 1400 miles of motorway in Britain (see Map 3). Bridges were built over the Forth (1964), the Severn (1966) and the Humber (1981).

Too many cars?

At the same time, cars in towns and cities were producing terrible conditions: noise, fumes, parked cars blocking streets, buildings being shaken to pieces (see Source 10). Attempts to deal with this problem include one-way systems, yellow lines and parking meters. The 1963 Buchanan Report recommended more bus-lanes, no-right-turn systems, urban throughways, by-passes and ring roads. Many people feel that a better public transport system would be a much cheaper solution, but the popularity of the car is difficult to overcome.

The effects of car ownership

The growth in car ownership has had an enormous effect on the life of the people in this country.

1 Most of all, the car has given people freedom to go where they want when they want. People can travel many miles for their leisure or entertainment. Shopping is

changing: High Street shops are being abandoned in favour of huge hypermarkets on good roads outside towns. Almost any organised leisure activity relies on support from people driving to it. People can have a wider social life than they could before.

2 People can live far from their work. This has led to the growth of suburbs and 'dormitory villages': places where working people sleep only, driving off to work every morning. This process was started by trams and trains, but the car has continued it.

3 Housing has had to be planned with the car in mind. In the 1930s there was ribbon development along roads (see Chapter 11, Source 12A). New towns have had to be built with the car in mind. The newest of these, Milton Keynes, is based on a network of fast roads. Houses have to be built with one, or even two, garages.

4 The social costs of car ownership are quite high. Over 6000 people die and thousands more are injured every year on the roads. Hospitals have to care for the injured. Motorways take up vast amounts of land, and urban motorways can make life in nearby housing intolerable. Lead from petrol exhaust fumes has been shown to have serious effects, especially on children, as it accumulates in the body.

Public Road Transport

In the early days of steam-power several inventors, including Murdock and Trevithick, used steam to drive vehicles on roads. In 1834 a regular steam-carriage service was set up in London. The carriages were fast (in 1906, in the USA, a steam-car reached 120 m.p.h.). They were also big and difficult to control. However, the real reason they did not succeed was the opposition of turnpike trusts and railways. The turnpike trusts, fearing that the heavy steam-carriages would churn up their road surfaces, made them pay very heavy tolls. The railways feared competition. In 1865 Parliament passed the Red Flag Act which said that any vehicle on the road which was not horse-drawn had to have someone walking in front of it with a red flag. It also imposed a speed limit of 4 m.p.h. in the country and 2 m.p.h. in the towns. This killed off steam-power as a means of road transport in Britain.

Trams and Buses

Horse-drawn buses were run in many cities from quite early in the 19th century. Manchester's started in 1824, and had 64 different routes by 1850. Trams, running on metal lines, could carry heavier loads, and the first horse-drawn trams appeared in 1860. There were problems with laying rails on the streets, however. The Tramways Act 1870 allowed the building of tramlines if they did not stick up above the roadway. But the real breakthrough in city transport came in 1885 when trams were electrified (see Source 11B). Electric trams were cheap to run, so fares were low: 2*d* or 3*d* (about 1p), or 1*s* (5p) for all-day unlimited travel. Trams could carry up to 70 people, and were very popular as the working people's way of getting around the city. There were 2500 miles of tramway in the various cities of Britain by 1914, and 3500 million passenger journeys per year, double the number of train journeys.

■ **SOURCE 11A** Horse-drawn bus, 1847

■ **SOURCE 11B** Trams and motor bus, 1920s

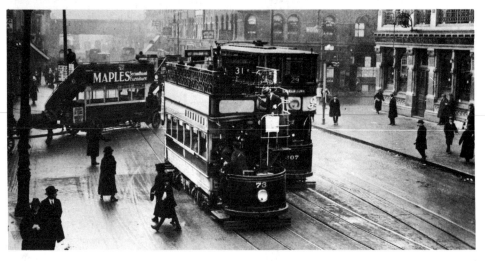

■ **SOURCE 11C** Early trolley bus, 1909

The first motor-buses were introduced in London in 1908, but were too unreliable to be successful. A new model, the Type B, began in 1910, and soon took over (see Source 11B). Horse-drawn buses were withdrawn from London and most city streets in 1914. After the First World War there were many improvements in bus design, as well as cheaper and better tyres. By 1928, 90 towns and cities had their own fleets of buses. In some places trolley-buses were used, combining the cheapness of the electric tram with the ease of movement of the bus (Source 11C).

In the First World War the Army used 1300 buses like the one in Source 11B. Many soldiers came home after the war was over, able to drive and maintain motor vehicles. Some became drivers on local buses, or for the bigger coach-hire firms. However, many bought their own buses and competed with the regular timetabled services. These 'pirate' buses would operate at peak hours only, to no timetable, and often were painted exactly the same colours as regular buses. They would race each other, causing accidents. Many were badly maintained, and the drivers were paid very low wages – 12/6 (62½p) for a 65-hour week in one case.

■ *SOURCE 12A*

No timetable existed and vehicles shuttled up and down in a continuous game of leapfrog, with an average frequency of less than a minute at peak times. Competition between individual omnibuses became general and convictions of drivers for dangerous driving and obstruction were frequent.

West Midland Traffic Commissioners, 1929, describing conditions in Stoke-on-Trent

 **QUESTIONS**

a) Explain briefly the differences between a tram, a bus and a trolley bus.
b) What are the differences between a modern double-decker bus and the bus shown in Source 11B?
c) Did the public benefit from the services described in Source 12A and Source 12B?

■ *SOURCE 12B* **Country buses, 1928**

The heyday of bus transport

To stop this, the Road Traffic Act 1930 was passed. It said that every vehicle, every driver and every service had to be licensed. This cut out some of the crazy competition and smaller operators.

Buses were more comfortable than trams, which were gradually taken out of service. The 1930s to the 1950s were the great years of the country bus. Villages far from railway stations could be served by buses, perhaps daily, or just weekly. The isolation of rural life, which was one of the reasons for the drift from the land to the towns (see Chapter 8, page 79), began to be broken. Together with subsidies to agriculture, it was the beginning of the revival of village life. In 1939, 10000 million passenger journeys were made on buses.

London had several types of public transport: buses, trams and tubes. In 1933 the London Passenger Transport Board was set up to plan all these service together. The idea was Herbert Morrison's – he was the Labour leader of London County Council. The LPTB was able to fix fares to suit different services and cross-subsidise, i.e. use profits from one part of the service to keep another going. New tube lines were built and new buses bought. Trams were gradually withdrawn.

Bus services decline

The 1950s and 1960s saw bus services begin to run into difficulties. The huge increase in car ownership (see page 112) meant fewer and fewer people using buses. Rural bus services were particularly hit, but town buses lost trade too. The National Bus Company made a loss in 1970, for the first time. Local authorities began to subsidise bus services more and more, but some were cut altogether.

■ *SOURCE 13* **Consequences of cutting country bus services**

Difficulties for young people attending Further Education classes, difficulties for those working in towns whose homes are in the country, difficulties for the elderly drawing pensions (a large number of rural Post Offices have closed in recent years), difficulties for the housewife who has to do her main shopping in towns, difficulties for those attending doctors' or dentists' surgeries, or needing to have prescriptions made up by the chemist, difficulties for those visiting patients in hospital or attending hospital for treatment.

Report of Women's Institutes, 1961

 *QUESTION*

Which groups of people are hit most when bus services are withdrawn?

■ SOURCE 14A Lorries and trucks, 1929

In spite of these warnings the decline in bus services has continued in the 1980s. Mrs Thatcher's Conservative government believed in letting services find their own level, without subsidy. The Transport Act 1986 de-regulated buses. It withdrew many of the controls put on bus services in the Road Traffic Act 1930. Any operator can now offer to run a bus on any route. As there are no subsidies, however, most operators are likely to operate the busiest, more profitable routes, and remoter areas are likely to remain without regular services.

Road Haulage

Before the First World War motor lorries were unreliable, expensive and little used. The war itself brought better lorries, and many soldiers learnt how to drive and maintain them. At the end of the war, 20000 ex-army lorries were sold off. This gave many people a start in running their own haulage business. Some large firms, such as Pickfords, survived from earlier days of wagons and canals. Many were firms of one man and one lorry.

The problems with pirate buses described above also occurred with lorries. One survey found 50% of lorries with serious mechanical defects. There was no control of the hours or training of drivers. The Road Traffic Act 1933 set up a system of licensing vehicles and drivers. Lorries also had to pay a higher road tax. The result was to raise standards, but also to help the larger firms.

Dramatic expansion

The expansion and success of road haulage has been almost completely at the expense of the railways. Lorry haulage was flexible: lorries could pick up goods from almost anywhere and deliver them in one journey to almost anywhere else: a door-to-door service that railways could not match. For most goods, road hauliers' rates were cheaper than rail freight, and journey times faster. Road haulage

■ SOURCE 14B Factories along the Great West Road, London, 1937

rates in fact fell by one third between 1919 and 1934, while railways had serious difficulty competing. Up to 100 million tons of goods were carried on the roads by 1936. There were 6 times as many lorries in 1940 as in 1914 – nearly half a million in all.

The growth of road haulage affected the location of new industries: it was more important to be on a main road than on a railway. This led to the growth of factories along main roads, such as the Great West Road (see Source 14B).

Changing control

The Second World War put the railways under great strain, as we have seen. Lorries were able to pick up trade which the railways couldn't handle. After the war, the Labour government intended to bring all forms of transport under public control, rather like the system for London under the LPTB. Along with nationalisation of the railways, all long-distance road hauliers were taken over. Altogether, 2900 businesses with 40000 lorries and many different depots were combined into British Road Services. The job was done by 1951, and BRS was able to make economies by planning the whole system. There were fewer lorries running empty, because return loads could be arranged, and better maintenance. However, the Conservatives won the 1951 election, committed to de-nationalising road haulage. The Road Haulage Association and the British Road Federation pressed for this to happen, and road haulage was de-nationalised in 1953.

Road haulage has continued to grow since 1953. The amount of goods carried on the roads increased by 60% in the 1950s. As Source 4D (page 109) shows, 83% of national freight was being carried on the roads by 1970. Lorries have grown bigger until the juggernaut – 40-ton vehicle – is now common. The tachograph was introduced as a safety measure. It records the mileage and the number of hours driven, thus enabling a check to be kept on speed, and also the tiredness of drivers. Heavy lorries are not popular with the public, but we are now utterly dependent on them for most of our industrial transport.

Water Transport

Shipping

Early steamships

Steam-power was applied to boats even before it was used on the railways. By 1850 steamships played an important part in coastal trade, as passenger boats and tugs. There were serious problems preventing the use of steamships on ocean-going services. One was reliability: a breakdown a few miles offshore was serious, but it would be disastrous in mid-Atlantic. Another was the fact that early steamboats were all paddle-steamers, which had difficulty running in heavy seas. Most serious of all, however, was the huge amount of coal needed to make long voyages. Early steam-engines used so much coal that there was hardly any room on board for cargo. Ships were still made of wood, so there were limits on the size of vessel which could be built. For these reasons *sailing* ships continued to dominate international trade. Norway and the USA, with cheap timber, had the largest fleets.

The first serious attempts to overcome these problems with steamships were made by the extraordinary inventor, Isambard Kingdom Brunel. Having designed the Great Western Railway from London to Bristol, he set about designing a steamship to take passengers on to New York. His 1500-ton paddle-steamer, the *Great Western*, did the journey in 14 days, in 1838. The same year Francis Pettitt-Smith invented the screw propeller. Brunel used this in the *Great Britain*, launched in 1845. It was the first iron ship, and the first with screw propellers, to cross the Atlantic. His final answer to the problem of carrying enough coal was the *Great Eastern*, launched, with some difficulty, in 1858. It was an enormous ship for its time, weighing 20000 tons. Not until 1901 was a larger ship launched. It was powered by paddles, sail and screw propellers, and its engines burnt 300 tons of

■ SOURCE 15A *Great Eastern*, 1858

■ SOURCE 15B Placing the paddle-shaft on the deck of the *Great Eastern*

coal a day. Nevertheless it was so large that it could still take 4000 passengers and 5000 tons of cargo, and cross the Atlantic in 11 days.

Sadly, the *Great Eastern* was dogged by bad luck. Five people were killed on her maiden voyage, the owners went bankrupt, and she ended her days as a cable-layer (see page 246). Sheer size did not seem to be an answer to the problems of ocean-going steamships.

? QUESTIONS

a) Why do you think the *Great Eastern* had sails as well as paddles and propellers?

b) The *Great Eastern* was a commercial failure. Is it of any interest to a historian?

SOURCE 16A Clipper under full sail, 1870s

The last days of sail

In fact the years 1850–1870 were the last great days of sailing ships. Most famous were the clippers, the fastest sailing ships ever built. The original design was American, but the British-built clippers had an iron frame with wooden planks. This made then even lighter and faster. Steam-winches allowed the crew to control an enormous spread of sail (see Source 16A). At a top speed of 16 knots they could overtake any steamboat of their day, and sail from Australia to Britain in 60 days. They were used to carry tea from China, wool and grain from Australia, and nitrate fertiliser from Chile. The most famous were the *Cutty Sark* and the *Thermopylae*.

SOURCE 16B Travel at sea in the 1850s

11 January, 1856: At dinner struck by a heavy sea, which created quite a commotion among the dishes, for all the contents were mixed up together. You have to hold on to your plate to keep it near you, hold on to your glass of water to avoid the unnecessary luxury of a shower-bath...

15 January: During the night another gale has sprung up ... Very little sail set. While on the main deck got several drenchings for the sea is coming right over the rail. I was amused by seeing the Pig (the only one on board) washed right along the deck by a sea; fortunately it did not go overboard.

❓ QUESTIONS

a) How many sails has the clipper in Source 16A? Why so many?

b) In Source 16B, why was very little sail set in the gale?

c) Why was there a pig on board?

Steel steamships

Eventually various inventions made the end of the sailing-ship inevitable. The most important was the compound engine, invented in 1804, but not developed until 1854 by John Elder. It used the steam from the main cylinder again to drive a second piston. The engine needed only two thirds as much coal, and ships could therefore be lighter, carry more cargo and go further. In 1865 a steamship went from London to Mauritius, 8000 miles, without re-loading with coal.

By the 1860s much cheaper steel was being made, so steel ships could be built. They were lighter than wooden ships and could withstand the pounding of the sea and the vibration of the engines. The screw propeller proved much better than the paddle-wheel, as Brunel had shown. The opening of the Suez Canal, in 1869, was a great help to steamships. Sailing ships could not sail through the Canal, and towing was too expensive. From 1869 more steamships than sailing ships were built, although sail was still used well into the 20th century: in 1914 one-quarter of the British merchant fleet were sailing ships.

The years from 1850 to 1914 were great years for British shipping. Britain's industry was leading the world, so there were raw materials to bring to Britain and manufactured goods to carry away (Source 17).

In addition there were tramp steamers: cargo boats which carried goods of any kind from port to port anywhere in the world. British-owned, they might not touch British shores from one year to another. The cable-telegraph allowed the owners to arrange cargoes and keep in touch.

British merchant shipping increased from 3.6 million tons in 1850 to 11.6 million tons in 1910. Nearly half the world's trade was carried in British ships by 1910. (See Chapter 9, pages 89–90 for details on the shipbuilding industry of the time.)

Safety at sea

Despite progress, travel at sea was still very dangerous. Many lives were lost every year. Some of these losses were caused by incompetent captains or ships overloaded or in a bad condition. The Merchant Shipping Act 1850 laid down basic standards of food and living space for the crew. The Act also required captains and mates to pass an examination. However, many ship-owners still often cared little about the condition of their ships.

SOURCE 18

I have had plenty of opportunity of seeing the sort of 'coffins' in which sailors are sent to sea .... One merchant who I could name lost

SOURCE 17 Increases in goods carried, 1850–1913

Imports	Increase (times)	Exports	Increase (times)
Cotton	3	Cotton goods	5
Wool	11	Iron and steel	6
Grain	7	Coal	24

two or three vessels every year, and generally all hands with the vessels. I have seen dozens of such vessels where the planks are so rotten that pieces of wood have to be driven into the seams .... They would make a passage across the Channel in the middle of winter with perhaps 18 inches of side above water .... Often the crew have refused to proceed in the ships, having regard for their own safety. Very often they were imprisoned for doing so.

Letter to Samuel Plimsoll MP, 1876

? QUESTION

a) Why could the crew be put in prison for refusing to go to sea in a 'coffin ship'?

Samuel Plimsoll took up the issue of safety at sea in Parliament. The Acts of 1875 and 1876 required a mark to be painted on the side of every ship to show how much load she was to carry. This mark is called the Plimsoll line, but at first the owners could place it where they wished. Only after 1890 did government inspectors decide where the line should go.

By the end of the century better lighthouses and lightships had been built, and regulations ensured that lifeboats were provided. The big shipowners who led the growth of British shipping saw the advantage of high safety standards. In 1875 Cunard could say they hadn't lost a life or a letter in 34 years.

New docks and harbours

The huge growth of shipping required docks to handle goods. Railway companies were involved in building several docks: Barrow-in-Furness, Grimsby, Hull, Cardiff and Southampton. Smaller ports declined as the better facilities at the large docks took more and more trade. By 1900, 75% of Britain's trade was handled by only 12 ports. Liverpool docks were well run by the Mersey Docks and Harbour Board, set up in 1857. This body controlled some 12 miles of quayside and kept the river clear. London docks were the biggest, but were not well organised. Trade increased from three-quarters of a million tons in 1820 to 10 million tons in 1901. New docks were built: West India, East India, Commercial, Surrey, St Katherine's, and the Millwall docks,

■ SOURCE 19A Liverpool Docks, built in 1845

completed in 1870. Not until 1909, however, were all of them brought together under the Port of London Authority.

■ SOURCE 19B London Docks

As you enter the dock the sight of the forest of masts in the distance and the tall chimneys vomiting clouds of black smoke ... has a most peculiar effect; While sheds with monster wheels arching through the roof look like the paddle-boxes of huge steamers. Along the quay you see men with their faces blue with indigo, then a group of flaxen-haired sailors chattering German, next a black sailor with a cotton handkerchief twisted around his head, then a mate, with green parrots in a wooden cage. Here you will see sitting on a bench a sorrowful-looking woman, with new bright cooking tins at her feet, telling you she is an emigrant preparing for her voyage.

Mayhew's London

? QUESTIONS

a) What can you tell about the trade of Liverpool in 1845, from Source 19A?
b) What can you tell about the trade of Liverpool now, from Source 19A?

Passenger ships

The other huge business in shipping was passenger liners. Until the 1950s these were the only way for people to cross the oceans. In the 19th century millions of Europeans emigrated, mainly to the USA, but also to Australia, Canada, New Zealand and South Africa. From 1845 to 1855, two and a half million people emigrated to the USA (see page 267). There was also a regular high-class passenger trade to the various parts of the British empire, especially India. The invention of the turbine engine by Parsons in 1884 greatly improved speeds. This was especially important on the Atlantic run between the USA and Europe. By the early 20th century large, fast luxury liners from Britain, France and Germany competed for the 'Blue Riband' – the award for the fastest crossing. This was won in 1907 by the Cunard ocean liner *Mauretania*. The huge changes in trans-Atlantic travel over 70 years can be seen in Source 20 (over).

The fact that sea travel was still dangerous, even in the 20th century, was shown in 1912, when the huge liner *Titanic* sank on her maiden voyage. There were not enough lifeboats and over 1500 people drowned.

■ *SOURCE 20*

Date	Ship	Construction	Size	Power	Journey time
1838	*Sirius*	Wooden	700 tons	Steam, paddle	16 days
1871	*Oceania*	Iron	3 800 tons	Steam, screw propeller	9½ days
1907	*Mauretania*	Steel	32 000 tons	Turbine, with screw propeller	4½ days

The decline of British shipping

During the First World War, the government took over what ships they needed, and paid very good rates. By 1917, 90% of imports were government-controlled, and shipowners made healthy profits. During the war 2.6 million tons of British ships were sunk.

The next 20 years were disastrous for British shipping. Other countries had built up their own industries and their own shipping fleets to support them. The goods carried by British ships – coal and cotton – (see Source 17) were just those industries in most trouble in those years. There were too many ships looking for too little trade, so the shipbuilding industry collapsed. Other countries subsidised their shipbuilders, or paid them to scrap old ships and build new ones. This was not done in Britain, and the profits of wartime trading were not put into building new ships either. The British share of world shipping fell from 43% in 1914, to 26% in 1938.

With few new ships, Britain was not prepared for changes in world trade. Oil tankers were 3% of world tonnage in 1914, 53% by 1938. Other countries, like Norway, Greece and Japan, were able to get into this business quickly. Diesel-engined vessels were introduced, too, and again Britain was slow off the mark in building them.

This decline in Britain's position was halted after the Second World War. New vessels were built and world trade recovered. Trans-Atlantic airliners brought an end to passenger liners by the 1960s, but oil tankers and freighters continued to increase in size. Containerised freight increased in popularity and brought the decline of old docks, such as London, which could not handle them. Container ports, such as Tilbury and Felixstowe, did well.

The world trade recession of the 1980s has meant that many ships are lying idle again.

Canals

Canal transport continued to decline from 1850 to the 1960s. As we saw in Chapter 6, railway companies bought up many canals in order to cripple them as competition. Narrow-boats were also very limited in what they could carry, because of their width. In the 1930s lorries were being built which could carry as much as a narrow-boat, but at five times the speed. In 1919, 22 million tons of freight were still being carried on canals; by 1938 this had fallen to 13 million tons.

Such a decline was not inevitable. In the 1880s in France 820 miles of new, wider canal were built, and over 5000 miles improved. There are still goods – heavy, bulky, non-perishable items – for which canals are the most suitable means of transport, and several European countries use them. In Britain, there was some canal improvement in the late 19th century: the Aire and Calde Navigation in South Yorkshire was made big enough for sea-going barges. The Manchester Ship Canal was built between 1887 and 1893, to bring ocean-going vessels into Manchester.

Such improvements were not carried out on other parts of the canal network. Nowadays canals in Britain are almost totally unused by commercial vessels, but are being restored for pleasure-boats.

❓ QUESTIONS

a) What kinds of goods would have been brought up to Manchester when the canal was first built?

b) Compare this picture with Chapter 6, Source 10D, page 51 which shows a narrow-boat canal. What are some of the advantages of broad canals that can be seen in Source 21?

c) Explain why most British canals remained as narrow-boat canals in the 19th century and were not widened.

■ *SOURCE 21* **Manchester Ship Canal, mid-20th century**

Air Transport

This chapter has described the rapid changes in rail, road and water transport since 1900. None of these changes have been as rapid as the growth of air transport. At the opening of the 20th century it seemed impossible that people would be able to fly, except in lighter-than-air vehicles, such as balloons. Nowadays millions of people travel by air as ordinary passengers.

Airships

Balloon flight became possible from the Montgolfier's flight in Paris in 1783. The trouble was that the passengers had no control over what direction they were moving in. Steam-engines were far too heavy and bulky to provide power in balloons. It was not until the petrol-engine was invented that powered lighter-than-air flight was possible Germany took the lead, building several Zeppelins in the years after 1900. They were used for civil air

travel and then, in the First World War, for bombing raids. After the war, other countries developed them. They were so large that a high standard of accommodation was possible.

■ SOURCE 22B Travel on the German airship *Hindenburg*

Outside the public rooms were 15-metre walkways connected by a cross-passage. These gave a walking distance of 60 metres. Outside the walkways were 6 large plexiglass windows, often left open as there was no draught, even at 95 m.p.h. Here the passengers stood or sat for hours, enthralled by the sight of foaming waves, tossing ships, rivers and cities.

Douglas Robinson, 1936

❓ QUESTIONS

a) Why was it possible to provide so much space on an airship?
b) What was the attraction of airship travel for the passengers?

Unfortunately the R101 crashed in 1930, and the *Hindenburg* caught

fire in 1937. Airship flight was discredited, and people turned instead to aircraft.

Aeroplanes

The Wright Brothers flew the first heavier-than-air machine for 12 seconds in 1903; for some years after only pioneers took to the air. Engines were weak, so aircraft were made of wood and canvas. As with several other forms of transport, the First World War provided a great boost. Aeroplanes gained rapidly in power, size and speed, and pilots and mechanics learnt their skills.

After the war, various attempts were made to set up commercial flights. Nearly all ended in failure, and the bankruptcy of the companies. There were several reasons for this: planes still only carried four or five passengers, so fares were expensive. Flight was still regarded as dangerous by most people, and certainly there were few navigation aids. Pilots used to navigate by following roads or railways, and night flying was impossible. This meant that flights were often cancelled – up to 25% of them on average and up to 40% in Scotland in winter. Speeds were low too – only about 150 m.p.h. With improvements in train services it was hardly worthwhile to travel by plane in a small island like Britain. Where aeroplanes could make a difference was in flights to other countries or to islands which were part of Britain. Routes to Paris, Brussels, Amsterdam and the Channel Islands were established by 1923.

Other countries believed in the future of air transport and subsidised their air companies. Britain followed suit in 1924, by setting up Imperial Airways. The British government aimed to keep up links with the British empire, in Africa and Asia. Imperial Airways flew to South Africa, Kenya, India and the Far East, as well as Europe. For some of these routes there were no airports, so flying-boats were used, which could land on a lake, or calm sea. These were very comfortable, with bunks for use at night (see Source 23A over).

Aircraft size and comfort increased, and so did the number of travellers. In 1919 there were 64 000 passengers per year,

■ SOURCE 22A R101, British airship, 1930

■ *SOURCE 23A* **Princess Flying Boat, 1930s**

153 000 by 1929, and 210 000 by 1939. British Airways was set up in 1935 to deal with European routes, but in 1939 it was amalgamated with Imperial Airways into the British Overseas Airways Corporation, BOAC.

■ *SOURCE 23B* **Flying in the 1930s**

We had to carry all the baggage on board and if the seats weren't fastened down tightly we had to screw them down. Then we had to dust the whole plane. Some of us had to join bucket brigades to help fuel the planes. If the weather got bad we would land in a field for a while and wait for the storm to clear up.

Interview with a former air stewardess, *New York Times*, 1970

■ *SOURCE 23C* **Steward serving drinks on a plane, 1930s**

? *QUESTIONS*

a) How does an air stewardess's job in the 1930s, as described in Source 23B, differ from the job today?
b) What does Source 23B tell you about aeroplanes in the 1930s?
c) Use these sources to describe the advantages and disadvantages of air travel in the 1930s.

The Second World War again brought improvements in air travel. Radar improved navigation enormously. The jet engine, invented by Sir Frank Whittle in 1930, was developed during the war. Afterwards it was used in turbo-jets, such as the Vickers Viscount: this used a jet engine to drive propellers. The de Havilland Comet was the first jet airliner, but there were several accidents following its maiden flight in 1952. The lead in aircraft design and manufacture passed to the USA, to firms like Boeing and McDonnell-Douglas.

Modern growth

The number of air travellers doubled every 10 years from 1960. Apart from people who travel for their work, there has been an enormous growth in numbers of people going on holiday by air. Large aircraft, capable of seating over 500 people, have been built. British Airways, formed in 1972, serves over 150 airports, the largest number of any airline in the world.

The growth of air travel has brought several new industries. Even so, because of the high costs of development, aircraft building has not been very profitable. Rolls Royce built the highly-successful RB211 engine, but went bankrupt in the process. They were taken over by the government in 1970. Concorde, an aircraft designed to carry passengers faster than ever before and capable of crossing the Atlantic in three and a half hours, has not been a commercial success. Only 16 have been built. They are expensive (£1000 million to build), take fewer passengers than traditional aircraft, and are very noisy.

The air transport business provides many jobs in the 1980s. Electronics firms make navigation aids. Construction firms build new airports, or new terminals at old ones. London Heathrow and Gatwick have expanded in recent years, and a third airport will be built at Stansted in Essex. Travel firms, ground staff and airline services have also increased in numbers to provide for the new industry.

Assignments

Empathy

1 Use Sources 1B – 1F to describe a journey from your home to Central London, in 1900. Describe what you saw, felt, ate, smelt and your reactions to these things.

2 Use Sources 23A, 23B and 23C to describe a journey in a passenger aircraft in the 1930s.

3 Car ownership is expensive: thousands die in accidents each year, and cars clog up our towns and cities. Yet more and more people are becoming car drivers. How do you explain this?

Understanding concepts

1 Causation

Faults of the railway system
Unfair competition
Advantages of petrol engine over steam engine
Two major wars
Other reasons

Use these five items to explain the decline of the railway system up to 1960.

2 Factors for change

Explain how wars in this century have led to changes in:
i rail **ii** car **iii** lorry and **iv** aeroplane transport in Britain.

3 Causation

The decline of sailing ships and their replacement by steamships had several causes.

a List the causes of the change.
b Were *all* the causes of equal importance?
c Which was the most important, in your opinion? Give reasons for your answer.

4 Cause/effect

Production line methods
Independent travel
The internal combustion engine
Accidents
Decline of buses
Higher wages and salaries

a Choose two of the above which were important *causes* of the growth in the use of motor cars. Explain your choice.
b Choose two of the above which were important *effects* of the growth in the use of motor-cars. Explain your choice.

Themes for discussion

1 There has been a huge rise in private transport such as cars and a decline in public transport such as buses and trains in the last 20 years.
a Is this desirable?
b Is this inevitable?

2 a Cars and lorries bring tremendous benefits to our way of life. What are they?
b Cars and lorries are also often very unpopular. In which situations?
c Is there any way out of these contradictions?

3 Discuss whether or not the government should play a part in transport policy. It might help if you consider each of the developments below and discuss whether government was involved and if so, whether its impact was positive or negative.
  i Building the railway network in the 1840s and 1850s (See Chapter 6);
  ii Growth of bus and lorry transport in the 1920s;
  iii Decline of the railways in the 1930s;
  iv Railways under nationalisation, 1948 to 1960;
  v The Beeching Report 1963 and its results;
  vi Traffic in towns in the last 20 years;
  vii Bus de-regulation, 1986.

11 The Growth of Cities 1700–1980s

SOURCE 1A Leeds, 1715

SOURCE 1B Modern aerial photograph of part of Manchester

Why Did Cities Grow?

Look at Sources 1A and 1B. Leeds in 1715 was a small town: the fields pressed in on the houses, and the hills could be seen from every street. Source 1B shows a typical modern city scene: factories, rows of houses, a canal, busy roads and no countryside in sight. There were towns in Britain in 1715, but most were only as big as Leeds, and only London was really large. In fact four out of five people lived in rural areas. Nowadays the reverse is true: four out of five people live in urban areas. Of all the changes which the Industrial Revolution brought, the greatest was this total change in the life-styles, homes and habits of the British people.

❓ QUESTIONS

a) What clues are there in Sources 1A and 1B which would tell you the date of each?
b) In Source 1B, find: the canal, church, factory chimneys, factories, shops, flats, offices.

From fields to factories

We saw in Chapter 1 that the population of Britain rose rapidly from 10.7 million in 1751 to 27.4 million in 1851. Most of these people were, of course, born in the countryside. Agriculture was improving and, in fact, the population of rural areas of Britain rose by 88% between 1751 and 1831. However, farming could not offer increased employment to match the increase in population. Agricultural wages were low and irregular. The new factories and workshops created by the Industrial Revolution, however, needed thousands of workers. The move to the cities began and became a flood: the population rose in urban areas between 1751 and 1831 by 129%.

At first people did not move very far: perhaps only about 10 miles, to the nearest town. Here they often moved in with friends or relations and could keep in contact with the family at home. However, most of the people who moved to towns were in the 15–25 age-group. They felt free to move on again if they saw better prospects. They were joined by people from very depressed parts of Great Britain, such as Ireland, and even from other parts of Europe (see Chapter 26). Cities grew and grew, drawing in people of many different races and cultures, nearly all of them country-born.

London saw the most remarkable growth: ⅓ million people went to live in London in the years 1831–41 alone. Most came from other parts of England, but there were, amongst them, 46 000 Irish, 8000 Scots and 26 000 Jews. By 1851 there were 100 000 Irish and 35 000 Jews in London.

■ *SOURCE 3* **The shift from rural to urban population**

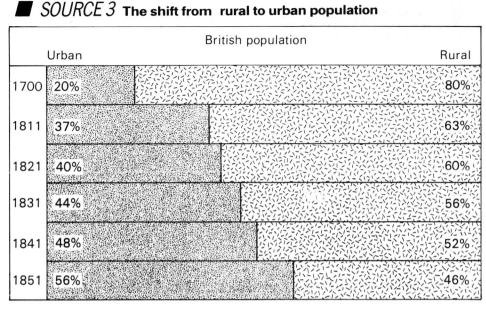

British population

	Urban	Rural
1700	20%	80%
1811	37%	63%
1821	40%	60%
1831	44%	56%
1841	48%	52%
1851	56%	46%

? *QUESTIONS*

a) What does Source 2 tell you about London at this time?
b) Limehouse is near London Docks. Why do you think there would be a number of different nationalities here?
c) Why do you think London attracted so many nationalities?
d) What facilities did the Strangers' Home offer?

People at the time watched the balance between town and country gradually swing over. By 1851 the majority of British people were townsfolk (see Source 3).

Which Towns and Cities Grew?

Industries do not always create towns. For example, mining and fishing are often carried out in villages. In Chapter 3, Source 3 (page 17) we read that the early textile industry was carried on in the rural cottages around Halifax. However, as soon as powered machines were invented, factories were built. Soon factory-owners were building bigger and bigger factories to make use of their powerful steam engines. They needed lots of workers, especially in the cotton textile industry. Lancashire experienced the most spectacular growth of population: in 1751 there were 318 000 people in the county but by 1821 the population topped 1 million. Most of these people lived in towns, the biggest of which was Manchester, with 303 000 people by 1851.

Early towns had no good public transport. Before the coming of the railway, the bus and the tram, workers had to live close to the factories. This produced the close packing of houses, factories, schools, shops and churches you can see in Sources 1B and 4A. The workers woke to the sound of the factory hooter, and their houses

■ *SOURCE 2* **The Strangers' Home, Limehouse, mid-19th century**

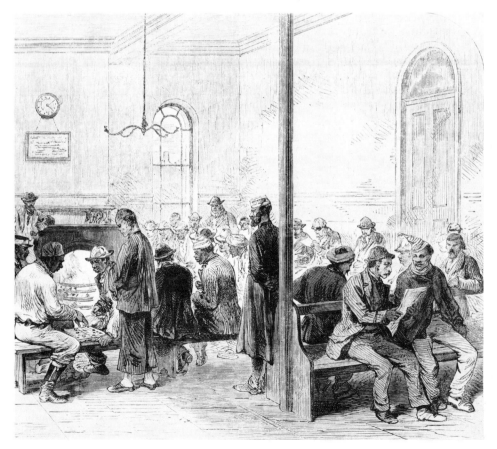

■ *SOURCE 4A* **Oldham – a Lancashire cotton-spinning town**

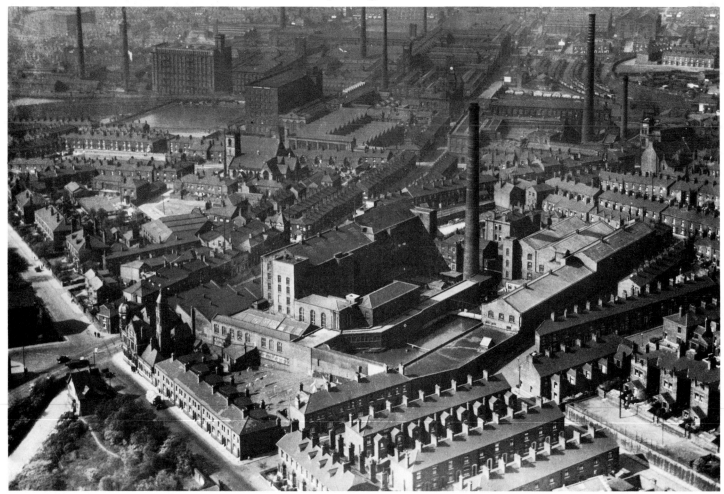

were blackened by the smoke from the factory chimneys. Because everything had to be in walking distance, these early city landscapes were called 'the walking city'. Even the countryside was in walking distance.

■ *SOURCE 4B*

Only half an hour's walk from Manchester was an old black and white farmhouse, with its rambling out-buildings. Here, in their seasons, may be seen the country business of hay-making, ploughing, etc. . . . . Here the worker, deafened with the voice of tongues and engines, may come to listen awhile to the delicious sounds of rural life: the lowing of cattle, the milk-maid's call, the clatter and cackle of poultry in the old farmyard.

Mrs Gaskell, *Mary Barton*, 1848

❓ *QUESTIONS*

a) Find the terraced housing and the factories in Source 4A.

b) What would be the advantages and disadvantages of home and work being so close together? List as many as you can.
c) What other buildings can you see in Source 4A?
d) What reasons does Mrs Gaskell give in Source 4B for town-dwellers to visit the country?
e) What other reasons can you think of? (Compare Source 4B with Source 4A.)
f) Source 4B is taken from a novel. Comment on its usefulness to a historian studying the towns of Britain in the 19th century.

The great cotton mills were certainly impressive, but it would be wrong to think everyone worked in them. Even in Lancashire the cotton industry employed only one third of the working population. Cities contained many other trades and industries. The finishing trades, specialist machine-makers and repairers gathered round the factories. In the engineering industry four fifths of the works employed

fewer than 10 people, but they clustered together near their suppliers and markets. The arrival of canals and railways increased this concentration. Businesses wanted to be near the wharves or railway stations. Cities provided other services: banks, lawyers and accountants, for example, which were also needed. Source 5 gives some of the towns and cities which expanded in this period.

■ *SOURCE 5* **Examples of urban population growth**

	1750	1851
London	657 000	2 491 000
Liverpool	22 000	376 000
Glasgow	23 000	345 000
Manchester	18 000	303 000
Birmingham	24 000	233 000
Leeds	10 000	172 000
Bristol	50 000	137 000
Newcastle	28 000	88 000
Preston	5 000	70 000
Norwich	35 000	68 000
Brighton	5 000	66 000

■ SOURCE 6 **Hastings, 1895**

? QUESTIONS

a) From Source 6, how can you tell that Hastings is only just beginning to grow?
b) What facilities for leisure activities are there in this picture?

The Problems of the Cities

Housing

With so many people wanting to work and live in towns, there was a tremendous need for housing. Older towns had large houses which were divided up. There were families on each floor, or even families in each room. The workers in the 'walking city' needed housing near to the factories. Builders soon realised they could make good profits from cheap housing, built quickly for high rents. Thousands of terraces of houses were built in this way. Many were jerry-built, that is badly built, with poor foundations, cheap materials, and very few facilities. However, they were built fast, and many Victorians were shocked as the towns spread out into the fields. In many towns in Northern England 'back-to-backs' were built: two rows of houses under one roof, with small rooms and poor ventilation.

? QUESTIONS

a) From Source 5, calculate which of these towns have shown the greatest percentage increase.
b) The list is written in the rank order for 1851, starting with the largest at the top of the list. Work out the rank order for 1750: which towns have moved up, or down, the list?
c) Mark all the towns on a blank map of Britain. Which are in the south and east, which are in the north and west?

Three of the towns on the list are in Lancashire – Liverpool, Manchester and Preston. A great deal of the output of the Industrial Revolution was exported, so ports such as London, Liverpool, Glasgow, Cardiff, Newcastle, Bristol and Hull expanded. Birmingham, Sheffield and the towns of the Black Country grew with the iron, steel and engineering industries.

You might have noticed that some towns on your list, such as Norwich, did not grow very fast. Norwich, along with York, Exeter, Bristol and Newcastle, had been an important centre before the Industrial Revolution. Then the new cities grew so fast that these old towns were overtaken.

It might surprise you that one of the biggest population growths in Source 5 is at Brighton. The main industry here was holidays. There was a huge increase in numbers of people taking seaside holidays in the 19th century, especially later on, when railways made it possible for people to travel to the coast quickly and easily. Before 1800 there was no interest in the seaside at all. Then towns grew up all around the coast. Brighton and Scarborough were the first, soon followed by Blackpool, Bournemouth, Torquay and many other places.

■ SOURCE 7A **'The March of Bricks and Mortar', by Cruikshank, 1829**

■ SOURCE 7B Back-to-backs in Nottingham, 1840s

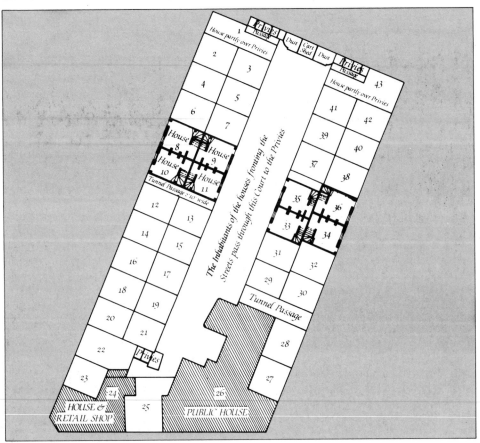

■ SOURCE 7C Bricklayers, 1840s

? QUESTIONS

a) In Source 7A (previous page) find the bricks, mortar and chimney pots; find also trees, haystacks and animals.

b) How does the cartoonist indicate that the houses are jerry-built?

c) What is Cruikshank's attitude to the growth of London?

d) How can you tell his attitude?

e) In Source 7B, find the privies. How many are there? What health hazard would this create?

f) What other health hazards were posed by these back-to-back dwellings?

g) In Source 7C, what kind of house is being built?

h) Do you think it is being built well?

i) The builders seem proud of their work: does that mean the house will be well-built?

j) How far does the evidence of Source 7C help to prove or disprove the truth of Cruikshank's cartoon, Source 7A?

k) What would you want to know about Source 7C to help your answer question j) further?

l) Source 7B is from a Report to Parliament: does that mean it is reliable evidence of housing in parts of Nottingham at that time?

m) Which of these three sources is the most useful to a historian trying to find out the truth about housing in cities in the early 19th century? Explain your answer.

If overcrowding was bad in English cities, in Scotland it was far worse. There was a tradition in Scotland of tenements: tall blocks of five, six or even seven storeys, with stairways (see Source 8).

One or two-roomed flats opened off the common stairs. This led to rather complicated addresses, such as 'Bridegate No. 29, back landing, stair first left, 3 up, right lobby, door facing'. People were horrified when it was revealed that 35% of the population of Finsbury, in London, lived more than two to a room. In Glasgow it was 55%, and in Dundee 63%.

Health

The overcrowding of people into houses built very close together was only part of a very serious health problem in all industrial towns and cities (see Chapter 13.) At that time no one understood the need for clean water, good drainage, sewage systems and refuse disposal. The builders of the industrial housing did not have to provide them, and the overcrowding made things worse.

■ *SOURCE 9A*

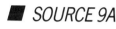

In one cul-de-sac in Leeds there are 34 houses, and in ordinary times, there dwell in these houses 340 persons, or ten to every house. The name of this place is Boot and Shoe Yard from whence the Commissioners removed, in the days of cholera, 75 cartloads of manure, which had been untouched for years.

To build the largest number of cottages on the smallest space seems to have been the original view of the speculators. Thus neighbourhoods have arisen in which there is neither water, nor offices [privies].

An Inquiry into the State and Condition of the Town of Leeds, 1842

■ *SOURCE 9B*

Suitable housing did not exist and the additional numbers were crammed into every nook and cranny from attic to cellar of old decaying property, or into cottages run up hastily in confined spaces with little or no access to light and air. Water and sanitation were often not provided at all, and where they were provided there was often a mixture of cesspools and wells, with an occasional overstocked graveyard or active slaughterhouse.... Since many industries now used coal furnaces and most domestic fires burned coal, from many towns a heavy sulphurous smoke was emitted to combine with other atmospheric conditions to make the fogs which were such a feature of Victorian England, and which probably slew thousands.

Such conditions were not new, nor probably were they worse than what had existed before. But as numbers increased, so these evils increased.

G. Kitson Clark, *The Making of Victorian England*, 1965 (adapted)

■ SOURCE 8 Tenements in Glasgow, 1868

❓ QUESTIONS

a) What dangers to health are mentioned in Source 9A?

b) What are the dangers to health mentioned in Source 9B?

c) Source 9A is a primary source, and Source 9B is a secondary source about 19th century housing. How can you tell?

d) Does the fact that Source 9B is secondary mean that it is less reliable than Source 9A?

e) How do you think the author of Source 9B reached the conclusions he gives in this extract?

The fact is that diseases flourished in all the industrial towns: typhus, tuberculosis, measles, smallpox, typhoid and cholera all took their toll. Even as late as 1893, when life expectancy in rural areas was 51 years, in Manchester it was 28 years. Babies and children were most at risk: the death rate of working-class under-fives in Preston in 1851 was 63 per 1000. There was also a close connection between overcrowding and death: areas with more than half the housing in back-to-backs had a death rate of 37 per 1000, those without back-to-backs 26 per 1000.

There was one thing which no photo, or diagram, or description of industrial cities can give us: the smell. In addition to the sewage and pollution from chimneys there were, in every city, cow-sheds and piggeries, breweries and glue factories, rotting vegetables from the market, smoking fish from the curers, and a background smell of decay from the overcrowded graveyards. It was in this environment that the millions of new city-dwellers lived their lives.

City Growth 1850–1945

Cities continued to grow, in size and in population, for many years after 1850.

■ SOURCE 10 Urban and rural population (millions)

	1841	1911
Urban areas	8.7	23.8
Rural areas	6.2	7.0

Most remarkable of all was the continuing growth of London, from 2.3 million in 1841 to 7.3 million in 1911, and over 9 million by 1945.

The continued growth of London and all the other big cities was made possible by improvements in transport (see Chapter 10). Horse-drawn buses, suburban trains, electric trams, motor buses and then motor cars all allowed people to live far from their workplace. Suburbs were originally built for the better-off who could afford to travel (see Chapter 12). Then, as transport became cheaper and faster, these commuters moved further out. City centres became places of work, entertainment and shopping only. The poor, finding their city centre homes demolished, moved into the older, inner suburbs. Some inner suburbs were also built from the start as working-class neighbourhoods.

As towns and cities grew in size, those near each other began to merge. The suburbs of one reached the suburbs of another, producing 'conurbations'. The conurbation in West Yorkshire, for example, includes Bradford, Huddersfield, Leeds, Halifax, Wakefield, Batley, Dewsbury, Pudsey, Shipley and other towns and villages which had previously been quite separate. The other six conurbations in Britain by the early 20th century were on Tyneside, Merseyside, Clydeside, West Midlands, Manchester and, of course, London.

Garden cities

As explained in Chapters 13 and 16, attempts were made to deal with the problems of city life, such as bad public health and poor housing. A highly original proposal to

deal with the problem was put forward in 1898 by Ebenezer Howard. He saw the rival attractions of town and country, and so suggested the idea of 'garden cities' to get the best of both worlds (see Source 11A). Each of his garden cities would be set in the countryside with plenty of open space. Business and industry would be provided but separated from housing (see Source 4A). Housing would be built to good designs with enough space for all. Companies would be formed to buy the land on which the garden cities would be built. Any profits which they made could be spent to the benefit of those who lived there. Each garden city should have about

■ SOURCE 11A Howard's 'Three Magnets', 1898

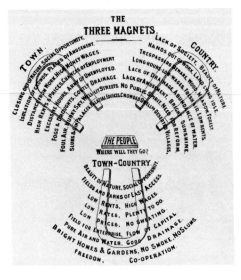

■ SOURCE 11B Centre and one section of a garden city, from Howard's book, 1898

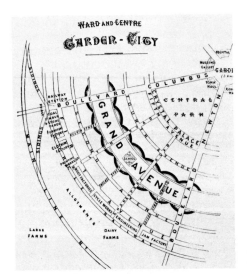

32 000 people, and the surrounding rural area, in decline in Howard's day, would benefit as well.

? QUESTIONS

a) Do you think Howard's ideas about what people want from town and country are as true today as they were in 1898?

b) How does the garden city (Source 11B) meet the aims of the town-country 'magnet' in Source 11A?

The Garden Cities Association was set up in 1899. It included several factory-owners who had built model housing for their workers, such as Cadbury, Rowntree and Lever. The first garden city was begun in Letchworth, in 1903, and the second at Welwyn, in 1919.

Cities Between the Wars

Britain between the wars was almost two countries, as Chapter 9 explains. In the old industrial towns and cities industry was depressed and unemployment was high. Housing Acts of 1919 and 1924 gave local councils the powers to clear slums and build council houses. One of the most famous schemes built at this time was at Quarry Hill, Leeds, (see page 174). Garden city-type suburbs were built at Hampstead (London), at Speke (Liverpool) and at Wythenshawe (Manchester). These only partly fulfilled Howard's plan as they were not independent towns, and much of the land was privately-owned.

The economic difficulties of the country in these years meant that there was not enough money available for councils to build much housing. The very areas with the worst slums were those with the most depressed industries. The Victorian housing of much of urban Britain simply became older and more decrepit.

However, there was no shortage of housing built privately for sale, particularly in the prosperous South and Midlands. Two and a half million houses were built in the years between the wars. As more were built, prices actually became cheaper. People who had good jobs were able to buy their own homes in the suburbs. In 1920 only 10% of the British people owned their own home; by 1939, 25% did.

The suburbs

Towns and cities began to sprawl even further out into the countryside (Source 12A). The popularity of the motor-car now meant that builders placed many of their new houses along main roads. This 'ribbon development', as it was called, came under strong criticism. The new suburbia was attacked too (see Sources 12C and 12D). Nevertheless, the people who bought these semi-detached houses usually liked them (Source 12B).

■ *SOURCE 12A* **1930s housing moving into the countryside**

■ *SOURCE 12B* **Suburban houses, 1930s**

■ *SOURCE 12C*

You know how these streets fester all over the suburbs. Always the same. Long, long rows of little semi-detached houses as much alike as council houses and generally uglier. The stucco front, and creosoted gate, the privet hedge, the green front door. The Laurels, the Myrtles, the Hawthorns, Mon Repos, Belle Vue.

George Orwell, writing in the 1930s

■ *SOURCE 12D*

Come friendly bombs and fall on Slough
It isn't fit for humans now
There isn't grass to graze a cow
Swarm over, Death.

John Betjeman, 1937

❓ QUESTIONS

a) Compare Source 12A with Source 7A. What similarities and what differences are there between the two situations?
b) Do John Betjeman and George Orwell dislike the same things about suburbs?
c) Why do you think people liked their suburban houses (Source 12B?
d) What criticisms would you make of the kind of housing and neighbourhood shown in Sources 12A and 12B?

The green belt

In the years just before and during the Second World War, plans were made to improve on the experiences of the 1930s. People saw the need to deal with the problem of housing in the cities. They also saw the dangers of the unplanned sprawl of the suburbs. In 1933 an Act was passed to prevent ribbon development. In 1938 a 'green belt' was created round London to prevent any further expansion into the countryside (see Source 13A). For the first time people were not allowed to build exactly what they liked where they liked. The government had taken much more control of people's lives in the war than they were used to. After the war similar powerful controls would be used to plan towns, cities and countryside.

Towns and Cities Since 1945

New towns

In 1944 the Abercrombie Plan for London suggested that the city's problems could be helped by building 'new towns' in the countryside beyond the 'green belt'. The New Towns Act of 1946 laid down plans for 12 such towns, 8 around London, 2 in Scotland, 1 in Wales and 1 in County Durham (see Map 1). Many of Howard's garden city ideas were included in the plans. Industry was separated from housing, which was surrounded by plenty of open space, and each New Town Corporation would own the land the town stood on.

After 1946 other new towns were started. The first new towns were intended to have about 50 000 people. Later new cities were planned, such as Milton Keynes and Telford, with a target of 200 000 people.

■ MAP 1 New towns since 1946

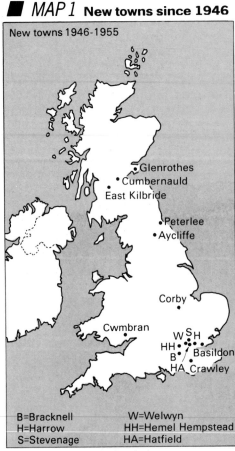

New towns 1946-1955

- Glenrothes
- Cumbernauld
- East Kilbride
- Peterlee
- Aycliffe
- Corby
- Cwmbran
- W S H
- HH
- B
- HA
- Basildon
- Crawley

B=Bracknell W=Welwyn
H=Harrow HH=Hemel Hempstead
S=Stevenage HA=Hatfield

New towns since 1955

- Livingstone
- Irvine
- Washington
- Skelmersdale
- Warrington
- Runcorn
- Telford
- Peterborough
- Newtown
- Northampton
- Redditch
- Milton Keynes

■ SOURCE 13A Abercrombie Plan for London, 1944

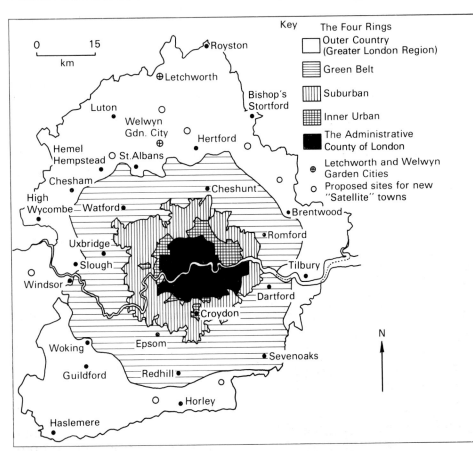

Key The Four Rings
- Outer Country (Greater London Region)
- Green Belt
- Suburban
- Inner Urban
- The Administrative County of London
- ⊕ Letchworth and Welwyn Garden Cities
- ○ Proposed sites for new "Satellite" towns

0 — 15 km

- Royston
- Letchworth
- Luton
- Bishop's Stortford
- Welwyn Gdn. City
- Hertford
- Hemel Hempstead
- St. Albans
- Chesham
- Cheshunt
- High Wycombe
- Watford
- Brentwood
- Uxbridge
- Romford
- Slough
- Tilbury
- Windsor
- Croydon
- Dartford
- Woking
- Epsom
- Sevenoaks
- Guildford
- Redhill
- Horley
- Haslemere

N

❓ QUESTIONS

a) In Source 13A, what is the purpose of the 'green belt'?

b) Compare Source 13A with the Map 1. Were the new towns built where Abercrombie suggested?

c) What has been done in Cwmbran New Town (Source 13B) to provide a good place to live?

d) Make a comparison of Sources 12B and 13B. Which would you prefer to live in?

The housing shortage

New towns did something to help the housing situation in cities, but a huge problem remained. In 1945 there was an acute housing shortage. German bombing had destroyed thousands of homes. Many more were quite unfit to live in. The Labour government of 1945–50 had 800 000 council houses built (see Chapter 16, page 176). The Conservative governments of the 1950s increased the number of private houses built from 200 000 per year to 400 000 per year. Despite these efforts, reports such as the Milner-Holland Report, in 1965, produced some disturbing statistics: 2 million households with no hot water, 2.8 million with no indoor toilet, 2.6 million with no bath.

■ *SOURCE 13B* **Housing in Cwmbran New Town, 1950s**

■ *SOURCE 14A* **26-storey block in East London, 1968**

Tower blocks

One solution which many councils were turning to by the 1960s was tower blocks (see Source 14A). Some architects said that building all the dwellings up in the air, freed all the ground level for parks, trees and open spaces. Others said that, instead of splitting up streets of people and sending them to remote new towns or housing estates, they could all stay together. Certainly tower blocks were the cheapest way of providing a lot of new housing, quickly.

? QUESTION

Explain why many people would rather live in the houses in Source 12D or 13B than in the flats in Source 14A.

Very soon it became clear that things had gone badly wrong with tower blocks. The Victorian street terraces they replaced may have been slums, but they had yards, gardens, sheds and quiet places to meet. Flats in the tower blocks had none of these. Lifts broke down, stranding people on upper floors. There were no places to store things, nowhere for children to play or for people to chat. Ground level was often not a leafy park at all, but a vandalised wasteland.

People in many European countries are used to flats, and live in them quite happily. The aim of most British people seems to be to have a house, at ground level, with a bit of space to call their own – like Sources 12B or 13B. For some types of household – single people, or childless couples – tower block flats may be quite suitable, but for others it can be a nightmare. Many people have moved out, and some tower blocks have been demolished, even though they were only a few years old.

Inner city problems

Cities, since the early days of the Industrial Revolution, have not been pleasant places for the poor to live. Yet they are often the only places the poor can find work. It is the same today. Inner city life is difficult: poor housing, high rents, high unemployment, low educational achievement and a high crime rate all create a circle from which it is very difficult to break out. Yet in 1986 Britain spent less money on housing than any other EEC country.

The main problem with building houses in inner cities today is the high cost of land. Businesses want to be in cities, so they compete with housing for land, and can pay higher rents. There has been a remarkable development of the London Docklands for housing, in recent years. But by the time the developers have bought the land, they have to build expensive houses in order to get their money back (see Source 14B). Ordinary Londoners on average wages cannot afford £100 000 for these flats.

? QUESTION

What advantages are there for rich people in living in these flats?

Are cities needed now?
One view of the problem of cities is that they were created by the Industrial Revolution, and are no longer needed. As Chapter 9 explains, Britain is no longer an industrial country, in fact no longer a major manufacturing country. This most recent change is reflected in Source 15. These figures represent a remarkable change from the pattern described in most of this chapter. What will happen to the cities, sometimes called the 'work-camps of the Industrial Revolution' in the future? Will governments try to revive them, by attracting new businesses to them, or will they be abandoned?

? QUESTIONS

a) Look at Source 15. Why are people moving from the cities?
b) Where are they going, and why?
c) What proportion of the total population now live in rural areas, and what proportion live in urban areas?
d) How does your answer to question c) compare with the pattern shown in Source 3 and Source 10?

■ **SOURCE 14B** **Luxury flats in London Docklands, 1987**

■ **SOURCE 15** **Changes in population distribution, 1971–81 (England and Wales)**

	Number (millions)	Percentage charge
London	6.7	– 10
Conurbations	11.2	– 5
Other large cities	2.8	– 5
Smaller cities	1.7	– 3
Industrial towns	6.7	+ 3
Resorts and retirement areas	3.3	+ 5
New towns	2.2	+15
Partly rural	9.5	+ 7
Rural	5.0	+10

Assignments

Local studies

1 Census returns can be used to investigate how towns and cities grew in the 19th century. You could make comparisons between two different streets in the same town. You could also compare the occupations and families of people in the same street from 1851 to 1881.

2 Town maps can also be used to compare the sizes of towns at different dates. Use maps of different dates, census returns, and your own observations to compare streets as they are now with how they looked in the past.

Empathy

1 Look at Sources 1B, 4A, 7B and 8.
   a Imagine you lived in one of the houses in Source 4A. Describe what it was like to live in 'the walking city'. What were the good and the bad things about life there?
   b In spite of the problems, people continued to move to urban areas. Why did they do this?

2 Look at Sources 12B, 13B, 14A and 14B. Get into groups of four. Imagine that one of you lives in each type of housing. Discuss the good and bad points of each. Think of as many aspects as possible: needs of children/old people, closeness to shops, peace and quiet, space for hobbies, etc.

3 Mrs Culpin lives in one of the houses in Source 4A. The council wants to demolish her house and build two tower blocks like those in Source 14A. Write a conversation between her and a council official who is trying to persuade her to move.

Understanding concepts

1 Factors causing change
Explain how changes in methods of transport have affected the growth of towns and cities through the last 200 years.

2 Causation
Explain how the following caused bad health in towns in the period 1750–1850:
   i overcrowding;
   ii poor housing;
   iii lack of water supply;
   iv lack of sewage system;
   v other factors.

3 Change/continuity
   a What were Ebenezer Howard's suggestions to solve the problem of cities?
   b How far were they put into effect?
   c How much impact have his ideas had on cities in Britain?

Themes for discussion

1 Compare the following:
   a Life in cities now;
   b Life in cities in 1850;
   c Life in the countryside.
Which lifestyle would you rather have? Why?

2 Cities seem to present serious problems for the people who live in them.
   a What are the problems?
   b What solutions can you offer?
   c Do you think the trend of people moving away from cities (see Source 15) will continue?

12 Life in a Victorian City

What is the population of the town or city you live in? For many of you it will be a six-figure number – 100 000 or more. In 1801 there was only one place in Britain with over 100 000 people – London. Even in 1841 there were only six such places. But by 1901 thirty places in Britain had reached this size. The reasons for this were given in Chapter 11. What was life like in a Victorian city?

Street Life

■ SOURCE 1A

Life in the streets seemed quite interesting. First thing in the morning the lamplighter came round with his long pole turning out the street lamps, and in the evening lighting them again. There were many hawkers singing their wares, gypsies to sell you something or offer to tell your fortune, the cats' meat man with his one-wheel barrow followed by hungry cats hoping he would drop a piece while he cut slices for a customer, the milkman ladling out milk from a churn on a barrow. Sunday was the day of the muffin man. He came round balancing a large tray on his head, packed with muffins and crumpets and ringing a bell while calling out 'Muffins!' In the afternoon there would be the winkle man, calling out from his barrow with winkles, shrimps and cockles. There was a ballad-singer who sang a popular song and sold copies of it for a penny, and again there was always the hurdy-gurdy man – an Italian with a small organ on a short pole and a monkey trained to turn the organ-handle.

***Memories of Albert Jacobs*, (born in Hoxton, London, 1889) pub. 1969**

❓ QUESTIONS

a) Source 1A is an old man writing about his childhood. How far can we trust the source? Explain your answer.

b) Sources 1B and 1C are photographs. Does that mean that they must be telling us the truth about life in the city streets? Explain your answer.

■ *SOURCE 1B* **19th century ice-cream seller**

■ *SOURCE 1C* **19th century mobile circus in a London street**

SOURCE 1D Traffic jam, engraving from mid-19th century

c) Source 1D is an artist's impression. Does that mean that the source must be biased in some way? Explain your answer.

d) Which of the four sources is the most helpful to you in giving you a picture of life on the streets?

e) Why would you find almost none of these scenes in a city street today?

Shops

When the industrial cities were beginning to grow, people did most of their shopping in markets, like the one in Source 2A. Most people had been born in the country and this was the kind of shopping they were used to. Usually the stall-holders made or grew the items they sold, or bought them locally. Later, shops grew up along the main streets. These shopkeepers did not make or grow the goods they sold, but bought them in. They could stock a bigger choice of goods than a market-stall. They used attractive displays, like the shop in Source 2B, and lots of advertisements. The growth of railways meant that shops could stock items from all over Britain.

The first Sainsbury's opened in 1869, the first Boot's in 1877 and the first Marks and Spencer's in 1894. These are called chain stores: shops in several places, all with the same name and selling the same goods, usually at cheap prices. Jesse Boot, for example, bought his medicines and pills in large quantities direct from the makers. He advertised all over town and sold them cheaply. His wife began to sell gifts for customers to take with them when they visited someone who was ill. She also ran a lending library. In this way the different departments of Boot's grew up. Michael Marks began as a Leeds market trader; his slogan was, 'Don't ask the price, it's a penny'. Then he teamed up with Tom Spencer and opened shops.

In city centres, department stores opened up. The most well-known London ones were Harrods and Selfridges. These shops were very large and sold almost everything in different parts of the shop.

However, most city-dwellers' needs were met by the little corner-shop (see Source 2C). In the days before fridges and freezers, people shopped every day, buying food in small quantities. Even in these small shops things were changing. Using the railways, big companies could supply shops all over Britain with their named goods, heavily advertised, such as Rowntrees, Colmans, Lyons, Tate and Lyle, Nestlé and many others.

■ *SOURCE 2A* **19th century poultry market in Manchester**

■ *SOURCE 2B* **19th century general store**

❓ QUESTION

a) List the advantages and disadvantages to a 19th century person of shopping in each of Sources 2A, 2B and 2C.

b) In what ways do markets, food-stores and cornershops today differ from those shown in these sources?

SOURCE 2C 19th century corner shop

SOURCE 3B The Old Oak, Hampstead, 19th century photograph

Pubs

SOURCE 3A

At one place I saw a revolving light with many burners playing most beautifully over the door; at another, about 50 or 60 jets in one lantern were throwing out their brilliant gleams. And over the doors of a third house were no less than three enormous lamps, lighting up the whole street.

They were in full glare on this Sunday evening, and through the doors of these infernal dens of drunkenness and mischief, crowds of miserable wretches were pouring in, that they might drink and die.

From the *Temperance Penny Magazine*, 1836

SOURCE 3C London gin-shop interior, 1852

? QUESTIONS

a) What is the attitude of the writer of Source 3A to pubs?
b) Explain how the pub in Source 3B would be an attractive place for people to go (look at Chapter 11, Sources 4A, 7B and 9B, for descriptions of houses).
c) What kinds of lamps are shown in Source 3B and described in Source 3A?

d) How can you tell what this attitude is?
e) What reasons can you suggest for this attitude to pubs?
f) Can you tell from his attitude what 'temperance' means?
g) What do you think is the attitude of the artist of Source 3C to pubs, if any?

h) How can you tell?
i) If Sources 3A and 3C are biased, does that mean they are no use to us in studying 19th-century pubs?

The bright lights of the city pubs attracted many people inside. The panelled walls, cut-glass windows, brass and pewter-topped tables were a great contrast to their over-crowded, dingy homes. The pubs offered interest and action, noise and warmth. There was music and singing, gambling and games. Most of all, there was alcohol to help you forget your problems, at least for an hour or two. Pubs hardly ever closed – only after 1864 were they made to close between 1 a.m. and 4 a.m.

It is no wonder that many Victorians were worried about the effects of alcoholism. They blamed the pubs for ruined families, neglected wives, hungry children and debts. Many people put their efforts into the Temperance Movement: working to ban alcohol.

Despite the Temperance Movement, the number of pubs grew as the cities grew. They had always been closely linked with travel, and grew up around the new railway stations. The trams usually ran to a turning-point at a pub. Even to this day several London Underground and suburban stations are named after pubs: e.g. Angel, Royal Oak, Elephant and Castle, Bricklayers Arms. Pubs were also built on main roads and city thoroughfares. In poorer areas there were beer-houses with plain wooden floors. Pubs were meeting places for clubs, societies and trade unions. They were places for popular sport, such as prize-fighting (an early, illegal kind of boxing), ratting, cock-fighting and horse-racing. Many pubs grew into music-halls, with different kinds of entertainment on a small stage: singers, dancers, comedians, jugglers, conjurers.

Public Buildings and Parks

Many industrial cities had started as small towns, even villages, and grown very fast. They did not have town halls or meeting-places big enough for their needs. Towards the end of the 19th century the local councils began to put this right. The councillors were usually very proud of their town or city and wanted the architecture to show this.

In addition to these grand and imposing town halls, the City Fathers, as councillors were often called, wanted to provide better facilities too. They were keen believers in education and self-improvement, so they built museums and free libraries. They also built concert halls in order that people might enjoy cultural events in their industrial cities. The centres of Liverpool, Manchester, Leeds, Bradford, Newcastle and many other towns and cities were soon filled with impressive buildings of this type.

? QUESTIONS

a) What impression has the architect tried to give to the people of Manchester in Source 4?
b) How has he done this?

One great problem of the new cities was the lack of open space. Councils set out to correct this by laying out parks. Sometimes the land was given by a local wealthy landowner, and the council would lay out gardens, ponds, seats and perhaps a bandstand for summer

■ *SOURCE 4* **Manchester Town Hall, 1885**

SOURCE 5A Horse-drawn tram, 1895

concerts.

Another type of open space which was badly needed was cemeteries. The old graveyards were soon filled as the population grew. Burying bodies on top of other bodies upset everyone greatly. The only answer was to set aside large new graveyards outside the city centres. About 3000 new graveyards were laid out between 1831 and 1861. As well as providing for the dead, these new cemeteries brought to the living a chance to see trees and grass.

Transport in the City

As described in Chapter 11, early industrial cities were called 'walking cities', because everyone walked to work. Indeed, there was no other transport for most people. The first change came with the horse-drawn tram (see Source 5A). Fares were cheap, and those who could afford it began to live outside the crowded city centre.

The city streets were still very crowded (see Source 1A). In fact slow-moving trams made matters worse. When the railway networks sprang up, they brought about a great change in the appearance and life of the cities.

SOURCE 5B

The railways have set us all moving far away from London – that is to say the special middle-class of Londoners, people ranging from three to five hundred a year. The upper ten thousand and the abject poor still live and sleep in the metropolis. The middle class betake themselves to far off spots like Richmond, Watford, Croydon or Slough. The smaller fry content themselves with semi-detached boxes at Putney, Kilburn, New Cross or Ealing, but the wealthier take a more extended scope and are found to go daily to and from the capital as far as even Reading and Brighton.

Letter to *The Architect*, 1873

? QUESTION

Which five different groups does this letter-writer identify?

SOURCE 5C 'Middlesex'

Gaily into Ruislip Gardens
Runs the red electric train
With a thousand Ta's and
    Pardon's
Daintily alights Elaine;
Hurries down the concrete
    station
With a frown of concentration,
Out into the outskirt's edges
Where a few surviving hedges
Keep alive our lost Elysium –
    rural Middlesex again.

John Betjeman, published in 1954

John Betjeman describes the early days of the Metropolitan Railway, just before the First World War. Like other suburban railways, it allowed people working in the city to live in or near the country. Not only in London, but in every large town and city, the railway led to the growth of suburbs. Further and further the city stretched out into the surrounding countryside, until it was many miles across. This sprawling growth posed problems for the later 20th century (see Chapter 11, pages 131–2).

Housing Types

Better transport meant that middle-class city dwellers could build houses on the edge of town. These new houses had big gardens and were set along wide roads that had trees on each side. The houses were big and solid, with lots of rooms.

SOURCE 6A Victorian villa

At the same time efforts were being made to provide better housing for working people. Prince Albert (Queen Victoria's husband) arranged for some new designs, such as that in Source 6B (over). This house has four apartments, each with a living-room, kitchen and three bedrooms.

Prince Albert's ideas were not taken up: builders preferred to make bigger profits from building more cheaply. As with many problems in industrial Britain, it took the government to force improvements through. The Artisans Dwellings Act 1875 laid down strict rules about thickness of walls, damp course, water supply and drainage. A better

■ *SOURCE 6B* **Improved house, 1851**

■ *SOURCE 6C* **Houses built after 1875**

■ *SOURCE 6D* **Railway arches and housing in Victorian times**

style of terraced housing began to appear (see Source 6C).

Only better-paid working people and clerical workers could afford the new houses in Source 6C. For the poorer city workers there was only the old housing, which was gradually getting worse. At least the people in Source 6D have a proper roof over their heads: there were (and still are) many people in the city with nowhere to live. Cities are a magnet for the poorest in society, the down-and-out. Many thousands were to be found sleeping rough in the poorest parts of Victorian cities; no one quite knows how many sleep rough in cities nowadays.

The railway arches carry middle-class commuters to their houses in the leafy suburbs. They tower over the slum housing and provide a damp and draughty refuge for the homeless.

⁇ QUESTIONS

a) Use Sources 6A–E to write a paragraph about the importance of transport in Victorian cities.

■ **SOURCE 6E** **Homeless people and railway arch, Victorian engraving**

b) Use the same sources to write a paragraph about differences between the classes in Victorian England.

Assignments

Empathy

1 You live in a country village in 1860, and have never visited a city before. Now you are spending a month staying with a friend in a city. Write a letter home to your parents describing what life is like.

2 a Draw a poster for a Temperance Society explaining the evils of alcohol and public houses.
  b Draw a poster for a pub, explaining what the attractions are.

3 a Source 1A seems to concentrate on the interesting side of city life, not the bad side. Why do you think this is?
  b What was the 'bad' side of city life?

Understanding Concepts

Change and Continuity
Take each of the sub-headings for the topics in this chapter and compare them with city life today.
  a In what ways have things changed?
  b In what ways are they the same?

Evidence

Look at all the sources in this chapter for evidence of differences between the classes in a Victorian city.
  a In what ways do each of the sources present problems of reliability for the historian?
  b What statements about class differences in a Victorian city can be truthfully made?

Theme for discussion

Would you like to have lived in a Victorian city? What would you have liked or disliked about it?

Urban Housing and Living Conditions

Living conditions in Britain's industrial areas in the early 19th century were appalling. The reasons for these conditions have been dealt with in Chapter 11. The result was a public health situation which was, literally, deadly. In Manchester in the 1840s, for example, 57% of babies failed to reach the age of 5.

▇ SOURCE 1 Average age of death, 1842

	Wiltshire – a mainly rural area	Liverpool
Professional persons, gentry and their families	50	35
Farmers, tradesmen and their families	48	22
Mechanics, labourers	33	15

Bad housing was not a new thing in Britain. There had been slums in London in the Middle Ages. Nor was bad housing only to be found in cities. Many farm labourers at this time lived in hovels which we would think were unfit for animals. The extra problem was overcrowding, which made the health situation much worse.

In Victorian cities, the demand for somewhere to live was so great that rents were high. People on ordinary wages could only afford to rent a room, or half a room, or a cellar, or only a bed, or even at the very worst, part of a bed. Of 1462 families surveyed in one parish in London, half had only one bed for the entire family, and 929 had only one room. For single men and women workers, tramps and casual labourers there were lodging houses. Leeds had 222 lodgings houses with an average of nine beds per room, and five lodgers to a bed.

It is not surprising that diseases such as typhus, carried by lice, tuberculosis, transmitted from one person's breath to another, and typhoid, spread by drinking polluted water, all flourished. These explain the figures in Source 1.

▇ QUESTIONS

a) What, in your own words, does Source 1 show?

b) Explain the reasons for differences between the columns for Wiltshire and for Liverpool.

c) Explain the reasons for differences between the classes in each area.

d) This table shows average age of death. Does it prove that lots of lower-class people in Liverpool died at 15? Explain your answer.

During the 20th century we have realised what a big task improving public health is. It requires better housing, higher wages, better food, better education, sound medical knowledge, pure water, improved drains, clean streets and efficient local government. However, people in the 1830s did not appreciate all these things.

▇ SOURCE 2A

In most of the inferior streets, chiefly inhabited by the working classes, few are paved at all, none of them properly. Dung heaps are found in several parts of the streets and open privies [lavatories] are seen in many directions. The chief sewage is in open channels .... Taking the general conditions I am obliged to pronounce it the most filthy town I visited.

Report on the Sanitary Condition of Bradford, 1844

▇ QUESTIONS

a) Which aspects of housing in Bradford are commented on in Source 2A?

b) Which of the list in the previous paragraph are not mentioned?

c) Why do you think some of the things which we know lead to bad public health were not referred to in Source 2A?

d) What would be particularly unhealthy about cellar-dwellings, such as those in Source 2B?

▇ SOURCE 2B Houses with separate cellar dwelling in Merthyr Tydfil. Not many Welsh houses had separate cellars, in fact, unlike Liverpool, where 40 000 people lived in cellars in 1840.

The Cholera Epidemic of 1831–2

In spite of the efforts of some doctors, Parliament and local government took little notice of public health problems before 1830. The middle and upper classes who ruled the country lived in rural areas, or in large houses on the edges of towns. The event which forced them to take notice was the cholera epidemic of 1831–2. Cholera was a new disease, causing sickness, diarrhoea and sweating. Death came within 36 hours or less. Although it affected the poor most, no one was safe: 32 000 died in the epidemic in a few months.

The cholera epidemic forced the government to take action. They set up a Central Board of Health and encouraged towns to set up Local Boards of Health. As Source 3A makes clear, Leeds was one which did so.

■ SOURCE 3A

On 26th May the first case of pure cholera occurred in Blue Bell Fold, a small, dirty cul-de-sac containing about twenty houses inhabited by poor families. Blue Bell Fold lies on the north side of the river between it and an offensive streamlet which conveys the refuse water from numerous mills and dyehouses.

The first case occurred in a child two years of age which having been in perfect health on the preceding day became suddenly ill on the morning of the 26th and died at 5 p.m. on the same day.

If the Board will refer to the map which accompanies this report they will at once see how the disease was worst in those parts of the town where there is often an entire want of sewage, drainage and paving.

Dr Baker, District Surgeon, Report to the Members of Leeds Board of Health, January 1833

? QUESTIONS

a) What does Source 3A tell us about how Leeds set about dealing with the cholera epidemic?
b) What does Dr Baker suggest about the causes of cholera?

■ SOURCE 3B Cholera in Exeter in 1832. The dead person's body is carried away, while the bedclothes are washed in the stream which provides other people's water-supply

c) How does he set about proving his argument?
d) What does Source 3B tell us about medical knowledge at the time?
e) Dr Baker seems to know that disease breeds in dirty conditions, yet the people in Source 3B seem to have little knowledge of public hygiene. How do you explain this?

Unfortunately, people did not know how to prevent cholera. The discovery that germs cause disease had not yet been made. (The Frenchman, Louis Pasteur, showed that this was so in 1864.) The Boards of Health issued lime for whitewashing houses. They also burnt barrels of tar and vinegar in the streets. These, of course, had little effect on the death rate.

There were two medical theories about disease at the time. One was that disease was transmitted by touch. Doctors therefore wanted to isolate diseased people. The other theory was that disease was caused by 'bad air' or 'poisonous miasma', as it was called. Doctors had correctly linked dirt with disease (as Dr Baker did in Source 3A). However, they believed that the disease was carried by the smell. Obviously both theories are close to the truth, but in the arguments between them mistakes were made.

? QUESTIONS

a) How do you think doctors had arrived at each theory?
b) How far does the 'poisonous miasma' theory explain the burning of tar?
c) Do you think it matters if the theories are wrong, provided they correctly link dirt and disease?

The cholera epidemic of 1831–2 revealed the lack of proper local government in many new industrial towns and cities. The Municipal Corporations Act was passed in 1835, setting up local councils in many places. But the enthusiasm to deal with the problems of health did not last long. By the mid-1830s the Central and Local Boards of Health were dissolved, and things went on as before.

How to Bring About Change?

The difficulty with trying to reform public health was the strength of opposition to change. People who owned slum houses did not want to pay for improvements. People who supplied water, at a price, did not want to improve its quality. People who made money out of selling the dung from the streets to farmers would lose their livelihood if sewers were dug. And who would pay for improvements? Better-off people, who would have to bear most of the cost, did not live in the bad areas. Their homes were healthy, so why should they pay? Businesses, such as mills, dye-works, tanneries and slaughterhouses, which polluted the rivers, were also reluctant to pay.

Public health problems would have to be dealt with by local government. But in many places this was a shambles, with lots of separate committees for different things and different parts of towns. Birmingham, for example, had separate bodies for street lighting, street paving and street cleaning, as well as four different surveyors, working independently. The main concern of local councils was to keep the rates as low as possible. A scheme to build a proper sewage system for Leeds, for example, was rejected in 1844 in favour of a cheaper scheme which emptied the sewage into the river. Local councils were very jealous of their local powers, and hated to be told what to do. Central government was therefore reluctant to issue instructions.

Edwin Chadwick

This opposition, and the lack of good medical knowledge, were major obstacles to reform. However, Edwin Chadwick, a man with a determination to overcome all the problems began to interest himself in public health in the 1840s. He had already carried out a total change of the Poor Law (Chapter 15, pages 163–7). While working for the Poor Law Commissioners he had also become interested in public health problems. He was trying to reduce the number of poor people by removing the causes of poverty. He believed that people who became ill were forced into poverty. He did not believe that poverty caused disease. He therefore set up an investigation into public health, using the medical officers of the Poor Law Unions to supply him with information.

His investigation concentrated on three aspects of health – drainage, refuse, and water supply. He realised that it was impossible, at that time, to tackle the problem of bad housing. Drains, in the 1840s, were designed to take rainwater away, not sewage. In fact, it was an offence, in many towns, to connect your house to the drains. Drains were often ditches or brick tunnels which would be cleared every few years by teams of men known as scavengers. New towns often had no drains: Merthyr Tydfil, in Wales, had 37 000 people in 1842, and no drains.

Householders were expected to make their own arrangements for getting rid of their own sewage. Some houses had cesspits, others had open privies (toilets), perhaps shared with several houses. The cesspits and privies would be cleared out only occasionally by scavengers. The dung was then piled into the street before being taken off to be sold to farmers.

■ **SOURCE 4A** **A Court for King Cholera, mid-19th century cartoon**

■ **SOURCE 4B**

The night-soil men, fortified with hard spirits, toured the town at nigh shovelling the contents of cess-pits into special carts which were hopefully, though not always, watertight. As dawn broke, they wended their way into the country to sell their reeking cargoes to local farmers, though not before stopping at the town's edge for some refreshment after their night's labours.

A. Phillips, *Ten Men of Colchester*, 1985

■ **SOURCE 4C** Jacob's Island, Bermondsey in the mid-19th century. **The wooden shacks are privies emptying into the stream. The stream also provides the water supply for many houses**

■ SOURCE 4D

Leeds is very ill supplied by that most needful element, water, by its public water works, which were established more than forty years since and adapted to the size of the town at that time .... Only 12 000 persons receive water from the waterworks. A population of upwards of 60 000 have no water supply except from wells and rainwater .... The water is raised from the river near Leeds Bridge and forced up by waterwheel to reservoirs. Its quality is very indifferent.

Leeds Directory, 1834

❓ QUESTIONS

a) Source 4A is exaggerated. What points was the artist trying to make in this cartoon?

b) What use would Source 4A be to a historian of public health in 19th century Britain?

c) According to Source 4B, how did the night-soil men tolerate their horrible job?

d) Source 4B is a history book about Colchester in the 19th century. It is therefore a secondary source. What use would it be to a historian of public health in 19th century Britain?

e) In what ways was the water supply of Leeds inadequate, according to Source 4D?

f) What had happened to Leeds to cause the problem?

g) Using Sources 4A–D, list the health hazards described.

h) Using the same four sources, describe the attitudes to public health which they show.

In tackling the problem of water supply Chadwick offended the people who had shares in private water companies. However, he was not to be put off. He pointed out that waterworks (as in Source 4D) only supplied a few people. Even for them the water supply was often only turned on for a few hours a day. The rest of the people used wells, streams, pumps or bought water from carriers. Wherever it came from, including the piped supply, the water was often impure.

The 1842 Report on Public Health

Chadwick's bold criticisms worried the other people who had carried out the investigation with him. *The Report on the Sanitary Condition of the Labouring Population* came out in 1842, under his name only. It pointed out the seriousness of the problem and the obstacles to putting it right. 'The annual loss from filth is greater than the loss from death or wounds in any wars in which the country has been engaged in modern times', argued Chadwick. He denied that it was the poor who were to blame through their own drunkenness and laziness for the condition they lived in. He said that bad conditions produced poverty and immorality, not the other way round. Unhealthy people were, he said: 'ignorant, passionate, violent and dangerous, with a tendency to moral, as well as physical deterioration'. He recommended that Parliament should enforce a system of sanitation improvement. This would cover paving of streets, drainage, water-supply, sewage and cleaning. It should be paid for out of the rates.

About 10 000 copies of his report were given away; 20 000 were bought. The country was shocked. But nothing was done. Parliament set up a Royal Commission on the Health of Towns in 1844 to check whether Chadwick's information was correct.

An attempt to bring in an Act in 1847 failed, owing to the opposition of MPs, who became known as the 'Dirty Party'.

■ SOURCE 5A

Athough I was not named in the Commission, I had to attend all the meetings, write out the questions put to witnesses and prepare the report. I persuaded Commissioners to go to see conditions for themselves. My annual holiday was taken up in visiting the worst parts of some of the worst towns. Dr Playfair has been knocked up by it and is seriously ill. Mr Smith has had dysentry. At Bristol Sir Henry de la Bêche had to stand at the end of an alley and vomit while Dr Playfair was looking at overflowing privies.

Chadwick, 1844

❓ QUESTIONS

a) What impression of Edwin Chadwick do you get from Source 5A and pages 146–7?

b) There is a saying about 'throwing pearls before swine'. It means offering something good to people who do not appreciate it. How has the cartoonist in Source 5B altered the saying?

c) What does the cartoonist think of the City of London Alderman? How does he make this clear?

■ *SOURCE 5B* **Lord Morpeth trying to persuade local councillors to take action, 1848**

Public Health Act 1848

Then, in 1848, cholera returned. Hurriedly the 'Dirty Party' withdrew its opposition. The Public Health Act 1848 was passed. It set up a General Board of Health, whose members were Chadwick, Shaftesbury and Lord Morpeth. A Local Board of Health could be set up when the death rate reached 23 per 1000 in a town, or if one tenth of the local people requested it. A local council (if there was one) could take on the powers of a Local Board of Health. These controlled sewage, drainage, roads, slaughter-houses, lodging-houses, water supply, as well as parks and cemeteries. All new houses were to have a WC or privy; older houses were to be connected to a drain or cesspit; no new cellar-houses were to be built.

The cholera epidemic of 1848–9 was even worse than the last one: 53 000 people died. It came too quickly for the measures of the Public Health Act to have any effect. The General Board of Health tried to do what it could, but met with the usual opposition. For example, when cholera reached the Tooting Poor Law District School, the General Board recommended that children be kept away. Two Poor Law Unions refused, and 180 children died.

Opposition continued after the cholera ended. Local councils refused to set up Local Boards of Health or, if they did, they refused to spend money. Any scheme of improvement cost a lot of money, and the rates went up. People hated being taken to court to remove dung-heaps from their private property. Working-class people liked to keep pigs in their backyards. They were angry when told that pigs were a health hazard and must be removed. Chadwick himself irritated many people. For example, he was convinced that small, glazed drainage pipes were the answer to sewage problems. Water would flush any solids out of them under pressure. Unfortunately, in these early years, water was not always very plentiful, and his small pipes became blocked. Chadwick also regarded public health as an engineering problem, a matter of drains and pipes, not a medical problem. He still believed in 'bad air' causing disease. In 1848 Dr Snow and Dr Budd had shown that cholera was transmitted by drinking water polluted with sewage. Chadwick and the General Board of Health ignored their findings.

The Times joined the campaign against Chadwick.

■ SOURCE 6

We prefer to take our chance with the cholera than be bullied into health. There is nothing a man hates so much as being cleansed against his will or having his floors swept, his hall whitewashed, his dungheaps cleared away and his thatch forced to give way to slate. It is a fact that many people have died from a good washing. The truth is that Mr Chadwick has a great many powers but it is not so easy to say what they can be applied to.

The Times, 1854

▣ QUESTIONS

a) List the reasons *The Times* gives for opposing Chadwick.

b) The attitudes in this source are ridiculous by late 20th century standards. What does this source tell us about mid-19th century attitudes to health, hygiene and the law?

c) Write a reply to this paragraph such as Chadwick could have written in his defence.

In 1854 Chadwick was dismissed from the General Board of Health, which was disbanded in 1858. By 1853 only 182 Local Boards, covering less than one sixth of the population, had been set up.

The trouble with the Public Health Act 1848 was that it was only 'permissive'; that is, towns could do certain things if they wished, but they did not have to. The General Board pressed for action, but was resisted. However, the powers were there for action if towns decided to take them.

Public health in London

In London a young doctor, Dr John Simon, was appointed Medical Officer of Health. He wrote a series of reports on housing, drains and water supplies. One of the main problems in London was the pollution of the River Thames. Most of the city's sewers emptied into it. Much of the water supply was taken from it. Dr Simon pointed out that in Southwark, which took its water from the Thames, the death rate was 130 per 10 000. Lambeth,

■ SOURCE 7A *Punch* cartoon, 1858

DIPHTHERIA.   SCROFULA.   CHOLERA.

FATHER THAMES INTRODUCING HIS OFFSPRING TO THE FAIR CITY OF LONDON
(A Design for a Fresco in the New Houses of Parliament.)

nearby, had a piped water supply from the Surrey Hills, and a death rate of 37 per 10000.

The newspapers took up the campaign to clean up the Thames (see Sources 7A and 7B). Matters reached a peak in 1858, the summer of the 'Great Stink': hot, dry weather lowered the water level and the river stank even more. The smell from sewage in the river actually stopped Parliament from sitting.

Joseph Bazalgette was appointed to build a sewage system from London which took the sewage down river, away from the city. This was completed in 1865 (Source 7C).

❓ QUESTIONS

a) In sources 7A and 7B, how does the cartoonist show his opposition to water pollution in the City?

b) Do you think the drawing in Source 7B was done before or after the discovery of the microscope? Give reasons for your answer.

c) What materials are being used to build sewers in Source 7C, and to what size?

Public Health Act 1875

Several factors brought a change at local and central government level in the late 1860s and 1870s. The link between germs and disease had finally been made and proved. The Reform Act 1867 gave the vote to working men in towns. Politicians therefore had to pay attention to their problems, the chief of which was bad living conditions. There was another cholera epidemic in 1865–6 in which 20000 died.

A Royal Commission on Public Health was set up in 1869. This revealed that conditions were just as bad in many towns as they had been at the time of Chadwick's investigations. A Local Government Board was set up in 1871 to supervise local control of public health. Then, in 1875 a Public Health Act was passed. This actually only brought together about 30 previous Acts on health. The difference was that it was not a 'permissive' Act: it was now compulsory to appoint sanitary inspectors, and a medical officer of health. Local government was given wide powers to lay sewers and drains, build reservoirs, parks,

■ *SOURCE 7B* **Punch cartoon, 1850s**

A DROP OF LONDON WATER.

■ *SOURCE 7C* **Sewers being built, 1862**

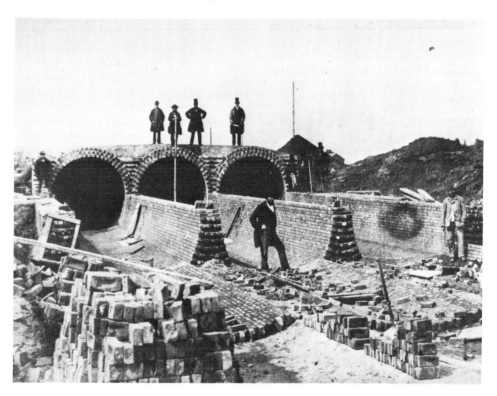

■ SOURCE 8 Lake Vyrnwy

swimming baths and public conveniences. Large cities began to look far away for sources of fresh water. Manchester set up reservoirs in the Lake District. Liverpool dammed a valley in Wales to form Lake Vyrnwy, in 1881, to supply the city's needs for clean water (see Source 8).

? QUESTIONS

a) Do you think a city has the right to take water from many miles away?

b) How do you feel about the Welsh people whose farms and houses were lost when the lake was formed?

Public Health Since 1875

By the latter part of the 19th century the government was prepared to tackle the housing problem. The 1875 Artisans Dwelling Act laid down standards of house buildings: size of rooms, sanitation, space between buildings, etc (Chapter 12, Source 6C, page 142). It also gave councils the power to clear slum areas. The city to take this up most dramatically was Birmingham. Under the mayor, Joseph Chamberlain, 40 acres of slums were cleared. The city was, in his words 'parked, paved, marketed, gas and watered, and improved'. The 1890 Housing Act gave stronger powers, and another Act in 1909 banned the building of back-to-back houses.

New local government structures were set up. In 1888, County Councils began, with County Boroughs to give similar powers to cities. In 1894 Urban District Councils and Rural District Councils were established, with public health powers. By 1900 the death rate was definitely failing (Chapter 7, page 68). It continued to fall in the 20th century as the new councils began to take all aspects of public health seriously. Today Environmental Health Departments have many jobs to do to keep us healthy. They deal with refuse disposal, water analysis, pollution of air and water, noise pollution, food inspection, pest control, disease control, slum clearance and such health provisions as maternity clinics and health visitors.

Central government also takes a part. In recent years they have carried out campaigns to stop smoking and insisted on all cigarette packets carrying a health warning. They are also working to stamp out drug addiction. Sometimes people are worried about a pollution problem and the government is slow to take action. This happened over the harmful effects of lead in petrol, only recently tackled.

In the 20th century, governments have realised that public health is a huge problem. Most of their attempts to deal with it concern the growth of the Welfare State, so are dealt with in Chapter 16. This does not mean the problem of bad living conditions has been solved, as Sources 9A and 9B make clear.

■ SOURCE 9A

Many of the houses in Merthyr Tydfil contained only two rooms, one up and one down, joined by a ricketty wooden staircase rotting into holes. Windows are small and low, and at two in the afternoon it is dark inside these houses. Ramshackle sheds, in cobbled yards, shared by several cottages, are the only sanitation. When I touched the back walls my hand came away, not merely damp but wet, although it was not raining.

Evening Standard, **1936**

■ SOURCE 9B

We have a small room in a disused army barracks which looks like a prison and feels like it.

We are infested with silverfish insects, and I am constantly scrubbing the floor to keep them away.

There are thirty families in this building, and there is hardly a child that has not been in hospital since arriving here. My own little ones have been in and out of hospital with bronchial and heart problems.

Shelter publication, 1986

? QUESTIONS

a) Both these sources were written long after the 1875 Public Health Act. Why do you think such housing was still found in the 1930s and is still found today?

b) Why does bad housing lead to bad health? Think of as many reasons as you can.

Assignments

Empathy

1 a Which groups and types of people opposed public health improvements in the 19th century?
  b What were their motives for doing so?
2 Get into groups of four. You are the members of a Town Council deciding whether to set up a Board of Health and spend money on a water supply system. Decide on your role, your attitude to the plans and debate the decision.

Understanding Concepts

1 Change/continuity
Improving health '… requires better housing, higher wages, better food, better education, sound medical knowledge, pure water, improved drains, clean streets and efficient local government.'

a Which of the items listed here were provided by 1890?
b Which of the items listed here were not provided by 1890?
c Why not?

2 Change/continuity
It took a long time to bring about changes in public health in British towns. What part did each of these factors play in holding up improvement:
  i lack of medical knowledge;
  ii unwillingness to spend money;
  iii unwillingness to interfere in people's lives;
  iv lack of good local government;
  v other factors.

3 Role of individuals
a Examine the role of Edwin Chadwick in Public Health improvements.
  i What were his motives in seeking to improve public health?
  ii Who were his opponents, and why did they oppose him?
  iii Why was he dismissed from the General Board of Health in 1854?
  iv What do we learn of his personality from the sources in this chapter?
b How much credit for public health improvement in Britain in the 19th century can be given to Chadwick, and how much to other people?

Themes for discussion

1 Why is public health such a large-scale problem?
2 Look at Chapter 7. When did public health improvements begin to affect the population at large?
3 Why is public health still an important part of local government?

▮ 14 ▮ Working Conditions and Reform in the 19th Century

Conditions Before the Industrial Revolution

Hard work, long hours and child labour did not start with the Industrial Revolution. When most people still worked on the land, hours of work were as long as the daylight lasted. There were a few hours' rest on Sundays and on the occasional holy days, also. When cloth was made in people's homes – under the 'domestic system' – working hours were again as long as the family chose to make them. Indeed it was, like farming, family work. Usually the men did the weaving, while women did the spinning and taught the children how to do carding and winding. Children were expected to play their part in helping the family earn its living. If a young person was learning a trade, he or she would become an apprentice,

living in the master's house as a junior member of the family, paid almost nothing.

There were some advantages to working at home, of course. The family were all together, and babies could be cared for. You could also work at your own pace. Weavers were notorious for 'observing Saint Monday' – taking Monday off, and even Tuesday too. They would then work long hours at the end of the week to make up. Work in a factory, on the other hand, meant starting and finishing by the bell, and many other strict rules. Sources 1B–C give an idea of what life was like for workers in the early days of industrialisation.

▮ SOURCE 1B 'The Factory Bell'

O happy man, oh happy thou
While toiling at thy spade and
  plough
While thou amidst thy pleasures
  roll

All at thy labour uncontrolled
Here at the mills in pressing
  crowds
The high-built chimneys puff
  black clouds
And all around the slaves do
  dwell
Who're called to labour by a bell.

▮ SOURCE 1C Factory rules

1 The door of the lodge will be closed ten minutes after the engine starts every morning, and no weaver will afterwards be admitted until breakfast-time. Any weaver who may be absent during that time shall forfeit 3*d* per loom.
2 ... Weavers leaving the room without the consent of the overlooker shall forfeit 3*d*.
9 All shuttles, brushes, oil-cans, wheels, windows etc., if broken, shall be paid for by the weaver.
11 If any hand in the mill is seen talking to another, whistling or singing, he will be fined sixpence.

'Published and dedicated to the working classes' by William Rashleigh MP, 1844

▮? QUESTIONS

a) In Source 1A, why was the mill built by a canal?
b) In Source 1B, who does the singer envy, and why?
c) What other complaints does the singer have, apart from the factory bell?
d) Do you think any of the rules in Source 1C are unfair?
e) Do you think any of the rules are fair?
f) Why do you think that these rules were published by an MP and dedicated to the working classes?
g) Does this fact affect their reliability and usefulness to a historian?
h) What questions would you want to ask before using Source 1C as reliable evidence of factory rules in the 19th century?

▮ SOURCE 1A Cotton factory in Manchester, 1835

Conditions During the Early Industrial Revolution

Child labour

The custom of families working together continued into the early Industrial Revolution. Crompton's spinning mule (see page 21) required one adult to work it, helped by several children who did things like cleaning, tying-up broken threads, removing full spindles, oiling, etc. Early power-looms, too, needed one adult worker and three or four children. The mill-owner paid the adults, who made their own arrangements for child-helpers. They brought in their own children, or paid others. Who they were, what they were paid, and how they were treated, was not the mill-owner's business.

It was the same in the mines. The custom in early, small pits, was for men to cut the coal and their wives and children to carry it away. In some coalfields the 'butty' system meant that one miner agreed with the pit-owner to mine a certain section of coal for a certain price. He would then pay other miners, including women and children, to carry coal, open and close doors and do other parts of the work. Again, the owner did not employ the children directly.

Thus people accepted the idea of child and female labour and long working hours. It seemed to be just part of the pattern of work which had been going on for centuries. The early 19th century, however, brought some changes of attitude among groups of people.

Some of the workers in Source 2A are about your age. What do you think it would be like working in this factory? You might think it would be interesting to make the machine work. You might think it would be good to have a full-time, paid job of your own. When you know that it was normal to work up to 16 hours a day, six days a week, that the temperature was often 27°C and that your wages, at 14 years of age, might be only 4s (20p) a week, you might not be so keen. You might think of the dangers of the whirring, rushing, unfenced machines. You might notice the small child carrying the heavy load, or the bare feet of the workers and like the idea even less.

Attitudes to child labour

But these are 20th century attitudes. What would early 19th century people think, when looking at the same picture? It would depend very much on who they were. Some people argued that there was nothing wrong with the situation in Source 2A: people should be free to choose to work or not, and it was up to the parents whether to send their children out to work. If they didn't like it, they could keep them at home. Factory owners would also regard the scene as quite normal. They insisted that certain jobs could only be done by children. They liked child workers because their wages were low; adult wages were also kept low because families received the children's pay as well.

Among the first people to raise objections to child labour in factories were doctors.

 SOURCE 2B

Children of very tender age are employed ... these children are too long confined to work in close rooms, often during the whole night; the air they breathe, from the oil, etc. ... is injurious .... Frequent changes from a warm and dense to a cold and thin atmosphere are causes of illness and particularly of the epidemic fever which is so generally met with in these factories.

He also wondered what would happen to the children when they grew up:

The females are wholly uninstructed in sewing, knitting and other domestic affairs requisite to make them ... frugal wives and mothers. This is a very great misfortune to them and the public.

Dr Aiken, 1795

Other doctors disagreed:

SOURCE 2C

They [the child workers] seemed to be always cheerful and alert, taking pleasure in the light play of their muscles .... The work of these lively elves seemed to resemble a sport .... As to exhaustion by the day's work they showed no trace of it on coming out of the mill in the evening; for they immediately began to skip about any neighbouring playground ... with the same keenness as boys issuing from school.

Dr Ure, 1835 (adapted)

? QUESTIONS

a) What is Dr Aiken's worry about the health of the children?
b) What would a modern doctor say about the reasons he gives for illness?
c) What physical dangers are there in Source 2A which he does not mention?
d) What worries him about the effects of factory work on girls?
e) What is Dr Ure's view of child labour, in Source 2C?
f) What evidence does he offer to support his view?

SOURCE 2A Inside a cotton-spinning factory in the 1840s

The attitude of some other people at that time to scenes like that in Source 2A was quite different. They were worried that people working such long hours, and with no chance of education, would know nothing of Christianity. To these 'Evangelicals' (see Chapter 23, page 243) industry was creating a new barbaric age, with no Christian beliefs or standards. They wanted to persuade the public, and Parliament, that laws must be passed to limit hours of work, and to prevent children from working. Others also wanted to improve the situation out of fear of revolution: they thought that workers should not be forced into intolerable conditions in case they rose up against the whole system. Sensitive members of the public at that time were offended by particular aspects of the factory system: cruelty to the children, deformity of the workers, for example. Many, such as Dr Aiken in Source 2B, wanted to enforce their view of women as gentle, domesticated beings. They disapproved of boys and girls, or men and women, working together and were shocked at hints of possible immorality.

As for working people themselves, they would have had quite different reactions to Source 2A. They knew that children in their families had always helped with their parents' work, as they had done when they were children. They also knew, all too well, that with wages low and the cost of living high, there was no choice but to send their children to work. They were only too aware of the dangers, the long hours and the bullying overseers. They knew far more about these things than many middle- and upper-class reformers. They also knew that the problem was not restricted to children or to women, but that work in factories and mines was appalling for *all* workers. You can read in Chapter 18 how working people tried to help themselves, through unions, demonstrations and other movements. This chapter is concerned with the efforts of reformers.

Reforming mill-owners

Some factory owners tried to set a good example. One of these was Robert Owen. Owen was a Welshman, the son of a draper. He had

■ SOURCE 3 Schoolroom in New Lanark, early 19th century

great business ability and was made manager of a textile mill at 19. In 1799, aged 29, he took over his father-in-law's huge mills at New Lanark in Scotland. Here he put into practice his ideas on how to run a business. He paid good wages, even when business was slack. He expected hard work and good time-keeping. Unlike most factory owners he refused to employ children under ten. He also cut the working hours in the factory to 10½ hours a day – quite short hours for that time. To everyone's surprise, New Lanark mills made a good profit. This was used to build decent houses, shops and schools for Owen's workers and their children.

? QUESTIONS

a) What kind of lesson is going on in Source 3?

b) Compare this schoolroom with that in Chapter 22, Source 4A page 228. What differences are there? Which do you think would give the best education?

Other mill-owners, such as Titus Salt of Bradford, also tried to look after their workers. Salt built the village of Saltaire for them. However, Owen and Salt were exceptional, and reformers looked to Parliament to pass laws to protect all workers.

At that time only better-off males in Britain had the vote. Most of them, even those living in factory areas, had no idea what went on in a factory. The reformers therefore

had to work on public opinion and MPs' feelings. They brought information to the notice of Parliament, but it was, of course, information which drew attention only to the horrors of factory life. It is this information, published in reports (called 'Blue Books') which is used by most school textbooks (including this one) to describe factory life. Such evidence, therefore, must be handled very cautiously.

Reforming Working Hours

As we saw in Chapter 3, the first factories in the cotton industry in the 1780s were water-powered. This meant that they were often placed in remote country areas. Local people in these places would not work under the discipline of these factories. The factory owners took on young children, usually orphans, from workhouses all over Britain. These children, some as young as five years old, were entirely fed, clothed and housed by the factory owner. They were signed up as apprentices and so were supposed to be learning a trade. The workhouse guardians were glad to get the children off their hands. With no parents to speak up for them, their conditions and treatment were often terrible. One orphan, Robert Blincoe, was sent from London to Litton Mill, in a remote part of Derbyshire. Here the young apprentices worked 13-hour shifts, often all night. Blincoe described how they were clothed in rags and so badly fed that they fought each other for a share of the pig swill.

Early attempts at reform

Robert Owen, and others, campaigned to get Parliament to prevent this kind of treatment. Even those who opposed parliamentary interference in working conditions could not argue that these orphans were free to choose whether to work or not. The Health and Morals of Apprentices Act was passed in 1802. It said that boys and girls should be housed separately, with not more than two to a bed. They must not work more than 12 hours a day, and no night shifts. They should receive two sets of clothing a year, be educated in reading, writing and arithmetic, and attend church. You can see from these terms just how bad conditions must have been.

However, the Act only applied to cotton mills, not to silk, wool or flax factories where conditions were just as bad. Also, there was no way of enforcing the Act: local JPs were supposed to, but they were often friends of the mill-owners. In any case, the law was almost irrelevant by the time it was passed. Improvements in steam-engines meant that

steam-powered mills were being built in coalfield areas, near to towns and cities. Workers brought their own children into the factories to help them. For example, out of 136 employees at one cotton-factory, 95 belonged to just 26 families. The children were wage-labourers, not apprentices, so the 1802 Act did not apply to them. The only gain was that the principle of passing a law to control conditions in factories had been established and could be used again.

❓ QUESTIONS

a) How does the cartoonist in Source 4A show his opposition to child labour in factories?
b) What uses could a historian of factory conditions make of this evidence?

From 1814 Robert Owen tried to get a strict law passed to protect children, but the only result was the 1819 Factory Act which said that no child under nine could be employed; no one aged nine to 18 could work at night, or more than 12 hours a day. Hobhouse's Act of 1825 laid down a maximum of nine hours on Saturday, and another Act in 1831 raised the age-limit on night shifts to 21.

These Acts did little to improve the situation. They still only applied to cotton mills. There was no system

of registering the ages of children. Parents and employers were both hostile to the law and combined to exaggerate the age of the children. There was no inspection of factories. The only way of bringing a case before the magistrates was to find a witness to an offence, but witnesses were often bullied into withdrawing their evidence. In the 1820s John Doherty of the Manchester Cotton Spinners Union brought 187 cases to court. Only 27 were convicted.

By the 1830s the whole issue had become much more serious. The factory system had extended to the woollen industry of Yorkshire. There were also 250000 employees in the cotton industry, of whom 30000 were under 13 and 75000 aged 13–18. The new, large factories employed fewer family units. This meant that many children were not working for their mother or father, but for a stranger. In many people's eyes, this made child labour quite a different matter. It was also a bad time for adults, with low wages and very long hours. The response was the Ten Hours Movement.

The Ten Hours Movement

In the textile areas of Yorkshire and Lancashire the trade unions campaigned for a ten hours' maximum for children. Because children worked in teams with adults, unions calculated that this would cut the adult worker's day to ten hours. 'Short-time' committees were set up to work for this aim. Their slogan was:

We will have the Ten Hours Bill Or the land will not be still.

Their allies among the middle classes were one or two mill-owners, some writers who opposed the whole idea of factories, and some Tory MPs. Richard Oastler raised the issue in a powerful letter to the *Leeds Mercury* in 1830 (Source 4B), in which he compared child labour with slavery in the plantations of the West Indies.

■ *SOURCE 4B*

Let the truth speak out .... Thousands of our fellow-creatures and fellow-subjects, both female and male, the inhabitants of a Yorkshire town are at this very moment

■ *SOURCE 4A* **Cartoon, early 19th century**

existing in a state of slavery more horrid than are the victims of that hellish system – Colonial Slavery. The very streets which receive the droppings of an Anti-Slavery Society are every morning wet by the tears of innocent victims at the accursed shrine of greed who are compelled, not by the cart-whip of the negro slave driver, but by the dread of the equally appalling strap of the overlooker to hasten half-dressed, but not half-fed to those magazines of British Infantile Slavery – the Worsted mills in the town and neighbourhood of Bradford.

Thousands of little children both male and female ... from seven to fourteen years are daily compelled to labour from six o'-clock in the morning to seven in the evening with only – Britons blush while you read it – with only thirty minutes allowed for eating and recreation.

Leeds Mercury, October 16, 1830

 QUESTIONS

a) What comparisons does Oastler make between 'Colonial Slavery' and 'Infantile Slavery'?

b) Give examples of the emotive language he uses to persuade people of his cause.

In 1831 Michael Sadler MP introduced a bill into Parliament calling for 10 hours maximum and huge fines for employers who broke the law. The government was on the side of the factory owners, who said that shorter hours meant higher prices for their goods. They insisted that Britain would lose trade. To delay the bill the government set up a Select Committee to hear evidence about factory conditions. However, supporters of the Ten Hours Bill arranged for witnesses to go to London, and coached them in their answers. MPs who supported Sadler asked leading questions.

■ *SOURCE 4C*

MP: Is it your impression that your growth has been very much stunted, your health injured, and your constitution thus early destroyed by excessive labour?

WITNESS: Yes, it is.

Opponents tried to show up the aims of the adult workers behind the call for a Ten Hours limit for children.

■ *SOURCE 4D*

I really do think it is absolutely necessary that children should be protected from excessive labour. That is the first point in my mind; and with a hope, I confess, that it will benefit myself and others as well.'

David Brook, cloth dresser and overlooker

Nevertheless, the Committee collected impressive evidence.

■ *SOURCE 4E*

5047: At what time in the morning, in the brisk time [i.e. when they were busy] did those girls go to the mills?

In the brisk time they have gone about three o'clock in the morning and ended at ten, or nearly half-past, at night.

5049: What intervals were allowed for rest or refreshment during those nineteen hours of labour?
Breakfast, quarter of an hour, and dinner half an hour, and drinking a quarter of an hour.

5054: Had you not great difficulty in awakening your children at this excessive hour?

Yes, in the early time we had to take them up asleep, and shake them, and when we got them on the floor, to dress them, before we got them off to work.

5065: Were the children excessively fatigued by this labour?

Many times. We have often cried when we have given them the little food we had to give them; we had to shake them, and they have fallen to sleep with the food still in their mouths.

5073: Have your children been strapped?

Yes, every one. The eldest daughter, when my wife came in she said her back was beaten nearly to a jelly.

Evidence of Samuel Coulson, 1831–2. (The numbers refer to the numbers of the questions asked.)

There was also lots of evidence of deformities, accidents and ill-health as a result of working machines for long hours.

 QUESTIONS

a) Why is the evidence in Source 4C not of much value?

b) How many hours did Samuel Coulson's children work during the brisk time?

c) How many hours' break did this include?

d) What effect did this have on the children?

e) What effect would Samuel Coulson's evidence have on public opinion when it had been published?

f) The short-time committees helped witnesses with their evidence. Does this mean that we should not trust statements such as these?

g) How would you check the general reliability of these sources?

h) What do these sources tell us about the attitude of parents to the cruelty of child labour in factories?

Before the Bill could become law, Parliament was dissolved. The evidence was published in a 'Blue Book' and the campaign continued. Petitions were sent to Parliament: 16000 signatures from Leeds, 12000 from Bradford and 5000 from Halifax. Sadler lost his seat in the next election, but Antony Ashley, later Earl of Shaftesbury, took over the leadership of the campaign. The government played for time again, setting up a Commission of Inquiry. This was like the Poor Law Commission (Chapter 15, page 163), with Commissioners sent out to collect evidence under oath. They were suspicious of the evidence sent to the Select Committee and tried to discredit it. Sometimes they were successful.

■ *SOURCE 4F*

I never meant to say what you have read to me, of my being so young when I worked at night. I was going 16, and I never worked so more than a month.

Evidence to Factory Commissioner, 1833

 QUESTIONS

a) Suggest reasons why the witness gave false evidence in the first place.

b) Can we believe the evidence this time?

c) Does this evidence discredit Sources 4C, 4D and 4E?

Some points the Commissioners made were fair: they pointed out that ill-health could not be blamed entirely on the factories. Living conditions in industrial towns were quite appalling and were probably the main cause of disease. Many members of the short-time committees refused to meet the Commissioners. They accused the government of trying to whitewash factory conditions. It is true that some evidence was biased in favour of the factory owners, but the Commissioners found that the complaints of bullying, ill-health, deformity and long hours were true.

One of the Commissioners, Edwin Chadwick, offered a compromise solution for the government. He was opposed to the unions' call for Ten Hours for adults, but saw that public opinion had been convinced that children's hours must be reduced. He therefore suggested a cut to eight hours for children aged nine to 13, with two hours compulsory school. By having three lots of child workers, working in relays, the factories could still work 24 hours, and adults would still have to work 12 to 16 hours. The compulsory schooling prevented children leaving one factory and going on to work at another. Ashley's hopes of linking a 10-hour day for children with a cut in adult hours were thus lost. Mill-owners saw the point and accepted the new hours.

The 1833 Factory Act

These became the terms of the 1833 Factory Act: no children to be employed under the age of nine; nine to 13-year-olds to work no more than eight hours a day, plus two hours' school; 13–18 year olds no more than 12 hours; no one under 18 to work at nights. With his usual thoroughness, Chadwick proposed that factory inspectors be employed to enforce the Act.

Middle-class public opinion, worried by the horror stories of child labour, was pleased. Present-day textbooks usually praise the Act, and it is true that it did bring some important changes. But the unions and short-time committees were bitterly disappointed. The failure of the Ten Hours campaign led many to support the growing Chartist movement (Chapter 18, page 194).

Problems with the Act

Enforcing the law was, for many years, quite a problem. At first four inspectors were appointed to cover the whole country. This meant an impossible workload: Rickards, for example, Inspector for Yorkshire and Lancashire, had 2142 mills to inspect. They met the opposition of the factory owners, parents, children, doctors and JPs. They were underpaid, and did not even receive their travelling expenses.

The worst problem was still that of a clear definition of age. There was an incentive to parents and owners to lie about ages nine, 13 and 18, as owners needed workers, and parents needed money. Parents would go from a doctor who refused to sign the age-certificate to one who would bend his conscience for the 6*d* (2½p) fee. Schooling was widely avoided. Owners and children expected to get away with not being caught breaking the law.

■ *SOURCE 5*

Mr Baker [an assistant inspector] proceeded, on arriving at the ... mill ... at once into one of the rooms (where, however, the cry of 'the Superintendent is coming' had already reached) and having observed two machines at work, with only one boy at each, but which absolutely required two, he cast his eye around the room and observed some person very busy about a bag of wool; he went up and found a boy who had been wrongly employed in the act of being concealed therein; his head and body had been already enclosed and the bag fastened over him, and Mr Baker only discovered him by his feet still protruding.

Report of a factory inspector about a visit to a woollen mill in Ossett, 1838

❓ *QUESTIONS*

a) How do we know that the inspector was making a surprise visit?

b) How did he know something was wrong?

Even if the case went to court, the normal fine was often only £1. Obviously most mill-owners could afford to pay this. Factory Inspector Horner, over four months in Lancashire in 1837, brought 504 prosecutions and gained 458 convictions, but in 343 cases the fine was only £1.

Only gradually did the situation improve. The 1844 Factory Act cut children's hours to seven per day, or ten every other day. Women aged 18–21 were not to work more than 69 hours per week. These terms probably brought a reduction in adult hours. The Act also helped the inspectors by increasing their numbers and paying travelling expenses. Agitation for shorter hours increased again in the late 1840s. A Ten Hour Act was passed in 1847, but could not be enforced. In the

■ *SOURCE 6A* Woman and child hauling coal in Lancashire

end, the Factory Act of 1853 laid down a working day of 6 a.m.–6 p.m. or 7 a.m.–7 p.m. With one and a half hours in breaks this gave a normal working day of 10½ hours.

Reforms in the Mines

Meanwhile Ashley turned his attention to the terrible working conditions for women and children in mines. Another Commission was set up, and a mass of evidence collected. It was published, with illustrations, in another 'Blue Book', in 1842. Sources 6A–6F are taken from this report. Source 6A is on the previous page.

■ SOURCE 6B

I have a belt round my waist, and a chain passing between my legs and I go on my hands and feet. The road is steep, and we have to hold by a rope .... The pit is very wet where I work and the water comes over our clog-tops sometimes .... I am not as strong as I was and cannot stand my work so well as I used to. I have drawn till I have had the skin off me; the belt and chain is worse when we are in the family way.

Betty Harris, aged 37

■ SOURCE 6C

I have wrought in the bowels of the earth 33 years. Have been married 23 years and had 9 children; six are alive, three died of typhus a few years since. Have had two dead born. A vast number of women have dead children and false births .... I have always been obliged to work below till forced to go home to bear the bairn .... We return as soon as we are able, never longer than 10 or 12 days: many less if they are much needed.

It is only horse work and it ruins the women; it crushes their haunches; bends their ankles and makes them old women at 40.

Jane Peacock Watson, aged 40

■ SOURCE 6D

I hurry in the clothes I have got on now (trousers and ragged jacket). The bald place upon my head is made by thrusting the corves. I hurry the corves a mile and more underground and back; they

■ SOURCE 6E Hurrier and trapper. A trapper opens the ventilation doors when a tub is pushed through

weigh 3 hundredweight; I hurry 11 a day. The getters that I work for are naked except for their caps; they beat me with their hands if I am not quick enough. The boys take liberties with me sometimes, they pull me about. I am the only girl in the pit. There are about 20 boys and 15 men. All the men are naked; I would rather work in mill than in coal-pit.

(Hurry – push tubs of coal; corves – tubs; getters – coal-diggers)

Patience Kershaw, aged 17

■ SOURCE 6F

I have been a trapper six months. I likes it very much. I goes at 5 and come away at 2, sometimes at 3. I get 4s [20p] a week and am quite content. Sometimes I falls asleep. If I'm caught sleeping I gets a hiding with a stick.

Thomas Thew, aged 10

? QUESTIONS

a) How far does Patience Kershaw (Source 6D) push the corves each day?

b) Thomas Thew (Source 6F) says he likes the job. Do you think that means it would be all right for children of his age to work underground?

c) Write a brief summary of the kinds of jobs women and children did in coal mines in Britain in 1840, as revealed in these sources.

d) On the basis of your summary, what would be the terms of a Mines Act you would pass to improve the situation?

e) The illustrations (Sources 6A and 6E) were drawn by an artist who had not, in fact, gone down a coalmine. On what has the artist based her illustrations? Does this mean that they are no use as historical evidence?

The report revealed working conditions of quite dreadful cruelty and barbarism. Women and children were being used as mere animals in crippling and degrading conditions. But we must be careful what conclusions we draw from this report. It would be quite wrong, for example, to think that the conditions described were typical of most pits in Britain. As we saw in Chapter 5, the use of tubs on rails, pit-ponies and cages had widely replaced the jobs done by Betty Harris (Source 6B) and Patience Kershaw (Source 6D). Modern estimates are that there were about 5000 to 6000 women miners, out of about 150 000 employed in the mines. Women were employed in Lancashire, East Scotland, West Yorkshire and South Wales, but in declining numbers; no women were employed in Northumberland, Durham, Cumberland, or the Midlands. Women and children were usually employed in small, old-fashioned pits, where the family or 'butty' system remained.

Ashley and his supporters knew how to shock their fellow-Victorians, too. For many of them, the things which touched their emotions were the tiny children left for hours in the dark, as trappers,

■ SOURCE 7 Pit lasses in Lancashire, late 19th century

and the suggestions of immorality (see Source 6D). The whole question of working conditions, safety and hours of work for men were not considered. Nor was any thought given to how women miners could earn a living if they could not go down the pit.

Mines Act 1842

Nevertheless, as Ashley said: 'The disgust is very great, thank God!' Although the mine-owners argued against it, the government could not prevent the Mines Act, passed in 1842. It said that no female could work underground, and that no one under 10 should go underground. An inspector was appointed to enforce the Act, but he tended to favour the owners. Not until 1850 were inspectors allowed down the pit. Nevertheless a start had been made on controlling this harsh and dangerous industry.

No doubt those who passed the Act expected women now banned

from coalmining to stay at home. However, many were single, or widows, or wanted to earn their own living. Mining usually took place in isolated areas where there were no other jobs to go to. A survey in Scotland found that of 2400 women miners thrown out of work, only 200 had other jobs by 1845. Women continued to work in the mining industry, doing jobs on the surface.

? QUESTIONS

a) Where was the photograph (Source 7) taken?
b) What jobs do these women do?

Efforts have been made up to the present day to stop women doing these jobs. The union wanted the jobs for men, and some reformers felt it was wrong for women to do hard physical labour. However, women have fought for the right to carry on earning their own living in the way they want to.

Further Reforms

Once the Factory and Mines Acts had made a start, reformers gradually increased the protection the law gave to children, women and eventually, adult male workers. The Factory Acts Extension Act of 1864 widened the control of the Factory Acts to other trades – pottery, matches, paper, dyeing and chemicals. The Workshop Regulation Act 1867 brought inspectors, and control of hours, to the thousands of tiny workshops. Anywhere employing more than five people was covered. (Note: only half the workers in industry worked in factories.) Further Acts in 1874 and 1878 brought in shorter hours up to the age of 14, and a ten-hour day for women and teenagers.

In the mines, most laws concentrated on safety. In 1855 laws controlling ventilation were tightened, and in 1862 single-shaft mines were declared illegal. In 1860 boys were not allowed underground until the age of 12 unless they could read and write. By 1872 mine-managers had to have a certificate to prove their ability to do their job.

Sweated labour

■ SOURCE 8A

The following is an account of my past experience as a City machinist. I obtained work at the following prices:

Flannel & cotton blouses, plain	1s dozen
Children's flannel & cotton blouses	8d dozen
Flannel & cotton nightdresses, with frills	2s 9d dozen
Flannelette bathing gowns, trimmed	3s dozen

After paying for my own cotton, and railway journey, I had 7s [35p] per week on average, sometimes less, and paid 5s [25p] for rent. I worked from 6 a.m. in the morning to 10 at night.

Letter to Anti-Sweating League, 1905

A major problem to seize reformers' attention in the late 19th century was 'sweated labour'. In various trades, such as garment-making, nail-making, lace-making and paper box-making, workers were paid piece-rates, i.e. the wage was based on how many they made. The pay was extremely low. The workers were usually women, or, in London, Jewish immigrants. They either worked at home or in overcrowded sweatshops. The Factory Acts and trade unions did not affect them.

After pressure from the Anti-Sweating League, and the Women's Industrial Council, the Trades Board Acts 1909 and 1913 were passed. Boards were set up for each trade, with representatives of employers, workers and the government. They laid down minimum rates of pay and conditions.

After the battles over the first Factory Acts, the idea that workers were free to make their own conditions began to decline. Nowadays the Health and Safety Executive makes detailed regulations for hours, conditions and safety in every part of industrial activity in Britain.

■ *SOURCE 8B* **Punch cartoon, 1845**

Assignments

Empathy

1 Several different groups wanted to reform condition in factories. What were the motives of each of these:
   i doctors;
   ii Evangelicals;
   iii some factory-owners;
   iv working people;
   v Tory landowners?
2 What does this chapter tell us about attitudes among Victorians towards:
   i women and
   ii children?
3 Imagine you are Samuel Coulson (Source 4E). Describe your life, your family, their work and how you feel about your daughters working.
4 Imagine you are the owner of a factory such as the one in Source 1A.
   a Why do you have rules such as those in Source 1C?
   b Why do you employ children?
   c Why are you opposed to any restriction in the working hours of any of your workers?

Understanding concepts

1 **Change/continuity**
   a How far did the 1833 Factory Act change working conditions in factories?
   b How far did the 1842 Mines Act change working conditions in mines?
   c What were the problems of enforcing these two Acts?

2 **Causation/motivation**
   a Who opposed the introduction of laws to restrict working conditions in factories?
   b What were their motives in doing so?
   c How did they prevent the 1833 Factory Act from including the terms that its supporters wanted?

Evidence

Sources 4A, 4B, 4C, 4E and 6A, 6B, 6C, 6D, 6E and 6F were designed to persuade people that working conditions in factories and mines needed reforming. They are, in different ways, examples of propaganda. Take each in turn and show the way they were designed to appeal to the Victorian public.

Themes for discussion

1 Do you think it was right to stop women from working down coal mines?
2 Do you think it is right to restrict the working hours of children at the present time?

15 *The Problem of Poverty 1700–1900*

The Causes of Poverty

What should we do about the poor? This question faces Britain today, as it has always done. The answer to it will depend on your views about the causes of poverty. If you think people are poor through their own fault, you will have one solution; if you think it is not their own fault, you will have another solution; if you think it varies from case to case, you will have to decide how and where to draw the line. In this chapter and the next one you can see how changing attitudes have brought changing policies throughout the period covered by this book.

Poverty was a serious problem in early 19th century Britain. In rural areas, mostly in the south of England, many farm labourers were very poor. The changes in agriculture described in Chapter 2 brought more employment in hoeing, harvesting, hedging and ditching. But the growing population meant that there were too many people looking for work, so wages were very low and work was often part-time only. In the past women had been able to earn money by spinning or making things at home. Now factories were taking over these jobs. The enclosure movement meant more work, but it took away the common grazing rights which had earlier helped country people make ends meet.

SOURCE 1A Farm labourer's cottage, early 19th century

■ SOURCE 1B A labourer's weekly budget, early 19th century

WAGES	
Husband 8s; Wife 6d; Total 8s 6d	
EXPENSES	
Flour for bread, 7½ gallons	6s 3d
Yeast	2½d
Salt	1½d
Bacon: 1 lb, boiled with vegetables (the stock, with bread, makes another meal for the children)	8d
Tea 1 oz	2d
Sugar 4 oz	6d
Butter 8 oz	4d
Soap 4 oz	2¼
Candles 5 oz	3d
Thread for mending clothes	3d
Total	8s 11¼d

■ SOURCE 1C

I don't want to argue about the good intentions [of enclosure]: poor people look at facts, not intentions; and the fact is by nineteen enclosure bills in twenty the poor are injured, in some cases grossly injured …

Go to an ale-house in an enclosed county and there you will see the origin of poverty. For whom are they to be sober? For whom are they to save? If I am hard-working, will I get permission to build a cottage? If I am sober shall I have land for a cow? You offer me no motives, you have nothing but a parish officer and the workhouse. Bring me another pot!

Arthur Young, 1801

? QUESTIONS

a) What signs of poverty are there in Source 1A?
b) Why would it be unwise to rely entirely on Source 1A to find out about poverty in rural England?
c) Does reading Sources 1B and 1C help us to make use of Source 1A?
d) In Source 1B, what is the main thing the family eats?
e) Does their income meet their expenses? How do you think they manage?
f) Are there any important items missing from their expenses?
g) What is Young's attitude to enclosures in Source 1C?
h) How could you find out if he is describing a true picture?

In industrial areas, mainly in the North, poverty had quite different causes. There were some craftsmen, such as the hand-loom weavers, whose jobs had been replaced by machines (see Chapter 3). There was also the problem of sudden changes in trade. If there was a slump, factory owners would lay workers off and would take them on again when they had more orders. With no dole or redundancy pay, the condition of these workers and their families became desperate in a short time.

The Poor Laws

The system for dealing with the poor at that time was based on the Poor Laws passed in the reign of Queen Elizabeth I in 1599 and 1601. These stated that each parish had to look after its own poor. The Justices of the Peace appointed overseers (or parish officers – see Source 1C) and levied a poor rate on every householder. Needy people who could work – called the 'able-bodied poor' – were set to work in a workhouse. People who were poor through old age or illness were given money, called 'outdoor relief', or were moved into an almshouse. Children were put out as apprentices in order to learn a trade. Beggars were punished. The Act of Settlement 1662 said that every poor person had to be looked after in the parish of their birth. This could lead to cruelty, as when overseers sometimes forced poor pregnant mothers to leave their parish. Gilbert's Act of 1782 allowed parishes to group together in unions to build better workhouses.

On the whole, and with the help of a good deal of local charity, the Elizabethan system worked up to the end of the 18th century. Then the changes in agriculture and population described at the beginning of this chapter really began to take effect and the problem became too big for the old system to cope with. Various schemes were tried in various parts of the country to deal with the large numbers of poor. One system which was quite common in parts of southern England was the Speenhamland or allowance system, devised by magistrates at Speenhamland in Berkshire.

■ SOURCE 2

At a general meeting of the Justices of this County on Wednesday May 6th, 1795, at the Pelican Inn in Speenhamland, it was resolved unanimously:

That the present state of the poor does require further assistance than has been generally given them …

The Magistrates make the following calculations and allowances for relief of all industrious men and their families who shall endeavour (as far as they can) for their own support and maintenance.

That is to say, when the gallon loaf shall cost 1s [5p],

Then every poor and industrious man shall have for his own support 3s [15p] weekly, either produced by his own or his family's labour, or an allowance from the poor rates; and for the support of his wife and every other of his family, 1s 6d [7½p] …

And as the price of bread rises or falls 3d [1¼p] to the man and 1d [½p] to every other of the family and every 1d [½p] which the loaf rise above 1s [5p].

**By Order of the Meeting
W. Budd, Deputy Clerk of the Peace**

? QUESTIONS

a) Explain in your own words how the system worked.
b) What were the motives of the JPs in working out the system?
c) Did the system make any distinction between people who were working and people who were not?
d) Do you think this would have an effect on people's willingness to work?

Other systems were the 'labour rate', by which a farmer could choose to pay a rate or employ a labourer. If he paid the labourer below the proper wage, it was made up out of the poor rates. About 20% of parishes used this system. Also used was the 'roundsman' system, where unemployed labourers had to go round the farmers asking for work before they could receive poor relief. In much of northern England the overseers simply paid money – outdoor relief – to poor families, to see them through the times when trade was bad.

The cost of looking after the poor was quite considerable, as Source 3A shows.

■ SOURCE 3A Costs of the poor rate over the whole of England and Wales

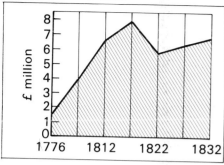

These totals hid local and regional differences as shown in Source 3B.

■ SOURCE 3B Amount of poor relief paid out per head of population, 1831

Region	Poor relief
Bradford	2s 11½d
Lancashire	4s 4¾d
Suffolk	18s 3¼d

? QUESTIONS

a) From Source 3A, what had happened to the cost of poor relief since 1776?
b) Why had this happened?
c) Which was the peak year?
d) What had happened since then?
e) From your own knowledge and from reading this book, what differences were there between Bradford, Lancashire and Suffolk in 1831?
f) How might these differences explain the different costs of poor relief?

Some writers, such as the Rev. Thomas Malthus, believed that it was a mistake to help the poor. Simple natural laws, he said, would solve the problem: overpopulation caused low wages; low wages caused hunger and death, so the population would fall and wages would rise again. In his view, to pay relief to the poor merely made the problem worse.

■ SOURCE 4

The labouring poor always live hand to mouth. Their wants of the moment are all they think about and they seldom think of the future. All they have above their needs of the moment goes, gener-

ally speaking, to the ale-house. The poor-laws of England may therefore be said to lessen both the power and the will to save among the common people and thus to weaken the incentive to soberness and hard work, and hence to happiness.

Malthus, *Essay on Population*, 1797

? QUESTIONS

a) What is Malthus's attitude to the poor?
b) Do you think what he says is true nowadays?
c) Do you think it was true then?

Many people agreed with Malthus that, in a nutshell, the Poor Laws created the poor. Other people were resentful of the high cost of poor relief and objected to the poor rate. For many, the Captain Swing riots of 1830 (Chapter 18, page 191) were the last straw: here were the very people who received all this poor relief rioting against those who paid the poor rate! The government decided to set up a Royal Commission to investigate the Poor Laws.

The Royal Commission into the Poor Laws

It was a huge topic to investigate: there were 15000 parishes in England and Wales. Clearly, the Commissioners needed to get a full and proper sample of what was going on all over the country. Also, to carry out a proper investigation they needed to have open minds about the Poor Laws and how they were working. Does the actual Report and its recommendations suggest that they did?

Three Commissioners and 26 Assistant Commissioners were appointed in 1832. In all, 3000 parishes were visited and 10% of parishes filled in a questionnaire. The most energetic Assistant Commissioner was Edwin Chadwick, who produced masses of evidence from his areas: part of London and rural Berkshire. Chadwick and Commissioner Nassau Senior wrote the report which came out in 1834. They were both followers of Malthus, though Chadwick was particularly influenced by the writer and thinker Jeremy Bentham. Above all, Chadwick hated waste and idleness.

The Speenhamland system was severely attacked in the Report. The Commissioners said that it discouraged hard work, helped the lazy and encouraged illegitimacy. They blamed it for forcing wages down, saying that farmers would not bother to pay proper wages, as they were made up to a decent level by the poor rate.

■ SOURCE 5A

In Coggeshall, Essex, a good labourer may earn 10s [50p]. Now consider the case of labourers with four children, for the subsistence of which family (according to the Chelmsford scale) 11s 6d [57½p] is required. Of this sum the good labourer earns 10s [50p] and receives from the parish 1s 6d [7½p]. The man who does not work, and who no one will employ, receives the whole from the parish.

Poor Law Commissioners' Report, 1834

■ SOURCE 5B

ASSISTANT COMMISSIONER: **In your parish are there many able-bodied men upon the parish [i.e. receiving poor relief]?**

THOMAS PEARCE, SUSSEX LABOURER: **There are a great many men in our parish who like it better than being at work.**

ASSISTANT COMMISSIONER: **Why do they like it better?**

THOMAS PEARCE: **They get the same money and don't do as much work. They don't work like me; and they be'ant at it so may hours, and they don't do so much work when they be at it.**

ASSISTANT COMMISSIONER: **How have you managed to live without parish relief?**

THOMAS PEARCE: **By working hard.**

Poor Law Commissioners' Report, 1834

The Report also quoted evidence from Cholesbury, a village which had gone bankrupt because of the poor rates.

? QUESTIONS

a) How widespread was the Speenhamland system?
b) Were there any other reasons for low wages?
c) How typical of the country as a whole were the areas investigated by Chadwick?
d) Does Source 5A contain facts or opinions?

e) Does Source 5B contain facts or opinions?

f) Do Sources 5A and 5B prove that the Speenhamland system caused laziness, low wages and illegitimacy?

g) There do not seem to have been any other villages which got into the same mess that Cholesbury did. Is there any point in reporting the problems of that village?

Historians have since criticised the Report for being unhistorical. That is, it blamed everything on the Poor Laws, when, as we know, historical events often have several causes. Recently, historians have also criticised the Report as unstatistical because the recommendations do not follow from the evidence that was collected.

The Report recommended simple, drastic changes. Chadwick wanted not merely to change the system but to change people's attitudes to work.

Recommendations made in the Report

1 To restore the self-respect of working people the poor had to be treated worse than the worst-paid labourer. Then people would choose to work rather than get poor relief, if they possibly could.

2 To test if people really needed relief, it would only be offered in a workhouse and would be so unattractive that people would only accept it if the alternative was starvation. Men and women would be separated; food would be adequate but uninteresting; discipline strict. This was called the 'workhouse test'.

3 All outdoor relief – payments to the poor in their own homes – should cease.

4 Chadwick recognised that there were some who simply could not get work: the ill, children and elderly. He proposed that they should be looked after in separate institutions.

5 Parishes should group together to form unions. Each union would have a workhouse, run by a Board of Guardians. These would be elected by those who paid the poor rate. A Central Poor Law Commission would be set up in London to inspect the work of the local guardians.

The 1834 Poor Law Amendment Act

The recommendations were included in the Poor Law Amendment Act of 1834. Three Commissioners were appointed, but Chadwick was not one of them. He had to be content with the post of Secretary. In this position he could urge the Boards of Guardians to carry out his plans. (This mixture of local and central power was typical of the time – see Chapter 13 on public health.)

■ SOURCE 6A

The members of the Board were very wise men .... So they established the rule that all poor should have the alternative of being starved by a gradual process in the house or by a quick one out of it. With this view they contracted with the waterworks to lay on an unlimited supply of water, and with a cornfactor to supply periodically small quantities of oatmeal; and issued three meals of thin gruel a day, with an onion twice a week and half a roll on Sundays.

They made a great many other wise and humane regulations: kindly undertook to divorce poor married persons ... and instead of compelling a man to support his family, took his family away from him and made him a bachelor.

Charles Dickens, *Oliver Twist*, 1838

■ SOURCE 6C Plan for a workhouse for 200, published by the Poor Law Commissioners, 1834

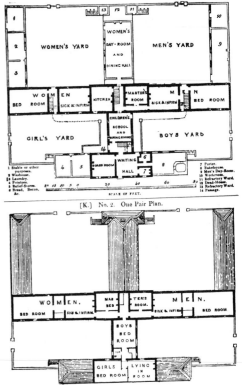

■ SOURCE 6B Dietary for adult paupers, 1838

		BREAKFAST.		DINNER.				SUPPER.	
		Bread.	Gruel.	Meat pudding with Vegetable	Suet pudding with potatoes.	Bread.	Cheese.	Broth.	Bread.	Cheese.
		oz.	Pints.	oz.	oz.	oz.	oz.	Pints.	oz.	oz.
SUNDAY.....	Men	6	1½			5	1		6	1
	Women	5	1½			7	1		5	1
MONDAY.....	Men	6	1½	16					6	1
	Women	5	1½	19					5	1
TUESDAY....	Men	6	1½			5	1	1½	6	1
	Women	5	1½			7	1	1½	5	1
WEDNESDAY,	Men	6	1½		16				6	1
	Women	5	1½						5	1
THURSDAY...	Men	6	1½			5	1		6	1
	Women	5	1½			7	1		5	1
FRIDAY.....	Men	6	1½	16					6	1
	Women	5	1½	19					5	1
SATURDAY...	Men	6	1½			5	1	1½	6	1
	Women	5	1½			7	1	1½	5	1

Old People, of Sixty Years of Age, and upwards, to be allowed 1 oz. of Tea, 5 oz. of Butter, and 7 oz. of Sugar per Week, in lieu of Gruel, for Breakfast.

Children under nine Years to be dieted at discretion; above Nine years to be allowed the same quantities as Women.

Sick to be dieted as directed by the Medical Officer.

[Woolby, Printer, Stowmarket.]

■ SOURCE 6D

Any pauper who shall neglect to observe such of the regulations herein contained as are applicable to and binding on him:

Or who shall make any noise when silence is ordered to be kept

Or shall use obscene or profane language

Or shall refuse or neglect to work

Or shall play at cards or other unseemly games of chance ...

Shall be deemed DISORDERLY ...

It shall be lawful for the master of the workhouse to punish any disorderly pauper by substituting, for not more than 48 hours, a meal consisting of 8 oz of bread or 1 lb of potatoes and by withholding from him during the same period all butter, cheese, tea, sugar, or broth.

Workhouse Rules of Conduct, 1838

■ SOURCE 6E A workhouse yard in the 1840s

■ SOURCE 6F

MR WAKELEY: **What work were you employed at when you were in the workhouse?**

CHARLES LEWIS: **I was employed breaking bones.**

MR WAKELY: **During the time you were so employed did you ever see any men gnaw anything or eat anything from these bones?**

CHARLES LEWIS: **I have seen them eat marrow out of these bones.**

MR WAKELY: **Did they state why they did it?**

CHARLES LEWIS: **I really believe they were hungry.**

MR WAKELY: **Did you yourself feel extremely hungry at this time?**

CHARLES LEWIS: **I did, but my stomach wouldn't take it.**

MR WAKELY: **Did you see any of the men gnaw the meat from the bones?**

CHARLES LEWIS: **Yes.**

Report of Parliamentary Select Committee into Andover Workhouse, 1846

? QUESTIONS

a) In Source 6A Dickens is being ironic (saying the opposite of what he means). What is his attitude to the new Poor Law, and how can you tell?

b) Comment on Source 6B from the point of view of:
  i) quantity.
  ii) interest.
  iii) nutritional value.

c) In what ways do Sources 6A and Source 6F seem to contradict the information given in Source 6B?

d) Explain these contradictions.

e) Which aspects of the new Poor Law can be seen to have been put into effect in Source 6C?

f) Which aspects cannot be shown in such a source?

g) What effect would the appearance of the building in Source 6C have, and why?

h) Do Sources 6D and 6E help us any further in finding out about the workhouse diet?

i) What further impression of workhouse life do Sources 6D and 6E provide?

The Poor Law Amendment Act was hated by the ordinary people of Britain for the next hundred years. Those who had to go to the workhouse hated the separation of husbands, wives and children most of all. They also hated having to wear the workhouse uniform. Chadwick's plans for putting the old, the sick, children and the mentally ill in different institutions from able-bodied paupers never came about. For elderly people in particular, the fear of ending up in the workhouse hung over them as they grew old.

■ SOURCE 6G Lambeth Workhouse in the 1890s

Although we were aware of the shame of going to the workhouse, when Mother told us about it both Sydney and I thought it adventurous .... Then the forlorn bewilderment of it struck me: for there we were made to separate, Mother going in one direction to the women's ward, and we in another to the children's.

How well I remember the poignant sadness of that first visiting day! The shock of seeing Mother enter the visiting room garbed in workhouse clothes. How forlorn and embarrassed she looked! In one week she had aged and grown thin, but her face lit up when she saw us ...

Extract from Charlie Chaplin's autobiography, 1965

❓ QUESTIONS

a) How did Charlie and his brother Sydney change their views about the workhouse when they got there?
b) What aspects of workhouse life upset him most?
c) What other unpleasant aspects of workhouse life mentioned in the paragraph above are referred to in this Source?

The effect of the new Poor Law

From 1834, Chadwick and the Commissioners set about putting the Act into effect. In all, 350 work-houses were built in the next five years.

Things went quite well in the south of England. Good harvests and an increase in employment building the new railways made the task easier. It was a different story in the North where the problem, as we have seen, was quite different. The Speenhamland system had not been used. Workers were happy with the system of outdoor relief which tided them over bad times in trade. Employers liked the system, too, because it gave them a ready supply of workers as soon as trade picked up. If the poor were forced into the workhouse, they could not start work again so easily. There was opposition all over the north. There were riots in Huddersfield, Dewsbury, Todmorden and Stockport. Richard Oastler spoke out against the new Poor Law and sermons were preached against it. The poor called the workhouses 'Bastilles' after the hated French prison stormed by the revolutionary crowds in 1789. Opposition to the new Poor Law was a big factor in the growing support for Chartism (see Chapter 18, page 194). Opposition also came from the Tories, who preferred the old system. Disraeli, soon to be leader of the Conservatives, complained that the Act 'made poverty a crime'.

■ *SOURCE 7A* **Riots at Stockport, 1842; rioters handing out bread**

■ *SOURCE 7B*

People who never could be made to work before have become good labourers, and do not express any dissatisfaction with the measure. In most parishes the moral character of the poor is improving: there is a readiness to be more orderly and well-behaved .... The great body of labouring poor throughout the Union have become reconciled to it; the workhouse is held in great dread; cases of bastardy are on the decline.

Report of the Market Harborough Union, Leicestershire, 1836

❓ QUESTIONS

a) Why did the rioters shown in Source 7A hate the workhouse?
b) In what ways is the writer of Source 7B pleased with the new Poor Law?
c) Why is he pleased that 'the workhouse is held in great dread'?

In financial terms the new Poor Law was a success. The cost of poor relief had dropped by as much as one-third by 1854. However, outdoor relief was never abolished. In difficult years the sheer numbers needing relief were so great that workhouses were swamped. Out-door relief was paid all over the country, especially in the North. In fact, it was soon realised that out-door relief was actually cheaper: in one London parish, calculations showed that it cost 4s 8d (23½p) a week to keep a pauper in a work-house, while paupers could be kept in their own homes for 2s 3d (11½p) outdoor relief per week.

As the 19th century went on, it became clear that the plans laid down in 1834 were not appropriate for an industrial society. Working people turned increasingly to self-help schemes: Friendly Societies, Unions, Co-operatives (Chapter 18, page 196). There was a growth in local charities too. In 1865, for example, £67 000 was distributed through charities. The Charity Organisation Society was set up in 1869 to provide help and advice. Radicals such as Lovett attacked this aspect of relief as encouraging 'hypocrisy and servility'. He may have been right, but it did help to keep many people out of the workhouse.

Increasingly, workhouses contained only orphans, the old, the sick and the insane. The principle of the 'workhouse test' was never intended to apply to them. Later in the 19th century changes were tried.

Schools were set up, orphans were placed in foster homes, hospitals were built. From 1862, separate wards had to be provided for the insane; from the 1880s married couples over 60 were allowed their own separate rooms. However the stigma of the workhouse remained, and Source 8 helps us understand why.

Chadwick and many early Victorians believed that poverty could be avoided by care and hard work. By the end of the 19th century many people realised that this was just not true, and began to press for a completely different approach to the problem (see Chapter 16).

■ *SOURCE 8* **New ward at Marylebone Workhouse, 1867**

Assignments

Empathy

1 Look at Sources 6A to 6F.
  a How would you feel if you had to live in a workhouse?
  b How do you think the poor felt about it at the time?
  c How would the author of Source 7B defend the system?
2 a What was the attitude of Chadwick and the Poor Law Commissioners to the old Poor Law?
  b What attitudes did they want the poor to have?
3 Explain why the following groups of people did not like the new Poor Law:
  i Poor people in rural areas, especially in the South;
  ii Poor people in urban areas, especially in the North;
  iii Some factory owners;
  iv Some Tory landowners.

Understanding concepts

1 **Causation/motivation**
  a What were the causes of poverty in early 19th century Britain?
  b What did the Poor Law Commissioners think were the causes of poverty?
  c Why did the Commissioners not understand the real causes?

2 **Similarity/difference**
  a What were the various methods used to deal with the poor under the old Poor Laws?
  b Why did many of the ruling classes in about 1830 wish to change the system for dealing with the poor?
  c How fair was the Report of the Poor Law Commissioners in its description of the old Poor Law?

3 **Change/continuity**
  a What were the terms of the Poor Law Amendment Act?
  b How successful was it in dealing with the problem of poverty?
  c What criticisms could be made of the Act by the later 19th century?

Theme for discussion

In what ways are attitudes to the poor today the same as they were in 1835? In what ways are they different?

16 The Making of the Welfare State

Class Differences

Life in Britain in 1900 for members of the upper and middle classes was very comfortable indeed.
A favourite form of upper-class entertainment was to invite guests to your country house for the weekend.

■ *SOURCE 1B*

On a lawn of brilliant green, he could see the sprinkled figures of his mother's guests, some sitting under the trees, some strolling about. He could hear their laughter and the tap of the croquet mallets. Round the garden spread the park: a herd of deer stood flicking their short tails in the shade of the beeches ...

[For tea] one just had scones, and egg sandwiches, and pâté sandwiches and cucumber sandwiches and chocolate cake and walnut cake and coffee cake and cake. Also there were little plates with china-handled knives to match from which people ate jam and toast ... the butler, the groom of the chambers, the under-butler and the footmen would move about offering food.

Vita Sackville-West, *The Edwardians,* **1960**

A lady from the comfortable upper-middle class describes moving into a new house in 1900:

■ *SOURCE 1C*

We proceeded to modernise it with a service lift, electric light and a telephone.

This house ... contained a large basement, three sitting rooms, a lounge-hall and seven bedrooms. All the rooms were warmed by coal-fires; there were nursery meals to be carried up and down, hot water to be taken to the bedrooms, and we entertained a good deal. Yet we found little difficulty in running the house with a staff consisting of a nurse, a parlourmaid, a housemaid and a cook. Later we kept a manservant for £70 a year. The cook earned £28. The nurse's salary was £40.

Mrs Peel, 1933

? QUESTIONS

a) A wealthy lifestyle depended on servants. How do Sources 1A, 1B and 1C make it clear that servants had a lot of work to do?
b) How could people afford so many servants?
c) Use these sources to write a letter from someone staying in an English country house for a weekend to a friend in the USA, describing what it was like. You may choose to be a guest, or a servant.

Below these lucky few came the working classes. But how many lived in poverty? It would have been quite easy for the people in Sources 1A–C to think that hardly anyone was poor. The Poor Law Amendment Act 1834 had provided workhouses. There had been Acts of Parliament to deal with health and housing (see Chapter 13). Real wages had risen in the second half of the 19th century. Most middle- and upper-class people could avoid coming across poverty in their daily lives, so they might be tempted to think the problem had been solved.

Finding Out About the Poor

A group of writers and investigators were determined to show that not only was poverty still present in Britain, but that it was widespread. One was Andrew Mearns, a Congregationalist minister, who wrote an angry book in 1883, *The Bitter Cry of Outcast London.*

■ SOURCE 2A

First, the information given does not refer to selected cases. Secondly, there has been absolutely no exaggeration. This must be to every Christian heart a loud and bitter cry, appealing for the help which it is the supreme mission of the Church to supply.

You have to penetrate courts reeking with poisonous and malodorous gases arising from the accumulation of sewage and refuse scattered in all directions .... You have to ascend rotten staircases. You have to grope your way along dark and filthy passages, swarming with vermin. Then you may gain admittance to the dens in which thousands of beings who belong as much as you do to the race for which Christ died, herd together.

Andrew Mearns, *The Bitter Cry of Outcast London*, 1883

Claims in the newspapers that a quarter of London's population lived in poverty made Charles Booth determined to prove that they were wrong. He was a wealthy ship-owner, and began a systematic investigation. His findings, filled 17 volumes, came out from 1889 to 1903 and were called *Life and Labour of the People in London*. He found various categories of poor, as shown in Source 2B.

■ SOURCE 2B

Class A – The Lowest Class. Street-sellers, criminals, loafers. Their life is the life of savages with extreme hardship ... 11 000 or 1¼% of the whole population.

Class B – Casual earnings – widows and deserted women – part-time labourers – many shiftless, helpless. 100 000 or 11¼%.

Class C – Occasional earnings – hit by trade depressions. 75 000 or 8%.

Class D – Low wages, less than 21/- a week [£1.05]. Wages barely enough to stay alive. This group includes dock labourers and gas workers. 129 000 or 14½%.

Charles Booth, *Life and Labour of the People in London*, 1889–1903

? QUESTIONS

a) What is the difference in attitude between Source 2A and 2B?

■ SOURCE 2C Poor family in the 1890s

b) How does Mearns, Source 2A, hope that the problem will be solved?
c) What percentage of the population does Booth put in classes A–D?
d) Is this more, or less than he expected to find?
e) How are both Sources 2B and 2C helpful in understanding poverty in Britain in 1900?

Booth's work was followed in 1901 by another survey. This was done by Seebohm Rowntree, a member of the Quaker chocolate family of York. Rowntree felt it necessary to define the 'poverty line' very carefully. For York he calculated that a family of husband, wife and three children could live on 21s 8d per week (£1.8½p).

■ SOURCE 2D

A family living upon the scale allowed for must never spend a penny on a railway fare or an omnibus. They must never go into the country unless they walk. They must never purchase a ½d newspaper or spend a penny to buy a ticket for a concert. They must write no letters to absent children, for they cannot afford to pay the postage. The children must have no pocket money for dolls, marbles or sweets. The father must smoke no tobacco and drink no

beer. The mother must never buy herself pretty clothes. Should a child fall ill it must be attended by the Poor Law doctor. Finally, the wage-earner must never be absent from his work for a single day.

S. Rowntree, *Poverty: A Study of Town Life*, 1901

? QUESTIONS

a) Why is it necessary to draw a precise line when calculating who is poor and who is not?
b) Do you think Rowntree's line is realistic? Why do you think he made it so strict?
c) Compare this source with Source 1B, Chapter 15, page 162. How can it be that people are poor on 21s 6d (£1.8½p) in 1901 and 8s 6d (42½p) in 1800?
d) What kind of things would you regard as bare necessities for a family today? How much money per week would a family of two parents and three children need to buy these things today?

The poverty line

Even on Rowntree's harsh – some might say impossible – definition of poverty he found 10% of York's population below the poverty line at all times. Another 18% were below it regularly, for a variety of reasons. Thus 28% of York's population, nearly half of its working class population, were living in poverty. Rowntree's survey pointed to a life cycle where many, perhaps most, working people hovered just one side or the other of the poverty line all their lives. A young unmarried person had her or his own wages and was all right. Marrying and having children pushed her or him below the poverty line. When the children started earning and left home, the couple crossed to the right side of the poverty line for a while. Then old age and falling earnings brought poverty again.

These and other surveys made two things clear. First, the problem of poverty had not been solved, but was as large as ever. Second, Victorian views about the causes of poverty being drink and idleness were just not true. Rowntree found the causes to be those shown in Source 2E.

■ *SOURCE 2E* Causes of poverty, according to Rowntree

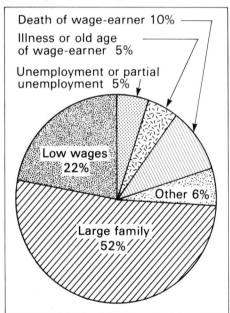

Death of wage-earner 10%
Illness or old age of wage-earner 5%
Unemployment or partial unemployment 5%
Low wages 22%
Other 6%
Large family 52%

Other factors also led the government to reconsider the problem of poverty around the turn of the century. Large numbers of young men from the poorer cities of Britain were found to be medically unfit to serve in the Army in the Boer War (1899–1902). The work of the Fabians and other socialists (Chapter 20, page 214) and the founding of the Labour Party in 1900 made many in Britain think about the needs of working people.

Liberal Reforms 1906–14

The Liberals did not campaign for welfare reforms in the 1906 election. Yet the Liberal government from 1906 to the outbreak of war in 1914 put through a series of measures to help all kinds of people. These reforms brought the government into people's lives in a way that it had never done before. They also provide the basic ideas behind much of our welfare provision up to the present day. What are the reasons for this?

Many older Liberals in 1906 still believed that the truly Liberal policy was to leave people alone in freedom to find their own solutions. Younger Liberals, such as Lloyd George (Chancellor of the Exchequer) and Winston Churchill (President of the Board of Trade) pointed out that people in abject poverty had no freedom to do anything except suffer. These Liberals had been influenced by the work of people like Mearns, Booth and Rowntree. They were impressed by the welfare schemes introduced in Germany. They set out to make the government provide the support that would enable everybody in Britain to live their lives in security and freedom.

The Labour Party claimed some credit for these reforms too. It is true that they had campaigned for many of the measures the Liberals introduced. However, there were only 29 Labour MPs in 1906. The Liberals had an overall majority in Parliament and did not have to rely on Labour votes. Nonetheless, they were concerned by the size of the Labour Party and tried to show that Liberals could look after working people just as well.

Children

There was a series of laws to help children. School meals could be provided from 1906, and 150000 a day were being served by 1914. School Medical checks started in 1907. The Children's Act 1908, called the 'Children's Charter', did several things to care for children who were in real trouble.

The Act set up juvenile courts and remand homes to treat children's crime as a social problem, rather than a problem of law and order.

■ *SOURCE 3A*

At Tower Bridge police court, X, seven years old, was charged on remand without proper guardianship or settled home. William Westcott, industrial schools officer, said he found the child in Tabard Street at 11 o'clock on a wet night. A crippled elderly woman, somewhat under the influence of drink, came up and said she was the child's mother... Witness made inquiries ... For some time past the woman had been using the child for the purposes of begging in the West End.

The Times, October 1906

? QUESTIONS

a) Why do you think the woman used the child to help her beg?
b) What do you think should be done about this situation?

Old people

In 1908 the first Old Age Pensions were introduced: 5s (25p) a week, over the age of 70, 7s 6d (37½p) for a married couple, paid to those earning less than 12s (60p) a week. This amount was hardly luxury. It was just enough to keep old people out of the workhouse. Still some opposed it in the House of Commons.

■ *SOURCE 3B*

We were challenged by the member for Preston who said, 'Would you declare that you are in favour of giving a pension of 5s a week to a drunken, thriftless, worthless man or woman?' My reply is very prompt. A man of seventy with nothing in the world is going to cut a pretty shine on 5s a week, whether his character be good or bad. Who are you, to be continually finding fault? Who amongst you has such a clear record as to be able to point to the wickedness of an old man of seventy? If a man is foolish enough to get old, and if he has not been artful enough to get rich, you have no right to punish him for it. They are veterans of industry, people of almost endless toil...

Will Crooks MP (the first person born in a workhouse to become an MP)

■ SOURCE 3C Pensions day in a country town, early 20th century

Pension Day 1 Jan 1909
Framlingham.

■ SOURCE 4A Cartoon, 1909: Lloyd George as the giant

RICH FARE.

The Giant Lloyd-Georgebuster: "FEE, FI, FO, FAT.
I SMELL THE BLOOD OF A PLUTOCRAT;
BE HE ALIVE OR BE HE DEAD,
I'LL GRIND HIS BONES TO MAKE MY BREAD."

■ SOURCE 4B Cartoon, 1908

CAUSE AND EFFECT.

SOCIAL LEGISLATION
1906-1908
TRADE DISPUTES ACT
WORKMEN'S
COMPENSATION ACT
SCHOOL CHILDREN'S
MEALS ACT
OLD AGE PENSIONS
UNEMPLOYED GRANT
£300.000
MINERS EIGHT HOURS BILL

Keir Hardie: 'Look at that list, Mr. Bull—not one of them would have been passed if it hadn't been for our Labour Party!'

■ SOURCE 4C Poster, 1911

THE DAWN OF HOPE.

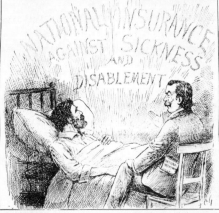

NATIONAL INSURANCE
AGAINST SICKNESS
AND
DISABLEMENT

Mr. LLOYD GEORGE'S National Health Insurance Bill provides for the insurance of the Worker in case of Sickness.

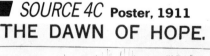

Support the Liberal Government
in their policy of
SOCIAL REFORM.

❓ QUESTIONS

a) What was the attitude of the MP for Preston in Source 3B?
b) How did Will Crooks argue against him?

Working people

Laws were passed to help people at work: the Trades Disputes Act 1906 reversed the Taff Vale Decision (Chapter 19, page 204). The Miners won an eight-hour day in 1908, and a minimum wage in 1912. The Shop Act 1911 guaranteed a half-day's holiday to all shop-workers. The Trade Boards Act 1909 regulated wages and hours in the 'sweated labour' trades – tailors, lace-makers, etc. The Labour Exchanges Act 1909 helped people find work.

The National Insurance Act of 1911

But the greatest effort the Liberals made was to try to tackle the problem revealed by Rowntree and Booth: poverty caused by illness or temporary unemployment. The National Insurance Act of 1911 was devised by Lloyd George and had two parts.

Part 1 concerned health insur-ance. Everyone earning under £160 a year had 4*d* (1.7p) a week deducted from their wages. The employer added 3*d* (1.25p) and the state 2*d* (0.8p). In return a worker could claim 10*s* (50p) a week sickness benefit for up to 26 weeks, and free medical care. The scheme was to be run by a Friendly Society, insurance company or union. In this way Lloyd George stuck to the Liberal idea of not making people rely on the government too much.

Part 2 of the National Insurance Act covered seven trades, such as building and shipbuilding, where occasional unemployment was a common problem. The worker paid 2½*d* (1p), the employer 2½*d* (1p) and the government about 1⅔*d* (0.7p). The benefit was 7*s* (35p) a week for 15 weeks, and about 2¼ million workers were covered.

All these schemes cost a great deal, and Lloyd George's budget of 1909 proposed large increases in income tax. The Conservatives in the House of Lords threw out the budget, which brought about a crisis in Parliament. In the end the budget was passed, and the 1911 Parliament Act cut the power of the House of Lords. Lloyd George showed clearly that he meant the rich to pay to keep the poor out of poverty.

? QUESTIONS

a) What is the attitude of the cartoonist to Lloyd George in Source 4A?
b) Explain how both the Labour Party, in Source 4B, and the Liberal Party, in Source 4C, tried to take credit for the reforms.

The reforms were only intended as a help to poor people – none of them were enough to live on. A 'lifebelt', a 'net over the abyss', were the phrases used. They were Liberal measures, not socialist, but by involving the government in the problem they provided a real foundation for the Welfare State which was to come later.

The Inter-war Years

During the First World War plans were made to continue the Liberals' reforms. These included abolishing the Poor Law, setting up a National Health Service, building council houses and increasing old-age pensions. There was also pressure to do more to help women. Apart from the Suffragette Movement (Chapter 21, page 222) there was an increasing interest in the needs of women. At that time this concentrated on the needs of mothers and babies before, during and after childbirth.

The Liberal reforms had only helped wage-earners, mostly men. The Midwives Act 1902 had begun the process of training midwives, although half were still untrained by 1916. In the 1890s Labour-controlled cities such as Bradford and Liverpool had set up mother-and-baby clinics. Florence Nightingale's idea of health visitors was also put into action at this time. However, working-class women wanted better medical treatment and more money, not just good advice. Women's groups, such as the Co-operative Women's Guild, campaigned for maternity benefits. The Eleanor Rathbone Society wanted family allowances.

■ SOURCE 5

Eleanor's sense of justice was disturbed: men and women appeared to be doing equal work, the women received less pay [as] men have families to keep. This barrier to the achievement of equal pay for equal work could only be removed by the acceptance of family allowances...

What struck her as the war years rolled by was the physical well-being and maternal efficiency yielded by small sums entrusted to the mother. Of course family allowances were the answer to the 'equal pay' impasse.*

*an impasse is a deadlock

Mary Stocks, *Eleanor Rathbone*, 1970

? QUESTIONS

a) Why was there deadlock over the equal pay issue?
b) In what way would the family allowances break it?
c) What sort of things would mother spend the money on?

Unfortunately most of these plans came to nothing. Britain, after 1920, began a period of economic depression which lasted until the Second World War. In these circumstances, governments did not want to increase spending on welfare.

Unemployment

Unemployment during the inter-war years averaged 14%, and reached 23% in the worst year, 1932. In some towns in the old industrial and mining areas it was much higher, reaching 70% or 80%.

■ SOURCE 6B

If only he had work. Just imagine what it would be like. On the whole my husband has worked about one year out of twelve and a half. His face was lovely when I married him but now he's skin and bones. When I married him he had a good job, earning from eight to ten pounds a week. He's a left-handed shop's riveter, a craft which should be earning him a lot of money. He fell out of work about four months after I was married, so I've hardly known what a week's wage was.

Shipbuilder's wife, 1934

■ SOURCE 6C

A working man does not disintegrate under the strain of poverty as a middle-class person does. Take, for instance, the fact that the working class think nothing of getting married on the dole. It annoys the old ladies of Brighton, but it is a proof of their essential good sense; they realise that losing your job does not mean that you cease to be a human being.

George Orwell, *Road to Wigan Pier*, 1937

■ SOURCE 6A Unemployed men, 1939

QUESTIONS

a) What is the mood of Sources 6A and 6B?

b) What effect does unemployment seem to have on people, from these sources?

c) George Orwell (Source 6C) was a writer. What is his attitude to the unemployed?

d) What does George Orwell mean by 'It annoys the old ladies of Brighton'?

e) Is there any evidence from the other two sources that George Orwell's opinion of the unemployed is correct?

Problems with the dole

In 1920 the National Insurance Act 1911 was extended to cover anyone earning less than £250 per year. This included most working people, but agricultural labourers, domestic servants and teachers were excluded. Also, the system, as in 1911, was based on a low unemployment rate – about 4% – and short-term unemployment: benefit was only paid for 15 weeks. Unemployment for the next twenty years was much higher than this, so fewer people were paying their contributions, while more people needed help. Many were unemployed for a long time, too. In West Auckland in 1935 only one in ten men had worked at all in the previous seven years, and in the Rhondda 45% had had no work for over five years. Both these difficulties were far greater than the National Insurance Scheme was designed to cope with.

Governments tried to deal with these problems in various ways. In 1921 unemployment benefit was extended to 47, then 52 weeks a year. This was the 'dole', as it was called. At 15s (75p) for men and 12s (60p) for women, per week, it was hardly enough to live on. It was also subject to two conditions: you had to be 'genuinely seeking work'. This was obviously impossible in some towns hard-hit by the Depression, but nevertheless one in twenty claimants lost benefit because they were held not to have looked for work.

The other condition was a 'means test'. The whole situation of the family was looked at, and if any one was earning anything at all, that was taken off the benefit paid. It might be that a child had a paper round, or

someone did a bit of cleaning of gardening. Perhaps the grown-up children of an unemployed person had jobs. In all cases the means test would cut the dole by that amount.

SOURCE 6D

Where the wife was earning but the husband unemployed there was evidently unhappiness. A printer, 42 years old, had lost his job. His wife was earning, so he only drew 5s [25p] Unemployment Assistance. She used to hear him tramping up and down the garden path, or up and down in the parlour, and it made her nearly mad to feel that she was keeping him by her earnings and they gained nothing by her work.

Pilgrim Trust Report, 1938

QUESTIONS

a) Explain in your own words why the wife felt upset at the situation.

b) Do you think a husband and wife would feel the same nowadays?

c) Do you think this kind of means test was fair?

Even if the family had some non-essential item, such as a piano, that had to be sold to raise money. In this way the old Poor Law attitude of making benefit the last resort, and trying to catch 'scroungers', still survived. Unemployed people were bitterly resentful of the means test. They were skilled workers in many cases, who only wanted a job, and had lost theirs through no fault of

their own. The form-filling, the personal questions, the snooping, the feeling that they had to prove that they weren't scroungers, all caused anger. In 1931, when the Depression was at its worst, the dole was cut from 30s (£1.50) for a married couple to 27s 6d (£1.37½).

The dole seems to have kept most families just above the poverty line. Their memories of the waste and humiliation of the 1930s, however, were to colour the policies of the years after 1945.

Council housing

During the First World War Lloyd George had promised to tackle one of the great evils affecting the poor of Britain – bad housing. He promised 'homes for heroes'. In 1919 Addison's Act gave government grants to local councils to build the first council houses. About 213 000 were built under this Act, but usually on the edge of towns, and to such a high standard that only better-off workers could afford the rents. The short Labour government of 1924 passed Wheatley's Act, which made local councils survey the housing need of their area and build houses to let at rents subsidised from the rates. About 520 000 houses were eventually built under this Act. There were still many slums, however, and a great shortage of good houses. Slum clearance programmes were begun in many cities, but the Depression forced heavy cuts in the

SOURCE 7A 1920s council housing in York

■ *SOURCE 7B* **Quarry Hill Flats, Leeds, opened 1938**

council house building programme. Eventually German
bombers in the Second World War
cleared far more slums than councils could.

■ *SOURCE 7C*

The first section where 938 families will ultimately live in municipal flats was opened by Alderman
J. Badley. Chairman of the Housing Committee, Alderman H. A.
Blackah, described the Quarry
Hill development.

He spoke of children's playgrounds, and gardens and many
other amenities which will be
available when the scheme is complete. There will be five children's
playgrounds.

'We believe the Lord Mayor will
yet see roses growing at Quarry
Hill,' he said. This observation
drew a smile from Alderman Badley, for he knew Quarry Hill when
it was one of the worst slums in
Leeds.

Every flat has a living room facing the sun and a back-to-back
range that will give warmth to the
living room and scullery.

Alderman Blackah said that
these were the finest tenements
built for the wage-earners of this
country.

Yorkshire Evening Post, 1938

? *QUESTIONS*

a) In what ways are both these
housing schemes an improvement on slums shown in Source
7B, Chapter 11 (page 128)?
b) What is the attitude of the Councillors in Source 7C to the new
flats?

c) Why do you think this is so?
d) In fact Quarry Hill Flats were not
popular and were later demolished. Suggest reasons why this
was so.
e) Does this mean that Alderman
Badley and Blackah were wrong
in what they say in Source 7C?
f) Imagine you were one of the new
tenants in Quarry Hill Flats.
Write a letter back to your old
neighbours in the slums where
you used to live, explaining the
good and bad points of where
you live now.

Plans for the future

The economic difficulties in inter-
war Britain prevented any further
efforts to deal with the housing
problem. However, during these
years local councils laid plans to
improve the housing situation in
their cities and towns.

Plans to improve old-age pensions, increasing the amount, and
lowering the age, were also made.
There was growing pressure to help
those people dependent on the
wage-earner – usually wives and
children. Reports showed how
much British women suffered during the 1930s.

■ *SOURCE 8*

**Mrs D. of Liverpool lives entirely
on tea and toast and margarine
with an egg at weekends and a
kipper twice a week. She has had
15 pregnancies of which two were
still-births and two children died
from pneumonia. There are nine
children living at home. The hus-**

band is mostly away, being a sailor. She suffers from rheumatism
for which she rubs on an ointment,
kidney trouble for which she was
in hospital six weeks but 'couldn't
stay longer owing to the children
at home', and anaemia for which
she takes 'Dr Williams' Pills'. The
Visitor says 'I sometimes wonder
to see Mrs D. alive at all, her children range from 19 to 4½ and as far
as I can see she never rests or eats'.

**Margery Spring Rice, *Working Class
Wives*, 1939**

? *QUESTIONS*

a) What effect does her way of life
have on Mrs D?
b) What kind of welfare support do
you think she needs?
c) What kind of help would she
receive today?

Source 8 shows clearly the link
between health, poverty and diet.
Many people, by the 1930s, were
talking of a huge increase in state
help to all, including a free health
service, which would be the only
way to help people like Mrs D. The
phrase 'Welfare State' was used in
the 1930s for the first time.

The Second World War and After

With the Second World War came
an end to unemployment but also a
host of new problems. Evacuation,
widowhood, mothers on their own,
homelessness and caring for elderly people all put new stresses on
the Assistance Board. New payments were made and new ideas
introduced. In 1941 the National
Milk Scheme provided free or half-
price milk to children and expec-
tant mothers. Concentrated orange
juice from the USA was supplied
from 1942. There was also a campaign to vaccinate all babies
against diphtheria.

The war also changed people's
ideas. Middle-class and country
people who gave homes to eva-
cuees were often shocked by their
poverty. The fact that children had
no proper shoes, did not know how
to use a bed, a bath or a toilet told
them a great deal about what life
was like in some British cities in the
1930s. The turmoil of war also

brought people together who would never have met otherwise. Everyone had to put up with terrible dangers, such as air-raids, and inconveniences, such as rationing. The feeling grew that this sharing for the good of the country must be continued after the war to make Britain a better country for all to live in. Some writers have said that the Welfare State grew out of this feeling. We have seen that the idea of a Welfare State was not invented in the war, but rested on ideas talked about ever since the First World War. However, the war did bring widespread discussion of these ideas and almost complete agreement that when the war was over great changes would have to come about.

The Beveridge Report, 1942

Sir William Beveridge was a civil servant who had worked on the Liberal reforms of 1911. He was asked by Ernest Bevin at the Ministry of Labour to investigate the national insurance system in Britain in order to tidy it up; Beveridge produced instead a thorough revision of the whole welfare system.

Beveridge said there were 'Five Giants on the road to progress'. The first giant was 'Want' – poverty. He pointed out that most poverty was caused by loss of earnings, and that the system to help people over these crises was far too patchy. He proposed a single system of insurance to cover any interruption of earnings – sickness, injury, pregnancy, child-caring or old age. The second giant was 'Disease' and he proposed a free health service for all citizens, not just wage-earners. The third giant was 'Squalor' – bad housing. He called for more and better homes to remove this terrible cause of so much hardship and illness. The fourth giant was 'Ignorance', requiring more and better schools. The fifth was 'Idleness' and he insisted that future governments must plan for full employment in the future.

Behind these attempts to slay the five giants for ever lay some new principles.

Beveridge's principles

1 Universality
Benefits were payable to all, rich or poor. In this way the hated means test was avoided. Your benefit was your right and it would be taxed.

2 Insurance
It was an insurance scheme into which everyone had to pay contributions while they were working. Beveridge was against what he called a 'Santa Claus State' – paying benefit from government funds alone. He thought this stopped people feeling responsible for their own lines.

3 Pro-women
Beveridge wanted to improve the position of women in several ways. Single women at work would pay the same contributions and receive the same benefits as men. Married women could choose whether to be treated in this way or as a dependant of their husband. He argued for grants for maternity and widowhood and benefits for divorced women and women at home looking after elderly parents. He insisted that housewives did important work: he wanted to pay sickness benefit to housewives who were ill.

4 Planning
As a Liberal he had always been against too much government interference in the life of the country. In the 1930s many British people looked at the planning which Stalin introduced into Russia with mixed feelings: they saw that it brought economic growth, but it greatly reduced people's freedom. By 1939 Beveridge felt that some government planning was necessary, to avoid such economic disasters as the 1930s Depression.

The Beveridge Report was immensely popular – it sold 635 000 copies and was widely-discussed.

? QUESTION

How does the cartoonist in Source 9A show his approval of Beveridge?

Beveridge knew what he was doing: appealing over the heads of government leaders to the public at large. Many people in the government were not happy with his sweeping proposals. However, with widespread public support for them, they could not be ignored.

The Conservative government, which ran the country for a few months after the war and before an election could be held, brought in the first change: family allowances. The payments were lower than Beveridge had calculated, only 5s (25p) per week, and were not paid for the first child in a family. Unions had long opposed family allowances, as they feared they would weaken claims for better wages. Eleanor Rathbone (see Source 5) and many mothers were delighted.

■ SOURCE 9A Cartoon, 1942

RIGHT TURN

The Labour Party and the Welfare State 1945–51

National Insurance

Labour won the 1945 election with a big majority, committed to many of Beveridge's proposals. The first was the National Insurance Act 1946, proposed by James Griffiths. All working people paid a contribution, recorded by a stamp on an insurance card. (This was computerised in the 1970s.) Everyone received the same rate of benefit for any interruption of earnings, whether through sickness, widowhood, unemployment, pregnancy, or old age. Maternity grants and death grants were paid, but Beveridge's proposals to cover divorced women, and women helping their parents, were not included. Nor was his idea for sickness benefit to be payable to housewives. Old-age pensions were paid to women at 60 and men at 65. These benefits were everyone's right, and were not means-tested: they demonstrated the principle of universality.

National Assistance

The National Assistance Act 1948 was to help anyone who was still in financial difficulties. There was an interview, to see how much was needed, and this put many people off. However, the earnings of other members of the family were not taken into account, as they had been before.

The National Health Service

The National Health Act 1946 (which was to come into effect in 1948) caused much more discussion. The Labour Minister of Health, Aneurin Bevan, inherited a rag-bag of a health system. About half the population – the wage-earners – were covered by the old National Insurance scheme. They got free medical care from a doctor on the approved panel. Their families were not covered, unless by their own insurance. For them as for Mrs D. in Source 8, medical care was almost out of the question. The rich, of course, could purchase medical, dental, ophthalmic, maternity and hospital treatment as they wished. There were also two kinds of hospitals: 1000 run by the local authorities and 1750 by charities.

Bevan criticised the existing system.

■ SOURCE 9B

A person ought not to be financially deterred from seeking medical assistance at the earliest possible stage by the financial anxiety of doctor's bills...

Our hospital organisation has grown up with no plan; it is unevenly distributed over the country .... In the older industrial districts of Britain hospital facilities are inadequate. Many hospitals are very much too small to provide general hospital treatment...

Furthermore – I want to be quite frank with the House – I believe it is repugnant to a civilised community for hospitals to have to rely upon private charity .... I have always felt a shudder of repulsion when I see nurses and sisters who ought to be at their work, going about the streets collecting money for the hospitals.

Bevan, speaking in the House of Commons, April 1946

⁇ QUESTIONS

a) List the criticisms Bevan makes of the health system in Britain.
b) How would each of the things he criticises prevent people from being healthy?

Bevan was opposed by the doctors, who feared that they would become just government officials. He had to make several compromises, but the National Health Service preserved his ideal of free health care for all. This included doctors, medicine, dentists, opticians and hospitals. Hospitals were brought under the Ministry of Health, although pay-beds were allowed for patients wishing to pay for private treatment. It was intended that most health care would be provided at health centres, where doctors, nurses and other medical services such as antenatal clinics could all be combined under one roof.

The need for free health care was revealed when the system started in 1948. There was a flood of patients looking for remedies after a lifetime of suffering. It was estimated, for example, that 6 million people needed glasses but didn't have them. Most women were found to have half or more of their teeth decayed. No wonder there was a rush.

Council housing

Plans to meet the need for housing ran into difficulties. There was a shortage of materials, and the Labour government insisted that priority was given to council-built housing. They also insisted on building to high standards. This brought much opposition from those who wanted houses built for sale. Nevertheless 800 000 houses were built in the first five years after the war, more than in any other European country. To meet the

■ SOURCE 9C Waiting for the doctor, 1940s

need for housing 157 000 'prefabs' were built – temporary prefabricated houses (built from sections made in a factory). The New Towns Act 1946 also helped the housing problem in cities by setting up twelve 'new towns' (see Chapter 11, page 132).

We have seen that there was massive support for certain welfare reforms at the end of the war. The system set up in the 1940s was popular and has remained largely unaltered by both Conservative and Labour governments since then. It gave people the basic security they needed, removing the anxiety and fear of poverty, old age, illness and the workhouse. The low unemployment and good wages of the 1950s and 1960s also helped people put memories of the awful Depression of the 1930s behind them.

Problems With the Welfare State

In fact prosperity brought its own problems: the benefits paid under National Insurance were fixed below the lowest pay level. This was to prevent people giving up work to live off the state. This meant that there was a large drop in many people's standards of living if they had to live on state benefit for any reason. In 1966 earnings-related benefits were brought in, so that people received a higher rate, depending on previous earnings, for six months. The high unemployment of the 1980s led to this being withdrawn in 1982. A second pension, the State Earnings Related Pension, was introduced in 1978 to do a similar thing for retired people who did not have their own pension.

Poverty in recent years

By the 1960s many people in the better-off parts of Britain felt that poverty had almost been driven out of the country. Then a series of reports revealed a different picture. Peter Townsend, basing his work on the surveys of Booth and Rowntree, revealed 6–9% of Britain's population to be living in poverty, with 22–28% on the margins. The Child Poverty Action Group, formed in 1965, claimed that 720 000 children were living in poverty. There

■ SOURCE 9D **Prefabs in London, 1940s**

■ SOURCE 10A **Poor family in slum housing, 1971**

seemed to be a widening gap between fit, employed people who were doing well and those who were, for no fault of their own, in difficulties: old-age pensioners, single-parent families, low-wage earners. The 1940s principle of universality did not seem to be able to help these people. In fact in 1979 four out of ten people on benefits needed Supplementary Benefit as well. (National Assistance was renamed Supplementary Benefit in 1966.) The number of people on National Assistance (or Supplementary Benefit) rose from 1.5 million in 1951 to 3.3 million in 1980. There was also a re-thinking of what poverty means.

■ SOURCE 10B

People must have an income which enables them to take part in the life of their community. They must be able to keep themselves reasonably fed, and well enough dressed to keep their self respect and attend interviews for jobs. Their homes must be reasonably warm; their children should not feel shamed by the quality of their clothing, the family must be able to visit relatives, read newspapers, retain their TV sets and their membership of trade unions and churches. And they must be able to live in a way which ensures that public officials, doctors, teachers, landlords and others treat them with the courtesy due to every member of the community.

Supplementary Benefit Commission Report, 1978

❓ QUESTIONS

a) How does this standard differ from Rowntree's (Source 2D)?
b) Why is it different?
c) Do you agree with the opinion of this Report?

Various attempts have been made to deal with this problem of continuing poverty. Many people did not claim all the benefits due to them, so in 1968 the whole health and welfare system was put into one department, the Department of Health and Social Security. This could look after all the needs of someone in difficulty. In 1971 Family Income Supplement was introduced. This gave cash grants, free school meals and free prescriptions to all those whose income, from work or benefit, was inadequate. It was an attempt to reach those in need, but, of course, broke the principle of universality.

The cost of the National Health Service

The cost of the National Health Service has brought concern to governments. The initial flood of patients in 1948 has hardly slackened since. New treatments, new drugs, new and higher standards of care all cost money. The initial principle of a free health service was broken in 1951 when prescription charges were introduced. Although Bevan and other ministers resigned in protest, the charges remained and have increased in recent years.

The increase in the number of elderly people has also put pressure on the Health Service. One result of the high demand for health care has been long waiting-lists for treatment, since the amount of money available has been severely limited. To avoid waiting, more and more people have taken out private medical insurance: half a million in 1955, 5 million by 1985. All parts of the Welfare State have faced problems in recent years. Nevertheless, the British people seem to be firmly in favour of a free National Health Service, decent old-age pensions and a widespread benefit system to help those in difficulties.

Assignments

Empathy

1 What attitudes are shown by *each* of the writers of Sources 2A, 2B and 2D, and the photographer of 2C:
  i towards the poor and
  ii towards the people who read their books or looked at their photographs?
2 What attitudes are shown by women and towards women in this chapter?
3 Imagine you are either the man in Source 6A or the woman in Source 6B. Describe the problems you face with unemployment, and how you feel about your life and future.
4 a What attitudes towards the poor have been seen in this chapter and in Chapter 15?
  b How much have attitudes changed?
  c How much do old 'Poor Law' attitudes still survive today?

Understanding concepts

1 **Causation/motivation**
  a What were the motives of the Liberal government of 1906 in carrying out the reforms that they did?
  b Show how these motives can be seen in the laws they passed.
  c In what ways do these reforms mark an end to 'laisser faire'?

2 **Causation/motivation**
  a What were the motives of the Labour government of 1945–50 in carrying out their welfare reforms?
  b Show how these motives can be seen in the laws they passed.
  c What was the importance, in relation to the reforms, of:
    i the 1930s Depression;
    ii The Second World War?

3 **Change/continuity**
  a How far is the welfare state as it exists today the same as it was thirty years ago?
  b How far, and in what ways, is it different?
  c What problems face the welfare state today?

Themes for discussion

1 Compare the Poor Law Amendment Act 1834, the Liberal Reforms, and the Labour welfare state measures. Look for differences and similarities in:
  i the problem of poverty
  ii the motives of the reformers
  iii the measures passed.
2 a How did the Second World War affect attitudes to welfare?
  b How far are these attitudes seen in the Beveridge Report?
  c Why weren't all the suggestions of the Beveridge Report put into effect?

17 Standards of Living and the Industrial Revolution

Were People Better Off?

In this chapter we want to try and answer the simple question: were the people of Britain better off as a result of the Industrial Revolution?

The trouble is that the arguments begin almost as soon as we have asked the question. What do we mean by 'better off', for example? In Britain today people argue about whether or not they are better off than they used to be.

■ SOURCE 1A Newspaper headlines, 1986

Wages continue to rise faster than prices

Poverty on the increase

? QUESTIONS

a) Do either of these headlines prove that Britain is better or worse off?
b) Explain how both these headlines could be true.

There were arguments even during the Industrial Revolution about whether it was making people better off or not.

■ SOURCE 1B

Before the Industrial Revolution the workers enjoyed a comfortable and peaceful existence .... Their standard of life was much better than that of the factory worker today.

F. Engels, 1845

■ SOURCE 1C

If we look back to the condition of the mass of the people ... even at the beginning of this century, and then look around us at the indications of greater comfort and respectability that meet us on every side, it is hardly possible to doubt that the elements of social improvement have been successfully at work and that there is an increased amount of comfort to the great bulk of the people.

G. R. Porter, *Progress of the Nation*, 1847

? QUESTIONS

a) Does either of these writers offer any evidence to support his claims?
b) What is the starting-point for the comparison they make in each case?
c) Suggest reasons why the two authors, both alive during this period, could disagree so completely about the Industrial Revolution.
d) Are these primary or secondary evidence of attitudes towards the Industrial Revolution?

Problems of evidence

The trouble with Sources 1B and 1C is that they do not offer any evidence to support their claims. In order to answer the 'standard of

■ SOURCE 1E Navvies building the first underground line, 1862

■ SOURCE 1D Old men in Cornwall, 1880s

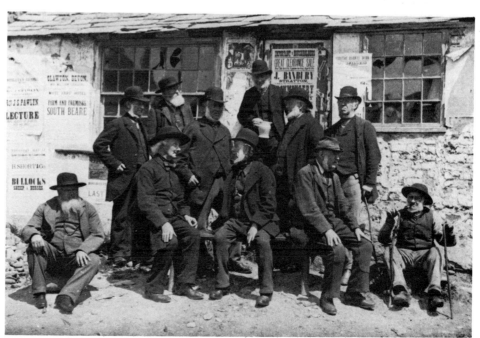

living' question, historians need precise, reliable evidence about wages and prices. We know the questions we would like to ask.

Take Source 1D. The man on the far right was said to have been a drummer-boy at the Battle of Waterloo, in 1815. That would mean he was born in about 1800. If only we could ask him whether he was better-off in 1880 than in his younger days!

What about the navvies in Source 1E? We would like to know how much they were paid, how many hours they worked, how many months per year they worked, how they spent their money.

? QUESTION

What other questions would you like to ask the people in Sources 1D and 1E?

Nowadays the government collects and publishes many statistics on wages and prices. This is because people expect the government to manage the economy of the country, and the government wants to know what is going on. In the past people did not expect the government to manage the economy. In fact they expected the government to keep out of people's lives and businesses. Before the 20th century, therefore, few statistics were collected on wages and prices. There is, however, lots of other evidence of different kinds, as we shall see.

Income

Today, government figures on income are taken mainly from taxation returns. The average income for Britain, and for different kinds of household in Britain, is shown in Source 2.

■ SOURCE 2 Incomes, 1983

	Annual income (£)
National average	7584
Household of 2 adults and 2 children	9480
Household of 2 adults	7389
Single parent with 1 child	5586
Household of 2 pensioners	4339

But how accurate is Source 2? Does everyone pay their income tax fairly? What about people with two jobs? People also have income from different places; not only their wage, but perhaps a pension, or Child Allowance, or a rent rebate. They may be paid in fringe benefits such as a car, medical insurance, discount on the firm's goods, cheap meals, etc. Fringe benefits do not appear in the figures in Source 2. The figures are averages, too: they may hide huge differences between rich and poor.

If there are these problems with present-day figures, the problems are much greater when we look at the past. Income tax was first collected in the Napoleonic Wars, but was abolished when the wars ended in 1815. It was regarded as such an interference in people's private business that all the records were burnt too. It was re-introduced in 1842, but very few people paid it at first. The present system of PAYE (Pay As You Earn) was not started until 1940.

Historians can, however, find some information on incomes. The records of some businesses tell us how much they paid in wages; some unions also collected information on wages. When there was a particular problem in one region or industry, the government itself carried out an enquiry. They heard evidence on oath from witnesses and published the results. We therefore have accurate, detailed information about hand-loom weavers and agricultural labourers, for example, as well as other trades. The trouble, of course, is that many of these statistics only refer to distress and hardship. People who are doing well do not complain, so their incomes may not be recorded.

■ SOURCE 3A Wages paid in the Manchester cotton industry, 1832

STATEMENT of the RATES of WAGES paid to PERSONS employed in COTTON MANUFACTURES in MANCHESTER in the year 1832.

[*From "Tables of the Revenue, &c. of the United Kingdom," Part II., 1833, p. 101.*]

	Rates of Wages.
COTTON MANUFACTURES.	Per Week.
Spinners, Men	20s. to 25s.
„ Women	10s. „ 15s.
Stretchers	25s. „ 26s.
Piecers (Boys and Girls)	4s. 7d. „ 7s.
Scavengers	1s 6d. „ 2s. 8d.
IN THE CARD ROOM:—	
Men	14s. 6d. „ 17s.
Young Women	9s. „ 9s. 6d.
Children	6s. „ 7s.
Throstle Spinners	5s. „ 9s. 6d.
Reelers	7s. „ 9s.
WEAVERS BY POWER:—	
Men	13s. „ 16s. 10d.
Women	8s. „ 12s.
Dressers, Men	28s. „ 30s.
Winders and Warpers	8s. „ 11s.
Mechanics	24s. „ 26s.

■ SOURCE 3B Wages paid in a worsted mill in Bradford, 1823–31 (1823–27 shown)

An ACCOUNT of the AVERAGE WEEKLY EARNINGS of WOOL COMBERS, &c. employed in a WORSTED MILL at BRADFORD, YORKSHIRE, in each year from 1823 to 1831.

[From "*Tables of the Revenue, &c. of the United Kingdom,*" Part III., 1834, p. 419.]

	Rates of Wages.				
	1823.	1824.	1825.	1826.	1827.
Wool Sorters	18s. to 24s	18s. to 24s.		18s. to 24s.	18s. to 24s.
	s. d.	s. d.		s. d.	s. d.
Wool Combers	12 2	12 7		12 0	12 8½
Weavers from 12 to 16 years old	12 1	9 10		7 6	8 1
„ 16 and upwards	13 8	13 2¼		10 3	11 1
Reelers of Worsted Yarn, Women	10 0	12 11		9 4	9 4
Warpers of Worsted Yarn, Women	12 0	12 0	Year of the turn out.	12 0	12 0
Hands working by the Day in Factories, from 9 to 11 years old, chiefly Girls.	s. d. s. d. 2 3 to 3 9	s. d. s. d. 2 3 to 3 9		s. d. s. d. 2 0 to 3 6	s. d. s. d. 2 0 to 3 6
Hands from 11 to 14, chiefly girls	3 9 „ 6 0	3 9 „ 6 0		3 6 „ 5 9	3 6 „ 5 9
Hands from 14 and upwards, Women	8 0 „ 8 6	8 0 „ 8 6		7 6 „ 7 0	8 0 & 7 0
Overlookers	18 0 „ 26 0	18 0 „ 26 0		18 0 „ 26 0	18 0 to 26 0

(The 'turn-out' was a dispute between the workers and the factory owner during which the factory owner locked the workers out of the factory.)

■ SOURCE 3C Wages paid to men at ironworks in Staffordshire, 1844–9

	Rate per ton	Probable earnings in 12 hours
Blast-furnace men	9d	5s
Forge and mill men	8s	6s

■ SOURCE 3D Earnings at Samuel Greg's Mill at Styal, Cheshire, 1790

Family	No. in family	Sex and age of workers	Jobs done	Average wage paid per week £ s d
Brierley	8	2 men, 2 women, 4 children	Packer, labourer, women and children carding	2 0 6
Swan	4	Man, 3 children	Head carder, children carding	18 2
Gallimore	3	Woman, young girl, child	Reeler, winders	12 8½

What do the figures for wages mean?

There are other problems with information about 19th-century wages. For example, do the wages include overtime? How many weeks per year did the worker get paid the wage shown? If there was no work, the employer would lay workers off. There was no dole and no records were kept. Farm labourers, for example, worked on average no more than about 8 months a year. Industrial wages were more regular, on the whole, but there were still serious depressions when factories were closed for months. Many workers were on 'piece-work' – that is, they were paid by how much they produced. For example, in the iron industry, blast-furnace workers were paid by the ton of iron produced (see Source 3C). Miners were paid by how much coal was dug. Farm labourers made a special price for getting in the harvest. Closely linked to this was the 'gang' or 'butty' system. Here the employer would agree a price for a job – weeding a field, or cutting a particular amount of coal – with the gang-leader or butty. Other workers would be paid by the gang-leader or butty to do the work.

Another form of group-working was the system of hiring families to work in the textile industry. This started, of course, when textiles were made at home, but continued into the factory system (see Source 3D). This leads us into the whole question of children's wages. Obviously they made quite a difference to a family's income, as Source 3F (over) shows. In agriculture the sums involved were not large (see Source 3G over). We don't know if the children kept these pennies for themselves, or handed them over to their hard-pressed parents. However, we can see that the *total* earnings of a family could be considerable.

■ SOURCE 3E Family making toys at home, 1900

■ SOURCE 3F Earnings for the family of W. W., a 17-year-old girl

	Wages per week		
	£	s	d
Eldest brother had been a piecer from the age of 9 up to 22, when he left off through ill-health			
Wages as piecer		8	6
Second, a sister, doubler		9	6
Third, a brother, works in a warehouse measuring calico, aged 20		9	6
Fourth, myself, doubler, aged 17		9	6
Fifth, brother, piecer		5	0
Sixth, sister, doffer		4	0
Seventh, is ill		–	
Eighth, a little boy, ill		–	
Ninth, a little girl		–	
Father, night watchman		18	0
Total	3	4	0

Thus the earnings of the family have always been considerable

Report of a Factory Commissioner, 1833

■ SOURCE 3G Women and children on arable land in the Isle of Thanet

Women are employed at:	Weeding in the corn. Hours: 7 to 5. Meals: one hour. Wages: 10*d* a day
	Turnip-pulling. Hours, meals, wages as above
	Stone-picking; thistle-picking. Hours, meals, wages as above
Boys are employed at:	Weeding the corn. Hours: 6 to 6. Meals: one hour and a half. Wages: 6*d* a day.
	Bird-scaring. Age 8. Hours, as above. Wages: 4*d* a day.
Girls are employed occasionally at:	Weeding, Stone-picking, turnip-topping. Wages: from 4*d* to 8*d* a day.

Report on women and children employed in agriculture, 1843

? QUESTIONS

a) What do Sources 3A–G tell us about comparative wage rates for men and women?

b) What are the problems in calculating actual wages when workers are paid by piecework?

c) How do Sources 3D, 3E and 3F show the advantages of having lots of children who can work?

d) How far do these three sources show us the disadvantages of having lots of young children?

e) Source 3D comes from Samuel Greg's mill at Styal. Greg was known to be a generous employer. How might this affect our understanding of the evidence in this Source?

f) Compare Sources 3F and 3G. Which seems to offer the best pay for women and children: agriculture or the cotton industry?

g) Which do you think would offer the most regular work?

Payments in kind

There are other reasons for differences between what the wage figures say and what workers actually got. They may have been paid in food or drink. Farm labourers often received beer or cider as part of their harvest wage. Workers could also suffer quite heavy fines for lateness, or bad work (see Chapter 14, Source 1C, page 262).

Many workers were often paid not in cash, but in 'truck'. They received tokens which could only be spent in the owner's shop. Prices in these 'truck' shops or 'tommy-shops' were often higher than normal. Some workers, such as miners and railway navvies, often ended up in debt to the tommy-shop. In fact, 'truck' had been illegal since the 15th century. Several Acts were passed in the 18th century, in 1831 and in 1842, to abolish it and pay wages in cash. Nevertheless the system lasted into the 20th century. There were, however, good truck systems: the Gregs of Styal sold fresh produce from their own farm to their mill workers, at low prices. Robert Owen provided food at low prices from his factory kitchen at New Lanark.

The general pattern of wages

Given all these difficulties it is very hard to say what happened to wages over the whole country. Sometimes quite good figures can be produced for one industry in one area. Source 4 shows some wild variations in wages, and life must have been very

■ SOURCE 4 Index of Black Country coal miners' wages, 1816–1900

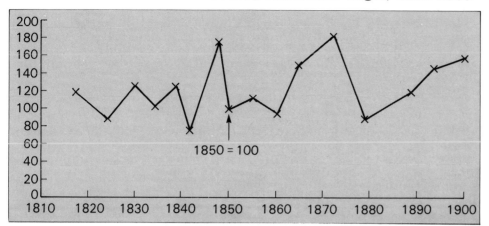

1850 = 100

difficult for the miners' families in the bad years. However, there seems to be a slight overall rise.

Doing the best we can with the figures available from many other industries and regions, it does seem that wages did increase from the 1750s to the 1860s. This was helped by the fact that employment in industry was more regular than in agriculture. There was also the opportunity, at least for men, to move into better-paid skilled jobs in industry.

Prices

There are therefore serious problems in deciding what wages were exactly. But even if we could decide, it would be no help in finding out if people were well-off unless we know what the money they earned could buy. It is no use simply saying that my salary when I started teaching in 1965 was £63 a month; you would want to know several things to decide whether I was well-off or not at that time. What did I *have to* spend money on? What did

I *want to* spend money on? Most of all, what would £63 buy in 1965?

The Retail Price Index

The government began trying to keep an accurate measure of prices in 1914. Prices were rising fast at that time because of shortages caused by the First World War. Politicians wanted to know just how rising prices affected people in order to fix wages. In 1937–8 a sample of 30 000 people was taken; detailed budgets of 8905 families were collected over four weeks. From this a 'basket' of items was made, and the prices of these could then be followed every month. These were measured by an 'index': a starting-point was chosen and the cost of an item was given the value 100. Changes in cost were then related to 100, so if the price doubled the index would record 200, and so on. The index was also weighted, because more was spent on some items, such as food, than on others, such as tobacco. This price index has been kept ever since. As the years go by the weighting has had to be altered as people's

spending habits change. The modern Family Expenditure Survey is based on a sample of about 8000 households, i.e. about 20 000 people.

■ QUESTIONS

Look at Source 5.
a) The weighting of food has decreased while that for housing has increased. This means that people are spending a smaller proportion of their money on food, and a larger proportion on housing. What has happened to the weightings for:
   i) tobacco?
   ii) clothing?
   iii) fuel and light?
b) Discuss this with your parents and other adults: does this weighting reflect their patterns of spending?
c) Prices have risen by three times from 1966 to 1984 (index 117 to 352). Some prices have risen more than this; for what items? Some have risen less; for what items?
d) You could compile your own index of goods and prices for teenagers. The more people you include, the more accurate it will be. How will you work out the weightings?

Family budgets

Obviously it is going to be impossible to make up something as careful and accurate as Source 5 for the Industrial Revolution period. However, evidence was collected by various people about how family incomes were spent. Charities, the Poor Law Commissioners and individuals who were worried about poverty all did this. The work of

■ SOURCE 5 Weighting of items: all weightings are proportions of 1000

	Food	Drink	Tobacco	Housing	Fuel/light	Household goods	Clothing	Transport	Other
1966	298	67	77	113	64	57	91	116	117
1984	201	75	36	149	65	69	70	158	177

Price indices: 1956 = 100

	Total	Food	Drink	Tobacco	Housing	Fuel/light	Household goods	Clothing	Transport	Other
1966	117	116	122	121	129	121	107	110	110	112
1984	352	326	388	490	401	479	257	214	375	360

Henry Mayhew, Charles Booth and Seebohm Rowntree is referred to in Chapter 16. They were extremely careful about collecting accurate information, and their findings had quite an important influence on the government. However, we must bear in mind that many of these enquiries were looking specifically at poverty. The information may not, therefore, reflect the habits, food and prices paid by better-off people.

■ *SOURCE 6A* Glasgow weaver's weekly diet. From Parliamentary Papers, 1834

	s	d
Oatmeal	1	4½
Potatoes		7½
Buttermilk		3
Herrings		3
Salt		½
Cheese		3½
Sugar		3½
Tea		2½
Oil		2½
Total	3	6½

■ *SOURCE 6B* Robert Crick and his family, Lavenham, Suffolk. From a Parliamentary Report, 1843

Name	Age	Earnings	
		s	d
Robert Crick	42	9	0
Wife	40		9
Boy	12	2	0
Boy	11	1	0
Boy	8	1	0
Girl	6		–
Boy	4		–
Total		13	9

	Expenditure	
	s	d
Bread	9	0
Potatoes	1	0
Rent	1	2
Tea		2
Sugar		3½
Soap		3
Blue		½
Thread		2
Candles		3
Salt		½
Coal and wood		9
Butter		4½
Cheese		3
Total	13	9

■ *SOURCE 6C* Factory Commissioners' Report, 1833

Mrs B., witness for the Factory Commissioners, 1833. Husband is a spinner and they have five children. Her eldest daughter works for her father as a piecer. At present her husband's earnings and her daughter's together amount to about 25s a week – at least she sees no more than 25s [£1.25]

(Note: Whatever sum her husband may bring home, his earnings as a fine spinner are certainly not less than 28s per week [£1.40]

Breakfast is generally porridge, bread and milk, on Sunday, tea and bread and butter. Dinner, on weekdays potatoes and bacon and bread, generally white. Sunday – a little meat, no butter, egg or pudding. Tea-time every day tea, bread and butter. Supper, porridge and milk – Sunday, sometimes a little bread and cheese.

	s	d
Butter, 1½ lb at 10d/1b	1	3
Tea 1½ oz		4½
Bread – makes it herself: 24 lb of flour and salt and yeast	4	6
Oatmeal, half a peck		6½
Bacon 1½ lb		9
Potatoes, 2 score at 8d a score	1	4
Milk, 2 pints a day, at 1½d each	1	9
Meat on Sunday, about 1 lb		7
Sugar, 1½ lb at 6d/lb		9
Pepper, mustard, extras		3
Soap, candles	1	0
Coal	1	6
Rent	3	6
Total	18	1
Leaves for clothes, school, sickness:	6	11

(Note: Read over this account to S.L. a worker, and a respectable witness. He thinks it somewhat below the average of comforts possessed by working families. Mostly they have tea and coffee for breakfast, and their dinners are generally fresh meat.)

? QUESTIONS

a) Why is it difficult to compare Source 6A with the other two sources in terms of what people bought?

b) Which items of spending are missing from Source 6A because it is simply a diet list?

c) What proportion of each of the three budgets is taken up by bread (or oatmeal in Source 6A)?

d) What would happen to Robert Crick's family (Source 6B) if one of the children was ill and couldn't work?

e) Who seems to be better off: the agricultural labourer (6B) or the textile factory worker (6C)?

f) Are budgets like these any help in calculating prices of goods?

g) What problems are there in using them for this purpose?

Family budgets like Sources 6A, 6B and 6C clearly tell us a good deal of interesting information. They tell us what people spent their money on, and how much they paid, at one moment in history. They do *not* tell us much about how prices changed over a long period. For this we can only find evidence from organisations, such as schools, hospitals or workhouses.

■ *SOURCE 7A* Greenwich Hospital, items for purchase

Bread per lb	Oatmeal per cwt
Flour per sack	Salt per bushel
Meat per cwt	Beer per barrel
Butter per lb	Candles per dozen
Cheese per lb	Coals per caldron [tub]
Peas per bushel	

(Note: prices for these items are available from 1795 to 1838.)

? QUESTION

What would be the problems in using prices from records like Source 7A to calculate prices paid by ordinary people?

■ *SOURCE 7B* **Two price indices, 1750–1850**

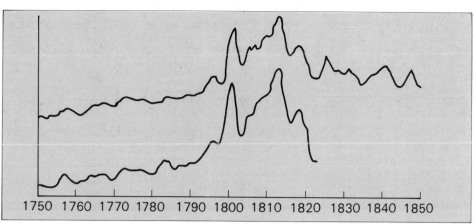

1750 1760 1770 1780 1790 1800 1810 1820 1830 1840 1850

The general pattern of prices

Using several of these kinds of evidence, historians have tried to draw up price indices for the period 1750–1850. Two versions of such a price index are shown in Source 7B.

Prices were obviously very high in the Napoleonic Wars and often high after that. There were wild variations, and a slight rise over the whole period. How did this affect people's lives? Sources 6A, 6B and 6C show that different people had different spending habits. Probably in years of high prices families bought mainly bread, and nearly everything else was squeezed out of their budgets. And in the good years? Perhaps they spent more money on 'luxuries' such as meat, eggs or coffee. Perhaps they kitted themselves out in decent clothes. Or perhaps they bought the same food and spent their spare cash in the pub.

Do all these calculations bring us any nearer to an answer to the question: were people better off? Attempts to find precise answers on modern lines seem to have failed. Is there some other form of evidence we could use?

Consumption

We know that during the 19th century consumption of many items of food and everyday articles went up. More sugar, tea, eggs, soap, leather, linen and cotton were bought, for example. The Industrial Revolution itself, as we know from Section A, reduced the prices of many manufactured items, such as fabrics, china and clothing. Savings banks were set up in the 19th century to give ordinary people a safe place to put their small savings. Deposits in savings banks went up from £3½ million in 1820, to £42 million by 1860 and £200 million by 1900. As Chapter 12 explains, shopping changed in the 19th century.

Markets were used less, and the number of specialised shops increased (see Source 8).

These pieces of information seem to suggest that people *were* better off. Of course it may be that it was the richer classes who consumed most of the goods, saved in the banks and bought Farmer Bates' meat. We know from the work of Seebohm Rowntree that there was still dire poverty when the 20th century began. We know of the terribly low wages paid to women in sweated labour right up to the First World War. But the signs are that more people were, indeed, better off. Probably the clearest sign of all is given in Chapter 11: people themselves chose to leave the countryside and move into the towns in huge numbers. Certainly, they appear to have expected to be better off in industrialised areas.

■ *SOURCE 8* **Farmer Bates' butcher's shop, late 19th century**

■ SOURCE 9

The historian can answer two questions about the Industrial Revolution in England: whether or not the workers' bundle of goods increased; whether or not the worker willingly gave up a rural, pre-industrial way of life for the way of life of an urban, industrial society. Evidence of wages, and of the movement of workers strongly suggests both that living standards improved, and that they welcomed the changed way of life.

R. M. Hartwell, *The Standard of Living Controversy*, 1973

? QUESTIONS

a) R. M. Hartwell is optimistic about the Industrial Revolution: he thinks things got better. On what basis does he comes to this conclusion?

b) This is a secondary source; where do you think R. M. Hartwell got his evidence from?

The Quality of Life

However, there is another aspect to this argument. Some historians agree that people may have become better off in terms of wages and goods, but they point to ways in which they were worse off in terms of the quality of life.

■ SOURCE 10A

We move from data which can be measured to those satisfactions which cannot. From food we are led to homes, from homes to health, from health to family life and thence to working conditions, hours, leisure and so on. From standard of life we pass to way of life. But the two are not the same .... People may consume more goods and be less happy and less free at the same time...

Over the period 1790–1840 there was a slight improvement in average material standards. Over the same period there was more exploitation, and increasing human misery. By 1840 most people were 'better-off' than their fore-runners had been 50 years before. But they had suffered, and continued to suffer this slight improvement as a catastrophic experience.

E. P. Thompson, *The Making of the English Working Class*, 1963

■ SOURCE 10B Working-class Londoners, 1896

? QUESTIONS

a) What are the 'satisfactions' which E. P. Thompson refers to which cannot be measured?

b) From your reading of this book, do you think he is right?

c) E. P. Thompson is pessimistic about the Industrial Revolution: he thinks things got worse. On what basis does he come to his conclusion?

In several other chapters you can find evidence that life for working people in industrial cities was, as E. P. Thompson says, 'catastrophic'. In Chapter 14 you read about the long hours and harsh discipline of factory work. In Chapter 11 you saw that the towns and cities were overcrowded, with appalling living conditions. In Chapter 21 you can read about the effects on women, confining them to low-paid, low-status jobs. In Chapter 18 you will see what efforts working people made to fight back, and how they were ruthlessly put in their place by the government. In Chapter 26 you can see how many expressed their opinion of life in industrial Britain by emigrating. Eventually the problems caused by industrialisation pushed the government into action. However, working conditions, housing and public health did not really show much improvement until the end of the century.

An empathetic view

However, we must be careful to look at these issues in the right way. The question is not how would we feel if we were suddenly picked up and dropped into an industrial city in Britain in 1830. The question is, how did people alive at that time, like those in Sources 1D, 1E and 10B, feel? In general, people today expect things to get better year by year; they expect to have a higher standard of living than their parents or grandparents. This was not so before industrialisation, when everyone's well-being depended on the success of the harvest, so the standard of living could not be expected to rise indefinitely. Much the same attitude survived into the 19th century.

When people moved into the towns and cities, how did they feel about the overcrowding? Did they worry about the dreadful diseases and high death rate? How did it compare with what they were used to? How did it compare with their expectations? You must make up your own mind about this, after studying this book. In the end your answer will depend as much on your skills in empathy as your skills in handling the evidence.

Assignments

Empathy

1 **a** Read Sources 6B and 6C. How would you feel if you had to manage on the budgets shown?
   b In what ways might people in the 19th century have felt the same as you, and in what ways might they have felt differently?
2 **a** Why is the 'standard of living' question as much a matter of empathy as of evidence?
   b Why is it helpful to read many of the other chapters in this book before reaching a decision on this question?

Understanding concepts

1 Change/continuity
'Standard of living' is a matter of wages and prices.
   a What problems are there in deciding what wages really were?
   b What problems are there in deciding how wages changed over time?
   c Why is it not enough just to decide what wages were?

2 Change/continuity
   a What is an index of prices?
   b What problems are there in deciding an index for a period in history?
   c Why do prices vary so wildly in the 19th century?
   d Why do prices not go up and down so rapidly nowadays?

Evidence

1 This chapter contains statistics, photographs and secondary sources of evidence.
   a In what ways is each of these sources most useful to a historian of standards of living?
   b What are the weaknesses of each as sources of evidence about standards of living?
2 'The question is, how did people ... like those in Sources 1D and 1E feel?' What evidence could be used to find this out?

Themes for discussion

1 Do you think this book offers a biased account or an unbiased account of the consequences of the Industrial Revolution?
2 What is *your* answer to these questions:
   a Did the standard of living of ordinary people in Britain rise or fall in the years 1800–1850?
   b Did people feel better-off or worse-off over this period?

18 Working-class Movements 1700–1850

Grievances and Protest

In Section A we saw how changes in industry affected the lives of most of the working people of Britain. Often their lives were changed for the worse. The grievances of working people all came down to the same thing: it was a struggle to live. A rise in the price of bread or a sudden slump in trade, causing an employer to lay off workers, meant disaster. Some craftsmen, such as the hand-loom weavers, lost their livelihood because their skill was replaced by machines. Other complaints involved unsafe working conditions, long hours and being cheated by employers. What could working people do about their grievances?

Ordinary people were not able to turn to the government for help. The 18th century view of society, and of government, was that a person's station in life had been decided by God. You were born to be a king or a factory worker, a duke or a labourer. It was therefore not only pointless, but sinful, to try to change things. It was also believed that only landowners, those who had a stake in the country, had any right to rule. Those who owned nothing could not be expected to take part in government. Therefore, only 4% of the adult male population could vote in elections (no women could vote at all). MPs had to own property in order to stand for Parliament. MPs were not paid, so no working person could think of standing for election.

This left working people with only two choices in trying to improve their situation. Firstly, they could accept that they had no power and try to persuade the ruling classes to help them. This could be done by peaceful petitions, meetings or negotiations. Alternatively, they could direct their anger into violent attacks on whatever they felt was causing their distress. This difference in methods, between peaceful persuasion and violent action, runs through the history of working people's movements (see also Chapters 19 and 20).

As well as disagreements about methods, there were disagreements about targets. Should working people try to change the system of government so that Parliament would represent them? The government could then be used to pass laws which would solve their problems. Or should they ignore Parliament and put pressure on employers to improve their wages and conditions? There were other alternatives: some people argued for a revolution to throw out all monarchs, aristocrats and bosses so that the land and the factories could be handed over to the workers. Others wanted to opt out of the whole industrial system and set up new communities of their own. Look for examples of these different targets, and different methods of reaching them, throughout this chapter.

In 1793 Lord Braxfield declared: 'The British Constitution is the best that ever was since the creation of the world, and it is not possible to make it any better.' Until about that date nearly all British people would have agreed with that statement. It was events in France that began to change some people's minds.

The French Revolution and Britain

When the French Revolution began, in 1789, it was welcomed in Britain. The early acts of the Revolution seemed to be bringing the French system of government more in line with the British. However, by 1793 the French Revolution had moved on: the King and hundreds of nobles had been executed and ideas of 'Liberty, Equality and Fraternity' were being put into practice. The British ruling classes then condemned the Revolution, and in 1793 declared war on France. Nevertheless, there was a great deal of interest in democratic ideas in England. The French Revolution had shown that the people could rise up and throw out their rulers. In

■ **SOURCE 1A** The execution of Louis XVI, 1793

Britain, groups were formed in many towns to discuss democratic ideas. Many of them wrote to France for further information, so were called Corresponding Societies. They were especially strong in London, Norwich, Sheffield and in Scotland. Newspapers were started to publish ideas for change. But the main reading matter among all the groups was Tom Paine's *Rights of Man*.

Tom Paine

Paine had been an admirer and supporter of the American Revolution of 1776. He had gone to live in America, but returned to visit France. His book, published in two parts in 1791 and 1792, was an attack on the whole basis of the British system of government, the King, the aristocrats and the Church.

■ SOURCE 1B

I disapprove of monarchical and aristocratic governments, however modified. Hereditary distinctions and privileges of any kind must work against human improvement. Hence it follows that I am not among the admirers of the British Constitution ...

Tom Paine, *Rights of Man*, 1792

■ SOURCE 1C

I consider the reform of Parliament by petition to Parliament to be a worn-out subject, about which the nation is tired .... The right belongs to the people, and the proper means is by a national convention, elected for the purpose by all the people.

Pamphlet by Paine, 1793

The *Rights of Man* had sold about 200 000 copies by 1793 – a huge number for that time, when there was no free education system to teach people to read. Corresponding Societies published shorter versions as pamphlets. Other radical writers also published their ideas.

■ SOURCE 1D

PEOPLE: What work do you do in this society?
PRIVILEGED CLASS: None: we are not made to work.
PEOPLE: How then have you acquired your wealth?

PRIVILEGED CLASS: By governing you.
PEOPLE: By governing us! We toil, and you enjoy; we produce and you spend; wealth flows from us and you absorb it.

Volnay, *Ruins of Empire*, published several times in the 1790s

❓ QUESTIONS

a) Who were the main targets of Paine's and Volnay's attacks?

b) On what grounds do Paine and Volnay base their criticisms?

c) Why does Paine, in Source 1C, reject the idea of petitions to Parliament?

d) What kind of system of government do Paine and Volnay seem to be suggesting?

e) How would Lord Braxfield, an upholder of the British Constitution, react to these ideas?

Government reaction

The British government was, not surprisingly, worried. They feared a revolution in Britain that would copy events in France. Britain had no police force, and the country was at war. Also, London was no longer the only centre of radical activity. Provincial towns and cities were involved, and the government had even less control outside the capital. They took drastic action: Corresponding Societies were banned. Tom Paine was arrested. Printers of radical books were imprisoned. Newspapers were taxed to make them too expensive for the poor to buy. The Combination Acts of 1799 and 1800 made trade unions illegal.

In fact, the only real threat to the government was in 1797 when there were mutinies in the navy at Spithead and the Nore. It is clear from what has been said that the supporters of radical ideas could read and bought newspapers and books. This excludes most labouring people at that time, who were not involved. Further, the movement was crushed by 1796.

This agitation of the 1790s affected working-class ideas and actions for many decades into the 19th century, however. The *Rights of Man* remained on many cottage bookshelves to convince anyone who read it that the system must be changed. No longer could Lord Braxfield, or his successors, count on the support of all working people

for a system of government which excluded them. For the next fifty years the most widespread movements of working people were those aiming, by peaceful means or not, at parliamentary reform.

Radical unrest, 1815–20

Radical ideas for the reform of Parliament were not killed off in the 1790s. This was soon clear after the wars against France ended in 1815. Trades such as iron and textiles, which had prospered in the war, had no orders. One-third of a million sailors and soldiers left the forces and began to look for work. The landowners dominating Parliament passed the Corn Laws. These kept up the price of corn by banning cheap imports (see Chapter 25). Mass unemployment, short-time working and high food prices brought demands for change. William Cobbett, the radical journalist, insisted that the focus for change should be Parliament.

The remedy consists wholly and solely of such a reform in the Commons ... as shall cause the members to be elected annually.

W. Cobbett, *Political Register*, November 2, 1816

Big protest demonstrations were held at Spa Fields, London, in 1816. The main speaker was the radical MP for Preston, Henry Hunt, called 'Orator' Hunt. Before he arrived at the second meeting, in December, another speaker led off a crowd of angry unemployed Londoners. They attacked gunshops, and rioting followed.

In the early part of 1817 unemployed Lancashire cotton workers began to march south; as they all carried blankets it was called the 'Blanketeers'' March. They got no further than Macclesfield, Cheshire, where they were stopped by soldiers, and the leaders were put in prison.

Some historians think that Britain was very near revolution at this point. There were determined leaders, desperate and hungry people and radical ideas. Certainly the government was very worried. The law of Habeas Corpus was suspended: this meant that people could be arrested and imprisoned without trial. Over a hundred radicals were put in prison; Cobbett fled, temporarily, to America; meetings were banned.

The fears of the Prime Minister, Lord Liverpool, were justified later in 1817 when nearly 300 villagers of Pentrich, in Derbyshire, rose in rebellion. Their leader, Brandreth, told them:

■ SOURCE 2

Every man his skill must try
He must turn out and not deny;
No bloody soldier must he dread
He must turn out and fight for
  bread.
The time is come you plainly see
The government opposed must
  be ...

? QUESTION

Suggest reasons why Brandreth's message was put in verse.

The Pentrich rebellion failed. They were met outside Nottingham by soldiers, and the leaders were put on trial. It seems that a government spy, Oliver, had joined them and led them on in order to catch them. The leaders were transported to the colonies or executed.

Peterloo

In 1819 a large meeting was due to be addressed in St Peter's Fields, Manchester, by 'Orator' Hunt. People had gathered from all over Lancashire, and the magistrates were warned. They had heard that men had been drilling like soldiers in preparation. The magistrates decided to arrest Hunt, and untrained soldiers went into the crowd. Violence broke out: 11 people were killed and 400 wounded. The incident became known as the Battle of Peterloo – a sarcastic reference to the Battle of Waterloo, four years earlier.

■ SOURCE 3A

I saw the main body proceeding towards St Peter's Fields, and never saw a gayer spectacle .... The 'marching order' of which so much was said afterwards was what we often see now in the procession of Sunday School children .... Our company laughed at the fears of the magistrates and the

remark was, that if the men intended mischief they would not have brought their wives, their sisters or their children with them.

A. Prentice, *Historical Sketches of Manchester*, 1851

The banners carried slogans such as 'Liberty and Fraternity', 'Parliaments Annual', 'Suffrage Universal' (votes for all adults).

? QUESTIONS

a) What impression of the march is given in Source 3A?
b) Samuel Bamford, a radical writer, supported the demonstrators, but admitted that some had practised drilling before the meeting. Why would this have worried, and frightened, the magistrates?
c) Does this excuse the magistrates' action?
d) Does Bamford's information contradict the impression of the march given in Source 3A?
e) Is Source 3A: (i) reliable, (ii) useful, and (iii) important in helping us understand the

events of Peterloo? Explain your answer.
f) What would have been the reactions of the magistrates to the words on the banners?
g) In what ways does Source 3B help us understand the events of Peterloo?
h) What questions would you want to ask about Source 3B in order to answer question f)?
i) Do historians have the right to judge such things as the actions of the magistrates at Peterloo?

The Six Acts

The government followed up Peterloo by passing the Six Acts. These tried to crush radical ideas still further by preventing the publication of books and pamphlets which criticised the government. Large meetings were banned. In the next year, 1820, a plan to assassinate the entire Cabinet, the Cato Street Conspiracy, was discovered. In Scotland there was a mass uprising in Glasgow: there was a general strike of most workers, a weavers' rebellion and demonstrations at the Carron ironworks. Once again the movement was crushed and the leaders executed.

After the dramatic events of the five years up to 1820 the movement for change subsided. A head-on attack on the government, sometimes peaceful and sometimes violent, had failed. Working people turned to other actions, and improvements in trade in the 1820s took the edge off their desperation.

Industrial Protests

The Luddites

Alongside these mainly peaceful demands for political change there were other actions by working people that were quite different. Violent attacks by groups of workers on the causes of distress were made. Throughout the textile trade, for example, new machinery represented a real threat to the livelihoods of craftsmen. In Nottinghamshire, in 1811, there was a rising of workers against the 'frames' – machines which replaced craftsmen's skills as stocking knitters. Workers broke into factories and smashed up machines. To protect themselves they made up the name of a leader – Ned Lud. (To this day the word 'Luddite' is used to describe someone who refuses to accept a new invention.)

■ *SOURCE 4A*

We the framework knitters declare to all hosiers, lace manufacturers and proprietors of frames that we will break and destroy all manner of frames whatsoever ... and all frames that do not pay the regular prices heretofore agreed.

Given under my hand this first day of January, 1812, at Ned Lud's office, Sherwood Forest.

The Luddite movement spread to Yorkshire, where shearing frames were attacked, and Lancashire where power-looms were the targets. Action subsided in 1812, but there were further outbreaks in 1826 and 1830. In Wales, at various times between 1820 and 1835 violence was used against employers who paid low wages, or who used English or Irish workers who would take low wages.

The Captain Swing riots

Much more serious, however, were the 'Captain Swing' riots of 1830. These took place in rural areas, where agricultural labourers resented the low wages and the introduction of threshing machines. Threshing by hand was an important source of employment in winter months, and machines robbed them of this work. Workers sent threatening letters to farmers, and burnt ricks, barns and machines. Again a made-up name, this time 'Captain Swing', hid the names of the letter-writers.

■ *SOURCE 4B*

Remember in Kent they have set fire all that would not submit and you will serve the same for we are determined to make you support the poor better than they have been suppered yet for they are all starving at present so pull down your thrashing machines or Fire without delay. For we are five thousand men and will not be stopt.

Captain Swing, 1830

? *QUESTIONS*

a) Why did the workers use a made-up name, such as 'Ned Lud', or 'Captain Swing'?
b) Why would the use of made-up names frighten employers?
c) Suggest reasons why these workers took violent action rather than making a peaceful protest.

■ *SOURCE 4D* Berkshire magistrate's notice, 1830

TO THE
Labouring Classes

THE Gentlemen, Yeomanry, Farmers, and others, having made known to you their intention of increasing your Wages to a satisfactory extent; and it having been resolved that Threshing Machines shall not be again used; it is referred to your good Sense that it will be most beneficial to your own permanent Interests to return to your usual honest occupations, and to withdraw yourselves from practices which tend to destroy the Property from whence the very means of your additional Wages are to be supplied.

Hungerford, 22nd November, 1830.

EMBERLIN AND HAROLD, PRINTERS, BOOKSELLERS, DRUGGISTS, &c. STAMP-OFFICE, MARLBOROUGH.

Trade Unions

These violent movements have been called 'collective bargaining by riot'. In collective bargaining a large number of workers get together to discuss their pay and conditions with their employer. If a single worker tried to do this, the employer could ignore or sack him or her. If many workers do it, they force the employer to take notice. There are several things that workers can do to press their point,

■ *SOURCE 4C* Rick-burning in Kent, 1830s

but in the last resort they can go on strike. This will mean that the employer loses money, as the factory is not producing anything. The usual way that workers get together for collective bargaining is in a union.

Early unions

Trade unions have a long history. In the 18th century there were societies of skilled workers, which helped their members in several ways. They prevented too many people learning a trade, for example. This kept up their own wages, because skilled workers were hard to get. They collected quite a high subscription, up to 1/- (5p) a week, from their members, which was used to pay benefits during times of illness or unemployment. They could combine against employers to keep up wages, but this was not common: they preferred to work with their employers in ensuring they got better treatment, as skilled workers, than the unskilled. Trades such as masons, coopers, tailors, printers and shoemakers were organised in this way.

By the 1790s the most skilled workers in the new industries, such as cotton-spinning, had formed unions as well. Some members were interested in radical ideas, like Tom Paine's, but they were mostly well-paid men who totally opposed violence and revolution.

The Combination Acts of 1799 and 1800 came from a government frightened of revolution. In fact, very few prosecutions were brought under the Acts. The only important case was against the printers of *The Times*, in 1810. Unions continued to exist, even to increase during the wartime trade boom. Nottingham, for example, was said to have 50 unions in 1812. The reason not much was heard about unions in the next few years was because, as we have seen, working people put their energies into other kinds of protest.

After 1820, when radicalism had faded and trade was better, there was pressure to legalise unions. This came especially from Francis Place, a London tailor, and Joseph Hume, a radical MP. As a result, the Combination Acts were repealed in 1824. This was followed by several strikes, so the government passed laws against picketting in 1825.

■ *SOURCE 5A* **Women's trade union membership card, 1833**

They also restricted union activities to negotiations about wages and hours only.

Attempts to form national unions

Unions were now legal, but very restricted. However, there were brief attempts to build a national union movement. John Doherty, a Lancashire cotton spinner, tried to unite all cotton workers in his 'Grand General Union of all Operative Spinners in the United Kingdom' in 1829. In the next year he set up the National Association for the Protection of Labour (NAPL).

■ *SOURCE 5B*

Agreed to by the meeting of delegates held in Manchester on Monday, Tuesday and Wednesday the 28th, 29th and 30th June, 1830:

Resolved:

1 **That the miserable condition to which, by repeated and unnecessary reductions of wages, the working people of this country are reduced, urges upon this meeting the necessity of adopting some means for preventing such reductions and securing to the workman a just and adequate reward for his labour.**
2 **That to achieve this object a Society shall be formed of all the organised Trades throughout the Kingdom.**
3 **That this Society be called 'The National Association for the Protection of Labour'.**

? QUESTIONS

a) What was the main reason for setting up the NAPL?
b) Do you think the NAPL would last?

Doherty claimed that the NAPL had 100 000 members, and started a newspaper. In fact the NAPL was only a 'union of unions': each union paid £1 to join and there were no individual members. By 1832 both his unions had collapsed. In the same year builders set up a 'Builders' Parliament', but this too did not survive. These mass unions tried to do more than just tackle issues of wages and conditions. They tried to change the whole economic system, and this is what attracted an extraordinary man of ideas, Robert Owen.

Robert Owen

Robert Owen believed that if workers were treated well they would work well and business would prosper (Chapter 14, page 154). Owen was among the first to point out that industry need not be a bad thing for ordinary people. He proved that it could bring prosperity and a better life, if people worked together.

Owen's belief in co-operation led him to live in America from 1824 to 1829. Here he set up a village, called New Harmony. All the villagers worked together and owned things together in what we nowadays call a commune. When this idea failed, Owen returned to Britain and set up his 'labour exchanges'. These were *not* like our own Unemployment Offices. His idea was that a worker should be paid according to the number of hours put into making something. Workers would bring the object made to one of his labour exchanges and be paid in notes for the hours of work (see Source 5C).

Such a system required lots of people to join it. This did not happen, and by 1834 the labour exchanges were shutting down. Owen then got interested in unions, and set up the Grand National Consolidated Trade Union. Anyone could join the GNCTU, and soon he was able to claim 800 000 members. Membership was only 3*d* (1¼p) a week. Owen, unusually

■ *SOURCE 5C* **A labour note, signed by Robert Owen, 1833**

NATIONAL EQUITABLE LABOUR EXCHANGE

BIRMINGHAM BRANCH

TRUTH.

ESTABLISHED 1833

to the STOREKEEPER of the EXCHANGE

N°   *July 22nd 1833   July 22nd 1833*   N°

Deliver to the Bearer Exchange Stores to the Value of Forty Hours *by Order of*

FORTY

Robert Owen GOVERNOR

Benj.ⁿ Woolfield DIRECTOR

SECRETARY

CHARLOTTE STREET, RATHBONE PLACE, LONDON.

for his time, treated women equally with men, and large numbers of women workers joined. His aim was to support any worker in a demand for better pay, but he also talked of a 'national holiday' – a general strike. He thought this would bring about the total collapse of the economic system. He hoped that this, in turn, would make everyone see the benefits of cooperation, rather than conflict.

■ *QUESTIONS*

a) Would you join in one of Owen's 'labour exchanges'? Give your reasons.

b) Did the NAPL (see Source 5B) and the labour exchanges work with the system, against it, or outside it?

The Tolpuddle 'Martyrs'

Employers were very worried by the GNCTU and the government decided to make an example of union members to discourage others. Six agricultural labourers at Tolpuddle, in Dorset, set up an agricultural workers' branch of the GNCTU. They were arrested and accused of swearing a secret oath – a crime under a wartime Act of 1797. The leader, George Loveless, said at his trial:

■ *SOURCE 5D*

My Lord, if we have broken the law, it was not done intentionally. We have injured no man's charac-ter, reputation, person or property. We were uniting together to preserve ourselves, our wives and our children from utter degradation and starvation. We challenge any man to prove we have acted different from that statement.

Loveless was a dignified man and a Methodist lay preacher, but he and four of his friends were sentenced to seven years' transportation to Australia. There was a national outcry and a huge protest in London, led by Robert Owen.

■ *QUESTIONS*

a) What do Sources 5C and 5D, and the sentence Loveless received, tell us about the government at the time?

b) Explain why the government acted in this way.

Loveless was brought back to Britain in 1836, but the GNCTU had collapsed in 1834, following the Tolpuddle Case. It was in many ways ahead of its time. There was no good, cheap transport system yet to keep its members together; its leaders were inexperienced. It included ideas which were very far-sighted, but could not stand up to the determined opposition of government and employers.

Robert Owen turned his attention to setting up more co-operative villages. Employers took to asking their workers to sign 'The Document' before taking them on. This document said that they were not union members, nor would they join a union. It was certainly not the end of trade unions, but working people turned away from them for a while.

■ *SOURCE 5E* **A meeting of protest against the deportation of the Tolpuddle Martyrs, 1834**

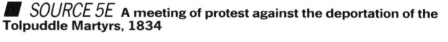

Reform of Parliament and Chartism

Working people took part in the agitation of 1830–2 leading to the great Reform Act. The leaders, however, were all from the middle classes, and there was never much likelihood of the vote being extended to everyone. There was a group called the National Union of the Working Classes, but it did not have much support. There were riots in Bristol, Derby and Nottingham, and a serious rising in Merthyr, but the leaders of the reform campaign just used these events to press the government into giving way. When the Act was eventually passed in 1832, it did not benefit working people. Forty-two towns which did not have MPs were given the right to elect them, including Leeds, Sheffield, Manchester and Birmingham. But only people who owned property were given the vote, so it was the middle class who benefited. The number of voters rose from about 150 000 before the Act to about 600 000.

The Charter

This disappointment led to a massive movement to make the country more democratic. In 1836 a group of skilled workers in the London Working Men's Association, led by Francis Place and William Lovett, drew up the six points of the Charter. These were:

1 Every man over 21 should have the right to vote.
2 There should be an equal number of voters for each election district (constituency).
3 Abolition of the property qualification to stand as an MP.
4 Payment of MPs.
5 Voting in secret.
6 Parliament elected every year.

For the next few years the attention and hopes of working people were concentrated on getting the Charter accepted. The reasons for their support varied, but everyone felt that if working people had a voice in Parliament then all other grievances could be put right. In the North, for example, there was

massive resentment of the new Poor Law (Chapter 15, page 165). In Birmingham there was a movement to reform the currency. There was opposition to the new police force set up by Sir Robert Peel. There were calls to pass laws to protect working conditions in factories. There were teetotallers campaigning against alcohol. Above all, there was a bitterness over the 1832 Act, and a feeling of betrayal. If it was logical to extend the vote to the middle classes, it was logical, as Tom Paine had explained long before, to extend it to everyone. Working people felt that they were on their own now that the middle classes had got what they wanted.

■ *SOURCE 6A*

It was the fond expectation of the people that a remedy for the greater part of their grievances would be found in the Reform Act of 1832. They regarded that act as a means whereby the will of the masses would be made real.

They have been bitterly and basely deceived.

The Reform Act has effected a transfer of power from one faction to another and left the people as helpless as before ...

Therefore: We demand [then follows the six points of the Charter].

The Monthly Liberator, June 13, 1838

A few towns, like Coventry, never joined the Chartist movement, and it was weak in Cornwall, where Methodism was strong, and in rural areas. However it was the biggest working-class movement of the 19th century.

■ *SOURCE 6B*

Chartism is no political movement where the main question is getting the ballot. This is the knife and fork question after all ... a bread and cheese question .... If any man asks me what I mean by universal suffrage I would answer that every working man in the land has the right to a good coat to his back, a comfortable abode in which to shelter himself and his family and a good dinner upon his table ...

J. R. Stephens in the *Manchester and Salford Advertiser*, March 25, 1838

■ *SOURCE 6C*

Universal suffrage there shall be — or our tyrants will find to their cost that we will have universal misery. We will make our country one vast howling wilderness of desolation and destruction rather than the tyrants shall carry out their infernal system .... Believe me, there is no argument like the sword – and the musket is unanswerable.

G. J. Harney, *Northern Star*, February 17, 1839

? QUESTIONS

a) Compare the reasons for Chartism given in each of these sources.
b) Compare the methods of achieving the points of the Charter suggested in Sources 6A and 6C.
c) Which do you think the writer of Source 6B would agree with?

Different tactics

With so many different hopes involved, it was inevitable that there should be disagreements over how to achieve the Charter. William Lovett intended that a huge petition would be presented to Parliament. He hoped that sufficient MPs would be won over to vote for it. But what if they didn't? There was a good deal of talk about using force (see Source 6C). The main leader of the Chartists in the north of England was Fergus O'Connor. He ran the Chartist newspaper *The Northern Star* and was a powerful speaker. His own attitude to using force was not always clear, but his phrase 'peacefully if we can, forcibly if we must' probably sums it up. Others, particularly in the desperate years of the 1840s, with unemployment and hunger widespread in the North, were more violent. However, no serious plans for national rebellion, or even peaceful resistance, were ever made.

Historians label peaceful Chartists, like Lovett, 'moral force' Chartists, and others, such as O'Connor, as 'physical force' Chartists. The trouble was that moral force depended on winning the support of MPs, who were middle- or upper-class. The speeches of O'Connor, and others, the huge torchlight pro-

■ *SOURCE 6D* **Newport Chartist rising, 1839**

revival of Chartist agitation. Once again there were huge processions and angry speeches. The government acted more sensibly than in the years 1815–20. The General in charge of the North, Napier, was sympathetic to the Chartists, but not to rebellion. He made it clear to Chartist leaders that there would be terrible bloodshed if they attempted a revolution. Eventually a huge meeting was held on Kennington Common, in London, in April 1848. The Chartists were going to march to Parliament with the petition, but the government banned the march and swore in 150 000 special constables under the old Duke of Wellington. O'Connor, to avoid conflict, sent the petition by cab.

The meeting was therefore a flop, and the petition, said to contain 6 million signatures, only contained 2 million, some of which were forged. Parliament rejected it.

The end of Chartism

Chartism really collapsed at that point. The village communities scheme was bankrupt. O'Connor became mentally ill. Many Chartists emigrated and some joined the early Socialist movement. However, Chartism was not a total failure. For masses of working people in the cities of Britain it was their first experience of organisation. They had learnt to run newspapers, hold meetings and work out their ideas. They had not been keen on using force, although many were moved by O'Connor's speeches. They had shown the government that working people had real grievances and must be listened to. Over the next fifty years, by their own actions and by government action, many of their hopes were realised.

cessions and the death's-heads on some of the banners frightened off the very people Lovett wished to win over.

The first petition, of 1.3 million signatures, was presented in 1839 and was rejected by Parliament. There had been talk of calling a general strike if this happened, but no effective plans were made for it. A thousand Welsh Chartists went to Newport, with weapons, to rescue their leader, Henry Vincent, who had been arrested. Soldiers opened fire on them, and 14 were killed. There was also a riot in Birmingham, where Lovett was arrested.

From then on Chartism came

under O'Connor's leadership. In 1842, a second petition, of 3.3 million signatures was presented and rejected. There was a wave of strikes and demonstrations in the North. These were called the 'plug plots' because strikers crippled the steam-engines (which powered the factories) by knocking out the boiler plugs.

As Chartism declined, O'Connor turned to setting up co-operative communities, as Robert Owen had tried to do. £112 000 was collected and five communities were set up, with 250 people.

The terrible distress of 1847 and 1848, and the revolutions of 1848 in various parts of Europe, led to a

■ *SOURCE 6F*

The Secretary of the LWMA was William Lovett, an example of one of the best types of Englishman. He was self-educated, well-read, possessed great moral courage .... Lovett hoped that the aim of the Charter could be achieved peacefully ...

[Caption to picture] Feargus O' Connor, the fiery leader of Chartism in the North of England.

Feargus O'Connor, an Irishman, then became leader of the

■ *SOURCE 6E* **Very early photograph of Chartists at Kennington, 1848**

movement …

Looking back one can see that a movement with two men of such conflicting outlooks as Lovett and O'Connor, and with such a wide variety of supporters, could hardly have hoped to succeed. Moreover the six points of Chartism were too big a programme to be accomplished at any one time …

From S. L. Case and D. J. Hall, *A Social and Economic History of Britain*, 1983

❓ QUESTIONS

a) How can you tell this is a secondary source about Chartism?

b) Give examples of opinions and facts from this source.

c) Why do you think the authors are so sympathetic to Lovett?

d) What is their attitude to O'Connor?

e) Do you agree with their reasons for the failure of Chartism?

f) How do you think the writers of a secondary source reach their conclusions?

Reasons for the failure of Chartism

1 'Moral force' or peaceful Chartism failed because MPs were put off by talk of violence from some Chartists.

2 'Physical force' or violent Chartism was more a matter of talk than action. Apart from the Newport Rising there were no plans, even for a general strike. Most Chartists did not actually want a revolution.

3 The aims of the Charter went too far for most MPs, and the Chartists did not do enough to win them over.

4 The government was against Chartism. They showed skill as well as determination in opposing it.

Chartism attempted to make a massive change in the situation of working people by giving them the vote. Two other types of organisation must be mentioned that quietly did a great deal to help working people in small but important ways.

Other Working-class Movements

Friendly Societies

Friendly Societies had existed since the 18th century. Each worker paid a small subscription and could claim some benefit during times of illness or unemployment. The family were also helped if the wage-earner died. Only the better-off workers could afford the subscription in the early years of the 19th century. Smaller societies, with lower subscriptions, began to reach the lower-paid after 1850. Soon over half the working people of Britain were subscribing, at a time when trade union membership was barely 10% of workers.

Co-operative societies

One of the most annoying aspects of early industrial life was the 'truck' system or 'tommy-shop'. Wages were paid in tickets or tokens which could only be changed at a certain shop, usually owned by the employer. Prices were high, and goods often of poor quality.

Robert Owen was a great supporter of co-operatives, as we have seen. He expected great things of them, hoping they would replace the entire capitalist system. He expected co-operative factories, farms, housing, villages and shops to be set up, and did indeed start some of these. At his peak in 1832 there were 500 co-operative shops.

However, Owen aimed too high, and his ideas crumbled. In 1844, in Rochdale, Lancashire, 28 flannel weavers simply gave £1.00 each to buy basic foodstuffs to be sold to local people. They bought good-quality items, and people learnt to rely on them. Any profit was given back to the shoppers as a dividend. From these small, but sound, beginnings, the co-operative movement grew.

Looking back over the whole of this period, working people appear to have gained very little. They still suffered from hunger in bad times, bad housing, bad health provision, no education, low wages and poor working conditions. Attempts to improve their lot by violence had achieved nothing. Any attempts to bring large-scale change, such as Chartism, were defeated. Only those organisations, such as Friendly Societies, co-operatives and some trade unions, which attempted small improvements, seem to have succeeded.

All this is true, but it does appear that some foundations were laid and lessons learnt. The years up to 1914 saw much greater changes and improvements, both by government action and by working people taking the initiative themselves.

Assignments

Empathy

1 a Write a letter from a group of Luddites to a factory-owner, threatening to smash his new machines if he doesn't remove them.

b Imagine some farms in your area have been set on fire by 'Captain Swing' gangs. Draw a poster threatening the rioters with transportation for their actions.

2 Look at Sources 3A and 3B. Describe the events of Peterloo from the points of view of:
i one of the people on the demonstration;
ii one of the soldiers.

3 Get into groups of four. You are all Chartists, at a meeting. One of you is a skilled worker, a believer in peaceful persuasion; one is a union member and wants to use a general strike; one is a middle-class radical who wants to get ready for an armed uprising; and one a young worker who is undecided. Have a discussion, explaining why you support the Charter and how you want to have its terms made law.

Understanding concepts

1 Cause/effect
What was the effect of the French Revolution:
i on the views of radicals in Britain about democracy;
ii on the government's view of democratic ideas?

2 Causation/motivation
There were many different working-class movements in these years. What were **i** the aims and **ii** the methods of *each* of the following:
a Luddites;
b The Cato St Conspiracy;
c Co-operatives;
d Corresponding Societies;
e G.N.C.T.U.;
f Friendly Societies?

3 Similarity/difference
Various forms of trade unions were set up in the years before 1850. On the whole they were not successful.
a Which types of unions were started?
b Why did they fail?
c Why was the government so hostile to trade unions?

4 Causation

Government opposition·
Split in tactics
Violence of some members
Aims too wide
Lack of organisation
Fear of revolution

a Choose two of the above factors and explain why you think each was an important *cause* of the failure of Chartism.
b Choose one of the above list and explain why you think it was *not* an important cause of the failure of Chartism.
c Add one reason, not on the list, why Chartism failed.

Themes for discussion

This chapter describes several different types of working-class movement in the early Industrial Revolution. Nearly all of them failed. Was this:
a because of their *aims* – what they set out to do? or
b because of their *means* – how they tried to achieve them?
c Was it *inevitable* that working-class movements would fail at this time in British History?

19 Trade Unions 1850–1980s

Early Unions

A hundred and fifty years ago only a small proportion of workers – about 5% – were in a union at all. Nowadays over 50% of all working people are in a union. It has been tempting for historians to describe this increase as a story of continuous steady growth. In fact, as we shall see, it is a story of ups and downs, of advances and setbacks. We shall also find that most of the arguments put forward for and against trade unions were just the same 150 years ago as they are now.

Many Victorians believed in the theory of 'laissez-faire', which means 'leave it alone', or 'don't interfere'. Economists, such as Ricardo, said that wages should be sorted out between employer and worker freely: there should be no interference from government, union, or anyone else. This might have been all right in theory, but in practice employers and workers did not negotiate on equal terms.

■ SOURCE 1A Strike in a Midlands coalfield, 1844

In 1844 the men left their work in April and immediate steps were taken to fill the places left vacant ... Men were brought from Wales under much better terms than those which had been refused to the men on the spot. Then came the evictions: the coal-owners own the cottages in which the pit-men live ... and eviction means the throwing out of people into the village street. Henry Barrass, eighty years of age, and his wife aged seventy-five, were turned out into the rain and the night. The men saw windows and doors being broken into pieces in order that the meagre household goods could be thrown into the street ...

A. Watson, *Life of Thomas Burt*, 1908. (Thomas Burt was an organiser of the Miners' Association, an early miners' union)

? QUESTIONS

a) Describe how the coal-owners broke the strike.
b) In what ways were the coal-owners more powerful than the miners?
c) What would be the effect of these events on the attitudes and feelings of the miners?
d) What would the miners' union have to do before it could win a strike in these conditions?

As Chapter 18, page 192, showed, trade unions had their roots in the societies of skilled workers which existed before the Industrial Revolution. It was the repeal of the Combination Acts in 1824 which brought an increase in union membership. Big unions, of all types of workers, like the Grand National Consolidated Trade Union (see page 192) frightened the government. They seemed to want to take over the country completely. Governments have felt this fear at other times too. After the Tolpuddle decision in 1834 (see page 193), the idea of big unions collapsed, and for the next few years most unions were small, local, and often did not last long.

Unions before 1825 found it very difficult to put pressure on an employer. If the union called a strike, employers could easily find other people willing to do the work. Strikers called these strike-breakers blacklegs. Unions were not allowed to picket – that is to stand outside a factory or mine and try to persuade blacklegs not to go in.

Even when they were in work, many workers, particularly unskilled workers, were so badly paid that they could not afford to pay much as a union subscription. This meant that unions did not have money to pay their members to support them during a strike. Thus unions could be completely crippled by a long strike and not recover for many years.

In this desperate situation some unions turned to violence, or threats.

■ SOURCE 1B Letter to Murray, a Dublin builder, in 1838, who brought in Scottish workers at lower wages than his own men were asking for

Dear Murray,

        This is to let you know that we are the boys that ignited your house, and we are happy to say that it did not go out until you had enough of it; But we intend very shortly to give you something that won't be telling you two-pence, you Bloody old robber; You may be on the look-out yourself, for we will come as a Thief in the Night; All the New Police in Dublin won't be able to save you, you cursed old robber ... We are not yet satisfied with your house being burnt, nor won't be satisfied till we kick the guts out of you ...

? QUESTIONS

a) What is the tone of this letter?
b) What does this tell you about working conditions in the building industry in Dublin?
c) The letter was quoted by Murray to a parliamentary investigation into unions. Why did he do this?
d) What effect would his evidence have on Parliament's opinion of unions?

As women were nearly all in unskilled work, or received lower pay for the same work, unions made little progress among women at this time. Victorian attitudes to women (see Chapter 21) also discouraged them from trying to improve their situation. Nevertheless, there were several female 'lodges' (branches) of the short-lived GNCTU. Only the Lancashire cotton weavers' unions had strong women's membership, about half of their 30 000 members in 1826.

'New model unions'

Some unions did grow during the 1850s and 1860s. They were for skilled men, who earned good wages and could afford the high entrance fee and high subscription of 1s (5p) a week. These unions were nationally organised, based in London. With a good income they could afford to pay a full-time Secretary. They could also afford to pay out benefits to their members during illness, unemployment or old age. Death grants were made to members and their wives to pay for their burial.

The first of these unions was the Amalgamated Society of Engineers, set up in 1851. In fact it was a joining together of many local groups of skilled engineers, machine-operators and mill-wrights – the most skilled men in the new industries. They had 12 000 members by the end of 1851, and 21 000 by 1860. Their membership card is shown in Source 2A.

? QUESTIONS

a) Which industries are shown on the card?
b) What impression of the union does this card give?

Similar unions of carpenters, bricklayers and iron-founders were formed. Their leaders began to work together in London, with the London Trades Council. Although they were called 'new model unions', there had been unions for skilled men, concentrating on benefits and co-operation, for centuries. These were now brought up to date in an age of better transport and communication. Historians usually say the new model unions

were peaceful and unwilling to strike. This was the impression they wanted to give (see Sources 2C and 2D). Certainly they did not set out to confront employers, but to work with them. As the best-paid men in the factory, ASE members did not want to stop work. However, it would be wrong to say that they were completely anti-strike: the ASE had a long strike in 1852 and often gave money to other unions to help them through a strike. They made 179 such grants in the 1860s.

Other early unions

Historians also write as if this little group of unions were the only unions of the time. This is not so. The Amalgamated Association of Cotton Spinners was very strong in Lancashire and had a number of serious strikes in the 1850s. Local miners' unions still flourished, with no connection with the London group. Miners in different coalfields had different problems, as their conditions of work were different. The mood of the time was moderate, seeking to co-operate with coal-owners.

■ SOURCE 2A Membership card for the ASE

AMALGAMATED SOCIETY OF ENGINEERS, MACHINISTS, MILLWRIGHTS SMITHS AND PATTERN MAKERS

BE UNITED AND INDUSTRIOUS

■ SOURCE 2B

Hitherto it has been a battle between masters and men about wages, now the miners are determined it shall be a battle between masters and men on the one hand, and the public on the other.

Miners' leader, 1844

The National Miners' Union, led by Alex MacDonald, and based on the Scottish, North-eastern and Welsh coalfields, was formed in 1863. It worked to persuade Parliament to pass laws to help miners over such matters as safety, hours of work, methods of pay, etc. In the Midlands coalfields, however, miners were more militant.

The fact that union activity was not always as peaceful as the new model unions wished was made clear in 1866. In what were called the Sheffield Outrages, workers in the cutlery industry attacked blacklegs, burnt their homes, and even killed one of them. The government set up a Royal Commission of Inquiry to investigate. Then, in 1867, in the case of Hornby v. Close, a union secretary was sued for making off with branch funds. Unions had thought that they were protected by the law in the same way as Friendly Societies (see Chapter 18). The judge ruled that they were not.

Trade unions were worried by these developments. In 1868 a meeting of all unions was called in Manchester, called the Trades Union Congress. The London unions did not go, but they did attend in 1869, and since then the TUC has been the 'parliament' of the whole union movement.

The law helps the unions

More important, the secretaries of the new model unions presented a very good picture of unions to the Royal Commission. They were helped in this by Thomas Hughes, a Christian Socialist and supporter of trade unions who was on the Commission. To some extent historians have believed the rosy picture they gave.

■ *SOURCE 2C*

'What are the objects of your association?'
'The object of this society is to raise funds for the support of its members in case of sickness, accident, old age, for the burial of members and their wives, emigration, loss of tools by fire water or theft and for assistance to members out of work ...'

Robert Applegarth, Secretary of the Amalgamated Society of Carpenters and Joiners, 1867

■ *SOURCE 2D*

MR HUGHES: It is very difficult for a strike to happen in your society, I believe? What measures have men to take, for example, before they can strike in your society?

MR ALLEN (Secretary of the ASE): They have to represent their grievances to the committee of their branch ...

MR HUGHES: But supposing the men who wished to go out had got the consent of their branch in their own town, what else would they have to do?

MR ALLEN: They would require to get the consent of the district committee, and the approval of the executive council.

Proceedings of the Royal Commission on Trade Unions, 1867

■ *SOURCE 2E* Union members attack the houses of blacklegs: an unidentified incident from the *Illustrated Midland News*

? *QUESTIONS*

a) What picture of a union is given in Source 2C and 2D?

b) How accurate a picture of the new model unions is given in these two sources?

c) How accurate a picture of the whole union movement is given in these two sources?

d) In what way does Thomas Hughes help Mr Allen in the impression he is trying to give in Source 2D?

e) How far does Source 2E contradict the impression Applegarth and Allen are trying to give?

f) Sources 2C and 2D are printed sources, available to historians studying trade unions. How might this affect the things historians write about trade unions?

The Royal Commission reported that trade unions were peaceful associations which should be given legal protection. The Trade Union Act 1871 gave unions this legal right. This reversed the effect of the Hornby v. Close case and protected their members' funds. However, the Criminal Law Amendment Act

of the same year prevented unions from any form of picketing. Picketing was essential to unions, and still is. The need to change this law led many unionists to think about being represented in Parliament (see Chapter 20). A TUC Parliamentary Committee was set up, and union members were encouraged to vote in the 1874 election against the Liberals who had passed the Act. The Conservatives won the election and passed the Conspiracy and Protection of Property Act of 1876 which permitted peaceful picketing.

These legal changes, and the improvement in the economy in the early 1870s, helped trade unions to grow a little. Working people found their jobs more secure for a while, and so they could afford subscriptions to a union. The Amalgamated Society of Railway Servants was founded in 1871, the Teachers in 1870, the Gas Workers in 1872. In 1874 Emma Paterson founded the Women's Trade Union League, which set up women's unions in several trades. It had nearly 40 women's unions in its membership by 1886, and sent delegates to the TUC from 1876.

■ SOURCE 3A Arch at a night meeting of labourers

The National Agricultural Labourers' Union was set up in 1872, and Arch had 100 000 members by the next year. Opposition came from all sides: farmers and landowning aristocrats were furious. The Bishop of Gloucester said Arch should be thrown in the village pond. To smash the union, farmers in Suffolk held a lock-out – refusing to employ any labourers. Soon 600 labourers were on strike. The NALU could not afford to support so many: their members were poor and funds were low. In the end, the labourers were forced to ask for work, NALU membership fell to about 20 000, but wages did improve. Arch went on to become an MP.

After 1875 business declined again. Employers forced down wages and extended hours. Unions tried to fight these changes, but often lost. Total union membership declined to about 600 000 (of whom only 37 000 were women). This was under 10% of the working population. Not until the late 1880s did an improvement in trade bring full employment again and a further increase in union activity.

New Unionism

This time the mood of the unions was different. Many of the leaders had been influenced by the ideas of Karl Marx (see also Chapter 20). Marx argued that the capitalist system took from the workers the real rewards of their labour. Their work left them poor, while their employers grew rich. Tom Mann criticised the unions, especially the new model unions, for not opposing the system.

■ SOURCE 4A

The true union policy of aggression seems entirely lost sight of; in fact the average unionist of today is a man with a fossilised intellect ... supporting a policy that plays into the hands of the capitalist exploiter.

Tom Mann, in a pamphlet published in 1886

Mann and another new union leader, Ben Tillett, put it even more simply in another pamphlet: 'It is the work of the trade unionist to stamp out poverty in the land.'

■ SOURCE 3B

After the harvest of 1871 had been reaped and the winter had set in the sufferings of the men became cruel and by 1872 there seemed to be two doors open to them. One ... led to a life of degradation in the workhouse; the other ... to the grave. Their poverty had fallen to starvation point and was past all bearing. They saw that if they were to rise out of their miserable state, they must force open a door of escape for themselves. Oppression and hunger and misery made them desperate, and desperation was the mother of the union.

Memoirs of Joseph Arch, 1898

Joseph Arch

A remarkable man, Joseph Arch, began to unionise the most downtrodden workers of all – farm labourers.

? QUESTIONS

a) Why do you think the meeting in Source 3A is held at night?
b) What difficulties were there in setting up a union of agricultural labourers that were not faced by a union of industrial workers?
c) Using Sources 3A and 3B imagine some of the questions and answers which Arch and his audience would exchange.

The match-girls' strike

This new attitude was seen first of all in the match-girls' strike of 1888. Women were paid very badly in all the jobs they did in Victorian Britain. The girls working at Bryant and May's match factory in East London were typical. For making boxes the rate was 2¼d (just under 1p) for 144; for making matches they received about 1d (under ½p) per hour. In addition they could be fined or hit by the foreman. Many suffered illness from the phosphorus in the matches. Annie Besant, a journalist and socialist, wrote articles about their conditions.

■ SOURCE 4B

Born in slums, driven to work while still children, undersized because underfed, oppressed because helpless, flung aside as soon as worked out, who cares if they die or go on the streets provided only that Bryant and May's shareholders get their 23%.

Annie Besant, in a newspaper article entitled 'White Slavery in London', 1888

■ SOURCE 4C Match-girls, 1888

■? QUESTIONS

a) What does Annie Besant mean by 'shareholders get their 23%'
b) Do you think that the photograph supports the impression given of the match-girls in Source 4B?
c) Which is the more reliable piece of evidence about the condition of the match-girls in 1888, Source 4B or 4C? Why?

The girls came out on strike, and Annie Besant helped them form a union. Her articles in papers gained them support, and her connections with other unions such as the Women's Trade Union League brought money to help. Within three weeks they had won: the fines were stopped and conditions improved.

Early in 1889 another union was formed among unskilled London workers: the gas workers. Men at the gasworks had heavy work shovelling coal, with long hours, at low pay. Will Thorne, another socialist,

helped by Eleanor Marx, Karl Marx's daughter, organised a gas-workers' union. Within six months there were 5000 members. The employers cut the hours without a strike being called.

The London dock strike

Later in 1889 came the most famous strike of all – the London dock strike. London was the busiest port in the country at that time. Most of the work of unloading ships was done by hand, as Source 5A shows. Although some of the skilled workers had unions, there were none for unskilled men. These dockers were taken on by the hour as required, by the foremen, in a humiliating system called 'The Cage'.

■ SOURCE 5B

We were driven into a shed, iron-barred from end to end, outside which a foreman walks up and

■ SOURCE 5A London Docks, 1880s

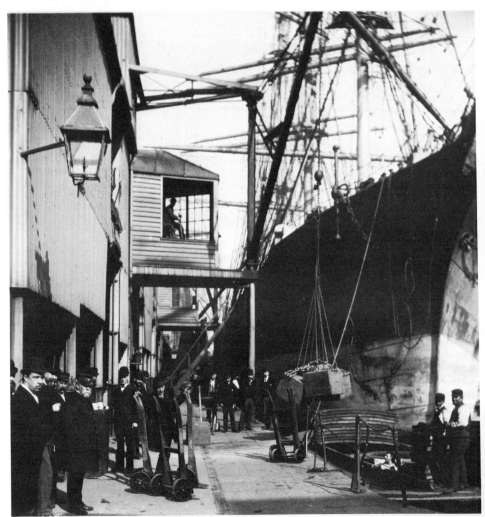

202

down with the air of a dealer in a cattle market, picking and choosing from a crowd of men, who in their eagerness to obtain employment, trample each other underfoot, and where they fight like beasts for a day's work.

Memoirs of Ben Tillett

Wages were as low as 5*d* (2p) an hour, and many men were starving. Often they could only work for an hour before having to go and get something to eat. In this weakened condition accidents to the men were common.

❓ QUESTIONS

a) Use Sources 5A and 5B to explain why it would be difficult to organise a union among these casual workers.

b) What problems would there be in organising a strike among such men?

Ben Tillett was secretary of a small union of tea warehousemen and began a strike for a pay increase to 6*d* (2½p) an hour: 'the dockers' tanner'. ('tanner' was Cockney slang for sixpence). Soon other dockers joined, and Tom Mann and John Burns helped organise the strike. Great processions were held in London and the whole docks were at a standstill. Their shortage of money for strike pay was helped

by a donation of £30 000 from trade unionists in Australia. In the end, Cardinal Manning helped to reach a settlement in which the dockers won their 'tanner'.

■ *SOURCE 5D*

Every industry was paralysed. Tens of thousands of tons of food was rotting in the ships lying in the Thames, which was overcrowded with vessels which could neither unload their cargo nor go elsewhere … It is satisfactory to have it proven that labour has the destinies of the world in its own hands … Hitherto, for the toiler one thing only in life was certain – his own misery and the hopelessness of ever escaping it. The tremendous influence of the union of riverside men on the country will give him faith in himself, and with that everything is possible in the future of the toiling millions of the mine, the workshop and the factory.

Reynolds News **September 1, 1889**

❓ QUESTIONS

a) Why were processions like the one in Source 5C important in winning the strike?

b) What clues does Source 5D give as to why the employers gave in?

c) What does the writer of Source 5D think will be the result of the strike?

d) What is the attitude of the writer of Source 5D to the strike?

Growth and difficulties

In one way *Reynolds News* was right: the years 1889–92 showed a great growth in union membership among unskilled workers. These 'new' unions – of gas and textile workers, dockers, the Miners' Federation, and builders' labourers – were based on a whole industry, not a skilled craft within an industry. They collected a low subscription from their poorly-paid members, and paid only one benefit: strike pay, in battles to win better pay and hours. John Burns noticed the difference between the 'new' union delegates at the TUC in 1890 – 'They looked like workmen, they were workmen' – and the delegates of the older craft unions, with their watch chains and top hats.

However, the older unions also gained members: the Railway Servants, for example, went up from 12 000 in 1888 to 30 000 in 1891. Several men's unions opened up their membership to women, and there were 118 000 women trade unionists by 1896. Total union membership doubled to 1½ million by 1892, with older craft unions still in a large majority. The TUC had, up to this time, voted on the basis of one vote per union. In 1894 the older, more moderate unions introduced the card vote: the delegates has as many votes as the union had members. At the time this worked against the 'new' socialist unions, which were smaller in size. Later, it would work to their advantage.

The 1890s were in many ways bad years for the unions. Employers launched a counter-attack and used blackleg labour to break strikes. Some unions could not survive: Will Thorne's Gas Workers' Union was crushed in 1890, and Ben Tillett's Dock Workers' Union collapsed in 1891. Fierce dock strikes in 1890–3 all failed. The NALU closed down in 1896. Even the great ASE, leader of the new model unions, was defeated in 1897–8 by a 'union of employers' – the Engineering Employers' Federation. In some ways the *Reynolds News* writer (Source 5D) was quite wrong: ordinary, unskilled workers did not make great strides following the 1889 dock strike. However, having organised once, there was the will to do it again when times were more favourable.

■ *SOURCE 5C* **Procession through London, 1889**

Many union leaders were beginning to feel – as some always had – that they must get Parliament to pass laws to help them. There was a move to get more working men into Parliament, and to set up a party for working people (see Chapter 20). This move was given a boost by the Taff Vale judgment in 1901.

The Taff Vale judgment

The Taff Vale Railway was a vital line running from large collieries right into the port of Cardiff. In 1900 railway workers there went on strike for better conditions. The railway managers refused to negotiate and brought in blackleg labour to break the strike. Four hundred court summonses were issued against the men for coming out on strike without proper notice. Sixty were fined.

The dispute was finally settled, but the court declared that the union was responsible for the loss of income to the railway company because of the strike. The company sued the union and was awarded £42 000. This judgment was disastrous for all unions, as it effectively prevented them from using strike action. The TUC pressed the Liberal Party to change the law if the Liberals won the next election; it also gave more support to the Labour Party. In due course the Trades Disputes Act 1906 made unions immune from being sued for losses caused by a strike.

Union Revival 1910–14

By 1910 a revival of employment, with low wages and rising prices, brought a new growth of union activity. Membership rose from 2.6 million in 1910 to 4.1 million by 1914. Female union membership grew to about 350 000 by 1914. The National Federation of Women Workers, set up in 1906, began for the first time to raise the issue of equal pay with men.

Syndicalism

In these years some union leaders and writers put forward the idea of syndicalism. This revolutionary theory said that unions should become larger and larger, perhaps by joining together, to fight for working people. In the end unions would be so powerful that they would call a strike of all the workers in the country, and take over industry and the government. A pamphlet, called *The Miners' Next Step*, put forward these ideas in 1912.

■ *SOURCE 6A*

One organisation to cover the whole mining industry in Great Britain, with one Central Executive.

The organisation shall carry out political action completely independent of all parties to seize whatever advantage it can for the working class.

Alliances should be formed with a view to amalgamating all workers into one union, to work for the taking over of all industries by the workers themselves.

The Miners' Next Step, 1912 (adapted)

? *QUESTIONS*

a) Why had miners found it difficult to unite into one national union before now?
b) Why would big unions be stronger?
c) What do you think the leaders of the new model unions would think of this statement?
d) What do you think Robert Owen would think of this statement?

Syndicalism clearly went further than the usual 'bread-and-butter' unionism found in the 19th century. However, such views were not common in the union movement as a whole. Some union leaders saw the advantages of having big unions, and alliances between unions, simply as a way of winning strikes more easily. The TUC was certainly not syndicalist, but moderate and poorly organised. Indeed Lenin, soon to lead the Russian Revolution of 1917, described British unions as 'insular, aristocratic and philistinely selfish'. The British government, however, was not prepared to make this distinction. They saw such union action as going beyond industrial disputes into a political action. Other governments have also taken a similar view, right up to the present day.

Certainly the strikes of these pre-war years were fierce and hard-fought. In 1911 a strike of dockers, railway porters and tram-drivers brought violence and two deaths. In the same year the government called in troops to run trains during a railway strike. From 1911 to 1912 a miners' strike closed the pits of South Wales, and troops were again sent in to keep the peace. A syndicalist strike in Dublin brought transport in the city to a standstill in 1913.

In 1913 there was an alliance

■ *SOURCE 6B* Confrontation of police and strikers, 1912

made – the so-called Triple Alliance – between unions of miners, railwaymen and transport workers. It seems clear that this was a purely practical arrangement: a strike in any one industry would hit the workers in the other two, as they were so closely linked. If they joined together, they could force a speedy settlement. Their leaders do not appear to have been planning a general strike, which was the syndicalists' main step towards taking over the state. Be that as it may, the government was very worried about the Triple Alliance, until war broke out in 1914, and the issue was shelved for a while.

The First World War and After

The war years, 1914–18, were mostly years of peace in industry. There were strikes on Clydeside and in South Wales, but generally unions and employers agreed to work together for the good of the country. The government took over mines, transport and 20 000 other workplaces.

Seventy-three Whitley Councils were set up to discuss pay and working conditions peacefully. Pay deals were negotiated in the railway, coal and transport industries. Local shop stewards became important. They could represent the workers in a particular factory in negotiations. Employers recognised unions as a good way of dealing with the work-force. Women were taken on in huge numbers and demanded the same pay as the men they had replaced. They did not achieve this, but women's pay generally rose during the war years. Union membership, rising fast before the war, continued to rise, particularly among women. There were 4.1 million trade unionists in 1914, 6.5 million in 1918, of whom over a million were women.

As soon as the war was over, industrial unrest returned. Prices had risen fast during the war, and workers looked to unions to win them better wages: 7.9 million people were in unions by 1919, 8.3 million in 1920. Unions joined together in bigger units. The largest was the Transport and General Workers' Union, set up in 1921 with

Ernie Bevin as Secretary. There was a police strike in 1918, and a successful railway strike in 1919. However, the main focus of discontent was the coal-mining industry.

The Coal Industry and the General Strike of 1926

The mines had been nationalised (run by the government) in the war. Wages were good and miners wanted this to continue. The Prime Minister, Lloyd George, set up a Royal Commission in 1919 under Sir John Sankey to look into this. It recommended continued nationalisation, but Lloyd George refused to put this into effect. He was under pressure from the mine-owners, and in 1921 the mines were handed back to them. This made the miners feel betrayed.

By this time the export price of coal was dropping fast, from nearly £4 a ton in 1920, to £1.75 a ton in late 1921, because of competition from foreign mines. The owners proposed cuts in pay and a longer working day. The miners called on their allies in the Triple Alliance to support them in a strike. However, the railwaymen and transport

workers refused to support them. Miners called this 'Black Friday'. They were forced back to work after a bitter strike.

In 1925 the price of coal dropped to below £1 a ton, and again the miners faced cuts in wages and one hour's work more per day. Their leader, A. J. Cook, adopted the slogan 'Not a penny off the pay, not a minute on the day'.

This time the Triple Alliance held firm, and a general strike seemed likely. The Prime Minister, Stanley Baldwin, bought time by giving a government subsidy to keep the miners' wages steady for nine

■ *SOURCE 7A* **Cartoon, 1921**

■ *SOURCE 7B* **Cartoon, 1925**

■ SOURCE 7C Cartoon, 1925

COAL MINE C° 25

INSERT £10,000,000
& THE MODEL WILL WORK.

Bernard Partridge

? QUESTIONS

a) What is the attitude of each of the cartoonists in Sources 7A–C.

b) In what ways do cartoons help historians understand a topic in history which no other type of evidence can?

months. The miners called this 'Red Friday', but it was not a permanent victory. When the nine months was up there would have to be a show-down, as neither miners nor owners were prepared to compromise.

Baldwin prepared for the crisis. He set up the Organisation for the Maintenance of Supplies (OMS), volunteers who would keep the country going. The Home Secretary, Joynson-Hicks, put the question on behalf of most of the government: 'Was England to be governed by Parliament, or by a handful of trade union leaders?' The Russian Revolution, only eight years earlier in 1917, frightened many middle-class British people into opposing the unions. The TUC feared wage cuts all through industry, so felt they had to support the miners. However, many of them had cold feet about a general strike.

The subsidy ran out in May 1926, and the government declared a state of emergency. This hardened the TUC, who issued instructions for a general strike. In turn, this hardened the government's attitude. When printers on the *Daily Mail* refused to print an attack on the TUC (see Source 8A), Baldwin called off discussions. The strike began on May 4, 1926.

Miners, railwaymen, transport workers, builders, chemical workers, printers, engineers, gas workers and shipbuilders came out on strike. Most transport and heavy industry stopped. People had to walk or drive to work. Out of 5½ million trade unionists, 4 million were called out, and nearly all obeyed the call.

■ SOURCE 8A

A general strike is not an industrial dispute. It is a revolutionary movement intended to inflict suffering upon the great mass of innocent people ... and put constraint upon the Government.

It is a movement which can only succeed by destroying the Government, and subverting the rights and liberties of the people.

Daily Mail editorial, intended for May 3, 1926, but not printed

■ SOURCE 8B

The General Council of the TUC wishes to emphasise the fact that this is an industrial dispute. It expects every member taking part to be exemplary in his conduct and not to give any opportunity for police interference.

TUC broadcast, 1926

■ SOURCE 8C Strikers' cartoon, 1926

T.U.C.

J.F.H.

The Constitution

A "PLEBS" STRIKE CARTOON.
THE ELEPHANT: *"Ooh! I must be careful not to tread on THAT!!"*

? QUESTIONS

a) Explain in your own words the two attitudes to the strike given in Sources 8A and 8B.

b) Write a paragraph to follow Source 8A explaining why you oppose the General Strike.

SOURCE 8D Waterloo Station deserted, 1926

SOURCE 8E OMS bus, guarded by soldiers, 1926

c) Write a paragraph to follow Source 8B explaining the TUC attitude to the General Strike.
d) What is the attitude of the strikers shown in Source 8C?
e) Do you think the TUC would agree with this?
f) Do you think the General Strike was inevitable from 1913?
g) Who do you think was to blame for it?
h) Do you think Baldwin was right to stop negotiating with the TUC after printers had refused to print Source 8A, or did he use the printers' action as an excuse?

Despite the use of soldiers (see Source 8E) the strike was generally peaceful. Strikers stopped some trains with OMS drivers by blocking the tracks. Some buses had their windows smashed. Some communists were arrested. There were very few injuries and no deaths. Both sides tried to put their point of view in emergency newspapers. The government brought out *The British Gazette*, edited by Winston Churchill. The TUC published *The British Worker*. The BBC, set up in 1922, tried to put both sides, but the government stopped Ramsay Macdonald, the Labour leader, from broadcasting.

Things seemed to be going well for the strikers. Very few went back to work. The OMS volunteers, middle-class people and students, kept essential supplies going. They couldn't carry on for ever, though, as they had jobs and studies to attend to. The country was not in chaos, but the strikers had shown their strength. Then, after only nine days, the TUC called off the General Strike on May 12.

Why did they do this? Certainly the miners had not been offered better terms. Nor had any guarantees been given that strikers would not be victimised when they went back to work. In fact, the TUC were very unhappy about the General Strike. They did not like being accused of attacking the Constitution. For them it was an industrial dispute to prevent wage cuts to miners, and perhaps other workers. However, they knew that some revolutionaries in the union movement did want to use the General Strike to overthrow the whole capitalist system, as the syndicalists suggested. For this reason the TUC never called out essential workers in health, water and sewage services. They were also very strict about peaceful picketing (See Source 8B). Caught between the government on the one hand and fear of the syndicalists on the other, and with no end in sight, the TUC backed down.

Results of the General Strike

Workers going back after the strike found that they were defeated. Wages were lowered, hours extended. The miners stuck out alone for six more months.

SOURCE 8F

The condition in most of the miners' homes in the Leicester area is almost beyond description. The children are obviously suffering from malnutrition. A large proportion of them have sores on their faces. They are nearly all pale ...

In the last village I visited two heartbroken mothers. One had a baby born on Sunday, for which she had been longing for years, and it had died on Monday. The district nurse said she could suggest no reason for its condition but the mother's weakness through lack of food.

Women's Committee for the Relief of Miners' Wives and Children, 1926

Eventually hunger forced the miners to drift back to work. They had to accept the longer hours, the lower pay. The memory of this strike, the bitterness, hardship and feelings of being betrayed, remained in miners' minds for two generations.

The government followed up their defeat of the General Strike. The Trades Disputes Act of 1927 banned 'sympathetic' strikes – strikes by one union on behalf of another. It restricted what kind of picketing was allowed. It also reversed the system of a unionist's payments to a political fund. Since 1913 (see Chapter 20) workers had to 'contract out', that is make a statement not to pay a political levy. Now they had to 'contract in', that is actually volunteer to pay it.

Throughout the 1920s and up to

■ *SOURCE 9A* **Women engineers at work, 1940s**

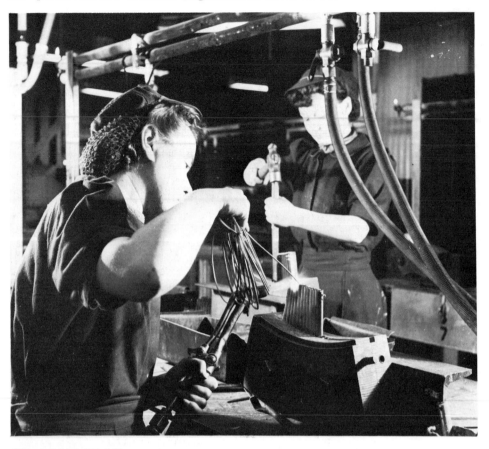

■ *SOURCE 9B* **Woman bus conductor during the war**

1934 trade union membership fell steadily. It was 4.8 million in 1928, 3.3 million in 1934. The main reason for this was serious unemployment (see Chapter 9). This was worst in the older, heavy industries such as coal, textiles and shipbuilding, which were just the industries with large union membership. However, some unions, in new industries, grew: the electricians' union, for example, doubled its membership in the 1930s.

The failures of the 1920s and the evils of mass unemployment turned many union members to the Communist Party. For most of the next few years much of unionists' time was taken up in struggles between communists and Labour supporters for control of the union.

The Second World War and After

The partnership between government and unions which had been set up in the First World War worked even more strongly in the Second. The Transport and General Workers' leader, Ernie Bevin, was made Minister of Labour. Unions accepted long hours for the good of the war effort. They even accepted 'dilution' – that is unskilled people working alongside trained workers, something they would never have allowed in peacetime. In return, Wages Boards fixed wages by agreement, and factories improved their medical and welfare facilities, with more inspectors. Joint Production Committees were set up, with workers sitting with employers to decide how to keep up production. Women moved into all industries on a large scale: in munitions from 7000 in 1939 to 260 000 by 1944, in engineering from 9% of workers to 34%. Their rates of pay were about three-quarters of the male rates.

Trade union membership rose to 8.8 million in 1946 and 9.5 million by 1950. The Labour government of 1945–51 worked closely with the unions. The Trades Disputes Act 1946 reversed the 1927 Act (see above). All unionists now had to 'contract out' of the political levy.

Nationalisation of railways, coal and other industries had long been a trade union objective. The welfare measures carried out by the Labour government were also part of union policy (Chapter 16, page 176). This calm, co-operative period lasted into the 1960s, despite a change to Conservative government after 1951.

Trade Unions Since 1960

Trade union membership seemed to have reached a standstill in 1960 at about 43% of the working population. This figure had been almost unchanged since 1950. Yet there was a sudden spurt of growth in the next 20 years. By 1970 there were 10.5 million trade unionists, by 1980 12.5 million. For the first time, in 1974, over 50% of workers were in trade unions. This was surprising in many ways. In the first place it was surprising because there was a great decline in the old, strongly unionised industries in these years. The number of miners, for example, fell by half: the railways were drastically cut by the Beeching programme (Chapter 10, page 109). The new members came from three groups who had not played a large part in the union movement before.

Increases in union membership

1 Women
More and more women were working, and so they saw the advantages of joining unions. In 1966 there were 2¼ million women trade unionists, 22% of all union members; by 1976 there were were 3½ million, nearly 30% of the whole.

2 Public service unions
The Confederation of Health Service Employees (COHSE) grew from 64 000 in 1964, to 215 000 in 1979. The National Union of Public Employees (NUPE) grew from 240 000 to 712 000 in the same period. Most of the members of these unions were low-paid workers and felt the need for union protection.

3 White collar workers
This group of workers, mainly middle-class, would never have

joined a union a generation earlier, but they felt they needed union protection at this time. Because of this, the National and Local Government Officers' Association (NALGO), the Association of Professional, Executive, Clerical and Computer Staffs (APEX), the Civil and Public Services Association (CPSA) and the Association of Scientific, Technical and Managerial Staffs (ASTMS) all gained thousands of new members. By 1980, 20% of white collar workers were in a union.

Such support for trade union membership seems even more surprising in view of the unpopularity of the unions at this time. Public opinion polls in the late 1970s showed enormous support for the view that unions had too much power and were responsible for Britain's problems. However there was also a widespread view that unions were necessary to protect workers. It seemed that many people hated unions and yet needed them. These were years of economic recession and crisis, and workers seem to have joined unions to protect their jobs and wages.

■ *SOURCE 10B*

What has happened is that those who sought higher living stand-

ards, or the mere continuation of the car and home ownership (which have risen in cost far more than prices in general) found that they could only obtain these by making full use of their trade union power, with the result that ordinary workers turned to aggressive union leaders to produce results.

Bacon and Eltis, 1976

■ *SOURCE 10C*

It's the same thing over and over again. There's no change in it, it wears you out ... There's no need to think ... You just carry on. You just endure it for the money. That's what we're paid for – to endure the boredom of it.

Hugh Benyon, *Working for Ford*, 1973

Trade unions and governments

With Labour governments in power in the years 1945–51, 1964–70 and 1974–79, the union movement was brought much closer to the government. The National Economic Development Council (Neddy), set up by Macmillan in 1962, has equal representation from employers, unions and government. Unionists, usually appointed through the TUC, also have places on ACAS (the Advisory, Conciliation and Arbitration Service), the MSC (Manpower Services Commission), the HSE (Health and Safety Executive) and many other influential bodies.

This close relationship has not been an easy one. Even Labour governments have sometimes had different priorities from the unions. The close relationship between unions and the Labour Party (see Chapter 20) made it difficult for unions and Conservative governments to work together. The economic problems facing Britain since the mid-1960s have increased these problems.

The economic crisis began soon after the Labour government came to power in 1964. They asked the TUC for a period of wage restraint to take them through the crisis. The TUC and union leaders agreed to co-operate, but there was much resentment at local level. There was an increasing number of short, local, unofficial or 'wildcat' strikes (that is, not agreed to by the national officers of the union). The effect was nothing like as serious as in the earlier years of this century. For example, in 1921 there were 763 strikes, but 86 million working days were lost. In 1970 there were over 4000 strikes, but only 11 million working days were lost. Nevertheless the government was worried. It produced a paper called *In Place of Strife* in 1969. This attempted to ban wildcat strikes, but it was never made law.

The Conservatives, under Edward Heath, won the 1970 election and set about trying to restrict union power. The Industrial Relations Act 1971 made agreements between unions and employers legally binding, required a ballot before any strike action and banned the 'closed shop' (a system by which anyone working in a particular place has to be a union member). There was to be a National Industrial Relations Court to enforce these measures. The union movement preferred to work without the intervention of the law, as they had done since Victorian times. They boycotted the Act and made it unworkable. Heath wanted to work in co-operation with unions, but became involved in a dispute with the miners. First in 1972, then in 1974,

■ *SOURCE 11* **Miners during the 1974 strike**

the miners struck for better wages.

Generations of bitterness dating back to 1926 and beyond came to the surface. Many people in Britain felt that the miners deserved better pay. Arthur Scargill, the Yorkshire miners' leader, developed the tactic of 'flying pickets', where groups of miners picketed ports and power-stations to prevent the movement of coal. The railway and power-station workers supported the miners. There were power cuts, and industry was reduced to working only three days a week. The miners won their strike and Heath lost the 1974 election. This time it was the Conservatives who carried their bitterness into the future.

In 1972 the TUC–Labour Party Liaison Committee was set up. With Labour back in power it was decided to continue it. They declared

a 'Social Contract': if the TUC persuaded its members to hold down wage demands, the Labour government would help working people through tax allowances and benefits. These were the days of 'beer and sandwiches at No. 10', when Prime Minister Harold Wilson worked with trade union leaders to solve industrial disputes. Things had moved a long way from Baldwin's attitude in 1926! The Bullock Report of 1976 produced proposals for union membership of the board of directors of all companies.

However, many trade unionists were not happy about this form of co-operation. They saw their job as unionists had always seen their job up to 1945: to get a better deal for their members. They objected to pay restraint; they did not want to be involved in running companies.

They saw their members' wages falling behind inflation while profits and managerial salaries increased. These feelings came to the surface in the winter of 1978–9, the 'winter of discontent'. There were several fierce strikes, for large pay rises, culminating in a 21% rise for lorry drivers. The strikes were successful for the union members, but the public was angered. Mrs Thatcher's promises to cut union power helped sweep her to power in the 1979 election.

Trade unions and the Thatcher government

The Employment Acts of 1980 and 1982 and the Trade Union Act 1984 made various changes. Secondary picketing – picketing at a place of work other than where the strike takes place – was declared illegal. A secret ballot of all members had to be held, and an 80% majority gained, before any industrial action

could be taken. There were also to be ballots to allow trade union members to decide whether they wished to set up a political fund – usually for the Labour Party.

Many Conservatives believed that union leaders caused strikes, so ballots would weaken their power for industrial action. In fact the ballots for political funds have all gone in favour of such funds. Ballots over strike action have often supported it. There were several ballots during the long teachers' dispute of 1985–6, and the teachers voted in favour of continuing the action.

Many employers have chosen not to use the protection now granted them by the law. But there have been some serious disputes. Print unions were involved in bitter and violent picketing in 1984 and 1986. The biggest battle, however, was the miners' strike of 1984–5. The government planned to close several pits as part of a plan to make

the coal industry profitable. Arthur Scargill, by then the leader of the NUM, called a national miners' strike. He used pickets at ports and coalmines, as he had done in 1974. This time Mrs Thatcher was determined to defeat the strike. Police were deployed in large numbers and coal imported to make sure supplies were kept up. The strike eventually collapsed after over a year.

As we have seen in this chapter, trade unions have always been controversial. Their legal rights continue to be the subject of new laws, and attitudes towards them are as divided as ever. However, unions have grown from being a tiny group of skilled workers, mainly men, to a major force in the lives of most working men and women in Britain. Whatever future form they take, trade unions are here to stay.

Assignments

Empathy

1 a What were the attitudes of most employees to trade unions in the years 1850–1900?
  b Why did many working people refuse to join unions in these years?
2 a What were the attitudes of the TUC towards the Miners Union in 1926?
  b Why did they call a General Strike?
  c Why did they call it off after 9 days?
3 Why did so many workers in the 1960s and 1970s:
  i criticise trade unions?
  ii join trade unions?

Understanding concepts

1 **Similarity/difference**
  a What impression of its activities did the ASE give to the Royal Commission?
  b What was the ASE really like?
  c What were other unions like at that time?

2 **Similarity/difference**
Compare these three 19th-century unions:

i ASE ii NALU iii Dockers Union.
Discuss: membership, subscription, leadership, aims, methods, success.

3 **Causation**

Syndicalism
Triple Alliance
Fall in coal prices
Nationalisation in the war
Red Friday
OMS
Daily Mail printers
Russian Revolution

  a Choose three of the above items which were important *long-term* causes of the General Strike of 1926 and explain your choice.
  b Choose three of the above items were important *short-term* causes of the General Strike of 1926, and explain your choice.

4 **Cause/effect**
1 a What were the causes of the failure of the General Strike?
  b What were the *short-term* results of the failure of the General Strike?

  c What were the *long-term* results of the failure?
  d What other reasons were there for the decline of union membership in the years between the wars?

5 **Change/continuity**
  a Compare relations between unions and governments;
    i in the Second World War;
    ii under the Labour governments of the 1960s and 1970s;
    iii under Mrs Thatcher's Conservative government.
  In what ways are these relations the same and in what ways are they different?

Themes for discussion

1 Why have trade unions always found it difficult to become part of British life, right from the 18th century to the present day?
2 Which different views of trade unions are held by:
  i different groups described in this chapter;
  ii different newspapers today;
  iii different members of your class?

20 The Rise of the Labour Party 1870s–1920s

Working People and Parliament

Working people turned their attention to Parliament at various times in the 19th century, as we have seen in Chapter 18. They felt that, if only workers could be properly represented in Parliament, it could pass laws to solve their problems. Tom Paine had claimed this right for them in 1792; it had been demanded at Peterloo in 1819; it was the basis of the great Chartist movement. After Chartism's collapse, however, many working people turned their attention away from Parliament for a while. They put their hopes into self-help movements, such as co-operatives and unions. They saw that they were totally excluded from taking part in Parliament. Only rich men had the vote, MPs were not paid and voting took place in public, so voters could be intimidated. There seemed no place for working people in political life when MPs of both parties, Liberal and Conservative, were all middle- or upper-class men.

Some unions, such as the miners, still felt, however, that on their own they could not make their employers improve their working conditions. They needed the law to help them. They therefore continued to look to Parliament for help – it had, after all, already acted to control hours and safety at work through the Factory Acts and Mines Acts (Chapter 14, pages 157–59). Gradually union supporters realised they had to work through Parliament to change laws that had been passed against them, such as the Criminal Law Amendment Act 1871 prohibiting picketing. The TUC set up a Parliamentary Committee in 1871. Unions also paid for 13 candidates in the 1874 election, of whom two, both miners, were elected.

The Reform Act 1884 gave the vote to most men in rural areas, and 28.5% of the population could now vote. Unions increased the number of their MPs to 11 in 1885. They sat with the Liberals and were called 'Lib-Labs', but with such tiny numbers their influence was small.

Most working people accepted the two-party system at that time, just as the new model unions accepted the industrial system and did not seek to change it. The workers often supported the party of their factory owner, or some local dignitary. The Liberals were probably the most likely to help working

people, but support for them was by no means certain. The Liberals were, after all, the party of business, even though there were a few radicals among them.

The Reform Act 1867 gave 1 million better-off working men the vote, and the Conservatives won the next election. Trade union support also helped the Conservatives win the 1874 election. It seemed that, in the words of Gilbert and Sullivan's song of 1882,

**Every boy and every gal
That's born into the world alive
Is either a little Liberal
Or else a little Conservative.**

■ *SOURCE 1A* **Agricultural labourers voting for the first time, 1884**

212

Socialism

Socialists believe that, on the whole, businesses – whether farms or factories, shops or banks – exploit the workers by using their labour to make profits for the rich. Socialists think that these places should be run for the benefit of the workers. Such ideas are not new: they were heard during the English Civil War and the French Revolution. Robert Owen believed in co-operative socialism, and some Chartists were socialists. In the 1880s, there was a revival of socialism among writers and thinkers. The Depression of those years seemed to show that the capitalist system was going wrong.

Many people were also influenced by the ideas of Karl Marx. Marx was a German who had been forced to flee to London. He wrote in German but his books were translated into English. The *Communist Manifesto* and his great work, *Das Kapital*, changed the world in the 20th century. First Russia, and then many other countries, threw out their old governments and set up communist systems. In Britain his ideas were taken up at once by several groups.

Early socialist groups

The first such group was the Democratic Federation, founded in 1881 by H. M. Hyndman. (It changed its name to the Social Democratic Federation in 1884.) Hyndman was a middle-class stockbroker, formerly a Liberal, who had been completely convinced by reading Marx's ideas.

■ *SOURCE 1B*

All history is the history of class struggle.

Society as a whole is splitting up into great hostile camps, into two great classes facing each other: the bourgeoisie and the proletariat.

The first step in the revolution by the working class is to raise the proletariat to the position of ruling class, to win the battle for democracy.

[Note: the bourgeoisie are the rich people with lots of money invested in business; the proletariat are the working people.]

Karl Marx, *Communist Manifesto*, 1848

■ *SOURCE 1C* Front page of *Justice*, the SDF paper, May 1896

? QUESTIONS

a) Which class struggle does Marx say is going on at that time?
b) How will the working class take over, does he say?
c) Look at Source 1C. Who is breaking the chains? What do the chains represent? Who is being freed?
d) Do you think Karl Marx would agree with the message of Source 1C?

Many people were interested in Marx's ideas and joined the SDF, including John Burns and Tom Mann (see Chapter 19). William Morris, the artist and writer, joined for a while before leaving to found his own Socialist League. The SDF organised demonstrations of unemployed workers. At one, in 1887, police were used to break up the march. This was called Bloody Sunday.

■ *SOURCE 1D* **Bloody Sunday riot, 13 November 1887**

Before Morris left the SDF, he and Hyndman wrote a little pamphlet, *Socialism for All*. They pointed out that £300 million was paid in wages every year, but £1000 million in rent, profit and interest went to the rich. It called for government takeover (nationalisation) of all land, industry, transport and banking. In the meantime, however, they called for better housing, reduced hours of work, jobs for the unemployed, free education. These more limited objectives attracted people to socialism who were put off by the violence of Bloody Sunday and the ruthlessness of Marxism.

The Fabian Society
Such a group was the Fabian Society, founded in 1884. It was named after the Roman general Fabius, who was famous for working patiently and slowly. Fabians included several writers, such as Annie Besant, George Bernard Shaw and Beatrice and Sidney Webb. Their many leaflets and pamphlets put across the need for socialist policies to help working people. They hoped to achieve them through Parliament, not by a Marxist revolution.

These socialist ideas had one thing in common: working people had different needs from the middle and upper classes. Gradually, working people came to realise that they could not look to the Liberal or Conservative parties for serious support. But in 1890 there were barely 2000 socialists in Britain. This was not enough to win a seat, let alone form a party. What was needed was a link between socialists and the growing trade union movement, with it large funds and mass support.

Keir Hardie

The man who brought this about was James Keir Hardie. He was a Scottish miner who became interested in socialism. In 1888 he was asked by miners in Mid-Lanark to stand for Parliament. He would have been a Lib-Lab, but the Liberal party bosses wanted someone else to stand for Mid-Lanark. Hardie was angry and decided to stand on his own. Liberal leaders tried to buy him off with the offer of a safe seat somewhere else. That was the last straw, and Hardie got together with some others to found the Scottish Labour Party in 1888.

In 1892 Keir Hardie was asked to stand as an independent socialist in West Ham, and won the seat. At that time MPs all wore top hats and morning dress, but Hardie arrived at the House of Commons in a check suit and deerstalker hat: the clothes of a Scottish miner. He called a conference in 1893 at Bradford, attended by the Scottish Labour Party, SDF and Fabians. They decided – with the Marxist SDF disagreeing – to set up the Independent Labour Party.

Although 600 local councillors were elected as Labour members in the next few years, ILP candidates were all defeated in the 1895 election. It was clearly a long way from being a party with mass support.

■ *SOURCE 2A*

The man who poses as a Liberal, and yet refuses to support shorter working hours, an improvement in the homes of the people, the organisation of relief works for the unemployed, and the restoration of land to its rightful owners, may call himself what he pleases, but he is an enemy, and as such is to be opposed.

Keir Hardie's speech in the Mid-Lanark election, 1888

■ SOURCE 2B **Election poster for the West Ham election, 1892**

VOTE FOR

Home Rule.
Democratic Government.
Justice to Labour.
No Monopoly.
No Landlordism.

Temperance Reform.
Healthy Homes.
Fair Rents.
Eight-Hour Day.
Work for the Unemployed.

KEIR HARDIE.

❓ QUESTIONS

a) How far does Keir Hardie's programme in Source 2A agree with his election poster in Source 2B?

b) Why might a Liberal not agree with the things Hardie is proposing in Source 2A?

The Unions and the Labour Party

Only a minority of trade unionists were and are socialists. However, the 1890s saw considerable efforts on the part of employers to weaken unions (see Chapter 19). The right of peaceful picketing was again under threat. Union leaders were also becoming disillusioned with the Liberals, who seemed reluctant to assist unions or help working-class grievances. This was not surprising, of course, as many Liberals were the very employers with whom the unions were struggling.

Labour Representation Committee

The TUC agreed in 1899 to call a conference 'to devise ways and means of securing the return of an increased number of Labour MPs to the next Parliament'. This met in London in 1900 and set up the Labour Representation Committee. There were seven union members, one ILP, two SDF and one Fabian. The Secretary was James Ramsey Macdonald. The unions would bear the expense of getting Labour MPs elected.

From the start the LRC was the result of compromise. The unions were very lukewarm in their support at first (fewer than 12 unions joined the LRC in 1900). They simply felt they had to defend themselves, as the Liberal Party was unwilling to help them. Of the socialists, many Fabians preferred to continue to work with the Liberals. The SDF wanted a declaration of class war, which the LRC rejected. It was really Keir Hardie, and the hard-working Ramsay Macdonald, who made the compromise work.

The Taff Vale Case in 1901 (Chapter 19, page 204) led many unions to support the LRC. The judgment seemed to prevent unions from ever being able to go on strike. All unions saw the need to make Parliament pass a law to reverse the decision. Ramsay Macdonald made a deal with Herbert Gladstone of the Liberals that the LRC would support the Liberals in Parliament if no Liberal stood against LRC candidates in 30 constituencies in the 1906 election. As a result 29 LRC members were returned. They changed their name to the Labour Party.

❓ QUESTIONS

a) What is the cartoonist's opinion of: Liberals, Labour, socialism?

b) How does he show these opinions?

c) What does he think the future holds? Was he right?

d) How useful is this cartoon to someone trying to understand the rise of the Labour Party?

■ SOURCE 3 **Cartoon, 1909**

The Labour Party up to 1914

In return for Labour support the Liberals passed the Trade Disputes Act 1906, reversing the Taff Vale Decision. However, for the rest of the period up to 1914 the Labour Party had little influence. Any new party has a difficult time getting established in our political system, as the SDP found in the 1980s. Many had hoped that the 1906 election would bring no overall victory to any party. In that position the little Labour Party would have been able to hold the balance of power. It would have been courted by both parties. In fact the Liberals, after 1906, had a majority of 84 over all other parties. This left the Labour Party with very little power at all. The SDF and ILP in fact left the Labour Party and later helped set up the Communist Party.

The powerlessness of the Labour Party was clear over the matter of the Osborne Judgment. In 1909 a railway union member, Osborne, objected to paying a union levy to the Labour Party, as he was a Lib–Lab. The court ruled that such a levy was illegal. This ruling hit the Labour Party's finances very badly, but the Liberals did nothing to help. In 1911 the Liberals passed the old Chartist demand of payment of MPs. This helped the Labour Party, as working men could now stand for Parliament, but it was not until 1913 that the Trade Union Act was passed. This allowed unions to pay a levy, but any individual worker could 'contract out' of paying it.

The Labour Party since the First World War

The Labour Party continued to grow after the First World War: 57 seats in 1918, 142 in 1922, 191 in 1923. In that year the Conservatives had 258 and the Liberals 158. Ramsay Macdonald was asked to form a government, with Liberal support. This first Labour government lasted for ten months only. However it did show that the Labour Party was a popular, mass party, and that it was a constitutional, not a revolutionary, party.

As we have seen, the Labour Representation Committee was set up in 1900 as a compromise between socialists and reformists. Unions provided the money and so had the largest say. This arrangement continues up to the present. It was when left-wing socialists seemed to be taking over the Labour Party in 1981 that moderates, led by David Owen and Shirley Williams, left to form the Social Democratic Party.

Unions have continued to work with the Labour Party – nowadays with more enthusiasm than in 1900. They realise that the Labour Party can help their members through its policies. Even more, they need the Labour Party to defend them when Conservatives pass laws to weaken unions, as both Mr Heath and Mrs Thatcher have done (Chapter 19, pages 210–11). Nearly all union leaders are Labour supporters, except for one or two Communists and, recently, SDP supporters.

Trade unions elect 12 members to the Labour Party's National Executive, and sponsor about half the Labour MPs. With declining party membership an increasing share of the finances of the Labour Party is provided by the unions – 80% in 1983. The Labour Party is probably more a trade union party today than it has ever been.

Assignments

Empathy

1 Get into groups of three. One of you is a trade unionist, one a middle-class Fabian, and one a member of the Social Democratic Federation. It is 1899. Discuss:
   i whether there should be a separate party for working people – a Labour Party;
   ii what its policies should be.
2 What were the attitudes of the following groups to the setting up of the Labour Party:
   i Socialists;
   ii trade unionists;
   iii Liberals?

Understanding concepts

1 **Factors causing change**
   a Choose 2 factors from the above list which you think are important causes of the rise of the Labour Party before the First World War, and explain your choice.

   > Trade union support
   > Keir Hardie
   > Socialist ideas
   > ILP
   > Karl Marx
   > Taff Vale Case

   b Choose one factor which you think is a less important reason for the early growth of the Labour Party and explain your choice.
   c Add one factor of your own, not on the list, which you think is an important cause of the early growth of the Labour Party.

2 **Factors causing change**
Why did the Labour Party start in 1900, rather than before or after that date? You should consider the importance of the following factors:

> Growth of trade union membership
> Socialist ideas
> Education for everyone
> Payment of MPs
> Role of Keir Hardie
> Disappointment with Liberal Party
> Failure of Chartism
> Reform Acts of 1867 and 1884

Theme for discussion

Which have been the most important means through which working people have improved their situation:
   i trade unions;
   ii Labour Party;
   iii co-operatives;
   iv other movements?

The Changing Role of Women 1800-1980s

Are Some More Equal than Others?

This book looks at the changes which have taken place in the lives of the people of this country since the early 18th century. 'The people of this country', of course, means women and men. When you were reading about stage-coaches and trains, you must have imagined women and men travelling in them. When you were reading about back-to-back houses and tower blocks, you must have pictured women and men living in them. Yet when you have read about individuals by name, whether inventors or writers, politicians or leaders, they have nearly all been men. Why?

The answer is that, throughout most of the period covered by this book, women have been regarded as unequal to men in nearly every way. This obviously affected women's role in many of the topics dealt with in other chapters, such as work, welfare, education and health. Clues as to the position of women can be seen in some of the source material. See, for example, Chapter 14, Source 6C, page 158, Chapter 16, Source 8, page 174, Chapter 19, Source 4B, page 202, Chapter 22, Source 2B page 226. Nearly all the pictures showing skilled use of machines in Chapters 3 and 9 show men. In this chapter we shall look at the position of women in British society and how it has changed over the years.

Women in the 19th Century

Before the Industrial Revolution, men and women worked together, in or around the home. The man was legally considered the head of the household, but each member of the family had his or her job to do. In the textile industry, under the domestic system, the men seem to have done the weaving, for example, while the women usually did the spinning. With the coming of factory production this pattern changed: people went out of the home to work. What was to be the position of women in this new situation?

The middle-class ideal

The middle-class ideal for women in the early 19th century is shown in Source 1A: a married woman, waiting at home for her husband to return from work. Her education would have covered reading and writing, embroidery and music: nothing that would really train her for a paid job, because she was not

SOURCE 1A Young wife at home in Victorian times

supposed to work outside the home. Her career was to be a dutiful wife and companion to her husband, a mother to his children, an organiser of his household.

■ *SOURCE 1B*

She must learn to adopt his taste, study his mood, bear his anger and irritability with grace, and submit to all his desires with all that grateful willingness which in a wife is the surest sign of a sound understanding.

***Woman as She is and Should be*, 1879**

? *QUESTIONS*

a) What evidence is there in Source 1A that the family is quite well-off?

b) What evidence is there that they are not rich?

c) Do these two sources, 1A and 1B agree in their view of women? Explain your answer.

d) What is your opinion of Source 1B?

e) Which do you think is the most useful to our understanding of a Victorian view of women, 1A or 1B?

This view of women was supported by the Church and by law. When a woman married, all her earnings and her possessions belonged to her husband. He was not committing an offence if he assaulted her. If they were divorced, she had no rights over their children, nor any share in their property.

Working-class women

Some people tried to extend this middle-class ideal of bread-winning men and home-based wives to the working classes. Middle-class reformers were shocked by women doing hard physical work and tried to forbid it, for example in coal-mining (see Chapter 14). They were also shocked by the independence which a job in a factory gave to women. In this they were supported by many working men, who didn't want to see women taking jobs which they themselves wanted. They made sure that the well-paid jobs were only open to men. Women were confined to poorly-paid jobs, or received less pay for the same

work. Most trade unions in the 19th century entirely opposed equal pay for men and women, because the men feared it would bring down their own wages. They even tried to oppose the whole idea of women doing paid jobs at all. They could then argue for a 'family wage' – a higher wage for men because they had to support their families.

■ *SOURCE 2A*

Fifty or sixty females, married and single, form themselves into clubs, apparently for protection; but in fact they meet together to drink, sing and smoke; they use, it is stated, the lowest, most disgusting language imaginable ... Why is it that this unnatural change is taking place? Because ... on women is imposed the duty and burden of supporting their husbands and families, a perversion of nature, which has the effect of introducing into families disorder and conflict.

Lord Shaftesbury, speaking in the House of Commons, 1844

■ *SOURCE 2B*

It was their duty as men and husbands to use their utmost efforts to bring about a condition of things where their wives would be in their proper sphere at home instead of being dragged into competition with the great and strong men of the world.

Speaker at the Trade Union Congress, 1877

■ *SOURCE 2C*

There can be little doubt that the greatest obstacle to economic freedom for women is the deeply-rooted idea, in the minds of many of them, and in the minds of all men, that they are merely playing at work for a time until they undertake the duties of wife and mother.

Ada Nield Chew, trade union organiser, 1912

? *QUESTIONS*

a) Why does Lord Shaftesbury, in Source 2A, find the idea of the women's clubs so terrible?

b) Why did trade unionists, like the one in Source 2B, not want women to work?

c) What does Source 2C tell us about women's own views of their position?

d) Do you think that the working

people referred to in Sources 2B and 2C would agree with the middle-class view of women seen in Sources 1A and 1B?

Women at work

The ideal of the non-working woman did not work out in practice. In 1851, half of all women in Britain were in paid work, and two-thirds of these working women supported themselves. There were three main reasons for this. First, there were many women who did not rely on a man to support them – unmarried women of all ages, as well as widows, divorcees and women whose husbands had left them. Second, wages were so low that most families simply could not survive on the man's earnings alone. All members of the family had to work: children, wives and mothers too. Third, some women chose to go to work to have money of their own.

The cotton textile industry of Lancashire was the only industry which employed women on a large scale. Even there, the supervisors were usually men, and the majority of the female workers were young and unmarried. Many women gave up their job if they married and had children. Women worked in a host of small trades, as dressmakers, bookbinders, artificial flower-makers, lace-makers, box-makers, shawl-makers, paper-makers, jam and pickle workers, tobacco workers (Chapter 8, Source 7, page 79). They had no unions to protect them. Their hours were long and their pay was low.

Domestic work

The most common job for a girl was as a domestic servant, and 1.3 million women were in service in Britain in the 1880s. The pay was so low – perhaps only £10 per year – that people who would not think of having a servant nowadays would have been able to employ one then. Girls started at about the age of 11. Because so many girls went into service, schools felt they had to train them for it. Girls did more needlework, domestic science and 'housewifery' than boys, who did more maths and woodwork.

After a while as a general maid, a girl might move on to a larger household, with more servants. The most senior women's job was as a cook,

■ **SOURCE 3A** Girls at school learning to do the laundry, 1908. The girl on the right is using a mangle to get water out of the clothes.

■ **SOURCE 3B** Housemaids and other servants, 1880s

earning £20 a year. Domestic work was physically hard, and the hours very long, with one day a month and a half day a week off. Servants lived in the house where they worked, in an attic, or basement, and had all their food and clothing provided. This also meant they were permanently under the eye of their master or mistress.

■ **SOURCE 3C**

Thursday, 28 September, 1871

Lighted the kitchen fire and the one in the dining room is begun now so I did that and swept the floors. Clean'd the steps and shook the mats. Wash'd me and got our breakfast. Wash'd up. Dusted the rooms and the hall. Rubb'd the brasswork in the W.C. and clean'd the little window. Clean'd the larder shelves and floor and rubbed the window. Clean'd the two copper coal scuttles and the scoops. Carried the one full o' coals into the dining room. Got the dinner by half past one ...

Diary of Hannah Cullwick

❓ **QUESTIONS**

a) Why do you think we no longer do laundry lessons at school, like in Source 3A?
b) What jobs do you think the various women and men in Source 3B did?
c) Do you think the servants in Source 3B look happy?
d) Why is the evidence of Hannah Cullwick (Source 3C) so useful to a historian?
e) Why do you think it is rare to find a housemaid's own view of her life?

Other jobs

Women in the country could get work on the land, often working in gangs at seasonal tasks: fruit-packing, weeding, hoeing, beet-lifting, hop-picking, etc. The work was hard, in all weathers (see also Chapter 8).

In towns, women were often forced to make a living in sweatshops. Since they were paid by the amount of work they did, the wages were terribly low, hardly enough to keep them alive (Chapter 14, Source 8A, page 159). Many girls became prostitutes simply in order to make enough money to live on.

This is one of the contradictions of Victorian Britain: sex was not mentioned in public, and men expected their wives to be faithful, yet there were many more prostitutes in cities than there are today.

■ SOURCE 3D Hop-picker, 1900

■ SOURCE 3E The 'Song of the Shirt'

With fingers heavy and worn,
With eyelids heavy and red
A woman sat in unwomanly rags
Plying her needle and thread:
Stitch! stitch! stitch!
In poverty, hunger and dirt,
And still with a voice of dolourous pitch
She sang the 'Song of the Shirt'.

Thomas Hood, 1843

❓ QUESTIONS

a) Compare Sources 3D and 1A. In what ways do the lives of the two women differ?

b) What questions would you want to ask of Source 3E before considering its value as historical evidence?

c) What possible use might Source 3E be to a historian?

Life at home

In these situations, women must have found the idea of marrying and giving up work quite attractive. They would also have been glad to get away from their parents' control (see Source 4A). But marriage only brought more back-breaking work. There was no cheap contraception available to working people at that time. This meant that women spent most of their 20s and 30s either pregnant or looking after babies and toddlers, or both. The effects of this on the health of women is looked at in Chapter 16.

In addition, everyday household tasks were far harder work than they are nowadays. Cooking, cleaning and, especially, washing were tiring and lengthy jobs. Women had little leisure time and rarely went out. It was also their responsibility to feed and clothe the family on whatever housekeeping money their husbands cared to give them. This must have been a great worry when wages were low and irregular. Often, if money was short, it was the mother who went without proper food.

■ SOURCE 4A

My mother came to the corner of the street and said, 'Come on, get yourself in. He's no better than he ought to be to keep you out after nine o'clock!' Nine o'clock! And when I was going to be married and how old was I – twenty-three!

Working-class woman in the Northwest, about 1900

■ SOURCE 4B

I am the mother of eleven children – six girls and five boys. I was only nineteen years old when my first baby was born . . . for twenty years I was nursing or expecting babies.

Mother in the 1890s

■ SOURCE 4C Washing day, 1910.

❓ QUESTIONS

a) Why do you think parents were so strict at that time? (Source 4A.)

b) Why would washday, using the equipment in Source 4C, be long and tiring?

c) Look at the clothes worn by the women in the sources in this chapter. Why would they make washday even harder work?

d) Use Sources 4B and 4C to describe the effects of 20 years of married life on the health and appearance of a working-class woman.

Changing attitudes to women

Towards the end of the 19th century attitudes began to change, first among the middle classes. Marriage came to be regarded more as a partnership of equals. The Married Women's Property Acts 1870 and 1882 allowed women to keep their own incomes and property when they married. In 1860 Charles Bradlaugh began to publish leaflets giving information about contraception; in 1877 he and Annie Besant were arrested for republishing a book about it. Doctors said using contraception would cause women to suffer 'a mania leading to suicide'. Men, they said, would suffer 'mental decay and loss of memory'. Despite these dire warnings, middle-class couples began to use contraception. (Most types were still too expensive for working-class couples to afford.) Middle-class families began to get smaller, bringing an improvement in the health and quality of life of middle-class women.

Demands for equality in education for women increased. Many girls' high schools were founded (see also Chapter 22). In 1870 girls were allowed to study at Cambridge University, although at first they lived 26 miles away and tutors went by train to teach them. Edinburgh Medical School opened to women in 1870, and London Medical School in 1878. The first woman doctor was Sophia Jex Blake, who was allowed to practise from 1877. The first woman to qualify as a doctor in Britain, against much opposition, was Elizabeth Garrett Anderson. Some men had claimed that studying hard damaged women's brains. These women proved that such ideas were nonsense.

Changes in women's jobs

It is, above all, a job and a wage which gives a person a chance to be independent. New careers opened up for women in the later 19th century. Florence Nightingale's work in the Crimean War led to the setting-up of a proper nursing school at St Thomas's Hospital in 1860. Other nursing schools followed, and it became a popular career for women. The expansion of education, especially after the Education Act 1870, brought a large increase in the number of women teachers. However, women teachers, like women civil servants, had to resign if they got married.

Jobs in nursing and teaching required extra education and appealed to middle-class girls. Other jobs did open up, though, for working-class girls too. The growth of shops and department stores (see Chapter 12) brought a demand for girls to work in them as shop assistants. The hours were very long – 80 or 90 a week in some cases. However, these hours were not as long as domestic service, and shopgirls were free in the evenings and on Sundays. They could dress smartly and at least were not living in, always under the eye of their boss.

Another type of job came in with the invention of the telephone and the typewriter. Women, trained to work these new machines, could get good jobs in offices and lead quite an independent life. The number of women office workers increased by 400% from 1861 to 1911.

Women and the Vote

In the last part of the 19th century, therefore, the position of women improved in several ways: in law, in education and in employment. One major male privilege remained – the right to vote in parliamentary elections. The campaign to achieve this right for women is the most famous part of the story of women's struggle for equality

The suffragists

A common view is that the campaign for votes for women started in about 1905 and was carried out entirely by Mrs Pankhurst and the suffragettes (see Source 5B over). In fact many women already had some voting rights. From 1834 they could vote on the same basis as men for Poor Law Guardians; they could vote for, and stand for, election to the School Boards when they were set up in 1870; they could vote in all kinds of local council elections from 1888. Only elections to Parliament were closed to them.

In 1867 John Stuart Mill had in-

■ *SOURCE 5A* **Suffragists' postcard, early 20th century**

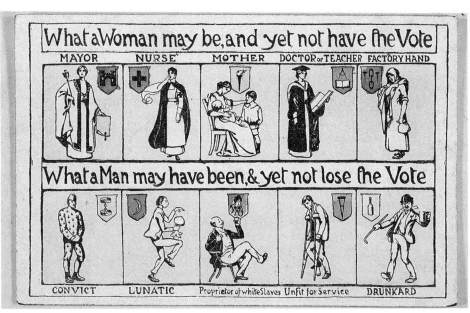

221

troduced a bill in the House of Commons to give the vote to women on the same basis as men. It was defeated, but similar bills were introduced nearly every year after that. Lydia Becker set up the Manchester Women's Suffrage Committee in 1867, and other suffrage committees were set up in other towns (suffrage means the right to vote). In 1897 all these suffrage societies were united in one national organisation – the National Union of Women's Suffrage Societies. Millicent Fawcett was their leader and there were over 500 local branches. Their tactics were peaceful: petitions, meetings, pamphlets, letters to politicians, etc. They were called suffragists.

The suffragettes

■ *SOURCE 5B*

On 10 October Mrs Emmelene Pankhurst . . . invited friends interested in promoting the cause of women's rights to a meeting at her Manchester home. They decided to band together to work for women's suffrage. Their activities soon made newspaper headlines, and the *Daily Mail* labelled the women 'suffragettes'.

School textbook, 1980

■ *SOURCE 5C* **Death of Emily Wilding Davison who threw herself under the horses' hooves during the 1913 Derby**

■ *SOURCE 5D* **Suffragette poster about the 'Cat and Mouse Act', 1913**

THE CAT AND MOUSE ACT
PASSED BY THE LIBERAL GOVERNMENT

BUY AND READ 'THE SUFFRAGETTE' PRICE 1P.

❓ *QUESTIONS*

a) What effect do you think the poster, Source 5A, would have on a (male) Liberal MP?

b) What impression of the women's suffrage movement is given in Source 5B?

c) Re-read the paragraph before Source 5B. In what ways is Source 5B misleading?

d) There are no real factual errors in Source 5B. However, what kind of bias does it show?

e) Using only Source 5C, explain what you think happened at the 1913 Derby.

f) What else would you want to know in order to get the whole truth?

g) In what ways is the poster, Source 5D, more emotional in its message than Source 5A?

There was much opposition to giving women equal voting rights. Queen Victoria called it 'a mad, wicked folly'. Of the two main political parties, most Liberals favoured votes for women, but their leaders were against it; Conservative leaders favoured it, but most of their party did not. The new, small Labour Party supported it, and Fabian socialists like George Bernard Shaw wrote plays to help the cause. Meanwhile the years went by and women still did not have the vote.

It was this frustrating situation which caused Mrs Pankhurst to break away from the suffragists and found the Women's Social and Political Union in 1903. Gradually their methods became more and more militant. They began by interrupting meetings, holding demonstrations and chaining themselves to railings in Downing Street. From 1912 the WSPU moved to more violent tactics: window-smashing, burning empty buildings and letter-

boxes, slashing paintings in art galleries and disrupting events such as the Derby (Source 5C). When they were arrested and sent to prison, they went on hunger strike. At first they were forcibly fed by having a tube put down their throats, a painful and revolting experience. There was an outcry: in 1913 an Act was passed allowing the prison authorities to release suffragettes and then, when they had recovered from their hunger strike, re-arrest them. Suffragettes called this the 'Cat and Mouse Act' (Source 5D).

The First World War

The vote had still not been won for women when the First World War broke out in 1914. In fact it may be that the suffragettes' violent tactics actually put off a number of Liberal MPs who might otherwise have supported the idea. Then, as the war went on and men were called up to fight, women took their places in the factories. Women were called on to do all kinds of jobs (see Source 6) which had been closed to them in peacetime. Most of the women who took on these jobs had been working women before the war, but some were volunteers. Usually they were paid less than the men they replaced.

It was impossible to deny the vote to women after their work to help win the war. But their voting rights were still very limited: in 1918 all men got the vote at 21, but for women the age was 30, and they had to be householders, or married to householders. Women could stand for Parliament; the first woman MP to take her seat was Lady Astor, in 1919. Only in 1928 did all women get the vote at 21, on the same basis as men.

Changes 1918–1960

Many of those who campaigned for women's suffrage did not see winning the vote as the end of the struggle. It was a way of helping women's position, at work and in the home. There was some progress in both of these areas in the years between the wars and up to the 1950s.

■ *SOURCE 6* **Women workers in a munitions factory in the First World War**

At work

Progress towards equality in the world of work depended on who you were and where you lived. The Sexual Disqualification Removal Act of 1919 opened up jobs at universities and the professions, such as law and architecture, to women. This was fine if you had the ability to enter them and your parents had the money to support you while you were studying.

For women without these advantages, it was the new industries which grew up in the 1920s and 1930s which brought them jobs. The old skills in old industries, which men had kept to themselves, did not apply in assembling radios, or telephones, for example. Women were happy to take jobs on assembly-lines at good pay. Banking and office-work continued to grow, and with them came more jobs for women. However, in the depressed areas, with older industries, there were few enough jobs for men, and almost none for women (see Chapter 9).

At home

Many women's organisations worked hard for women at home during this time. They campaigned

for child allowances, and proper health and welfare benefits for women (see Chapter 16). There were improvements in health care, with trained midwives and health visitors. From 1930 National Birth Control Clinics were started, offering free advice on contraception (see Chapter 7). Poorer people could now limit their family size, and this helped mothers' health. Child allowances started in 1945, and the National Health Service in 1948.

For women who were at home, new inventions at least helped take some of the drudgery out of housework. Vacuum cleaners were invented in the 19th century, but in 1906 cost £35. By the 1930s they were being made for less than one-tenth of this price. As Source 7C shows, washing machines took a lot of hard work out of this weekly task. Electricity and hot running water also helped make housework easier. Packaged food, in tins, and then later, frozen foods helped with the time-consuming job of preparing meals.

Gradually, attitudes began to change a little, too. Women had more confidence to live their own lives. The 1920s fashions, with short skirts and short hair suited the independent girl who earned her

■ SOURCE 7A Woman car driver, 1930s

own living and wanted to enjoy herself. The number of women in domestic service greatly decreased between the wars. There were other jobs available now, and women were not prepared to be ordered about in the same way. The cheap motor-car also gave women more independence.

■ SOURCE 7C Washing-machine advertisement, *Radio Times*, 1950

£25 (plus £6.5.0. tax) Hire Purchase available

HEAVY, TIRING WASHING DAYS A THING OF THE PAST

NEW Hoover Electric Washing Machine

does the full weekly wash for a large family

The new Hoover Electric Washing Machine saves hours of hard drudgery every week. It washes everything astonishingly quickly and *spotlessly clean*. Works on an entirely new " gentle-with-the-clothes " principle, and is such a handy size it will stand under the average draining board. You will be delighted, too, with the wringer — cleverly sprung to take even large, bulky articles.

So don't wear yourself out any longer. See your Hoover Dealer and order a Hoover Electric Washing Machine *now*. Hire Purchase available.

Remember, it does the full weekly wash for a large family

And it's made by **HOOVER** TRADE MARK

MAKERS OF THE WORLD'S BEST CLEANER

■ SOURCE 7B

How the Historian of 100 years ago would be confounded if he could return and see the world of women today. He would find women engineers, architects, lawyers, accountants, doctors, dentists, vets, librarians, journalists, scientists, tax inspectors and factory inspectors.

Helen Venner, *Daily Telegraph*, 1937

In the Second World War women were called up to serve, either in the armed services, or in important civilian jobs. As in the First World War they became a vital part of the workforce. Some of the opposition towards married women working was broken down by the war. As in the First World War however, women got less pay for the jobs which men used to do. After the war women found themselves excluded from many jobs again when the men returned. Nevertheless, by the 1950s the battle for women's rights was largely regarded as won.

Equal or Not?

Then, from the 1960s, women began to point out how far short of equality they still were. For example, it had been possible for women to enter the professions for many years; yet in 1980 only 8% of barristers, 4% of architects and 1% of accountants were women. One of the most serious inequalities was in Parliament itself. In 1983, nearly 65 years after women were allowed to become MPs, only 23 out of the 650 elected to the House of Commons were women. Moreover, although there were more women wage-earners in Britain than ever before, they tended to do the low-paid jobs. In 1975, 97% of canteen assistants, 92% of nurses, 92% of cleaners and 81% of shop assistants were women. Average earnings for women were less than four-fifths of average earnings for men, and still are.

Clearly there is more to equality than just allowing women to compete with men. It is also a question of attitudes, and these are very much harder to change. Women writers and thinkers, in what is sometimes called the 'women's movement', have exposed those prejudices and inequalities that still cause discrimination against women in all aspects of life, ranging from education to income tax.

Some of these attitudes can be tackled by the law. The Equal Pay Act 1969 came into effect in 1975, making it illegal to pay women less than men for the same job. Women trade unionists had worked hard over many years to overcome objections made by their male colleagues. This Act helped them to insist on their right to a fair wage. The Sex Discrimination Act 1975 made it illegal to refuse a woman a job simply because of gender. It set up the Equal Opportunities Commission to investigate cases of discrimination. It is not easy to prove something like discrimination, but at least the Act makes it very clear to employers what their attitude ought to be. The Sex Discrimination Act has also had an important effect on schools. All subjects now have to be open to girls and boys. Schools also try to encourage non-sexist attitudes in young people.

Many people recognise that the main problem to be dealt with is child care. As long as everyone expects women to take sole charge of this task, they will be discriminated against at work and find it hard to achieve equality. On a personal level, they will always have to choose between jobs and children. Some employers have offered crèches for their employees' children. Some jobs are now offered on a sharing basis, so mothers can work without having to work full-time. In a few couples the man has chosen to take the main responsibility for the children so that the woman can continue with her job. In these ways the last remnants of the Victorian ideal of women, which tried to turn them into mere decorative objects, is being slowly broken down.

Assignments

Empathy

1 Look at Sources 3B and 3C. Imagine you have just started work as a servant in a large house.
   a Describe what you have to do in your job and describe your feelings about it.
   b What are your hopes for the future?
   c Your younger brother has just started work on the railways: how do you feel about this, and the fact that he earns more than you?
2 Read Sources 2A, 2B and 2C. What might be the attitudes of the following towards a woman who wanted her own independent career:
   i an upper class man;
   ii a working class man;
   iii a middle class woman and
   iv a working class woman?
3 Get into groups of three. It is 1912, and one of you is a suffragist, one a militant suffragette and one a male MP considering whether to vote in favour of women's suffrage. Discuss the aims, methods and reactions of each of the three.
4 Look at Source 6.
   a Imagine a conversation between one of the women working here and a male foreman. They discuss the work and what it involves, pay and hours of work.
   b It is now 1919. Men are returning from the forces looking for jobs. Write a second conversation between the same two people in this new situation.
5 Read Source 7B. What would be the reaction to this statement of
   i a woman from the 1850s and
   ii a woman of the 1980s?

Understandiing concepts

1 **Similarity/difference**
   a How were women supposed to behave in mid-Victorian Britain with regard to: work, education, home, men?
   b Why was it impossible for working-class women to behave in this way?

2 **Similarity/difference**
   a What jobs did women do in mid-Victorian Britain?
   b In what ways were they treated worse than men?
   c What was the life of a married woman of *either* the middle class *or* the working class?

3 **Change/continuity**
   a In what ways did the position of women change in the period 1880–1914 as regards:
      i work;
      ii education;
      iii marriage;
      iv childbearing?
   b In what ways was it still the same?

4 **Causation**
   a Why did women fail to win the vote before 1914?
   b Why did women gain the right to vote in 1918?
   c Why were women not given the same voting rights as men in 1918?

5 **Factors causing change**
How have changes in the following affected the position of women in Britain in the 20th century:
   i education;
   ii household machines;
   iii contraception;
   iv fashion;
   v the law?

Themes for discussion

1 a What obstacles still prevent women from being treated as the equals of men in all walks of life?
   b How can they be overcome?
2 From your reading of other chapters in this book, do you think the Industrial Revolution made the position of women better or worse?

22 Education for a Changing Britain 1700-1980s

Everyone in Britain today between the ages of 5 and 16 has to be in some form of education. For most children and young people this means a state school – one run by the local education authority and paid for out of the rates. In the late 18th century there were no state schools at all; in fact there were only a few schools of any kind in the whole of England and Wales. The majority of men and women could not read, or write their own name. The Scots regarded education more highly. There were local schools in most Scottish towns and villages, paid for by the local rates. As a result, more people in Scotland could read and write. Because of its separate history, education in Scotland is not covered here.

As we shall see, the growth of state education was not simple or easy. Nor has there been much agreement about what schools are for, and what they should teach.

■ SOURCE 1A Schools in Leeds in the 1820s

There were very few schools, and many of the teachers could not have passed our present Board Schools Sixth Standard*. Some taught nothing but reading and spelling, or knitting and sewing; others only reading and writing from printed copies, as they could not write so well themselves ... Writing was looked upon by many parents as a mere luxury for the rich only ...

[Note: Board Schools Sixth Standard: a level reached by 13-year-olds in the 1870s, roughly the same as that reached by 10–11-year-olds nowadays.]
Joseph Lawson, 1887

■ SOURCE 1B A comprehensive school's 'Aims', 1987

What do we mean by 'progress' for each pupil?

We mean that all pupils, as they study ... will steadily increase their understanding and appreciation of the world about them.

We also mean that they will develop their ability to think for themselves, gain skills, work co-operatively with others, and take responsibility for their own work.

? QUESTION

Compare the aims of the schools in Sources 1A and 1B. How have schools changed?

Education in the 18th Century

Public schools

The sons of the rich were either taught at home by a tutor, or went to 'public school'. These schools, such as Eton, Harrow, Winchester and Shrewsbury had, in fact, been started centuries earlier as schools for the poor. However, the quality of education they offered had attracted the better-off, and the rising fees gradually excluded all but the rich. All the teachers were Church of England clergymen, and most of the time was spent studying the Classics – Latin and Greek. These schools were at a low point at this time, with bullying, caning, bad food and poor teaching. There was a full-scale rebellion at Harrow in 1808, and a riot at Winchester in 1818 which had to be put down by the army.

Upper-class girls rarely went to school. Their tutors, or governesses, taught them reading, writing, music, painting, dancing, and perhaps French, at home.

Grammar schools

In the 19th century, middle-class boys might go to a grammar school, if there was one in their town. These schools, too, had often been going for many centuries, and again the pupils spent most of the time studying the Classics. Some parents in Leeds wanted their sons to learn mathematics, and accounting, which might be useful to them in business. They were told that this was against the rules under which Leeds Grammar School was set up. Grammar schools were also in decline at this time, sometimes down to only two or three pupils.

Private schools

There were some small private schools, which were good or bad according to the person who ran them. Charles Dickens made great fun of how ignorant some of these private schoolteachers could be, in his novel *Nicholas Nickleby*.

■ SOURCE 2A Imaginary school, Dotheboys Hall, run by Wackford Squeers

We go upon the practical mode of teaching ... C-L-E-A-N, clean, verb, active, to make bright. W-I-N, win, D-E-R, der, winder, a casement. When a boy knows this out of a book he goes and does it.

Charles Dickens, *Nicholas Nickleby*, 1839

■ SOURCE 2B Advertisements for schools, 1836

EDUCATION – ESTABLISHMENT for young LADIES, within 2 miles of Hyde-park-corner. Terms 20 guineas per annum, which includes instruction in the English and French languages, writing and arithmetic, geography, history, pianoforte, singing and dancing. The house offers very superior accommodation, and has a large garden. Address, post paid, to Y.Z., at A. Osborne's, 37, Eagle Street, Red Lion-square.

EDUCATION – By Mr Shaw, at Bowes Academy, Greta-bridge, Yorkshire. YOUTH are carefully INSTRUCTED in the English, Latin and Greek languages, writing, common and decimal arithmetic, bookkeeping, mensuration, surveying, geometry, geography and navigation, with the most useful branches of the mathematics and provided with board, clothes, and every necessary, at 20 guineas per annum cash. No extra charges. No vacations. Further particulars may be known on application to Mr J Metcalfe, agent, 38, Great Marylebone-Street. Mr Shaw attends at the George and Blue Boar, Holborn from 12 to 2 daily.

QUESTIONS

a) How does Charles Dickens make fun of Wackford Squeers in Source 2A?

b) What is the value of this source to a historian?

c) Using Source 2B, describe how girls' and boys' private education differed.

d) Why do you think this was so?

e) Dotheboys Hall (Source 2A) was supposed to be based on Bowes Academy (Source 2B). Does this link help you understand either Source 2A or 2B any better?

Because grammar and public schools were for members of the Church of England only, Dissenters (see Chapter 23) set up their own schools in the 18th century. These were the best schools of their time, with an up-to-date curriculum, including science, geography, maths, languages and book-keeping. Many such schools were run by Quakers. Famous industrialists such as Boulton, Roebuck and Wilkinson, and scientists such as Priestley and Dalton went to these 'Dissenting Academies', as they were called.

Charity schools

For working-class children there was no free education and very few schools at all, even if parents were willing to pay. Some schools were set up by charities. The Society for the Propagation of Christian Knowledge (SPCK), which now runs many bookshops, was set up in 1699 to found more charity schools. For a few pennies a week the charity schools taught reading, writing, arithmetic and religion as well as some local craft, such as weaving or shoemaking. Pupils usually had to wear a uniform. Many charity schools were in decline by 1800, but a few did give working-class children their only real chance of a proper education.

Other schools

More common than the charity schools were dame schools, for younger children, and common day schools for older ones. Both these types of school were set up by anyone who had the space in their

SOURCE 2C Dame school, mid-19th century painting

home (or even if they didn't – see Source 2D) and who needed the money. Fees were low – 4d (1½p) to 10d (4p) a week. What the children learnt depended on the person who ran the school, but many were no more than child-minders. As one village 'dame' said: 'It is not much they pay me and it is not much I teach them'.

SOURCE 2D Inspector's visit to a common day school in Birmingham, 1838

On a perch sat a cock and two hens; underneath ... was a dog-kennel ... occupied by three black terriers whose barking added to the noise of the children, and the cackling of the fowls was almost deafening. There was only one small window, at which sat the master, obstructing three-quarters of the light ...

QUESTIONS

a) The artist who painted Source 2C was probably trying to give a good impression of a dame school. How does he do this?

b) What is your impression of Source 2C? Would you like to attend such a school?

c) How does Source 2C compare with a modern primary school?

d) Source 2D is obviously critical of the day school. Is there anything we can learn from these two biased Sources, 2C and 2D?

As Source 2D shows, many people were very critical of common day schools in the 19th century. It is their reports which supply us with most of our information about such schools and they may be biased. Recently some writers have suggested that they may have given a better education than the school system set up by the Victorians to replace them.

The Impact of the Industrial Revolution

The Industrial Revolution brought demands for changes in education, as it changed every other aspect of society. On the one hand, industry needed more educated people. It needed clerks to keep accounts, write bills, keep up with orders and run the offices. It needed skilled craftsmen who could do calculations and read working diagrams. On the other hand, industry created new towns and cities (see Chapter 11). Thousands of children were growing up in these places, without any education at all. Such schools as existed were too small, and many children were at work every weekday anyway. For many middle-class people this situation seemed to present a serious problem of lawlessness, immorality and crime.

More schools seemed to be one way of tackling the problem, so that children could be disciplined.

The Sunday Schools movement

Controlling the problem was the motive behind the Sunday Schools movement. The first Sunday School was set up by Robert Raikes in 1780 in Gloucester. One Sunday he came across a group of factory children playing and shouting in the street on their day off. He decided to set up a Sunday School for them, to teach reading, Christianity, obedience and good manners. His idea was taken up widely. Manchester, for example, had 42 schools, with 5171 children by 1787. Half a million children were going to Sunday Schools in England and Wales by 1818, 1½ million by 1833. In the 1780s, Welsh chapels set up Sunday Schools teaching children to read in Welsh.

■ SOURCE 3A Welsh reading book, 1850

■ SOURCE 3B Rules of Bridgnorth Sunday School, 1795

8 The objects of this charity be poor persons of each sex and of any age above seven years who shall be taught to read.

14 That the teacher and scholars attend divine service on the morning and afternoon of every Sunday.

15 That the teachers shall take care that the scholars come clean to school; and if any scholar be guilty of lying, swearing, stealing, talking indecently, or otherwise misbehaving himself the teacher shall point out the evil of such conduct ...

? QUESTIONS

a) What are the children to be taught at Bridgnorth Sunday School?
b) How far do the rules here support the motives of Robert Raikes in setting up the Sunday School in Gloucester?

The monitorial system

The cost of Sunday Schools was low, as the teachers were usually volunteers. Churches and chapels became interested in running schools during the week too, but that would mean paying salaries to lots of teachers. This problem was overcome by the monitorial system. This was invented by two people at much the same time: Andrew Bell, of the Church of England, and Joseph Lancaster, a Quaker. Under this system the teacher taught a lesson to some older pupils, called monitors. They then each taught a group of children. Senior monitors, called ushers, did jobs such as keeping the register.

The main advantage of this system was that it was extremely cheap. One teacher could teach up to 200 children; at one Manchester school there were over 1000 pupils and three teachers. It was, however, very mechanical, and the children did not learn much beyond basic skills in the 3Rs – reading, writing and arithmetic.

■ SOURCE 4B The monitorial system at work

A monitor is appointed to each class. The books are laid by each monitor at the end of her desk. Each writer, in passing up the desk takes her book and holding it up before her remains standing ... The command is then given by the monitor to 'Front', – 'Lay down – books', 'Hands down', 'Look – in', 'Open – books', 'Hands down'. The monitors now distribute the copies and pens. At the word 'Begin', the writing commences; they are not allowed to exceed five lines. Each monitor then goes from girl to girl pointing out defects by comparing it with the copy slip.

Manual of Teaching, 1821

? QUESTIONS

a) How many adult teachers, how many monitors and roughly how

■ SOURCE 4A The monitorial system, early 19th century

many children are there in Source 4A?

b) What subjects are being studied in Source 4A?

c) Would you like to be a monitor?

d) How does the classroom differ from your own?

e) Do you think you would learn much under the monitorial system as shown in Source 4A?

f) Read Source 4B. What other criticisms would you make of teaching and learning by the monitorial system?

g) Imagine you are a pupil in these sources and are keen to learn. Describe the lessons and your reactions to them.

Voluntary schools

Rivalry between the Church of England and the Dissenters or Nonconformists was growing at this time (see Chapter 23). The joint Sunday School Society collapsed over this rivalry in 1800. Each group wanted to make sure the children educated in their schools received their own religious ideas. Both groups included quite well-off members: the Church of England included many landowners, who had become rich through agricultural improvements and high food prices in the Napoleonic Wars. They set up the National Society in 1811. The Nonconformists included many industrialists. They set up the British and Foreign Schools Society in 1808.

The two societies began to collect money and to build schools, all operating on the monitorial system. Because they were paid for by voluntary donations, they were called voluntary schools. These were day schools, for boys and girls, charging about 1*d* (½p) per child per week. Religious instruction was a central part of the education they offered, as you would expect from schools set up by religious societies. All the British Society schools had non-denominational religious teaching, that is, not taking any one line on religion. The full title of the National Society was the National Society for Promoting the Education of the Poor in the Principles of the Established Church. As you would expect, therefore, National Schools taught their pupils the Church of England view of religion.

■ *SOURCE 4C* Schoolchildren, early 20th century. These were the kinds of children Shaftesbury was trying to provide schools for 50 years earlier

Ragged schools

Although these voluntary schools were cheap, there were many children whose parents were so poor that they could not afford to send their children even to them. To try and reach some of these children John Pound, a Portsmouth cobbler, set up the Ragged Schools Union in 1844. Lord Shaftesbury became the leader of this movement, which by 1870 had 132 schools, with 20000 children. The ragged schools were free, and taught the 3Rs.

? QUESTIONS

a) What signs of poverty do the children in Source 4C show?

b) Suggest reasons why they were so poor.

c) Why would it be difficult for them to learn anything at school?

Poor Law schools

In addition to these different efforts to provide schools, there were two other kinds of school which working-class children might be attending by 1850. Firstly there were Poor Law schools. The Poor Law Amendment Act 1834 (see Chapter 15, page 164) encouraged Boards of Guardians to set up schools. It was hoped that education would help solve the problem of poverty. Unfortunately most workhouses had no school, or a school that was so bad it was worse than nothing.

James Kay-Shuttleworth, who was interested in education, saw how bad things were when he was Poor Law Commissioner to Norfolk and Suffolk in the 1830s. Later on, he set up a school for Poor Law children at Norwood. The girls were prepared for domestic service, and the boys for a career in the navy. This was encouraged by erecting the mast and guns of *HMS Excellent* on the school playground. Few Boards of Guardians took up his idea, however: only three London and six rural Poor Law School Districts were formed. One Guardian said that providing education was 'like putting the torch of knowledge into the hands of rick-burners'.

Factory schools

The other type of school that working-class children might go to was a factory school. The Acts of 1802 and 1833 insisted on some education for children who worked in some factories. Robert Owen, at New Lanark, set up excellent schools as part of his plan to improve the conditions of his workers (Chapter 14, Source 3, page 154). Sir John Guest, at Merthyr Tydfil, set up several schools, educating 1041 pupils by 1850, and other factory owners did the same. However, the standard of factory schools was generally low. Factory Inspector Horner, reporting on Lancashire in 1857, classified only 76 schools out of 427 as 'good'. Of the rest, 26 were 'tolerably good', 146 'inferior', 112 worse than that, and 66 so bad they were 'a fraud upon the poor ignorant parents who pay the school fees'.

Government grant

Several times during the early part of the 19th century attempts were made to set up schools in every parish, to be paid for out of the rates. These early efforts at education all failed because of various kinds of opposition. Some people, particularly in the years just after the French Revolution, thought that any kind of education for the working classes was wrong.

SOURCE 5

Giving education to the working classes would be bad for their morals and happiness. It would lead them to despise their lot in life instead of making them good servants in agriculture and other work to which their rank in society had destined them; instead of teaching them obedience it would make them difficult. It would enable them to read seditious pamphlets, vicious books, and publications against Christianity.

Davies Giddy MP, House of Commons, 1807

? QUESTIONS

a) What bad effects does this MP think education would have?
b) What do you think of his views of education?

Others opposed plans for any kind of state education, as it would extend the power of the government over people's lives. They said it was up to the parents to decide if their children were educated, and the government should not interfere with this. The disagreements between the religious groups also prevented any progress. Any plan which brought the parish priest into running the schools was opposed by the Nonconformists. Any plan for non-denominational schools was opposed by the Church of England.

Yet there were far more children in the country than the societies and charities were able to deal with. In 1833, as the supporters of state education pointed out, only a third of children attended a day school at all (half attended a Sunday School). In rural areas up to three-quarters of children did not go to school. The government therefore decided in 1833 to make a grant of £20 000 for education. It would be paid to the British and National Societies. In the same year they made a grant of £70 000 to rebuild the Royal Stables – so you can see they didn't think schools were very important. Nevertheless, this tiny grant marks the beginning of government's involvement in education.

The grant was put up to £30 000 in 1839 and increased a great deal in the next few years. A Committee on Education was set up to control the grant, with James Kay-Shuttleworth as its Secretary. Inspectors were then appointed to visit schools, to report to the government and advise teachers. Kay-Shuttleworth set up a teacher-training college at Battersea, in 1840, using his own money. He also tried to improve the training of teachers by setting up a system of pupil-teachers, in 1846. These were clever young people aged about 13, who were given a five-year apprenticeship in the basic skills of teaching. There were 10 000 of them by the 1850s. The best pupil-teachers could win a full Queen's Scholarship for a two-year training course at a college.

The number of pupils at school increased a great deal over these years. In 1815 there were 564 National Schools, with 98 000 pupils. By 1830 there were 3670 National Schools, with 346 000 pupils and by 1851 there were 17 015 National Schools with 956 000 pupils. In 1851 there were also 1500 British Schools, with 225 000 pupils. With grammar schools, public schools and private schools, probably about one-third of all children in England and Wales attended school by 1851.

Schools in the Later 19th Century

Public schools

The move to improve education in the 19th century also affected the public schools. These schools were intended for the leaders, not the workers, of industrial Britain. New headmasters such as Samuel Butler, Head of Shrewsbury

SOURCE 6A Radley public school in about 1859

1798–1839, and Thomas Arnold, Head of Rugby 1828–42, brought several sweeping changes. Lessons were widened to include maths, geography and history, although the classics still played a large part. Team games were thought to be important, for encouraging team spirit, leadership and discipline. Customs such as 'fagging' – younger boys made to act as servants to older boys – continued, but were more strictly controlled. The aim was to make each boy a kind of 'Christian gentleman' – well-mannered, religious, loyal, patriotic and ready to take responsibility.

The Clarendon Report, an investigation into public schools in 1864, recommended that they should broaden their curriculum to include science. This, however, was not widely taken up.

In addition to reforms of existing schools, 54 new public schools were founded in the 19th century. The sons of the new, rich industrialists were sent to them, to mingle with the sons of older landowning families. Few of them went back into industry, but instead chose the army, or the Civil Service. These young men eventually ran the country and its growing empire overseas. Senior posts in the Church of England, the law and banking were also really only open to public schoolboys. This situation has continued, with relatively little change, up to the present day.

Education for girls

There was also an interest in girls' education. Cheltenham Ladies College was set up in 1854, and North London Collegiate School in 1850. In 1872 the Girls Public Day School Trust was started by Maria Grey. This built over 30 schools in England. There were plenty of team games at these schools, but the main emphasis was on a high academic standard. The pressure for women's rights in the early 20th century owed much to the standards set by these schools.

State schools

Those who wanted every child to go to school continued to put pressure on the government. The Victorians were great collectors of statistics, and these seemed to show how far short the various schools fell of

■ SOURCE 6B A School for Young Ladies, 1890

providing education for everybody.

James Kay-Shuttleworth wanted to show that there was a shortage of schools, so he calculated on the basis of the number of children aged 3–15 in the population. It would have been more realistic to use ages 5–11, as these were the normal school years at that time. His calculations made the number of children not at school seem much larger.

? QUESTIONS

a) Source 7 shows the number of children at school and also the total population of the cities. How does this make it difficult to draw conclusions as to what proportion of children in the cities were at school?

b) Why do you think an ancient city like York has a bigger proportion of its population at school than the new industrial cities?

■ SOURCE 7 Number of children at school in three cities, 1836

	Number at day and dame schools	Number at other, better schools	Total number at school	Total population
Liverpool	11 336	14 024	25 360	230 000
Birmingham	8 180	4 697	12 877	180 000
York	1 494	2 697	4 191	25 000

The Newcastle Commission

The government responded by setting up the Newcastle Commission, which investigated education from 1858 to 1861. Some idea of the attitude of the times is given in its instructions. It had to find out what had to be done to provide 'sound and cheap elementary instruction to all classes of people'. The government also wanted to see if education could be given to 'those who, even in the humbler classes, are found endowed with superior mental powers'.

The limits of elementary education were outlined by one of the Commission's witnesses, Rev. James Fraser.

■ SOURCE 8A

I doubt whether it would be desirable, with a view to the real interests of the peasant boy, to keep him at school until he was 14 or 15 ... It is quite possible to teach a child all that it is necessary for him to possess by the time he is 10 years old. He shall be able to spell correctly the words that he will ordinarily have to use, he shall read ... the paragraph in the newspaper that he cares to read with sufficient ease to be a pleasure to himself and to convey information to listeners; if gone to live at a distance from home, he shall write his mother a letter that should be both legible and intelligible. He knows enough of arithmetic to make out a ... bill; if he hears talk of foreign countries he has some notions as to the part of the habitable globe in which they lie; he has acquaintance enough of the Holy Scriptures to follow the arguments of a plain Saxon sermon and to know what are the duties required of him to his Maker and his fellow man.

Newcastle Commission's Report, 1861

? QUESTIONS

a) What subjects does Rev. James Fraser want to be taught?

b) What subjects in your present curriculum are not included in Fraser's plans?

c) Do you think he would agree with the views of education given in:
   i) Source 3B?
   ii) Source 5?
   iii) Source 1B?

d) Fraser's view of education does not seem to show any advance on that described in Source 1A from 40 years earlier. Can you explain this lack of progress?

The Newcastle Commission found that only 10% of all children were in a school which could be called satisfactory. Attendance was very poor, because of bad health among children, and also the need to work, either in factories or on the land. Up to 42% of all children attended for less than one year of their lives.

The first result of the Newcastle Commission was a change in the method of paying the government grant to a school. The principle now adopted was 'payment by results'. Under this system an inspector tested all the pupils in the school in the 3Rs. The grant was then calculated according to how many reached the required standard, provided they had attended regularly.

■ *SOURCE 8B*

The Managers of schools may claim at the end of each year:
a the sum of 4/- [20p] per scholar
b for every scholar who has attended more than 200 morning and afternoon meetings of the school. If more than 6 years of age 8/- [40p] subject to examination.

Standard III
Reading: a short paragraph from an elementary reading book used in the school.

Writing: a sentence from the same paragraph, slowly read once and then dictated in single words.

Arithmetic: a sum in any of the four rules.

[Note: Standard III children were aged about 9 or 10. The 'four rules' are addition, subtraction, multiplication and division.]

Revised Code, 1862

? *QUESTIONS*

a) How far does this source carry out the aims of education as described by the Rev. James Fraser, Source 8A?

b) What effect would this type of inspection have on teaching in the schools?

c) Why would there be pressure on teachers to cheat, under this system?

d) How does the standard compare with what is expected of a nine- or ten-year-old today?

You can see that the aims of the Newcastle Commission were being put into practice: a very basic education, provided as cheaply as possible. As Robert Lowe said to Parliament when he described the system, 'If it is not cheap it shall be efficient, and if it is not efficient it shall be cheap'. This 'payment by results' lasted until 1897. It may have improved standards in some bad schools, but in general it made schools very dull. Teachers felt discouraged from doing anything but the basic skills in the 3Rs.

Still there were not enough schools. The Newcastle Commission had looked at education abroad, and reported that in many countries schools were provided for everyone. Industrialists worried that the better-educated foreigners would steal British trade. Yet others argued that children needed school discipline in order to become suitable workers. The argument that parents should have the right to decide was defeated because in many areas there were simply not enough schools anyway. The main problem remained the question of religion and the rivalry of the two Societies.

? *QUESTIONS*

a) Who are the people quarrelling in the doorway in Source 8C?

b) Explain the attitude of *Punch* to education.

Although the arguments had been going on for fifty years, the government was finally pushed into action by the 1867 Reform Act. This gave the vote to most men in towns and cities, and it was felt that education was necessary to make sure they used their vote wisely.

■ *SOURCE 8C Punch* cartoon, 1860s

"OBSTRUCTIVES."

MR. PUNCH (*to Bull A1*). "YES, IT'S ALL VERY WELL TO SAY, 'GO TO SCHOOL!' HOW ARE THEY TO GO TO SCHOOL WITH THOSE PEOPLE QUARRELLING IN THE DOORWAY? WHY DON'T YOU MAKE 'EM 'MOVE ON'?"

The 1870 Education Act

The 1870 Education Act was introduced by W. E. Forster, a Quaker, and son-in-law of the great Thomas Arnold, Head of Rugby School. Each district of the country was investigated, and if the existing schools had enough places, nothing needed to be done. If there was a shortage of places, a school board was set up to build and run schools. The religious problem was overcome by having non-denominational religious teaching in Board Schools. In the voluntary schools (whose grants were doubled by the Act), religious teaching was to be at the beginning or end of the school day. Parents could therefore withdraw their children if they wished.

School boards could make their schools compulsory, if they wished, and free, if they wished. However, free, compulsory education was still not provided for all children. This was mainly because it would obviously take time to put the new system into operation.

Sandon's Act 1876, and Mundella's Act 1880, made education compulsory from the ages of 5 to 10. In 1893 the leaving age was raised to 11, and in 1899 to 12. By the 1890s many school boards had stopped charging fees, and in 1891 fees were abolished in all state schools.

School life

What was education like in the schools of late 19th century England and Wales?

You can see from Source 9B that classes were large and often all the children were taught in one room. Many children from poorer families came to school dirty, hungry and badly-clothed (see also Source 4C). Compulsory school brought the problem of child poverty to people's attention, and led to the move for school meals and school medical inspections.

■ **SOURCE 9B** Children at a National School in Bristol, 1895

■ **SOURCE 9A** London Board School, built 1874

■ **SOURCE 9C** Reading book, from the early 19th century

6   TOM THUMB'S PLAY-BOOK.

A was an Archer, and shot at a Frog.

B was a Butcher, and had a great Dog.

C was a Captain all cover'd with Lace.

D was a Drunkard, and had a red Face.

E was

? QUESTIONS

a) In what ways does the school in Source 9A differ from your school building?

b) In what ways does the classroom in Source 9B differ from your classroom?

c) Do you think children would have found it easy to learn to read from books like the one shown in Source 9C?

Sometimes there was a lesson on a subject apart from the 3Rs. This was called an 'object lesson'. Here is an object lesson on clay.

■ SOURCE 9D **From a teaching manual, late 19th century**

(Show one of the lumps of dry clay.)

'Who can tell me what this is?' – 'It is a piece of clay.'

'Where did it come from?'

(Make the class tell where they have met with clay.)

'We have a common name for all substances which we get out of the earth in this way. We call them minerals. Clay is a mineral.'

(Break the lump into small pieces and distribute round the class.)'

■ SOURCE 9E **From a country school log-book**

The teaching is again unsatisfactory, for although there has been a slight improvement in arithmetic, I must recommend a reduction in grant. It is true that 5 standards, and an infant class, with only one Monitress as an assistant, make a hard task, it is difficult to believe the results need to have been so poor. Animal pictures are wanted and desks for the infants would be useful. An easel, and maps are also wanted.

Vicar's report, 1881

Fieldwork, gathering stones, cow-keeping and farm-work has reduced the average. 35 out of 61 attended. Many children are always ill with coughs and colds and stay at home half the year.

Vicar's report, 1890

■ SOURCE 9F

Her Majesty's Inspector of Schools came once a year on a date of which previous notice had been given. There was no singing or quarrelling on the way to school that morning. The children, in clean pinafores and well-blackened boots walked deep in thought; or, with open spelling or table books in hand, tried to make up in an hour for all their wasted yesterdays.

The Inspector was an elderly clergyman, a little man with an immense paunch and tiny grey eyes like gimlets ... His voice was an exasperated roar and ... he looked at the rows of children as if

he hated them ... The very sound of his voice scattered the few wits of the less gifted and even those who could have done better were too terrified to collect their thoughts or keep their hands from trembling.

A village National School, 1880s

? QUESTIONS

a) Source 9D does not sound very interesting, but the children enjoyed these lessons very much. Why do you think this was?

b) Why is the vicar reducing the grant in Source 9E?

c) What difficulties does the teacher have in meeting the standard required?

d) Do you think the school in Source 9E is a British, National or Board School? How can you tell?

e) What effect did the inspection (Source 9F) have on the children?

f) Do you think 'payment by results' was a fair way of judging schools? (See also Source 8B.)

g) Using all these sources, describe the difficulties of being **(i)** a teacher and **(ii)** a pupil in a school in the 1880s.

Higher education

The growth of interest in education in the 19th century extended to the universities and higher education, too. In 1800 there were only two universities in England: Oxford and Cambridge. (Scotland had four: Edinburgh, Glasgow, Aberdeen and St Andrews, and these had close links with the new industries.) The colleges of Oxford and Cambridge were open only to male members of the Church of England. Industrial Britain passed them by, and many of the dons, and their students, spent their time hunting and drinking.

In 1828 London University was founded. In 1851 Manchester University was started, and in the 1870s Birmingham, Newcastle, Leeds, Sheffield, Liverpool and Nottingham (see Source 10). Colleges, which later became universities, were set up at Cardiff and Swansea. These new universities included engineering and science departments, and worked with local industry. Women began to demand and receive university education from

the 1870s. At first they were taught separately from male students. In 1871 the Universities Test Act opened universities to students who were not members of the Church of England.

In many towns, mechanics' institutes were set up. These were places where working people could study, usually in the evenings. Lecture programmes were arranged, and there was often a good library as well.

? QUESTION

Study Source 10. Which industries did Yorkshire College cooperate with closely in its early days? Why was this?

Education in 1900

Sources 9A–F give a clear view of the problems and weaknesses of schools in the late 19th century. Nevertheless, a start had finally been made on providing education for every child. By 1900, 2500 school boards had been set up, running 5700 schools for nearly 2½ million pupils. The voluntary schools had also expanded to meet the challenge, with 14 500 schools and places for 3 million pupils by 1900. The most important basic statistic – level of literacy – showed a great improvement.

■ SOURCE 11 **Percentage of illiteracy in England and Wales, based on signatures or marks on marriage registers**

	Men (%)	Women(%)
1840	35	50
1870	20	27
1896	6	7

? QUESTIONS

a) Account for the differences between 1840 and 1870, and between 1870 and 1896.

b) Which period of years has shown the greatest improvement? Why was this so?

c) Account for the differences between men and women as shown in Source 11.

d) Do you think this use of marriage registers is a good indicator of the level of illiteracy?

This improvement in standards

SOURCE 10 Appeal broadsheet (1880) for the University of Leeds, founded in the 1870s as the Yorkshire College. The top drawing shows the design for the complete college. The bottom drawings show the new buildings for the Department of Textile Industries, opened in 1880.

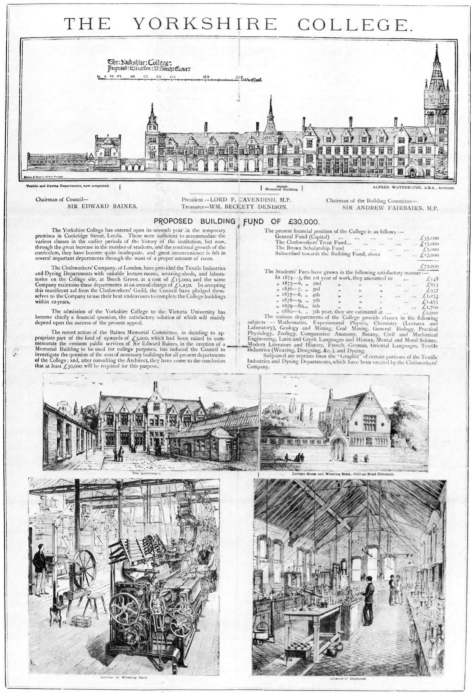

brought a demand for education for working-class children beyond the age of 11. Teachers were often sorry to see bright children forced to leave at 11 to go to work. Such children could stay on to 13 but, as we have seen, conditions in elementary schools did not give the teachers much time to teach them. Pressures began to arise for such pupils to be able to go on to another, more advanced school until the age of 14 or 15 – a secondary school.

The Growth of Secondary Education

Various types of school were offering secondary education in 1900: grammar schools, technical schools, and higher grade board schools. Grammar schools had changed in the last part of the 19th

century. The Taunton Commission of 1868 investigated them and recommended many changes. Some, such as Oundle School, became public schools. Others, such as Manchester Grammar School, concentrated on high academic standards. The classics were still taught to every pupil, but now maths, science, languages, geography and history were included. For working-class children the problem was that the grammar schools charged fees which were much higher than working-class parents could afford. There were, however, a tiny number of free scholarships.

Technical schools were started in 1889, run by the County Councils. They gave a practical and scientific education, but there were not many of them.

Lastly, some school boards had begun to build and run secondary or higher grade schools. Seventy-nine such boards had done so by 1900, and were proud of their schools. Then, in 1901, the Cockerton Case declared that it was illegal for school boards to run secondary schools. They had been set up in 1870 to run elementary schools only.

The 1902 Balfour Act

Clearly the government had to sort out this confusion. Many radicals and socialists liked the school boards. As the members were elected, this gave a chance for women, working-class people and socialists to serve in public office. However, the government disagreed. The 1902 Education Act called Balfour's Act, abolished the school boards. All schools – as well as technical schools and colleges – came under the County Council or County Borough as the local education authority (l.e.a.). This system has remained the same ever since.

The Act also gave a chance for working-class children to go on to secondary education. Scholarships were available for clever pupils to attend grammar schools. This was seen as an 'educational ladder' whereby working-class children could work their way to a grammar school. A grammar-school education was the opening to middle-class careers, such as banking, insurance, local government or teaching. By an Act of 1907 a quarter of the places at grammar schools had to be free. Of course, working-class children had to compete with all other children for these free places.

The Education Act 1918

After the First World War there was an increasing demand, pressed most strongly by the Labour Party, for 'secondary education for all'. Fisher's 1918 Education Act raised the school-leaving age to 14. It also proposed that nursery schools should be provided for children aged from 3 to 5, and part-time education to 18. Like so many hopes at the end of the war, these came to nothing in the great Depression of the inter-war years.

In 1930 only about 1 in 8 children from an elementary school went to a secondary school, and 1 in 240 from an elementary school went to a university. Not all elementary-school children came from working-class homes, so you can see that the 'educational ladder' was a narrow and difficult one. About 80% of children attended the same school for their whole education from 5 to 14.

■ *SOURCE 12A* **Boys at a grammar school, 1920s**

■ *SOURCE 12B* **A village school in the 1920s**

Our village school was poor and crowded, but in the end I relished it. It had a lively reek of steaming life: boys' boots, girls' hair, stoves and sweat, blue ink, white chalk and shavings. We learnt nothing abstract or tenuous there – just simple patterns of facts and letters ... no more than was needed to measure a shed, write out a bill, read a swine-disease warning. Through the dead hours of the morning, through the long afternoons, we chanted away at our tables: 'Twelve-inches-one-foot. Three-feet-make-a-yard. Fourteen-pounds-make-a-stone. Eight-stone-a-hundredweight.' Unhearing, unquestioning we rocked to our chanting, hammering the gold nails home: 'Twice-two-are-four. One-God-is-love. One-lord-is-King ... One-King-is-George. One-George-is-Fifth.' So it was always; had been, would be for ever; we asked no questions; we didn't hear what we said; yet neither did we ever forget it.

Laurie Lee, *Cider with Rosie*, 1959

? *QUESTIONS*

a) Describe the main differences between the two schools in Sources 12A and 12B.

b) Laurie Lee in Source 12B describes a limited education, not very different from that suggested by Rev. J. Fraser in 1860 (Source 8A). In what ways was his education in the 1920s much the same as in mid-Victorian times?

c) Explain why there was so little change in 60 years.

The Hadow Report, 1926, criticised these all-age schools. It put forward a system of primary education to age 11, and secondary education for all, from 11 to 14, of two types: grammar schools and secondary modern schools. By 1939 two-thirds of the country had this pattern of schools. The Spens Report, 1935, said that an examination at the age of 11 should decide whether a child should go to a grammar school or a secondary modern school. It also proposed raising the school-leaving age to 15, then 16. This suggestion was blocked by the coming of the Second World War.

The 1944 Butler Act

Education was severely disrupted by the war, with 2 million children evacuated and a shortage of teachers. However, in education, as in other fields the war brought a determination to build a better world after the fighting was over. In 1944 R. A. Butler's Education Act was passed. This, at last, gave free secondary education for all. Children would be tested at 11, and then attend a grammar school, technical school or secondary modern school.

The grammar schools still based themselves on public schools, and their teaching was geared to university entrance. There were not many technical schools. The rest of the children – 70 to 90% of them, depending on the area – went to secondary modern schools. Here, teaching concentrated on basic skills in Maths and English, with lots of time in practical subjects. All three schools were supposed to be equal, but, from the first, grammar schools were regarded as 'better' schools.

Comprehensive schools

By the 1950s this division at the age of 11 was being widely criticised. Secondary modern schools were not regarded very highly by parents and employers. Eleven seemed a very young age to determine a person's whole future. Some so-called 'failures' at secondary modern schools went on to pass GCE O level examinations and even got to university. Pressure on primary schools to concentrate on the 11+ exam affected all that they tried to do.

For these reasons several areas began to introduce comprehensive schools – schools for all children regardless of their ability. The Labour government encouraged this development. By 1980 over 90% of secondary schools in England and Wales were comprehensive.

■ SOURCE 13B

In a street there are a dozen children approaching eleven-plus who have been friends since they were five. Probably all the parents are hoping the child will get to grammar school. Primary School Head teachers are asked to provide a great deal of English, arithmetic and even intelligence tests. Parents compare marks, help with homework, arrange extra coaching. Then, after the exam, three or four lucky boys and girls go to the schools everyone wants, and the rest, who have failed, go to the other schools.

H. R. Chetwynd, 1960

■ SOURCE 13C

Thomas Bennett School takes the whole of one Crawley neighbourhood and gets its share of able and stupid children. It started in 1958.

But already 31% of the children had 5 or more O levels after 6 years – the national average is 12.8%. And of the 70 taking A levels, 23 would have been graded 'Secondary Modern' at 11.

Lynne Teasdale, who came from Hampshire, had failed the 11 plus and entered a low stream. Suddenly she discovered science. 'Straight away I just understood it. It seemed logical and that was it.' Next year she will go to university.

The Observer, April 1965

❓ QUESTIONS

a) What can you tell about comprehensive schools from Source 13A?

b) What criticisms of the effects of the 11+ are given in Source 13B?

c) What benefits of the comprehensive system are given in Source 13C?

d) Source 13C concentrates on exam results: what other ways are there to measure the success of a school?

e) From your own knowledge, and what you have read, do you think the widespread abolition of selective education has been a good idea?

Other changes have also been made to try to help all children achieve the best they are capable of. The school-leaving age was raised to 15 in 1947, and 16 in 1973. In the 1960s many more children were staying on at school after the age of 15 anyway. The GCE O level exam, introduced in 1951, was designed to be taken by the cleverest 20% of pupils only, so the Certificate of Secondary Education (CSE) was started in 1965. By the 1980s, when most children were in comprehensive schools, it was obviously wrong to have two different examinations for 16-years olds. The GCSE exam, open to all pupils, replaced both the other examinations and will be taken for the first time in 1988.

Public schools

The public schools continued through most of the 20th century much as they were in late Victorian times. However, from the 1960s there have been some changes. Some boys' schools now admit girls,

■ SOURCE 13A London's first purpose-built comprehensive school at Kidbrooke, opened in 1954

too, especially in the sixth form. Under competition from the excellent facilities offered by many state schools, public schools have spent money on modernisation. Laboratories, computers and technology rooms have been added.

For those parents who choose to pay for their children's education there is a completely separate school system. Preparatory schools cover the years 7–13, at the end of which a child takes the Common Entrance examination. This decides which school the child will go on to, and, sometimes, if he or she has won a scholarship to help with the fees. For their money, which may amount to £10 000 per year, or

even more, parents buy certain benefits: smaller classes, for example. Although only 6% of children attend them, public schools still have a powerful influence.

Higher education

The steady growth of universities and technical colleges in the 19th century continued into the early 20th century. The Robbins Report, 1963, pointed out that fewer British people went into higher education than in most other developed countries. Several new universities were founded, starting with Sussex in 1961. Several Colleges of Advanced Technology were formed, and these

became polytechnics, also able to award degrees. Usually the 'polys' have a more scientific or practical element in their courses than universities do. There were 17 universities in Britain in 1945 and 45 by 1979.

One further remarkable development was the Open University, started in 1969. Students work in their own homes from course books, and radio and TV broadcasts. The Open University specialises in helping students who missed out on education when they were younger. Over 40 000 people have been awarded OU degrees since it started.

Assignments

Empathy

1 There were several different attitudes towards education in the 19th century.
  a Which different attitudes were to be found, and which types of people held them?
  b What did working people expect from education in the 19th century?

2 Look at Sources 9A–9F. Imagine you are at school at that time: describe what your school day is like, what you are learning, what you feel about your teachers and the other pupils.

3 Look at Sources 13A–13C.
  a What were the effects of the 11+ exam on parents' and pupils attitudes?
  b What were the feelings of those who passed, and those who failed the exam?
  c What did comprehensive schools try to do for the motivation of pupils?

Understanding concepts

1 **Similarity/difference**
  a What kinds of schools were there in England in the early 19th century?
  b What were the faults of each kind?
  c Why did the Industrial Revolution bring about a need for better education?

2 **Causation/motivation**
  a What were the motives of those who set up Sunday Schools?
  b What were the motives of those who ran voluntary schools?
  c What were the motives behind the 1870 Education Act?
  d Some people had been campaigning for a system of education for all children since the 1820s, yet this was not achieved until the 1870 Act. Why did it take so long?

3 **Change/continuity**
  a What were state schools like:

  i in the 1890s;
  ii in the 1930s?
  b What kind of state secondary education was available
  i in the 1930s;
  ii in the 1950s;
  iii in the 1970s?
  c Why did it take so long for secondary education for all to be achieved?

Themes for discussion

1 a What do you think should be the *aims* of an education system?
  b Do you agree with any of the statements of aims in this chapter?

2 Public – fee-paying – schools have continued right through this period.
  a Why do parents choose to spend money on sending their children to fee-paying schools?
  b What effect does this have on:
  i state schools;
  ii Britain?

23 The Decline of Religion 1700–1980s

SOURCE 1 Middle-class family at prayers, 19th century

SOURCE 2A A Victorian parson with his family and servants (the parson is standing on the left)

Role of the Church

Source 1 shows a middle-class man reading morning prayers with his family and servants. Most middle- and upper-class families did this every day in Victorian Britain. Working-class people were rarely able to take time to do this, although a large proportion of them went to church or chapel regularly. Even those who didn't worship every Sunday probably thought of themselves as Christians. Religion certainly played a much larger part in the life of the country than it does now. As Chapters 14, 19 and 22 show, factory reform, trade unions and education were deeply influenced by religion. There was even a religious side to party politics.

? QUESTION

Which are family and which are servants in Source 1?

The Church of England

The biggest and most powerful church throughout the time-span of this book was the Church of England. In the century after 1750 it was much more powerful than it is today. All posts in the Army and Navy, the Civil Service and the law were only open to Anglicans, as were the universities of Oxford and Cambridge. MPs and members of town corporations had to be Anglicans. The Church of England had close links with the Crown, as the monarch was (and is) Head of Church. Bishops, then as now, had seats in the House of Lords, and many of them were members of the aristocracy.

The basic unit of the Church of England was the village church. Here, too, the upper-class connections were made clear. The parson, with the squire, ruled the village. In fact in some villages the squire was also the parson (in which case they were called squarsons). In 1800 a quarter of all JPs were clergymen. The parson collected tithes from the farmers – a tenth of all their produce. The class differences of the villages were made clear in Church, as the better-off could rent a pew which was nearer the front, and more comfortable than the rest.

 SOURCE 2B

Some of the pews for the rich were padded, lined, cushioned, supplied with every comfort. The poor, on the other hand, were seated on stools in the aisles; many of the seats were without backs, to prevent the occupants from falling asleep during the sermon, and the cold, damp stone beneath their feet was the only place to kneel during the prayers.

Glyde, *Ipswich* in 1850

SOURCE 2C **Verse from a Victorian hymn, 'All Things Bright and Beautiful'**

The rich man in his parlour
The poor man at his gate,
God made the low and mighty
And ordered their estate.

? QUESTIONS

a) Which are family, and which are servants in Source 2A?
b) What impression of the Church of England would be given by the appearance of the church as described in Source 2B?
c) What is the message of the verse quoted in Source 2C?

The message that the parson preached was obedience: God had made the rich to own the land and give orders, and the poor to work and obey them. The close link between the parson and the upper classes was always evident: Holy Communion was given to the upper-class members of the congregation first, while labourers and their families waited. Also, the poorer villagers, many of whom could not read at all, found it difficult to follow the Prayer Book.

Nevertheless, most villagers did attend church, mainly from custom and habit, although there were other reasons too. Many were the

tenants, or farm labourers, of the squire, the parson or one of their rich farmer friends. To fail to show your face in church was to risk losing your farm, or your job, and thus your home, too. Poor villagers attended in some places in order to qualify for an annual charity handout of coal, bread, or blankets.

The Church of England in difficulties

The Church of England's system of reaching the people through the village parson did not always work very well by the late 18th century. In large areas of Wales, the West and the North, villages were too scattered and the pay too low to attract good ministers. Clergy were trained at Oxford and Cambridge universities. The standards of education there had declined, so many of them did not do their job properly. Many parsons preferred to spend their time hunting with the squire. They appointed a curate on a low salary to take the services.

Much more serious for the Church of England were the changes taking place in Britain as a result of industrialisation. As shown in Chapter 11, people were moving from the country to the towns and cities in ever-increasing numbers. Of course, there were parish churches in towns, but few parsons made much of an effort to contact the newly-arrived factory workers. Even if they had tried to, the Church would have been unable to cope

with the huge and rapid increase in numbers. No effort was made to build new churches in industrial towns. In some industrial towns and mining villages therefore, religion had no influence on people's lives.

The Methodists

John Wesley

Into this gap came the Methodists, led by their founder, John Wesley (1703–91). Wesley trained as a Church of England priest at Oxford. He was a keen student and, with some friends, he worked out a course of prayers and religious exercises. These were done *methodically*, and thus Wesley and his followers earned the name of Methodists.

Wesley's struggle to lead a religious life continued after leaving Oxford. In 1736 he went to the USA, to Georgia, and on his return in 1738 he had a deep religious experience, of which he said, 'I felt my heart strangely warmed. I felt that I did trust in Christ and an assurance was given me that He had taken my sins and saved me from the law of sin and death.'

From that point Wesley began a life of travelling and preaching. He rode thousands of miles, visiting miners in Cornwall, factory towns in Lancashire, fishing villages and great cities. Everywhere he went he preached to the people, wherever they would gather to listen to him.

SOURCE 3A **Gwennap Pit, near Redruth, Cornwall, where Wesley often preached**

■ SOURCE 3B

We reached Gwennap a little before six and found the plain covered from end to end: it was estimated that there were ten thousand people. I could not conclude until it was so dark we could scarce see one another; and there was on all sides the deepest attention; none speaking, stirring, or scarce looking aside. Surely here, in a temple not made by human hands, was God worshipped in the beauty of Holiness.

John Wesley's Journal, 1773

? QUESTIONS

a) From Source 3A, what kind of area does Gwennap appear to be in?

b) Most of Wesley's listeners at Gwennap would be tin-miners and their families. What do you think was the Church of England's attitude to such people?

c) Wesley preached at Gwennap 17 times in his career. How do you think that would affect his relationship with the local parish priest?

d) How does the scene described in Source 3B compare with the description of a Church of England church, Source 2B?

Wesley preached 40 000 sermons in the last 53 years of his life, an average of over two a day. He did not preach in churches, but in the open air, in fields, from the tops of walls and on hillsides. His message was simple: repent, stop drinking, gambling, swearing, and lead a sober Christian life, or you will go to hell. Often he met violence and abuse, but he persisted. His direct message appealed to many people.

Another great preacher, George Whitfield, joined him. John Wesley's brother, Charles, composed many good hymns, which added to the power and excitement of his meetings.

Methodism

Wesley always wanted to stay in the Church of England. He supported its beliefs and only preached out of doors when local priests refused to let him preach from their pulpits. Reluctantly, however, he split from the Church of England in 1784 and started the Methodist Church. The system of organisation he worked out was ideally suited to the rapidly-changing industrial communities where his support lay. A local group, or 'class' of 12 people was formed, and would meet in each other's homes, or in barns or warehouses. One of them could be elected as a preacher. Several classes could combine into a society which could then build a chapel and appoint a minister, if they wished.

The stirring hymns and simple but powerful sermons Wesley preached had a tremendous effect on people. Men and women often danced, cried or fainted at his meetings and came away determined to change their ways and to convert others. The system of classes gave power to working people to run their own church. Many became powerful lay preachers themselves. (A lay preacher is someone who preaches and takes a service, but is not an ordained, full-time minister.) Methodism continued to grow after Wesley's death in 1791. There were a quarter of a million Methodists in Britain in 1815, and another quarter of a million abroad, mostly in the USA.

Other Dissenters

Other groups had broken away from the Church of England in the 17th century and continued to exist into the 18th century. The main ones were Congregationalists, Presbyterians, Baptists, Unitarians and Quakers. Together with the Methodists, they were called Dissenters or Nonconformists. Their members were generally more middle-class than the early Methodists. They, too, made some effort to reach out to the new groups of workers in the towns and cities. As a result, the new industrial areas often had several chapels but no church.

■ SOURCE 4B Interior of a nonconformist chapel

This movement away from the Church of England was especially strong in Wales. The Church had always been weak in Wales, with badly-paid clergy and poor organisation. Welsh-speaking tenant farmers objected to being forced to attend the Church of England by the landowner.

■ SOURCE 4A Moriah Baptist Chapel, South Wales

■ *SOURCE 4C* **Letter from a landowner in Carmarthen to his tenants, 1860**

Having been placed by God here as a landowner, I feel the responsibility of my situation, to make use of the property entrusted to my care by choosing those persons to be my tenants who can and will support our Church. Deeply impressed with these considerations, I feel morally bound to set before you two alternatives, namely, either to attend our Church services with your family, or quit the farm which you hold of me.

? **QUESTIONS**

a) The Welsh called this practice 'the screw'. Explain in your own words what 'the screw' was.

b) What effect would a letter like this have on a Welsh-speaking Methodist tenant?

Nonconformists, especially the Methodists and Baptists, found ready support in Wales. Their members were mostly ordinary people, and so were often Welsh-speaking. The Nonconformists' chapels were thus closely linked with Welsh nationalism and had firm local roots. They provided education, libraries, choirs, religion and a focus for social life. By 1880 Nonconformists outnumbered Anglicans in Wales by three to one.

Nonconformism, more especially Methodism, was a powerful force in England too. The chapels gave working people a chance to organise themselves and take responsibility. Lay preachers learnt not to be afraid to speak in public. Their confidence, their upright and trustworthy way of life made them obvious choices as trade union officials. Joseph Arch, and many officials of the National Agricultural Labourers Union, were Methodist lay preachers.

Chapels also formed the basis of people's social life. A Norfolk labourer recalled: 'A lot of people used to come from nearby villages for the Chapel Anniversary, for in those days there was little other entertainment beyond going for a walk or to church or chapel.'

Nonconformists attacked the older, more violent sports such as dog-fights, bear-baiting and ratting. These were usually accompanied by drinking and gambling. The chapels organised brass-band contests, outings, talks and lots of tea-parties.

Some people argue that Methodism distracted working people from the awfulness of their lives. By giving them a purpose, and a hope for life after death, it prevented a revolution in Britain. Others argue that Methodism actually helped working people form their own organisations and discover their own power.

Revival in the Church of England

By the 1830s and 1840s the Church of England began to take stock of its position. Britain was no longer a country of cosy villages, with the parsons telling the labourers how to behave. Huge new cities had grown up. Millions of people in them either had no knowledge of religion, or had joined the Nonconformists. The rapid growth of Methodism showed up the failure of the Church of England to reach these people. The links between the Church and the upper classes were not necessarily an advantage, as the Vicar of Leeds pointed out (Source 5A).

■ *SOURCE 5A*

The people in rural areas are generally indifferent to the Church – luke-warmness is their sin. But in industrial areas the Church is the object of hate to the working classes. They consider themselves to be an oppressed people ... they consider the Church to belong to their oppressors. Hence they hate it, and consider a man of the working classes who is a Churchman to be a traitor ...

Letter, July 1843 (adapted)

? *QUESTIONS*

a) What was the attitude of the working classes to the Church in towns, according to Source 5A?

b) How far does the fact that the letter (Source 5A) was written by the Vicar of Leeds make you more willing to accept its reliability?

c) According to Source 5B, what was the most popular sect in 1851:

  i in England and Wales?
  ii in Leeds?

d) Explain the difference between your answers to c) i and c) ii.

e) Why do you think there was a difference in the percentage who actually attended a place of worship , between the country as a whole, and Leeds?

f) People were shocked that so few were going to church at all. Does this table give us any information about whether the country was getting more, or less, religious?

g) What can this table tell us about religion in rural areas?

h) How far does the table support the views of the Vicar of Leeds (Source 5A)?

■ *SOURCE 5B* **Results of the 1851 religious census: percentage of believers among the population**

	England and Wales	Leeds
Church of England	52	34
Methodists	21	42
Other Nonconformists	20	13
Roman Catholics	4	6
% of total population who attend a place of worship	58	47

Effects of the 1851 religious census

The census was disturbing for many reasons. First, only a little over half the population attended any form of church or chapel. The figures for industrial cities like Leeds were even more disturbing, with less than half the population at church. Parts of London showed less than one third. Also worrying to Anglicans was the information that, even among practising Christians, barely half went to the Church of England. Again, the figures were worse for industrial areas, where Methodism was now the main faith.

Various groups within the Church of England tried to make changes. The Oxford Movement revived interest in ritual. Its members felt that the Church should emphasise its ancient roots and moving ceremonies. Another group, the Evangeli-

SOURCE 5C St Mary Magdalene, Paddington, built in 1873

men. By 1900 a Church of England vicar was more likely to be playing tennis with local farmers than shooting with the squire; more likely to be cycling round the parish than driving round in a pony and trap.

The Salvation Army

Another organisation which rapidly made a reputation for working for the most unfortunate in society was the Salvation Army. The Army's founder, William Booth, began as a Methodist. He opened a mission in Whitechapel in 1865 (Source 6). He soon realised that the poor had to be fed before they were capable of listening to his sermons. The idea of an Army, with ranks, bands and uniforms, came to him in 1878, and he formed the Salvation Army. They have continued their work with the very poor, alcoholics and homeless ever since.

■ SOURCE 6 Whitechapel Mission, 1870

cals, had a wider influence. They believed that the church had to get out into the industrial towns and cities and help the working people. One of the leading Evangelicals was Lord Shaftesbury, who campaigned to reform conditions in factories and mines. He was also President of the Ragged Schools Union. Another Evangelical was William Wilberforce, the anti-slavery campaigner. The Christian Socialists also built links between the Church and working people.

Many churches were built in working-class areas to try to reach working people. The church in 5C had colourful services, with music and ritual. The clergy also set up a working men's club, a choir school and other ordinary schools.

? QUESTION

Why has the church in Source 5C been built with pointed-arched windows, like a much older building?

Even in rural areas the Church changed. Pew rents were abolished in most churches. The Tithe Commutation Act 1836 changed the payment of tithe to a fixed cash amount. As a result the link between parsons and farmers was weakened. With the farming depression of the late 19th century, (see Chapter 8), tithe payments dropped. The £100 average tithe payment in 1835 was worth only £67 by 1901. With falling incomes, the life of a village priest stopped attracting as many upper-class

? QUESTIONS

a) What things do the two Salvation Army buildings in Source 6 offer?

b) Why do you think Booth chose to go to Whitechapel, in the poorest part of London?

The Decline of Religion

In 1859 Charles Darwin published his *Origin of Species*, putting forward his theory of evolution. This said that all living things had evolved from basic organisms over millions of years. Darwin did not intend to attack religion, but many people thought his theory undermined the Christian beliefs that God had made the world in six days. As other scientific ideas became popular, so other religious beliefs – miracles, for example – came under attack.

Another religious survey, carried out, in 1882, revealed a considerable decline in church or chapel attendances, since 1851 (Source 5B). Only 37% of the population now attended, and in some urban areas it was only 10%. The Church of England saw the greatest decline, while the Nonconformists stayed much the same as in 1851. Roman Catholicism had followed the immigration of Irish workers into British towns and cities (see Chapter 26). Roman Catholic churches were built in the poorer parts of towns,

where their people lived, and this survey showed an increase in their numbers. Altogether, though, the tight hold on people's lives which the churches enjoyed in the early 19th century was loosening. A lack of enthusiasm for religion affected all classes. It was even felt that Queen Victoria's own son, Edward, Prince of Wales, was uninterested in religion and leading a fairly immoral life. The decline affected rural areas too.

■ SOURCE 7 Description of a village at the end of the 19th century

If Lark Rise people had been asked their religion, the answer of nine out of ten would have been 'Church of England' for practically all of them were christened, married and buried as such, although in adult life few went to church between the baptisms of their offspring. The children were shepherded there after Sunday School, and about a dozen adults attended regularly. The rest stayed at home, the women cooking and nursing and the men, after shaving and cutting each other's hair, spent the rest of the day eating, sleeping, reading the newspaper and strolling round to see how their neighbours' pigs and gardens were looking.

F. Thompson, *Lark Rise to Candleford***, 1945**

In the 20th century the steady decline of the influence of religion and the churches has continued. Today less than 10% of the population go to a church or chapel regularly. Because the Church of England was originally the largest church, it has had the most to lose: in 1960 it had 3 million members, in 1980 1.8 million – although the fall in numbers seems to have stopped there.

For the majority of the population, Sunday is a holiday, a time to relax and enjoy leisure activities. Science has provided answers to many of the great mysteries of life, to which religion at one time seemed to have the only key. A generally better standard of living has softened the sharp need for a spiritual message which once led people to walk miles to hear Wesley preach. Britain is now a multi-cultural society, too. Trends in immigration since 1945 (see Chapter 26) have meant that many British people now belong to non-Christian religious faiths.

Assignments

Empathy

1 **a** What were the attitudes of the Church of England towards the different classes in rural society at the beginning of this period?
  b What were the attitudes of the Church of England towards industrial areas at the beginning of this period?
  c How did both these attitudes change through the 19th century?
2 You have just been to hear John Wesley preach to a crowd of people.
  a Describe what happened and what he said.
  b Describe the effect of the meeting on yourself, and other people.

Understanding concepts

1 **Similarity/difference**
  a Why was the Church of England unable to adapt to the changes in British life caused by industrialisation?
  b How was Methodism better organised to cope?
  c How did the Church of England try to change to meet the new situation?

2 **Change/continuity**
  a Why did Methodism appeal so strongly to people in Industrial Britain?
  b Why has the appeal of all types of religion declined in the last 150 years?

Theme for discussion

From your reading of this book, how much has British Social and Economic History in the last 200 years been affected by religion, or by people with a strong religious belief?

24

Communications 1800–1980s

Speed of Change

If you watch the news on television tonight you will see moving, colour pictures of events that have taken place today all over Britain and in other countries. In the early 19th century news travelled far more slowly. The battle of Trafalgar took place on October 22, 1805, but the news did not reach London until November 6. It then took several more days to reach other parts of Britain. It is this tremendous change in the methods and speed of sending messages, in words and pictures, which we shall be dealing with in this chapter. The change took place because of a number of spectacular inventions, sometimes called the 'second wave' of inventions (the 'first wave' being those described in Section A). It often took several inventors, working on the same idea over many years, to turn the basic discovery into a machine which worked. Look for this time-lag between the discovery and application of the inventions described in this chapter, and try to explain what caused it.

Post, Telegraph and Telephone

The post

From the 16th century there had been a mail service for the use of the government. For that reason it was called the Royal Mail, and private citizens could pay to have their letters taken with official ones. Improvements in coaches and turnpike roads (see Chapter 6) increased the speed of the Royal Mail. But the system for using it was chaotic and very expensive. The charges depended on the weight of the letter and the distance it was carried. An ordinary letter could cost 1*s* (5p), which was a day's

wages for a working person. This was not paid by the sender, but by the receiver of the letter, who had to pay the postman for it. Further, many towns had no post office.

The growth of business and trade in Britain brought a need for a better system. By the 1830s railways brought the opportunity for a much faster service. Rowland Hill proposed a 'penny post' and the idea was begun in 1840. The sender of the letter bought a stamp for 1*d* (½p) and fixed it to the letter. This was not only cheaper but saved enormous amounts of time and effort.

SOURCE 1A Penny Black stamp, 1840

SOURCE 1B First pillar-box, 1855

a) Whose head is on the stamp?
b) Look at a modern British stamp and one from another country. Why do you think the name of the country is not put on British stamps?
c) The new 'penny post' was a great success. Why were people so ready to make use of it?

Rowland Hill also invented the sticky-backed stamp, and the perforated sheet, so that individual stamps could just be torn off as needed. The number of letters sent increased from 76 million in 1838 to 642 million in 1867.

The telegraph

Back in the 18th century the discovery was made that electric signals could be sent along wires. In 1837 William Cooke and Charles Wheat-

SOURCE 2A The five-needle telegraph, 1837

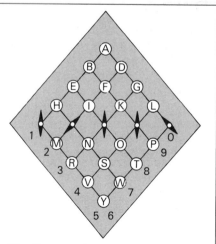

The five needles can be turned by electric currents either to right or left. When one needle alone is operated a number is indicated. When two needles are operated together a letter is indicated. For example needles 2 and 5, operated together, as shown, point to letter D. If the same needles were operated one after another they would indicate numbers 2 and 0.

■ *SOURCE 2B* **Great Eastern laying trans-Atlantic cable, 1866**

stone invented the five-needle telegraph (Source 2A). Electric currents moved the needles in pairs to point to different letters of the alphabet. In this way messages could be sent instantly.

The telegraph was first used by the railways to send information about trains. The advantages for business were soon realised, however. A telegraph cable was laid under the English Channel in 1850, so messages could be transmitted between London and Paris. In 1866, after various unsuccessful attempts, a trans-Atlantic cable was laid (see Source 2B). By that time the needle system had been dropped in favour of Morse code, an alphabet of dots and dashes invented by an American, Samuel Morse. In 1869 the Post Office took over all telegraph systems in Britain.

? *QUESTIONS*

a) In what way was the telegraph a better method of communication than sending a letter?
b) In what way was it not as useful as sending a letter?

The telephone

The Morse code required specialist operators to send and receive it. The next stage was to invent a system to allow ordinary speech to be transmitted. A Scot living in the USA, Alexander Graham Bell, invented a method of turning speech into electrical waves in 1876. By 1879 there were telephone exchanges in London, Liverpool and Manchester.

■ *SOURCE 3A* **Early telephone**

■ *SOURCE 3B* **London telephone exchange, 1883**

At first there were private telephone companies; in 1912 the Post Office took over all these, except the service in Hull. Telephones were widely used in business. They provided office jobs for women at a time when women were looking for work outside the home. Private telephones were not as common in Britain as in the USA, however. In 1920, only 2% of all homes in Britain had a telephone. The trans-Atlantic telephone link was set up in 1927. In 1958 Subscriber Trunk Dialling (STD) was begun, allowing users to dial their own long-distance, or trunk, calls. (Before then all trunk calls had to be connected by the operator.)

❓ *QUESTIONS*

a) British people were slow to make use of the telephone. Why do you think this was?

b) A telephone call provides rapid communication. Why do people still send letters?

The number of telephone calls increased rapidly after the Second World War: in 1930 there were 1.3 billion calls made per year, with a further half a million long-distance calls; by 1981 there were 20 billion calls and 117 million long-distance calls. In 1981 the telephone service was separated from the Post Office

and called British Telecom. This meant that the Post Office's control over the whole system was broken. In 1985 the government privatised British Telecom, and other companies were allowed to compete with it.

Newspapers

The British read more newspapers than any other country in Europe. The existence of popular national, daily and local newspapers has come about for several reasons.

Weekly news sheets began in the 17th century, and the first daily paper was *Daily Courant*, begun in 1702. By 1815 there were about 250 newspapers in existence, but they were nearly all local papers. The lack of fast, cheap transport meant that the news could not be gathered, nor papers sold, over a wide area. Papers were expensive, too, because there were taxes on advertisements, newsprint and newspapers themselves. These taxes were partly imposed because the government did not want to be criticised in print. Few people could read anyway, and this, together with the price, meant that most newspaper readers came from the better-off classes. Nevertheless, by

the mid-19th century newspapers were becoming quite important. Reports of the government's mishandling of the Crimean War in *The Times* led to a change of government in 1854.

Great changes took place in newspapers in the second half of the 19th century. The taxes on them were removed in the 1850s. The invention of the telegraph meant that news could be collected rapidly from any part of Britain, or even Europe. The news agency, Reuters, was set up in 1851 to collect news and sell it to newspapers. Railways could carry newspapers printed in London to any part of Britain by the next morning. National newspapers began to become more important than local ones.

More and more people could now read, especially after the Education Act 1870. Businesses were also looking for more ways of advertising. Alfred Harmsworth saw that the newspapers of the time were still written for upper-class readers. There were long, serious articles, and few pictures. He believed a cheap newspaper would sell well to the millions of ordinary people who had learnt to read. If it did, he could carry lots of advertisements, and the money from these would allow him to keep the price low. He launched the *Daily Mail* in 1896, at

SOURCE 4A Page from the *Daily Mail*, 1896

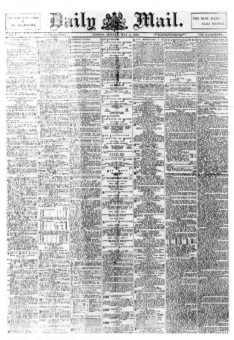

SOURCE 4B Page from the *Sun*, 1987

SOURCE 4C Linotype machine, invented in 1886

the price of ½*d* (0.25p). Using new steam-powered printing presses he could print half a million copies a day. The *Daily Express* followed in 1900 and the *Daily Mirror* in 1904.

These papers were not 'sensational' by modern standards (see Sources 4A and 4B). However, they were more chatty and less serious than any other newspapers of the time.

With the coming of television the sales of some newspapers declined and they stopped publication. In the 1970s the *Sun* became the best-selling paper at over 4 million copies per day. It offers very little

news apart from stories about the private lives of T.V. stars and the royal family.

Modern 1980s technology has changed the newspaper industry. The skilled Linotype machine operator (see Source 4C) is now no longer needed. Journalists can type their stories direct into the computer system. Computerised typesetting can produce newspapers so cheaply that all production costs can be covered by advertisements and the newspapers can be given away, not sold. Colour pictures can also be included. This streamlining has led to clashes between some newspaper owners and the printers' unions, who see their members' jobs disappearing.

? *QUESTIONS*

a) What differences are there between the two newspapers in Sources 4A and 4B?

b) Why do you think newspapers have changed in this way?

c) The linotype operator's skills are becoming obsolete. What other inventions have you read about in this book which have made some skills obsolete?

Radio

In 1864, a scientist, James Clark Maxwell, proved the existence of radio waves. Later, Hertz, another scientist, carried out experiments in transmitting them. An Italian scientist, Marconi, came to Britain to develop his ideas for radio transmission. He carried out successful experiments on Salisbury Plain in 1896. In 1901 he attempted to send a radio signal from Cornwall across the Atlantic to Newfoundland. The signal, the letter 's' in Morse, was faintly heard, proving that radio waves followed the curve of the earth. Other inventions, such as the thermionic valve, invented by J. A. Fleming in 1904, and the amplifier, invented by Lee de Forest in 1907, improved the equipment.

At first radio was mainly used by ships at sea, but also by the police, army and Post Office. It was a radio message sent to the captain of a trans-Atlantic liner which enabled the police to arrest Dr Crippen, the murderer, in 1910. It was the radio call for help sent out by the sinking *Titanic*, in 1912, that brought other

SOURCE 5A Rise and fall in the number of radio licences (millions)

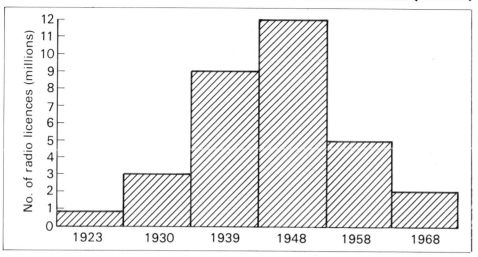

ships to the rescue and saved 700 lives.

At that time radio was called the 'wireless' to distinguish it from the telephone, which needed wires to link the transmitter and receiver. Early users of radios had both receivers and transmitters. For this reason they were controlled by the Post Office and owners had to pay a licence of 5s (25p). Then, from 1920, Marconi's company in Chelmsford began broadcasting their own programmes. People only needed a radio receiver to hear them, and listened through headphones. From 1922 the British Broadcasting Company put out regular programmes; in 1926 the government set up the British Broadcasting Corporation – the BBC – with a monopoly of all radio broadcasting.

The growth of radio

Unlike almost all other countries, Britain had a radio broadcasting system paid for not by advertisements, like newspapers, but by the licence fee. The government was worried about the effect advertisements would have on the quality of programmes. They put in control of the BBC a man who believed that broadcasting had a serious purpose, Lord Reith. Under his control the BBC built up a wide range of types of programme: music of all kinds, talks, comedy shows, quizzes, discussions, drama and documentaries. Reith was a clergyman's son, and made sure Sunday programmes had a strong religious tone. He also banned comedians who told 'dirty' jokes.

SOURCE 5B BBC radio programmes for Christmas Day, 1934

10.45 Christmas Morning Service
1.00 Troxy Grand Orchestra
1.55 Empire Exchange
3.00 The King
3.15 Pini's Tango Orchestra
3.55 John Armstrong (tenor)
4.15 BBC Northern Orchestra
5.15 Dance Music

SOURCE 5C

On the programme side, alongside huge dollops of light music, light entertainment and sport were doses of first-class music, drama and talks. The result was to educate people to enjoy new pleasures. This has been most obvious in music. The name Bach was enough to raise a laugh from a music-hall audience in the early days. Nowadays records of Bach are asked for in 'Family Favourites'.

In talks and school broadcasts the BBC went further than any other radio organisation in the world.

V. Ogilvie, *Our Times*, published 1953

SOURCE 5D Family group gathered for tea by the radio, 1930

? QUESTIONS

a) Do the figures in Source 5A prove that BBC radio was popular up to the late 1940s?

b) Do they prove that Lord Reith's approach to broadcasting was the right one?

c) Does the picture, Source 5D prove that radio was popular?

d) Compare Source 5B with the programmes on Radio One for last Christmas Day. What differences and similarities are there?

e) What is the attitude of the writer of Source 5C to radio? Do you agree with him?

f) What do these four sources tell you about the differences in people's attitudes and tastes between nowadays and the 1930s and 1940s?

During the Second World War radio became an essential service. Winston Churchill's famous radio speeches rallied the British people; people were eager for news, and special announcements of victories or defeats were made; entertainment also made people forget the war. Other countries, tired of propaganda from Nazi-controlled radio stations, listened to the BBC Foreign Service for news. People whose countries had been overrun by enemies listened to their leaders broadcast to them from exile in London. It was at this time that the BBC's good reputation was made.

By 1960 people were changing from radio to television. They were also getting tired of the stuffy attitude of 'Auntie' BBC. Young people, eager to hear more pop music than the BBC was prepared to play, tuned in to pirate radio stations. Because of the BBC monopoly, it was illegal for anyone else to broadcast from within Britain. Pirate radio stations were installed on ships anchored just outside British waters. They took advertising, played pop records and gained a wide audience. In the face of this competition BBC radio was modernised and reorganised into Radios One, Two, Three and Four, each with a different style. There has also been a growth of BBC and commercial local radio stations.

Recording sound

The first machine to record sound was invented by the American, Thomas Edison, in 1876. He called it a 'phonograph', and it played cylinders.

QUESTIONS

a) What kind of sounds did the phonograph play?

b) At the price of £2 2s (£2.10) in 1900, who would buy such a machine?

Phonographs became very popular, and many famous artists were recorded. Later the disc, turning at 78 revolutions per minute, was invented and used until the 1950s. There were great improvements in the 1960s in sound recording and reproduction techniques. Sound

■ **SOURCE 6** **Advertisement for a phonograph, 1900**

WHAT WILL YOU DO

IN THE

LONG, COLD, DARK, SHIVERY EVENINGS,

WHEN YOUR HEALTH AND CONVENIENCE COMPEL YOU TO STAY

INDOORS ?

WHY!!! HAVE A PHONOGRAPH, OF COURSE.

It is the FINEST ENTERTAINER in the WORLD.

There is nothing equal to it in the whole Realm of Art.

It imitates any and every Musical Instrument, any and every natural sound, faithfully :

the HUMAN VOICE, the NOISE OF THE CATARACT, the BOOM OF THE GUN, the VOICES OF BIRDS OR ANIMALS.

From

£2 2s.

THE GREATEST MIMIC.

A Valuable Teacher of Acoustics. Most Interesting to Old or Young A Pleasure and Charm to the Suffering, bringing to them the Brightness and Amusements of the outside World by its faithful reproductions of Operas, New Songs, Speeches, &c.

EVERY HOME WILL sooner or later have its **PHONOGRAPH** as a **NECESSITY.**
HAVE YOURS NOW; you will enjoy it longer.

Brought within the reach of every family by Mr. Edison's last production at **£2 2s.**

Send for our Illustrated Catalogues to

EDISON - BELL CONSOLIDATED PHONOGRAPH CO., LD.,
Or to our Licensees— 39, Charing Cross Road, **W.C**
EDISONIA LD., 25 to 22, Banner Street. and City Show-Rooms, 21, Cheapside, E.C., **LONDON.**

was recorded in stereo, diamond styluses were used to give high-fidelity reproduction, and the 33⅓ r.p.m. long-playing disc became widely used. These improvements, with increasing prosperity and the growth of interest in 'pop' music, brought a huge boom in the recorded music industry. Recent technical improvements include digital recordings and the compact disc, read by laser and not a stylus.

Recordings on wire had been made in 1898, and the first recordings on tape were made in 1935. Tape-recorders were used in radio stations, but the invention of the cheap audio-cassette in the 1960s made this a popular means of listening to recorded music. Cheap transistors and compact batteries have meant that radios and tape-recorders can now be made small, light and portable.

■ *SOURCE 7A* **Cinema, built in the 1930s**

Cinema

The first successful photographs were taken by Edward Fox-Talbot in 1839. In the early days of photography the subjects had to remain still for long exposure times – up to 10 minutes. Many early photographs have been included in this book, and the long exposure times account for the serious expressions on people's faces. Cameras were also very heavy and bulky in the early days, but by the end of the century fast film, handy-sized cameras and rolls of film had all been invented.

Photographs and pictures on glass provided a popular form of entertainment in Victorian times – the 'magic lantern show'. The first films showing movement were made by the Lumière bothers in

Paris in the 1890s. This proved such a popular attraction that the idea spread all over the world. There were 400 cinemas in London alone by 1914.

The great boom in the film industry took place between the wars. Films had to be made out of doors in good sunlight, and one place where this was usually available was Hollywood, in southern California. Film companies and film stars, including British actors like Charlie Chaplin, flocked to Hollywood. From 1927 the government said that one film in five had to be British-made, but these films were far less popular than the romances, adventures and comedies put out by Hollywood. Sound films began in 1927.

By the 1930s most towns had at least one cinema, and probably two double bills of films a week. Many people went once or twice a week,

whatever was showing. For 6*d* (2½p) or 1*s* (5p) you could sit in warmth and comfort and escape from the Depression into the glamour of films.

In 1946 there were 4700 cinemas in Britain, and audiences of 30 million a week. By 1968 there were 2000 cinemas and 2 million attendances. The cause of this change was, of course, television, which offered even more entertainment than the cinema at an even lower price, every night of the week. At first the film industry fought back with big-screen, big-cast films that television could not handle. But homes were getting much more comfortable, television was improving and a visit to the cinema was becoming more expensive. Cinemas continued to close, and the video boom of the mid-1980s seemed to spell the end for all except a few.

■ SOURCE 7B **Cinema programmes in 1958**

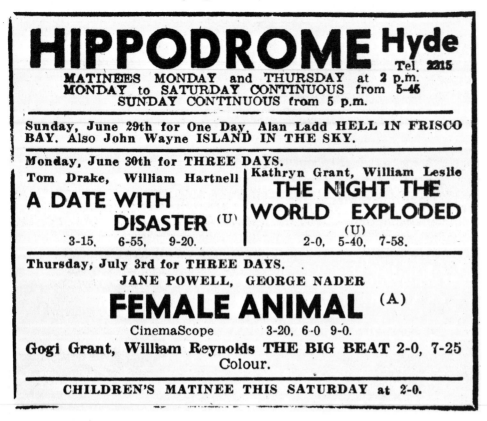

HIPPODROME Hyde

Tel. 2215

MATINEES MONDAY and THURSDAY at 2 p.m.
MONDAY to SATURDAY CONTINUOUS from 5-45
SUNDAY CONTINUOUS from 5 p.m.

Sunday, June 29th for One Day. Alan Ladd HELL IN FRISCO BAY. Also John Wayne ISLAND IN THE SKY.

Monday, June 30th for THREE DAYS.

Tom Drake, William Hartnell
A DATE WITH DISASTER (U)
3-15, 6-55, 9-20.

Kathryn Grant, William Leslie
THE NIGHT THE WORLD EXPLODED (U)
2-0, 5-40, 7-58.

Thursday, July 3rd for THREE DAYS.
JANE POWELL, GEORGE NADER
FEMALE ANIMAL (A)
CinemaScope   3-20, 6-0 9-0.

Gogi Grant, William Reynolds THE BIG BEAT 2-0, 7-25
Colour.

CHILDREN'S MATINEE THIS SATURDAY at 2-0.

? QUESTIONS

a) Cinemas aimed to provide popular entertainment. How did this aim affect:
   i) the design of cinemas and
   ii) the type of films made?

Television

The first television pictures were successfully shown in 1926, by a system invented by John Logie Baird. However, the system that became the basis of all our modern television was developed in 1935 by Isaac Schoenberg. This was based on the cathode-ray tube, invented in 1897. The BBC began to broadcast TV programmes from 1936. However, the television sets were large and expensive, with tiny screens. Only about 20 000 people, all in the London area, had sets when the war broke out and TV programmes stopped.

The service was resumed after the war, but it was really the televising of the coronation of Queen Elizabeth II in 1953 which began the growth of TV. The Coronation was watched by 25 million people, many of whom had bought a set specially for the occasion. From the 1950s companies began to hire out televisions, as they were too expensive for many people to buy. Then in the 1960s printed circuits and transistors brought better pictures and cheaper, more reliable sets. By 1965 there were 13 million sets in Britain and 85% of homes had one; by 1977 95% of homes had a television.

In 1955 commercial television started. The various original commercial companies sold advertising time and used this income to make programmes. These companies were controlled by one body, the Independent Television Authority (renamed the Independent Broadcasting Authority from 1973), to ensure the standard of their programmes was kept up. The BBC still depended on the licence fee, and competition from commercial television caused a re-thinking of its rather old-fashioned programmes. Under Hugh Carleton-Greene, Director-General from 1961, the BBC began to modernise its output with lively interviews, hard-hitting comedy and documentaries on important subjects. BBC2 began in 1964, so that the BBC had two channels on which to offer both popular and specialist programmes. Colour was introduced in 1969, Channel 4 in 1982 and breakfast-time television in 1983.

■ SOURCE 8

In the Second World War ... the BBC said what most people were prepared to hear; it brought them the voices of the leaders, and of Churchill in particular, and it introduced many of them to the pleasures of music and drama which they had never experienced before.... It was not the BBC which brought about the divisions in society, but its programmes reflected them. It began to publish things which some people didn't want to hear.... the BBC, to some people seemed to be deliberately seeking out targets to knock. At the same time, the BBC did not altogether escape criticism from the opposite direction, that it was old-fashioned, clinging to the values of a society that was passing.

Interview with Hugh Carleton-Greene, 1973

? QUESTIONS

a) What comparison does Hugh Carleton-Greene make between the BBC in the war years and in the 1960s?
b) What types of criticism has the BBC had?
c) Which, if any, of these criticisms of the BBC do you agree with?

Today nearly everybody watches television regularly. A survey in 1982 found that people spent nearly half their leisure time watching television. Satellites (of which the first was Telstar, launched in 1962) can bring pictures of events in any part of the world into the home. Most people get their news information from TV; they also see national occasions, sport and entertainment. The popularity and cheapness of video-recorders makes it likely that people will spend even more time watching television. Of all the many startling and clever inventions described in this chapter, it is the one which has had the greatest effect on the social life of the people of Britain.

Information Technology

This chapter has described several methods of communication. Some carry printed or written words, some carry conversation, some carry pictures. As well as communicating, people in many jobs need to store information. They also need to study it and take decisions about it.

In the past, this has mostly been done on paper. Businesses and government departments have kept masses of paper files. Letters have been typed and written.

In recent years, computers have brought about many changes. Information on computer can be stored more easily – on discs. It can be studied or processed more quickly. It can also be transmitted a great deal more quickly. People working in different parts of the country, or abroad, can exchange information – words, diagrams, figures – between their computers. This information is transmitted through the telephone system, which itself is controlled by computers. This Integrated Services Digital Network is growing rapidly, as more and more people find it makes their jobs easier. At the same time, of course, some people, employed as typists or filing clerks, are losing their jobs.

Assignments

Empathy

1 It is 1890 and you have just had a telephone, like the one in Source 3A, installed in your house. Describe your feelings as you make your first telephone call.
2 The cinema was very popular in the 1940s, but it has now become a little-used facility. How much is this due to new inventions? How much is it due to changes in people's habits and attitudes?

Understanding concepts

1 Cause/effect
What have been the most important results of each of the following:
  i the Penny Post;
  ii the telephone;
  iii the telegraph;
  iv radio;
  v recording;
  vi the home computer?

2 Similarity/difference
Several inventions described in this chapter have been used in different ways by:
  i ordinary people;
  ii businesses;
  iii others.
How have these three types of use been applied to:
  i letters;
  ii telephone;
  iii radio;
  iv computers?

3 Change/continuity
Several of the inventions described in this chapter have made some jobs unnecessary, so people have lost their employment (e.g. linotype operators). They have also created new jobs.
  a Which jobs have become, or may become unnecessary as the use of computers and information technology spreads?
  b Which new jobs have been, or will be created?

Themes for discussion

1 Which invention described in this chapter do you think has had most impact on the lives of the British people?
2 The inventions described in this chapter have made faster and better communication between people possible. Why has industrialisation made such a change necessary? How has it made such a change possible?

25

British Trade and Policy 1700–1980s

■ **SOURCE 1A** Goods produced at home and abroad

What is Trade?

■ **SOURCE 1B** Headline from *The Guardian*, December 1986

Increased Spending Goes on Imported Goods

❓ QUESTIONS

a) Which of the goods in Source 1A do you think are produced in Britain, and which are produced abroad?

b) Think of some food which you like that cannot be produced in Britain.

c) What other things do you use in your daily life at home or at school which cannot be produced in Britain?

d) What other things do you use in your daily life which were made abroad, but which *can* be produced in Britain?

e) Compare your answers to all these questions with the rest of your class.

f) Look at Source 1B. Why do you think it may cause problems if British people buy too many imported goods?

We all buy some goods made in foreign countries, because we cannot make them here, because we prefer the foreign goods, or because they are cheaper. These goods are called imports. Britain buys imports from other countries. But how does this country pay for them?

We sell British-made goods abroad. These are called exports. Because Britain needs so much in the way of imports – especially food, and raw materials for our industry – exports are very important. This chapter looks at the pattern of British imports and exports, or British trade, over the last 250 years.

Free trade or protectionism?

Over these 250 years, and right into the present, there has been argument about how trade should be carried out. Free trade is when goods are imported and exported between countries quite freely. The problem with this is that one country may be able to produce something much more cheaply than another. Everyone will buy the cheap goods, their home industry will collapse and lots of people will be put out of work. To stop this happening countries sometimes adopt a policy of protectionism. They make certain things coming into their country pay a duty, called a tariff. This then makes imports more expensive than the same things made at home, so the home industry is 'protected'. British trading policy has moved between protectionism and free trade over the last 250 years, and this chapter looks at the reasons for the changes.

British Trade in the 18th Century

Britain in the 18th century had strong protectionist policies. These were designed to protect British industry and shipping, and British colonies. Several European countries had set up colonies all over the world in the 16th and 17th centuries. Britain had colonies in West Africa, India, the West Indies and, especially, North America. A series of laws, the Navigation Acts 1651, 1660 and 1663, ensured that all the benefits of the colonies came to Britain. All colonial goods had to be brought to Britain to be sold, or re-exported elsewhere. All goods sold to the colonies had to come from Britain.

The Navigation Acts also protected the British shipping fleet (which was also the basis of the Navy): all goods coming to Britain had to be brought in British ships, or ships of the country the goods came from. There were also heavy tariffs on hundreds of items, in order to protect British industry. In addition, the export of machinery was forbidden, and skilled workers were not allowed to emigrate to foreign countries.

The Atlantic trade

Through the 18th century Britain's Atlantic trade, especially with North America, increased (see Map 1). Valuable colonial products, such as sugar from the West Indies, and cotton and tobacco from the American colonies, came to Britain. By the 1780s the population of the American colonies had grown to about 4 million. It provided a large – and protected – market for British manufactured goods, such as woollen and cotton textiles, hardware and other industrial products.

? QUESTIONS

a) Which was Britain's best customer at the end of the 17th century?

b) Which was Britain's best customer for manufactured goods 75 years later?

Britain benefitted a great deal from the law which required all

MAP 1 Britain's North Atlantic trade, 1770

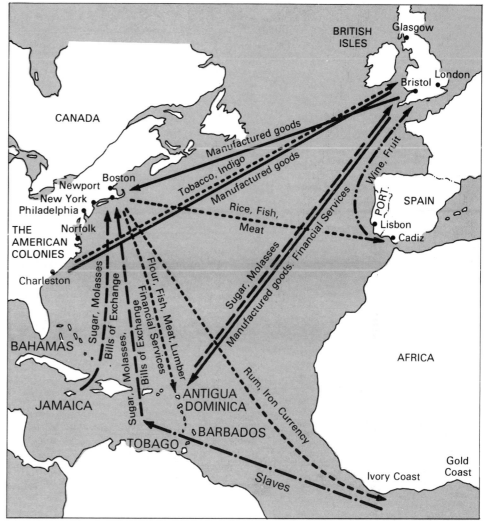

SOURCE 2A Value of British exports of manufactured goods (thousands of pounds)

	1699–1701	1772–4
Woollen goods		
To Europe	2745	2630
To Ireland and Channel Isles	26	219
To America and Africa	185	1148
To Far East	89	189
Other manufactured goods		
Europe	456	987
To Ireland and Channel Isles	60	280
To America and Africa	290	2533
To Far East	22	501

goods from British colonies to come to Britain before being re-exported elsewhere. In 1770 British exports were worth £14.3 million, of which £4.8 million was earned from re-exports.

The War of American Independence made little difference to this pattern of trade. After 1776 the USA could buy and sell where they liked, but Britain was still by far their best customer and supplier. As explained in Chapter 3, these were the years of the huge growth of cotton plantations in the southern USA. The cotton supplied the Lancashire cotton industry, and the plantation owners grew rich. They spent their money on a wide range of goods, most of them made in Britain or made elsewhere and supplied via Britain. The increase in the amount of raw cotton imports led to huge increases in shipping and port facilities in Britain. This trade needed banking, insurance and loan services, all of which Britain provided and profited from.

Protectionism and the Industrial Revolution

Some people think that the strongly protectionist policies of the 18th century helped bring about the Industrial Revolution. They argue that new industries were protected while they were getting started; also that British traders became rich and had money to invest in new enterprises. However, many of the protectionist laws were quite ineffective. Smuggling was common, and it is estimated that smuggled goods reached 30% of the value of official trade. Everyone took part, and the government forces were quite inadequate to stop it.

■ *SOURCE 2B* 'Smugglers' Song'

Them that asks no questions isn't told a lie
Watch the wall, my darling,
    while the Gentlemen go by!
Five and twenty ponies,
Trotting through the dark –
Brandy for the Parson
'Baccy for the Clerk;
Laces for a lady, letters for a spy.
Watch the wall, my darling,
    while the Gentlemen go by!

Rudyard Kipling, 1890s

⁇ *QUESTIONS*

a) Which are the items being smuggled, according to this source?
b) Which respectable people will receive the smuggled goods?
c) This source is a poem, written long after smuggling came to an end. Does it have any value as historical evidence? Explain your answer.
d) Does it have any value as evidence of how smuggling was regarded in Kipling's day?

The laws preventing the export of machinery and the emigration of skilled workers were not effective either.

Running the colonies themselves

was expensive: over the period 1760–76 Britain spent more on colonial wars than she earned by colonial trade. Nevertheless, a great deal of money was made in trade in the 18th century, and some of this was used to support Britain's industrial growth. It was the ports of the western side of Britain which benefited most, especially Bristol, Liverpool and Glasgow. The population of Bristol doubled between 1700 and 1750. Liverpool had under 7000 people in 1700, but 30000 by 1750.

Money from Glasgow went into Scotland's ironworks, coalmines and textile factories. Money from Liverpool was invested in industry in Lancashire. Abraham Darby (see Chapter 4) was backed by money from Bristol Quaker merchants. Capital for the Cyfarthfa ironworks in South Wales was provided by London merchants, Anthony Bacon and Richard Crawshay. Wealthy merchants also bought country estates and invested in agricultural improvements (see Chapter 2).

The Movement for Free Trade

Adam Smith and William Pitt the Younger

In a book published in 1776, called *The Wealth of Nations*, the writer Adam Smith put forward the idea of free trade. He argued that each country could produce some goods cheaply and export them. Goods that could be produced elsewhere cheaply should be imported.

■ *SOURCE 3*

The tailor does not attempt to make his own shoes, but buys them from the shoemaker. The shoemaker does not attempt to make his own clothes, but employs a tailor ... What is sensible in every family can hardly be wrong in a great kingdom.

A. Smith, *The Wealth of Nations*, 1776 (adapted)

⁇ *QUESTIONS*

a) How does Adam Smith explain Free Trade in Source 3?
b) What arguments would people

in favour of protectionism put against him?
c) Is it true that 'great kingdoms' should behave in the same way as families?

Adam Smith said that tariffs just made the prices of some things unnecessarily high and encouraged smuggling. He realised that the government made most of its money from tariffs, but pointed out that it was not necessary to put tariffs on so many things. (Even bullrushes had their import duty at that time!) A small tariff on a few basic essentials would raise the same amount, he said.

William Pitt the Younger, Prime Minister from 1784, agreed with Adam Smith. He wanted to stop smuggling, so he cut the duty on tea from 119% to 12.5%. Some of the favourite items for smugglers to bring in were French-made luxuries, such as wine, brandy and silk. Pitt made a trade treaty with France in 1786, cutting the tariffs on these items. In return the French lowered their tariffs on British textiles and other manufactured goods. This was just the kind of freedom which Adam Smith had in mind, with each country selling what it could make well. However, the coming of war in 1793 meant that the British government needed money. Tariffs were increased again to new levels, and the free trade movement ceased.

The Corn Laws

During the period of the Napoleonic Wars prices of corn were high, mainly because of poor harvests. Farmers were afraid that when the war ended cheap corn would flood into Britain from Europe and America. Prices would tumble down and they would lose out. They therefore used their power in Parliament to get the Corn Laws passed in 1815. These banned the import of foreign corn unless there was a shortage and the price went up above a certain level (£4 a quarter).

British traders and manufacturers were against the Corn Laws right from the start. They had two objections to the Corn Laws. Firstly, they kept up the price of corn. This was good for farmers, but bad for working people because it meant high bread prices. High bread prices meant that working people demanded higher wages in order to eat. Industrialists wanted to pay lower wages, so that they could sell their goods abroad more cheaply. More export sales would bring more jobs for working people and more profits for industrialists.

The second objection also concerned exports. British industry by the early 19th century depended on selling goods abroad. But foreign countries had to be able to sell something to Britain in order to buy British goods. For many countries the main thing they had to sell was corn. If they could not sell corn to Britain because of the Corn Laws, they could not buy British goods. For all these reasons British manufacturers were supporters of Free Trade.

The Free Trade movement was helped by William Huskisson, MP for Liverpool and President of the Board of Trade 1823–7. He lowered the tariffs on raw materials, such as cotton and iron ore. He reduced tariffs on imported manufactures in the hope that other countries would do the same. He also attempted to do something about the Corn Laws by introducing a sliding scale of tariffs in 1828: the import tariff decreased as the price of corn rose.

More and more businessmen were coming to see the benefits that Free Trade would bring. When trade was depressed in the late 1830s, northern industrialists began an organised campaign in favour of Free Trade and particularly against the Corn Laws.

The Anti-Corn Law League
The Anti-Corn Law League was started in Manchester in 1839, with support from rich manufacturers and the middle classes. Around 9 million leaflets were posted all over the country, using the new Penny Post (see Chapter 24, page 245). Speakers used the new railways to visit towns all over Britain. Among the most famous were Richard Cobden and John Bright, both of whom became Liberal MPs. It became a battle between the old Britain of farmers and landowners on one side, and the people who saw a new future for Britain as a great industrial, trading nation on the other. To Cobden and Bright, a Quaker, Free Trade was the way to

achieve international peace and understanding too.

Reduction of other tariffs
The Prime Minister from 1841 to 1846 was Sir Robert Peel, the son of a Lancashire cotton-mill owner. He began to remove a great deal of the protective tariff system. By 1845 he had removed all export tariffs and nearly all tariffs on imports of raw material. Over 600 items had import tariffs removed entirely, and the rate was lowered to 10% on nearly everything else. He realised that the government would lose income from this, so in 1842 income tax was introduced, at 7*d* (3p) in the pound on incomes over £150 per year.

All Peel's reforms took Britain a long way towards becoming a Free Trade country, but the Corn Laws remained. The Reform Bill 1832 had loosened the hold of the landowners and farmers to an extent. However, this group still had a majority in Parliament, whatever their importance in the country as a whole. In fact, the Corn Laws never really worked properly. Corn was often imported and kept in warehouses until the price reached £4 a

quarter. It was then released, and prices tumbled crazily. Often the inspectors did not report prices fairly. Nevertheless, British farmers felt the Laws gave them some protection.

Repeal of the Corn Laws, 1846
By 1845 Peel had been convinced by the arguments of Free Traders such as Cobden (see Source 4A). However he was leader of the Conservative Party, which was mainly made up of landowners. Then in 1845 the corn harvest in Britain was bad because of heavy rain, and the Irish potato crop failed because of potato blight. By late 1845 there was starvation in Ireland (Source 4B).

? QUESTIONS

a) In Source 4A, Cobden is striding along, and Peel is the little boy. Explain what the cartoonist is trying to say.

b) Why couldn't Peel go as far and as fast as Cobden?

c) Why did the plight of the Irish in Source 4B (over) change the whole situation of food imports into Britain?

■ SOURCE 4A *Punch* cartoon, 1845

PAPA COBDEN TAKING MASTER ROBERT A FREE TRADE WALK.

PAPA COBDEN.—" Come along, MASTER ROBERT, do step out."
MASTER ROBERT.—" That's all very well, but you know I cannot go so fast as you do."

■ SOURCE 4B Starving Irish people, 1845

■ SOURCE 4C *Punch* cartoon, 1846

THE BRITISH LION IN 1850;

OR, THE EFFECTS OF FREE TRADE.

Peel decided that large amounts of foreign corn would have to be imported to save the Irish from starvation. This would mean removing the Corn Laws. His party split on the issue, but his own followers, with Liberal support, out-voted the rest of the Conservatives. The Corn Laws were repealed in 1846.

British Trade 1850–1914

The final steps towards Free Trade

The final steps to make Britain a free-trading country were taken by William Gladstone, Chancellor of the Exchequer 1852–5 and 1859–66. Tariffs were removed on all except a small number of items, such as tea, where they were kept in order to provide money for the government.

As Chapter 9 explains, these were the years of Britain's great industrial and trading prosperity. As the 'workshop of the world', Britain did not need protectionism. Raw materials could be imported cheaply. British manufactured goods were the best and cheapest in the world, so they could be sold easily. The value of British exports rose from £47 million in 1843 to £200 million in 1870. Even the farmers, who had been so anxious to keep the protection of the Corn Laws, prospered (Chapter 8, page 73).

? QUESTIONS

a) What seem to be the effects of Free Trade, according to the cartoon in Source 4C?
b) The cartoon was published at the time of the arguments for and against repealing the Corn Laws. What side does *Punch* seem to be on?
c) Was the cartoonist right about the effects of Free Trade after 1850?

Britain's decreasing share of world trade

By the 1870s other countries were beginning to catch up with Britain. The USA had huge natural resources and a large population. The shortage of skilled labour in the USA meant that American manufacturers invested in modern mass-production methods. This meant that, in the long run, their goods cost less than British goods, which were still being manufactured by older, more expensive methods. By the early 20th century Germany, too, had overtaken Britain, and other European countries were not far behind.

Britain continued to sell more textiles, iron, steel and coal than she had ever done before. But as other countries industrialised, they excluded Britain from their markets and she had to rely more and more on sales to less-developed countries. Britain also failed to get a large share of world trade in new industries: chemical and electrical engineering, motor cars (Chapter 9, pages 99–101.) Overall, Britain's share of world trade declined over this period.

The Tariff Reform League

Some business people began to feel the effects of foreign competition. Politicians were worried to see German and other foreign-made items sold in Britain. Joseph Chamberlain formed the Tariff Reform League in 1903. He wanted to bring back some form of protection. He pointed out that foreign countries shielded their home industries by putting up protective tariffs. Now that Britain was facing increasing world competition, why shouldn't we do the same? Chamberlain wanted to have Free Trade only with British colonies: they would supply raw materials and provide a market for our goods. He called this idea 'imperial preference'.

However, the Liberal Party still believed firmly in Free Trade. In the election of 1906 they used the same arguments about the price of bread that the Anti-Corn Law League had used 60 years earlier.

With the kind of election material shown in Source 4D, was it surprising that the Liberals won a huge majority at the 1906 election? Tariff reform and protection remained unpopular for the time being.

Invisible exports

Although British industry and agriculture were feeling the effects of

■ *SOURCE 4D* **Election poster, 1906. Pearce was a Liberal candidate**

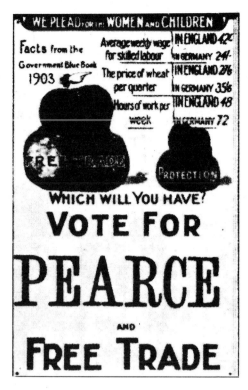

foreign competition by the late 19th century, there was still a huge income from invisible exports. During the years of Britain's domination of world trade, the City of London became the financial centre of the world. Banking and insurance, loans and shipping facilities were arranged in London for schemes all over the world. In 1914, 45% of the money borrowed on the international markets was raised in London. There were also enormous amounts of money invested abroad by British investors. This brought money back into Britain as interest. These exports were 'invisible' because money came into the country without any goods changing hands.

Source 5 shows that Britain had always imported more than was exported. The balance of payments, however, was massively tipped in Britain's favour by these invisible exports. Shipping accounted for a

good deal of the income from services – £100 million in 1911–13; insurance brought in another £25 million

Trading Conditions 1914–39

The First World War, not surprisingly, caused a major disruption to foreign trade. Britain turned most of her industrial effort to making war materials. The USA and other countries supplied Britain with the imports no longer being made here. At the same time, British exports declined. To overcome this huge imbalance, Britain borrowed large sums from the USA and sold off many foreign investments.

When the war ended, British industrialists found that many other countries had developed their own industries, or found new suppliers. Many had more modern machinery, so cheaper production costs. There was a brief boom in 1918–21 as countries re-stocked after the war, but this soon ended. These were difficult years for British trade and industry (see Chapter 9). World trade was now very competitive, and British manufacturers were not well placed to compete. In addition, products which had formed the basis of British exports, such as cotton and coal, were being replaced by substitutes.

British government policy did not help much. Britain was still committed to Free Trade, even though the situation which had made Free Trade such a successful policy had now disappeared. The government also wanted to strengthen Britain's position as a financial centre, and returned to the Gold Standard. This meant that the British pound was backed by gold, and stood at a high value against other currencies. Unfortunately, this brought high interest rates, so industrialists found it difficult to borrow money for new

■ *SOURCE 5* **Britain's balance of payments 1836–1940 (£ million**

	Imports	Exports	Trading balance	Income from services	Income from investment	Balance of trade
1836–40	74	50	– 24	19	8	+ 3
1856–60	158	124	– 34	44	17	+ 27
1911–13	623	489	–134	153	188	+207

equipment. It also meant high export prices, so foreign sales were difficult.

Reintroduction of tariffs

The USA took such a lead over other countries during the First World War that world trade now depended on the US market. When the Wall Street Crash brought depression in the USA, world trade declined from $2998 million in 1929 to $992 million in 1933 – a 67% fall. Many countries imposed tariffs to protect their own industry, and Britain was forced to do the same. The Import Duties Act 1932 put duties of 10% on raw materials, excluding food, rubber, cotton and wool. Duties of 33.33% were put on many manufactured items. Trade with the colonies was protected by the Ottawa Agreement of 1932. This offered favourable treatment to trade between Britain and the Empire. Behind this tariff wall some parts of British industry, such as motor-manufacturing, did quite well.

Britain's Trade Since 1939

Britain faced the same difficulties in the Second World War as in the First. Again, American loans and sales of foreign investments kept the country going. The long-term effect of these, however, was to lower the income from invisible exports.

Nevertheless, Britain in the early 1950s was still an importer of food and raw materials and an exporter of manufactured goods and financial services. This is no longer the case today. Britain now imports not only food and raw materials, but also manufactured goods. In 1978 imports of motor cars were 35% of sales, by 1984 they were 51%. For all manufactured goods, imports rose from 26% in 1978 to 34% in 1984. In particular fields, such as office equipment, imports now account for about double the sales of home-produced goods. In textiles we now import twice as much as we export. Manufactured goods exports and invisible exports have declined. The only item which keeps the balance of trade from

going deeply into the red is the export sale of oil. By 1984 oil exports were worth four times car exports.

The European Economic Community

At the same time as these tremendous changes, Britain's own position as a trading nation has changed because of the Common Market. At the end of the Second World War, the countries of Western Europe realised they had more to gain by working together than by fighting wars. In 1951 the European Coal and Steel Community was formed. The members were Germany, France, Italy, Belgium, Netherlands and Luxembourg. They agreed to work together in the vital production of coal and steel. Production in the ECSC rose by 25% up to 1954.

In 1957, the European Economic Community (EEC) was formed, by the Treaty of Rome, with the same six members as the ECSC. They agreed to work towards free trade between themselves and to apply the same tariffs on all trade with non-members. This would give them protection against other

countries but a large open European market among themselves. This was achieved in 1968. They agreed to work together in nuclear power, through Euratom. They also agreed to work towards common policies on welfare, tax, agriculture, transport, etc.

Britain was interested in the EEC, but still had half her trade with the Commonwealth in 1957. Sugar from the West Indies, meat and butter from New Zealand and corn from Canada and Australia were basic items of British trade. Gradually this pattern changed as trade with Europe grew. Britain helped set up the European Free Trade Association in 1960 with Austria, Sweden, Switzerland, Denmark, Norway and Portugal. However, EFTA members traded more with the EEC than with each other.

In 1961, Harold Macmillan, the British Prime Minister, applied for Britain to join the EEC. Five of the six EEC members were in favour, but General de Gaulle, President of France, was against. He felt Britain was still too closely tied up with the Commonwealth and the USA. The same thing happened in 1967 when Prime Minister Harold Wilson applied again.

■ *SOURCE 6A* **Cartoon from 1961**

"AH, I HEAR YOU WANT TO JOIN OUR CLUB AND PLAY FOR EUROPE, AFTER ALL . . ."

SOURCE 6B Cartoon from 1967

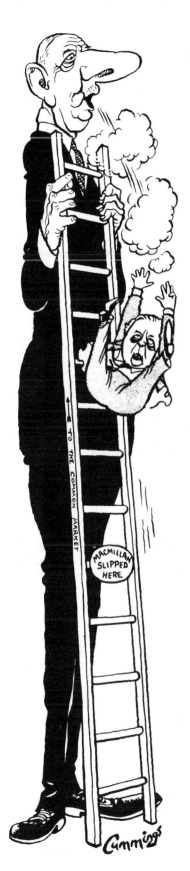

General de Gaulle fell from power in 1969, and Prime Minister Edward Heath made another application to join the EEC 1970. This was successful and Britain became a member in 1973. Harold Wilson renegotiated the terms of membership in 1975.

Unfortunately, Britain joined the EEC just when it was of least benefit. By 1973 it had been going 16 years, and the six original members had shaped it their way. Britain had a different trading pattern from other European countries, and this has worked to our disadvantage. Contributions to the EEC budget are calculated on the basis of who does the most trade outside the EEC. Thus Britain, not by any means the richest member, pays the most. As much as 70% of the EEC budget goes on the Common Agricultural Policy (CAP). British agriculture is very efficient (Chapter 8, page 83), so we receive little in the way of CAP money. At the same time the Free Trade between EEC members opens up Britain as a market for European manufacturers. Many of these are more efficient and can produce at lower cost than their British rivals.

The decline of British industry and the reasons for it are dealt with in Chapter 9. In the 19th century, British industry led the world, and Free Trade was the way to benefit from this lead. What should we do now? Mrs Thatcher's Conservative government, in power from 1979, has held to the policy of Free Trade. It believes that weak industries should be left to go out of business and that new ones will thrive on competition. Other people argue that Britain should bring in import controls and protective tariffs to help British industry in difficult times. But if we did this, how would other countries react?

Assignments

Empathy

1 Get into groups of four. Two of you are business people, two are farmers. It is 1840. The business people want free trade and the repeal of the Corn Laws. The farmers want to keep the Corn Laws. Discuss your views and your reasons for them.
2 Look at Source 4D. Design a poster to oppose this one, giving the arguments in favour of protection.

Understanding concepts

1 **Cause/effect**
   a What was the system of protection set up by the Navigation Acts?
   b What were the effects on Britain?
   c What were the effects on the beginnings of industrialisation in Britain?

2 **Causation/motivation**
   a What were the aims of the Anti-Corn Law League?
   b What were its methods?
   c What were Sir Robert Peel's motives for repealing the Corn Laws?

3 **Change/continuity**
   a The Common Market was set up in 1957. Britain did not join until 1973. Why the long delay?
   b What have been the results of membership:
     i for British industry;
     ii for British agriculture;
     iii for British people?

4 **Causation/motivation**
The arguments between free trade and protection have continued in the 20th century. What was British trading policy, and why, in each of these periods:
i 1900–1914;
ii 1930s;
iii 1980s?

Themes for discussion

1 Trace the movements between protection and free trade in this chapter. Do you agree with the statement that protection is the best policy for a country unless it is an obvious world leader?
2 Which trading policy do you think Britain should adopt at the present time – Free Trade, or protection?

261

26 Migration and Multi-cultural Britain 1700–1980s

■ *SOURCE 1* **City street, 1987**

Population Movements

The British people are made up of many different races and cultures. This has always been true. Waves of people settled in Britain before the Romans, then came Anglo-Saxon, Viking and Norman settlers. Dutch immigrants came to Britain in the 15th century, Jews and Huguenot French in the 17th. There were also about 20000 black people in Britain by the 18th century. At the same time, in the 17th and 18th centuries, British people began to emigrate in quite large numbers to colonies in various parts of the world. About 350000 had gone to America by 1780. In the last 200 years these movements of people have increased. Faster, better means of transport have meant that more people can travel, and they can travel further.

Why migrate?

Seeking 'freedom'

Why do large numbers of people leave the place where they were born to go and settle in a strange land? Sometimes the government in their home country does not let them live, or worship, in the way they want. This was true of the Huguenots who came here and the British who went to America in the 17th century. In our own day, it has been true of Hungarians who left their country in 1956, Chileans in 1972 and Tamils in 1987.

Economic reasons

But the main reason for emigration or immigration is economic. People leave their homes because life has become intolerable through poverty and hunger; they see that another place offers them hope of a job and a better life. In Chapter 11 we saw how the people of Britain moved from the countryside to the towns. Population was rising in rural areas with the result that jobs were few and wages low. At first they moved to the nearest town, then to an industrial city further away. For many, however, this was not the answer. America, Canada, Australia, New Zealand, and other areas, seemed to offer a better life than anywhere in Britain.

Emigration in the 19th Century

The new lands offered good employment prospects to those with the necessary skills.

SOURCE 2A

As to the classes to which British America offers attractions as emigrants, much will depend upon individual character. The settlers who do best are men of steady habits, used to hard work.

Working farmers with £200 to £600 may buy farms of 20 to 30 acres, which can be cultivated in the same way as in the UK. Joiners, stonemasons, saddlers, tailors, shoemakers, blacksmiths, millwrights and, (in the seaports) coopers may always find employment.

Selected documents of Canadian history (adapted), 1783–1855

SOURCE 2C The emigrant's last sight of home, 1858

SOURCE 2B *Punch* cartoon, 1840

HERE   AND   THERE;

OR, EMIGRATION A REMEDY.

■ *SOURCE 2D* **Scottish emigrants leaving for Canada, a 19th century painting**

■ *SOURCE 2D* **Scottish emigrants leaving for Canada, a 19th century painting**

? QUESTIONS

a) Why do you think land was cheaper in Canada than in Britain (Source 2A)?

b) Why was there a shortage of skilled craftsmen in the colonies?

c) What effect would this shortage have on wages in Canada?

d) What kind of people does the writer of Source 2A want to encourage to emigrate?

e) What might have been the effect of Source 2B:
   i) on a farm worker who had hardly enough to live on?
   ii) on a farmer worried about the cost of the Poor Rate?

f) What are the feelings of the emigrants as portrayed by the artists in Sources 2C and 2D?

g) What do Source 2C and 2D tell us:
   i) about emigrants?
   ii) about Victorian views of emigrants?

Official encouragement

Other groups of people, who had no intention of going themselves, encouraged emigration. In rural areas many landlords in the 1820s were worried about the rising costs of looking after the poor (page 163). They sometimes subsidised the fares of poor labourers to assist their emigation. Trade unions, too, helped their members emigrate. Unions were worried about low wages: if there were fewer workers, then those who were left could bargain for better pay. The government was worried about the rising population causing poverty and unrest. They wanted to get rid of what they called 'redundant' population. They also wanted settlers to develop the colonies, and grow the raw materials for British industry. In 1835 a grant of £20 was made to any young, married mechanic or labourer wanting to go to Australia. Many early emigrants were single men. In order to encourage them to set up permanent homes in the colonies, single women were given help in emigrating. In 1833 young women between 18 and 30 'of good health and character' were offered the subsidised fare of £6 to go to Australia.

The difficulties faced

Crooks

Despite this encouragement, the hazards and difficulties faced by emigrants in the 19th century were enormous. The emigrants, often young people who had never left their village before, were tricked and exploited at every stage. When they arrived at the port their ship would leave from, they were 'befriended' by local crooks. These people would earn large commissions by directing them to certain hotels to await their departure, or 'help' them buy tickets at inflated prices. Sometimes they would persuade the emigrants that British money was no use where they were going. They would change it at unfair rates, or persuade them to buy unnecessary items for the voyage (see Source 3A).

Bad conditions on board ship

At first the emigrant ships were ordinary sailing ships, often leaky old tubs. Britain imported more from the colonies than was exported, so there was room for extra

■ *SOURCE 3A* Emigrants embarking at Waterloo Docks, Liverpool, 1850

passengers on the outward trip. Temporary berths were set up and conditions were often dreadful. Then Passenger Acts of 1803 and 1828 laid down basic requirements of space and food to be provided. By the middle years of the century specialist emigrant ships were being built. The American 'Black Ball' and 'Red Swallowtail' lines were the most famous.

Even on these ships conditions were often bad. The emigrants paid a fare of under £5 so they were crammed in by the ship-owners. Perhaps 700 passengers would live together in the 'steerage' deck for the 35 days of the trip. There were complaints about overcrowding, poor food and water (see Sources 3B and 3D), mixed berths and favouritism by the crew. Female emigrants also complained of sexual harrassment from captains and ship's officers. Safety was inadequate, so there was very high loss of life if anything went wrong. For example, fire broke out on the 'Ocean Monarch' just after leaving Liverpool in August 1848 and 176 people died. The first steamer to carry emigrants, the 'City of Glasgow', was lost in 1854 with 430 people on board. Later, in 1912,

■ **SOURCE 3B Handing out food in the steerage, 1872**

■ *SOURCE 3C* **Dancing between decks, 1850**

there were still not enough lifeboats on the 'Titanic' when it sank, and over 700 emigrants died.

SOURCE 3D

Our water has for some time past been very bad, when it was drawn out of the casks it was no cleaner than that of a dirty gutter after a shower of rain, so that its appearance alone was enough to sicken one. But its dirty appearance was not its worst quality. It had such a rancid smell that to be in the same neighbourhood was enough to turn one's stomach.

Rev. William Bell, on the 'Rothiemurchus', from Leith to Quebec, 1817

? QUESTIONS

a) What do you think would be the feelings of the emigrants in Source 2C on seeing the scene in Source 3A when they arrived at port?
b) How can you tell that the people in Source 3A are emigrants, and not any other kind of traveller?
c) In what ways do Sources 3B, 3C and 3D give conflicting pictures of life on an emigrant ship?
d) Why do you think we have more evidence of complaints than scenes such as Source 3C?
e) How could you find out whether Source 3C is more or less reliable than other sources?
f) Look at Source 3E. Why would cholera be a terrible danger on an emigrant ship?
g) What else does Source 3E tell us about conditions on an emigrant ship?

Patterns of emigration

Despite all these problems, emigrants left Britain in very large numbers. 193 000 left in the 1820s, 671 000 in the 1830s and then there was a flood which continued well into the 20th century.

? QUESTIONS

a) Look at Source 4. Which areas were popular in the mid-19th century and which became popular later?
b) How can you tell that the USA began to restrict immigration in the early 20th century?

■ SOURCE 3E Cholera poster, 1853

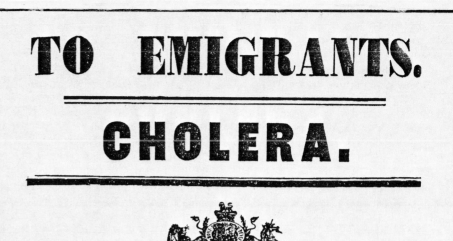

■ SOURCE 4 Numbers and destinations of emigrants from England, Scotland and Wales, selected years

Selected years	USA	Canada	Australia	Other	Total
1861–70	442 000	90 000	184 000	37 000	753 000
1881–90	1 088 000	257 000	317 000	162 000	1 824 000
1911–20	379 000	822 000	352 000	275 000	1 828 000
Total 1851–1920	4 651 000	2 856 000	2 102 000	1 606 000	11 215 000

There are some regional variations hidden in these figures. Scots went particularly to Canada. Welsh emigrants set up a successful colony, almost like part of Wales, in Patagonia, in Argentina. The most popular place in the 'Other' group in Source 4 from the late 19th century, was South Africa. The emigration shown in Source 4 was just part of a huge movement of people out of Europe in these years.

Immigrants to Britain in the 19th Century

Irish immigrants

There was already some emigration from Ireland in the early 19th century, to Britain and to other parts of the world. Then the Great Famine of 1842–6 brought starvation (page 257). Many Irish people decided to leave: it was more a flight than an emigration: 100 000 left in 1846, 250 000 in 1851. Probably 5 million Irish people left in the years 1820–1920. Many villages had only the old men and women left. Irishmen usually emigrated first, sending for their families as soon as they could afford to (see Source 5).

? QUESTION

Why was it customary for the men to go alone, first?

The pattern of Irish migration was really the same as for other rural parts of Britain. The population moved to industrial towns and cities, as well as to new lands. The arrival of large numbers of Irish immigrants in British towns and cities upset many people. Although Ireland was at that time part of Britain, they were regarded as foreigners. The hostility of local people, and the desire of the Irish immigrants to stay together, meant that parts of some cities were soon almost exclusively Irish. Their readiness to take low-paid jobs meant that those areas had the lowest rents and worst housing. Their willingness to work for low pay also brought hostility from other working people. The Irish were thus the first to experience what it was like to be an immigrant in a British city. Racist attitudes began to appear.

■ SOURCE 6

The rapid growth of the cotton industry has attracted workers here from every part of the kingdom, and Ireland has poured forth the most destitute of their hordes to supply the constantly increasing demand for labour. This immigration has been a serious evil . . .

The example which the Irish have given, of barbarous habits and savage lack of care, have demoralised the people . . .

In some districts of the town exist evils so remarkable as to require more minute description. A portion of low swampy ground, liable to be frequently flooded . . . is enclosed by a high bank . . . and a bend of the River Medlock . . . This unhealthy spot lies so low that the chimneys of its houses are little above the level of the road. About two hundred of these are inhabited . . . by the lowest Irish.

Want of cleanliness, of forethought and carefulness are found in alliance with drunkenness, reckless habits and disease.

J. P. Kay Shuttleworth, 'The Moral and Physical Condition of the Working-classes Employed in the Cotton Manufacture in Manchester', 1832

? QUESTIONS

a) Give examples of the emotional language used to describe the Irish.
b) Racism uses 'stereotypes'. It gives general labels to all members of a particular group of people, instead of looking at them as individuals. What kind of stereotype does Kay Shuttleworth make of the Irish in Manchester?
c) Could the Irish be blamed for the condition of the housing?
d) Look at Source 7B. How have attitudes to the Irish changed by 1902? Why do you think this is?

Jewish immigration

Another group of immigrants who suffered from much the same problems in housing and discrimination were Jews. Since at least the 17th century there had been a small Jewish community in Britain, numbering about 35 000. Then in the 1880s Jews began to be persecuted in Russia and Eastern Europe. In danger of their lives, they fled, first to Germany, then to Britain. It is difficult to say how many settled in Britain because most went on to the USA. Fares from Britain to the USA were much cheaper than from Ger-

■ SOURCE 5 Irish emigrant mothers and children, 1902

many. However, probably about 3000 per year stayed in Britain from the 1880s, rising to about 10000 per year 1899–1902. The Jewish population of Britain was probably over 250000 in 1901, out of a total of 41500000.

These Jewish immigrants were largely concentrated in the poorer parts of London (60%), Leeds (7%) and the towns of Lancashire (12%). Speaking little or no English at first, and with a different religion, it was inevitable that they gathered together. In London they worked in the East London clothing trade, usually for long hours at terrible wages. Anti-semitic (anti-Jewish) attitudes had been present in Britain for a long time, but were now strongly heard (see Source 7A). The growth of racist attitudes following Jewish immigration led to the passing of the 1905 Aliens Act.

SOURCE 7A

People of any other nation, after being in England for a short time, assimilate with the native race and by and by lose nearly all their foreign trace. But the Jews never do. A Jew is always a Jew.

East London Advertiser, 1899

SOURCE 7B

Samuel Street used to be a street occupied by poor English and Irish. In the afternoons you would see the steps cleaned inside and the women in their clean white aprons in summertime beside the doors, perhaps at needlework with their little children about. Now it is a setting mass of refuse and filth.

Evidence to the Royal Commission on Alien Immigration, 1902

SOURCE 7C

Where work is slack and difficult to get, a small addition of low-living foreigners will cause a fall in the entire wages of the neighbourhood...

(The Jew's) superior calculating intellect, which is a natural heritage is used to enable him to take advantage of every weakness, folly and vice of the society in which he lives.

J. A. Hobson, *The Problem of Poverty*, 1892

❓ QUESTIONS

a) What accusations are made of the Jews in these three sources in matters of
   i) housing
   ii) work and
   iii) being different?
b) What racist stereotypes can be seen in these sources?
c) Source 7A speaks of 'assimilation'. This means adapting to the way of life of the people among whom you are living, and not standing out. Do you think the Irish and Jewish people have become assimilated into British life?

Migration Patterns After 1918

Emigration

During World War 1 and the inter-war years emigration and immigration declined. The USA imposed strict immigration controls. The Depression also hit Canada and Australia, making them less attractive as places to go and live. A proportion of migrants has always gone home after a while (see Source 10B below). Possibly 30% of emigrants returned to Britain in these years.

When the world economy began to recover after the Second World War emigration began again. Australia, New Zealand, Canada and the USA were popular, but at this time South Africa and Rhodesia (now Zimbabwe) took quite large numbers too. These countries wanted skilled workers from Britain, so offered cheap fares, e.g. £10 to Australia for emigrants. The economic difficulties of Britain in the 1950s and early 1970s also encouraged British people to try their luck elsewhere. In the 1980s many thousands of British workers looked for jobs all over the world, especially in Europe and the Middle East.

Immigration

The British Union of Fascists tried to stir up race hated in the East End of London in 1936. However, this was generally a period when older groups of settlers became more

accepted into British life.

After the Second World War, though, there was a change in the pattern of immigration into Britain. In June 1948, 492 Jamaicans came to Britain on the 'Empire Windrush'. A few more West Indians came later that year and in 1949, and perhaps 1000 came in 1950. Larger numbers came in the mid-1950s, including wives and children of men who had come earlier – 24000 in 1954, 26000 in 1956. By 1958 about 125000 West Indians had come to live and work in Britain. At the same time, people from India and Pakistan came to settle in Britain – about 55000 of them by 1958.

They came for exactly the same economic reasons as other immigrants before them. There was unemployment and poverty in the West Indies; independence in India and Pakistan in 1947 caused disruption and unemployment. Britain was calling out for workers. London Transport began to recruit staff in Barbados in 1956 and from 1966 in Trinidad and Jamaica too. The British Hotels and Restaurants Association, also short of workers, began to sign up people from Barbados. Conservative Minister of Health, Enoch Powell welcomed West Indian nurses to help the shortage of nurses in British hospitals. Many employers lent their new staff the fare to Britain, which was repaid out of wages. It was the same story in India and Pakistan, where workers were recruited from country areas.

There had been black people in Britain for centuries. They had fought in the British army and navy and had contributed to British life (see Sources 8A–C). Sometimes there had been outbursts of prejudice against them. Often this had been connected with jobs: white seamen trying to stop black seamen getting work, for example. This had led to serious violence in Cardiff, Liverpool and South Shields in 1919, and again in Liverpool in 1948.

Throughout the years of the British Empire and Commonwealth, the people of British colonies were regarded as British citizens. They held British passports and were not affected by the 1905 Aliens Act.

West Indians, particularly, regarded themselves as British, and were loyal and patriotic.

■ *SOURCE 8A* **Naval pensioners at Greenwich, 1830**

■ *SOURCE 8B* **Mary Seacole, (1805–1881) nurse in the Crimean War**

■ *SOURCE 8C* **William Cuffey, (1788–1870) Chartist**

Attitudes Towards Immigrants

Racism

The West Indians who arrived in the 1950s were disappointed with the treatment they received. Most were skilled workers, but found themselves forced to take unskilled jobs which local white people would not do. They met deep prejudice in all sorts of ways: in housing, pubs, restaurants, education and at work. Some white workers operated a 'colour bar' to prevent blacks being taken on. They were often abused in the streets, and sometimes attacked. Asian immigrants found it even harder. Sometimes they knew

■ SOURCE 9A

The first generation Asian immigrant to Britain was not used to an industrial society. His presence was resented, and he suffered racialist insults and indignities. He was denied a decent house and a job equal to his abilities. He was often not promoted to a higher position.

Dr Bhikhu Parekh, BBC, 1978

■ SOURCE 9B

Since I came here I never met a single English person who had any colour prejudice. Once, I walked the whole length of a street looking for a room, and everyone told me that he or she had no prejudice against coloured people. It was the neighbour who was stupid. If we could only find the neighbour we could solve the entire problem. But to find him is the trouble! Neighbours are the worst people to live beside in this country.

From a play by A. G. Bennett, 1959

■ SOURCE 9C

Edgbaston Road used to be such a lovely road ... you used to have nannies up that way, you know. Really good class people used to live there, and it was a pleasure to walk in that area. Now they've taken over and the place is a slum ... Their habits are pretty terrible, they use the front garden as a rubbish dump, and heaven knows what they do in the toilets.

Smethwick housewife, 1961

? QUESTIONS

a) What kinds of discrimination are described in Sources 9A and 9B?
b) How do the English people in Source 9B hide their racism?
c) What attitude does the speaker in Source 9B adopt towards racism?
d) Look at Sources 6 and 7B, and compare them with Source 9C. What similarities are there?
e) What racist stereotypes does the speaker in Source 9C have?

little English and had less in common with white people in Britain than West Indians did.

Growing racism in Britain led to riots in 1958 in Nottingham and in North Kensington. Race hatred was stirred up by the British National Party (which became the National Front in 1966). White youths, looking for trouble, attacked black people and their homes. There was also an increasing call for immigration controls, from both Labour and Conservative politicians. From 1959 a group of Conservative MPs formed the Birmingham Immigration Control Association. Others spoke out against immigration control, such as Labour Party Chairman, Tom Driberg.

■ SOURCE 10A

People talk about a colour problem in Britain. How can there be a colour problem here? Even after all the immigration of the last few years there are only 190 000 coloured people in our population of over 50 million – that is only four in every thousand. The real problem is not black skins, but white prejudice.

Tom Driberg at TUC Conference, 1958

The 'numbers game'

He was right that, despite all the talk of being 'swamped' by black people, the actual numbers were very small. The government had no accurate statistics about emigration and immigration of people with British passports at that time, only of aliens. West Indians, Indians and Pakistanis were British Commonwealth citizens with British passports. When figures were collected, they showed a complex pattern of movement.

? QUESTIONS

a) Look at Source 10B. Which was the most popular country for British emigrants in 1964?
b) Which was the most popular destination in 1984?
c) What was the overall effect of immigration and emigration in 1964?
d) What proportion of Indians, Pakistanis, Sri Lankans and West Indians were emigrants, as opposed to immigrants, in 1964, and in 1984?
e) Does the information in Source 10B support what the speaker in Source 10A is trying to say?
f) Explain the last sentence of Source 10A.

Many people argue that numbers are not a relevant issue anyway. What is important is how people are treated, whatever their colour and wherever they were born.

■ SOURCE 10B Migration into and out of the UK, 1964 and 1984

Country of last, or future residence	1964		1984	
	In	Out	In	Out
Australia	15 000	80 000	13 000	18 000
New Zealand	6 000	16 000	9 000	6 000
Canada	9 000	31 000	6 000	5 000
India, Pakistan and Ceylon (Sri Lanka)	28 000	9 000	22 000	4 000
West Indies	19 000	7 000	2 000	3 000
Africa	22 000	17 000	14 000	1 000
South Africa	2 000	13 000	8 000	8 000
Western Europe	12 000	23 000	22 000	21 000
TOTAL (all countries)	211 000	271 000	201 000	164 000

Discrimination and Integration

Immigration control

The first Commonwealth Immigration Act was passed in 1962. People, even with British passports, could only enter Britain if they had a work permit, or were 'dependents' (wife, children or aged parents) of such a person. Those who had British parents or grandparents could come in freely. In this way the law discriminated on grounds of colour of skin: Canadians, Australians, New Zealanders, for example, were not subject to the same controls as West Indians, Indians, Pakistanis or black Africans.

Labour leader, Hugh Gaitskell called the Act 'miserable, shameful and shabby'. However, when they came to power in 1964 the Labour Party kept immigration controls. They felt that it was partly a matter of numbers. Therefore their policy was to restrict black immigration still further, but work for integration within Britain. Their 1965 Race Relations Act set up the Race Relations Board to promote racial harmony and prevent discrimination. It also cut the number of work permits issued.

The 1968 Commonwealth Immigration Act specifically limited the entry of British passport holders of Asian descent living in Kenya. In fact, the Kenyan Asians were descended from workers taken across from India to Kenya in the 19th century by the British. They were needed at that time to work the coffee and tobacco plantations. When Kenya became independent in 1963 the Asians were given guarantees that they would be able to come to Britain. Now they were being persecuted in Kenya and the British government saw that other African states could adopt the same policies. Britain feared that if they were let into Britain freely, Asians from all over Africa would want to come. Only 1500 per year were allowed in, and once more the 'grandfather clause' ensured that the restriction did not apply to whites.

British entry into the Common Market complicated the issue of who was a British citizen still further. The 1971 Immigration Act defined 'patrials' as those who held British citizenship by birth, or who had a parent or grandparent born in the UK, or who had lived here for five years. Only patrials could come and go freely in Britain and the Common Market. Again the Act contained the 'grandfather clause' – those with a British grandparent could come into Britain freely. This made it possible for white South Africans to get into Britain, even though South Africa had left the Commonwealth in 1961. Those who did not have a British grandparent (i.e. black people) could only come to Britain if they had a specific job, even if they had a British passport.

Since 1972 immigration controls have remained, and the 1983 Nationality Act confirmed these.

■ *SOURCE 11A* **Immigrants at Heathrow, 1968**

Race Relations Acts

Governments have tried to deal with racial discrimination by passing laws against it. The 1965 Race Relations Act made it illegal to practise discrimination in pubs, restaurants or hotels. It also became illegal to stir up racial hatred. The Race Relations Board was set up to deal with complaints. Immediately the weaknesses of the Act were seen: black people suffered from discrimination most of all in housing and in jobs, which were outside the Act. Of 327 complaints dealt with by the Race Relations Board from February 1966 to March 1967, only 89 came within the Act. 101 complaints concerned discrimination in jobs, and 37 in housing.

The 1968 Race Relations Act increased the powers of the Board; it could now make its own investigations, instead of waiting to receive complaints. The Act also set up the Community Relations Commission to promote 'harmonious community relations'. In 1976 a new Race Relations Act set up the Commission for Racial Equality, with even wider powers.

The aims of these Acts were defined by Roy Jenkins, the Home Secretary, as 'integration'.

■ SOURCE 11B

I define integration ... not as a flattening process of assimilation but as equal opportunity, accompanied by cultural diversity, in an atmosphere of mutual tolerance. This is the goal.

Roy Jenkins, May 23rd, 1966

? QUESTIONS

a) What do you think Roy Jenkins means by 'a flattening process of assimilation'?

b) What does he see as the difference between 'assimilation' and 'integration'?

Unfortunately the other part of government policy – immigration controls on black people – works against the policy of 'integration'. In the first place it affects the position of all coloured people in Britain, however long they have been here.

■ SOURCE 11C

In spite of my years of residence in Britain, any service I may have given the community in war or peace, any contribution I might make or wish to make, or any feeling of belonging I might have towards Britain and the British, I, like all other coloured persons in Britain, am considered an immigrant. Although this term indicates that we have got into Britain, it describes a continuing condition in which we have no real hope of ever enjoying the desired change to full responsible citizenship.

E. R. Braithwaite, distinguished West Indian teacher and writer, who first came to Britain in the RAF in the Second World War, writing in 1967 (adapted)

The need to abolish racist attitudes

With immigration laws based on racism still in effect, many whites feel they can get away with racist attitudes. For non-whites, bodies like the Race Relations Board and the Community Relations Commission have little impact on their lives. The people they meet daily – employers, officials, police – often display racist attitudes. Young black people who were born in Britain find this particularly hard to take.

■ SOURCE 11E

The only home we know is Britain ... All the ... white agencies have now adopted the ... label 'second generation immigrants' for Black Britons. By the use of such labelling devices the vicious circle of racial discrimination continues ... Merely because of the colour of their skin, black children become second class citizens, doomed to a life of ... exploitation.

We will not put up with racist behaviour. Rather than submit we will react ...

We are now heading towards a complete breakdown in communication between white and black society. This process began in the early sixties and gathered momentum ... with the country's expressed wish to tighten up controls and ostracise ... black immigrants and Black Britons alike. We cannot help but feel that white society is knifing us in the back ... As the breakdown in communication becomes more absolute, passive resistance could give way to more violent forms of behaviour.

Chris Mullard, 1973

The violence pointed to in the last sentence of Source 11E did erupt. In Southall in 1979, in Bristol in 1980, then in Brixton (London) and Toxteth (Liverpool) in 1981, as well as in dozens of other cities, riots

■ SOURCE 11D Brixton riots, 1981

broke out in which blacks were actively involved, although whites also played a part. There were other outbreaks of serious violence in several areas through the 1980s.

Britain is a multi-cultural society but attitudes among politicians, employers and people generally will have to change before racial discrimination is abolished and equal opportunities are offered to all people, whatever the colour of their skin.

Assignments

Empathy

1 a What kinds of people emigrated from Britain in the 19th century?
 b What were their reasons for emigrating?
 c What were the attitudes to emigration of:
  i trade unionists;
  ii landowners?
2 a What were the hopes and fears of British emigrants in the 19th century?
 b What problems and hazards did they meet before arriving at their destination?
 c If there were such difficulties to face, why did they go in large numbers?
3 a What were the hopes and fears of immigrants coming to Britain in the 1940s and 1950s?
 b What problems and hazards did they meet on their arrival in Britain?

 c What have been the attitudes of British governments to these problems and hazards?

Understanding concepts

1 Causation/motivation
What have been the motives of each of the following groups for migrating to and from Britain:
 a British emigrants in the 19th century?
 b Irish immigrants in the 19th century?
 c British emigrants in the 1950s?
 d West Indian immigrants in the 1950s?

2 Causation/motivation
 a What immigration policies have British governments adopted since 1962?
 b What have been the reasons for these policies?
 c What have been the results of these policies for:

  i white immigrants **ii** black immigrants?

Themes for discussion

1 a What similarities and differences have there been in attitudes among some British people towards:
  i 19th century Irish immigrants;
  ii Jewish immigrants around 1900;
  iii West Indian and Asian immigrants since 1950?
 b Is there any difference in each case between short-term and long-term attitudes?
2 a How far is Britain today a multi-cultural society?
 b How far do white British people accept that it is a multi-cultural society?
 c What problems do black people face in being treated equally with white British people?

Index

Acts of Parliament

Acknowledgements

The publishers would like to thank the following for permission to reproduce photographs:

Aerofilms: Ch9 Sources 8c, 25; Ch10 Source 15b; Ch11 Source 4a; Ch22 Source 13a

Arkwright Society: Ch3 Source 7b

Austin Rover: Ch9 source 9g

Barnaby's Picture Library: Ch5 Sources 1a, 1c, 1d, 1e, 1f; Ch8 Sources 13a, 14b; Ch11 Source 12d

BBC Hulton Picture Library: Ch3 Source 2b; Ch6 Sources 10b, 19d, 20b; Ch8 Source 6; Ch9 Sources 2a, 13b, 13d, 25b; Ch10 Sources 8a, 12b, 15a, 22a, 23c; Ch11 Source 12a; Ch13 Sources 4c,7c; Ch14 Source 3; Ch15 Sources 6e, 7b, 8; Ch16 Sources 1a, 4c, 6a, 9c, 10a; Ch18 Source 5a; Ch19 Sources 4c, 5a, 6b, 9b, 11; Ch20 Source 1c; Ch21 Sources 3b, 7a; Ch22 Sources 9a, 12c; Ch24 Sources 3b, 5d; Ch25 Source 4b

BBC Radio Times: Ch21 Source 7c

Bedfordshire Record Office: Ch2 Source 8b

Berkshire Record Office: Ch18 Source 4d

Bracegirdle Collection: Ironbridge Gorge Museum: Ch6 Source 10a

British Airways: Ch10 Source 23a

British Library: Ch1 Source 4a; Ch3 Source 10; Ch17 Source 3a, 3b; Ch26 Source 8c, 9c

British Museum: Ch11 Source 7a; Ch26 Source 9a

Acknowledgements

British Petroleum Company plc: Ch9 Source 8d
British Waterways Board: Ch6 Sources 10d, 10e
B T Batsford: Ch24 Source 7b; Ch9 Source 4f
Boots plc: Ch9 Source 12
Buckinghamshire Record Office: Ch2 Source 8a
City of Birmingham Museum and Art Gallery: Ch5 Source 8b
City of Liverpool: Ch10 Source 19a
Communist Party Picture Library: Ch20 Source 1c
Compassion in World Farming: Ch8 Source 14B
Country Life : Ch4 Source 3
Courtaulds: Ch9 Source   10
Crown Copyright: Ch24 Source 1a
Cwmbran Development Corporation: Ch11 Source 13b
DHSS: Ch7 Source 4d
Elton Collection: Ironbridge Gorge Museum: Ch5 Source 6b; Ch6 Sources
    5b, 7
Freightliners: Ch10 Source 5b
GLC Photo Library: Ch21 Source 3a
Greater Manchester Museum of Science and Industry: Ch3 Sources 6a, 7a
Great Western Railway Museum, Swindon: Ch6 source 26
Guildhall Library: Ch17 Source 1e
Hallgarth Collection: Ch8 Source 8
Heatherbank Museum of Social Work: Ch11 Sources 8, 11a, 11b
John Hillelson Agency Ltd: Ch12 Source 2b
HM The Queen: Ch3 Source 1; Ch9 Source 1; Ch18 Source 6e
Hoover: Ch9 Source 14a
Philip J. Kelley: Ch 10 Source 4b
ICI: Ch9 Source 15b
Imperial War Museum: Ch8 Sources 11a, 12
Institute of Agricultural History and Museum of English Rural Life: Ch2
    Sources 1c, 1b, 5a, 5b, 5d, 6, 11; Ch8 Sources 2c, 2d, 2e, 2f; Ch17
    Sources 1c, 3e
Ironbridge Gorge Museum: Ch4 Sources 2b, 5a, 5b, 7b, 7c.
Lanman Museum, Framlingham Castle, Suffolk: Ch16 Source 3c
Leeds Central Library: Ch11 Source 1a: Ch16 Source 7b
Liverpool Record Office: Ch13 Source 8
Jeremy Lowe from 'Welsh Industrial Workers Housing 1175–1875, National
    Museum of Wales, Cardiff 1985" Ch13 Source 2b
Labour Party Library: Ch20 Source 2b
Linotype Ltd: Ch24 Source 4c
London Express News and Features Services: Ch16 Source 9a; Ch25
    Sources 5, 5b
London Dockland Development Corporation: Ch11 Source 14b
London Regional Transport: Ch10 Sources 1g, 11a, 11b, 11c
Mail Newspapers plc: Ch24 Source 4a
Mansell Collection: Ch3 Sources 2c, 5a; Ch4 Source 5d; Ch6 Sources 9a,
    15, 16a, 16b 24b, 27; Ch10 Sources 16a; Ch12 Sources 1d, 6b, 6d, 6e;
    Ch13 Source 4a; Ch14 Sources 1a, 4a, 6a, 8b; Ch16 Sources 1a, 5e; Ch22
    Source 4a; Ch24 Source 2b
Manchester Public Libraries: Ch3 Sources 8, 9c; Ch4 Source 7d; Ch11
    Source 7c Ch14 Source 2a: Ch18 Source 3b
Mary Evans Picture Library: Ch6 Source 16e; Ch12 Source 2c; Ch14 Source
    6e; Ch15 Source 1a; Ch19 Source 3a: Ch21 Source 5b, 6
Master and Fellows of St John's College Cambridge: Ch23 Source 1
Master and Fellows of Trinity College Cambridge: Ch14 Source 7
Museum of London: Ch21 Source 3d
National Coal Board: Ch5 Sources 3a, 3b, 6e: Ch9 Sources 6c, 6b, 6d
National Dairy Council: Ch6 Source 25
National Farmer's Union: Ch8 Source 14a
National Film Archive London: Ch24 Source 7a

280

National Monuments Record for Wales: Ch23 Source 4b
National Motor Museum: Ch9 Sources 9b, 9d, 9e
National Museum of Labour History: Ch19 Source 2a, 7b, 8e; Ch21 Source 3d
National Library of Wales, Aberystwyth: Ch22 Source 3a
National Railway Museum: Ch6 Sources 13a, 16f; Ch10 Sources 1b, 1e, 1f, 3b
National Trust: Ch5 Source 1b
Peter Newark's Historical Pictures: Sources 20, 20a, 22
Newcastle City Libraries: Ch6 Source 13c: Ch22 Source 9c
Photo Source: Ch11 Source 14a
Popperfoto: Ch1 Sources 1a, 1b, 1c, 1d
Press Association: Ch19 Sources 8d, 10c; Ch26 Source 1c
Public Record Office: Ch1 Source 7
Punch Publications; Ch13 Sources 7a, 7b; Ch16 Source 4a; Ch19 Source 7a, 7c; Ch20 Source 3; Ch22 Source 8c; Ch25 Source 4a, 4c; Ch26 Source 2b
Radley College: Ch22 Source 6a
Rex Features Ltd: Ch24 Source 4b
Royal Commission on Historical Monuments: Ch2 Source 10: Ch12 Source 6a: Ch23 Source 5c
Richard Sale: Ch23 Source 4b
The Salvation Army Archives and Research Centre: Ch23 Source 6
The Science Museum: Ch5 Sources 6c, 8a: Ch6 Sources 16c, 16d, 18a; Ch10 Sources 1a, 15a
Shaftesbury Society: Ch22 Source 4c
Sheffield City Museum: Ch9 Sources 3b, 3a
Trades Union Congress: Ch18 Source 5c
Topham: Ch19 Source 9a
Truro County Museum and Art Gallery: Ch23 Source 3a
University of Cambridge, Committee of Aerial Photography: Ch2 Source 8d
University of Leeds: Ch22 Source 10
Welsh Industrial and Maritime Museum: Ch4 Source 6a; Ch5 Source 3c, 4
Weybridge Museum; Ch21 Source 4c
George Washington Wilson Collections, Aberdeen University Library: Ch11 Source 6

From books

Ch4 Source 2a *Understanding the Modern World*, Allen and Unwin Ltd
Ch12 Sources 1b, 1c, 3b, 3c; Ch17 Source 8a *Victorian City*, Routledge and Kegan Paul
Ch8 Source 5 *Victorian Countryside*, Routledge and Kegan Paul
Ch12 Source 6c *Longman Secondary History Packs, Housing and Living Conditions*, Longman
Ch13 Source 3b, 5b; *Schools Council History 13–16 Project – Medicine Through Time*, Holmes McDougall
Ch15 Source 6c *Edwin Chadwick Poor Law and Public Health*, Longman
Ch19 Source 2a; Ch21 Source 1a *Changing Society in Victorian England 1850 — 1900*, Longman
Source 8c: '*How and Why: The General Strike*', Dryad Press Ltd.
Ch22 Source 6b *Ordinary Lives* Virago. Unable to trace copyright holder
Ch25 Source 4d *Machines, Money and Men*, Hart-Davies Educational
Ch3 Source 9b *Britain's Industrial Revolution*, Heinemann Educational
Ch26 Source 8b *Black Settlers in Britain*, Heinemann Educational

Every effort has been made to contact the holders of copyright material but if any have been inadvertently overlooked the publishers will be pleased to make the necessary arrangements at the first opportunity.

Conversion Charts

Money

Old currency: 1 penny (1d) × 12 = 1 shilling (1s) × 20 = 1 pound (£)
Modern currency: 1 penny (1p) × 100 = 1 pound (£)
Therefore:

1d = about ½p	1s 6d = 7½p
2½d = about 1p	2s = 10p
4d = about 1½p	2s 6d = 12½p
5d = about 2p	3s = 15p
6d = 2½p	4s = 20p
7½d = about 3p	5s = 25p
9d = about 3½p	6s = 30p
10d = about 4p	7s = 35p
11d = about 4½p	8s = 40p
1s = 5p	9s = 45p
	10s = 50p
	15s = 75p
	£1 9s 6d = £1.47½p

Weights and measures

1 ounce (oz)	= 2.8 grams
1 pound (lb)	= 0.45 kilos
1 hundredweight (cwt)	= 51 kilos
1 ton	= 1,016 kilos
16 ounces	= 1 pound
112 pounds	= 1 hundredweight
20 hundredweight	= 1 ton

1 gallon	=	4.55 litres
1 bushel	=	36.4 litres
8 gallons	=	1 bushel